CHRIST VERSUS SATAN IN OUR DAILY LIVES

Robert J. Spitzer, S.J., Ph.D.

CHRIST VERSUS SATAN IN OUR DAILY LIVES

The Cosmic Struggle
between Good and Evil

Volume One of the Trilogy:
Called Out of Darkness: Contending with Evil
through the Church, Virtue, and Prayer

IGNATIUS PRESS   SAN FRANCISCO

Nihil Obstat: Reverend Joseph Son Nguyen, M.Div., MA, BCC, S.T.D.
　　　　　　 Censor Librorum

Imprimatur: +The Most Reverend Kevin J. Vann, J.C.D., O.D.
　　　　　　 Bishop, Diocese of Orange
　　　　　　 August 28, 2020

Cover art:
Detail from *The Three Crosses*, etching by Rembrandt van Rijn, 1653.
Image in the public domain

Cover design by John Herreid

© 2020 by Ignatius Press, San Francisco
All rights reserved
ISBN 978-1-62164-417-0 (PB)
ISBN 978-1-64229-137-7 (eBook)
Library of Congress Catalogue number 2020938409
Printed in the United States of America ∞

*In loving memory of my mother and father, who showed me
the path out of darkness through faith and virtue.*

*And to my many brothers in the Society of Jesus who provided
wisdom and modeled holiness through their faith and friendship,
particularly Father Thomas King, S.J.; Father Gordon Moreland, S.J.;
Father James Schall, S.J.; Father John Navone, S.J.;
Father Joseph Koterski, S.J.; Father William Watson, S.J.;
Father David Leigh, S.J.; and Father Patrick Conroy, S.J.*

You are a chosen race, a royal priesthood, a holy nation, God's own people, that you may declare the wonderful deeds of him who called you out of darkness into his marvelous light.

—1 Peter 2:9

CONTENTS

Acknowledgments 15

Introduction to the Trilogy 17

  I. How the Quartet Connects to the Trilogy:
Three Dimensions of Conversion 19

 II. Moral Conversion—the Reason for This Trilogy 24

    A. Volume I—The Recognition of Spiritual Evil
and Its Tactics 26

    B. Volume II—Engagement in Spiritual and Moral
Conversion 30

    C. Volume III—Formation of Conscience through
the Teaching of Christ and the Church 33

 III. Conclusion 37

Part One:
The Reality of Divine Goodness and Spiritual Evil

Introduction to Part One 43

Chapter One: The God of Love Is with Us 45

Introduction 45

  I. The Guidance, Power, and Inspiration of the Holy Spirit 46

    A. A Peace beyond All Understanding 47

      1. Peace in Times of Suffering 48

      2. Peace in Times of Persecution 49

      3. The Peace Necessary for Good Judgment 50

    B. Inspiration and Guidance 51

      1. Words of Help and Edification 51

      2. The *Sensus Fidei* 53

      3. Guidance on Our Way 55

C. Transformation in the Heart of Christ 57

D. Working with the Holy Spirit 61

II. Visions and Revelations—and Their Distinction from Psychologically Induced Phenomena 63

III. Christian Mysticism 70

    A. The Purgative Stage of Contemplative Life 74

    B. The Illuminative Stage of the Contemplative Life 78

    C. The Lord's Presence and Consolation in Contemplative Life 81

    D. The Passive Dark Night of the Spirit ("The Dark Night of the Soul") 83

    E. The Unitive Stage of Contemplative Life 85

IV. Conclusion 87

Chapter Two: Jesus' Victory over Satan 89

Introduction 89

  I. Satan and Demons in the Old and New Testaments 91

 II. Jesus' Defeat of Satan in the Temptations in the Desert 92

III. Jesus' Prolific Ministry of Exorcism 98

IV. Jesus' Teachings about Satan and His Power 106

    A. The Beelzebul Controversy (Mt 12:22–32; Mk 3:22–29; Lk 11:14–23) 106

    B. "I Saw Satan Fall Like Lightning" (Lk 10:18) 110

    C. The Sermon on the Mount 112

    D. Three Parables—"The Sower" (Mt 13:1–23; Mk 4:1–20; Lk 8:4–15), "The Weeds" (Mt 13:24–30, 36–43), and "The Sheep and Goats" (Mt 25:31–46) 113

  V. The Church and the Ongoing Victory over Satan 119

 VI. Jesus' Passion and Death: The Ultimate Defeat of Satan 126

VII. Conclusion 132

Chapter Three: The Devil Is Real   134

Introduction   134

  I. Evidence of the Preternatural, Supernatural, and
Angelic Spirits   134

  II. The Signs of Demonic Possession   142

    A. Paranormal Manifestations of Demonic Possession   144

    B. Behavioral Manifestations   146

    C. Effects of the Possessed Person on Other People   146

  III. Two Documented Cases of Possession   147

    A. The Case of "Julia" (2007)   148

    B. The Case of "Robbie Mannheim" (1949)   152

      1. Paranormal and Demonic Phenomena Manifested
in and around Robbie Mannheim prior to
March 16, 1949   155

      2. The Thirty Exorcisms of Robbie Mannheim
Commencing March 16, 1949   163

      3. A Psychiatric Assessment of the Facts behind
the Robbie Mannheim Case   171

  IV. What Are the Causes of Possession and Why Does
God Allow It?   174

  V. How Does Possession Take Place?   178

  VI. Conclusion   181

Part Two:
Satan's Tactics: From Temptation and
Deception to the Eight Deadly Sins

Introduction to Part Two   185

Chapter Four: How the Devil Works   187

Introduction   187

  I. Spiritual Maturity, the Cosmic Struggle, and the Lord's
Loving Perspective   187

  II. Two Common Defenses against Evil   195

III. A Brief Explanation of Human Freedom 200

IV. Temptation 204

    A. How Temptation Works 205

    B. Three Cardinal Virtues 207

    C. How the Evil One Tailors Temptation for Each Individual 211

        1. The First Group—No Religious or Moral Conversion 218

        2. The Second Group—Weak or Tepid Religious and Moral Conversion 219

        3. The Third Group—Striving toward Strong Religious and Moral Conversion 224

        4. The Fourth Group—Strong Religious and Moral Conversion 229

    D. The Evil One's Preparation for Effective Temptations 231

    E. How the Evil One Works within the Culture to Promote Large-Scale Temptation 237

V. Deception, Discouragement, and Discernment 246

    A. Consolation and Desolation 247

    B. Rules for Discerning Deceptions in Our Spiritual Feelings 252

        1. Never Make a Major Decision in Times of Desolation 252

        2. False Consolations for Individuals in the Third Group 254

    C. Beware of the Evil One Posturing as an Angel of Light 256

VI. Conclusion 259

Chapter Five: The Deadly Sins—Part I: Gluttony, Greed, Lust, Sloth, and Vanity 261

Introduction 261

  I. Gluttony 264

  II. Greed (Avarice) 269

III. Lust 278

IV. Sloth (Acedia) 290

V. Vanity 294

VI. Conclusion 306

Chapter Six: The Deadly Sins—Part II:
Anger, Envy, and Pride 308

Introduction 308

  I. Anger 309

 II. Envy 315

III. Pride (*Superbia*) 326

   A. Explanation of Pride and Its Five Stages of
      Destructiveness 327

   B. The Destructiveness of Pride in the Bible 333

   C. The Destructiveness of Pride in Literature 342

IV. Conclusion 358

Appendix:
Scientifically Validated Miracles Associated
with the Blessed Virgin Mary, Saints,
and the Holy Eucharist

Introduction 363

  I. Three Marian Apparitions 366

   A. The Apparition of Our Lady of Guadalupe 367

   B. The Apparition of Our Lady of Lourdes 371

      1. The Miraculous Cures 373

      2. Marie Bailly and Alexis Carrel—1902 375

      3. Gabriel Gargam—1901 377

      4. John Traynor—1923 379

      5. Conclusion 380

   C. The Apparition of Our Lady of Fatima 383

 II. Validated Miracles through the Intercession of
     Contemporary Saints 388

    A. A Miracle Attributed to Saint Padre Pio   388

    B. A Miracle Attributed to Blessed Fulton J. Sheen   390

    C. A Miracle Attributed to Pope Saint John Paul II   392

 III. A Contemporary Eucharistic Miracle   393

 IV. Conclusion   395

Bibliography   401

Name Index   415

Subject Index   421

Scripture Index   435

ACKNOWLEDGMENTS

I am most grateful to Joan Jacoby, whose invaluable work brought mere thoughts into reality through her excellent editing suggestions and research. It is not easy to do research for a blind scholar, transcribe multiple copies of his dictation, clean up the manuscript, and endure his many edits, but she did so with great patience, care, competence, and contribution—a true manifestation of her virtue and dedication.

I am also grateful to Kathy Wilmes and Gabriella Negrete for their input and considerable assistance in preparing the manuscript.

I would also like to express my appreciation to the board and benefactors of the Magis Institute who gave me the time and resources to complete this Trilogy on spiritual and moral conversion.

INTRODUCTION TO THE TRILOGY

We are building a dictatorship of relativism that does not recognize anything as definitive and whose ultimate standard consists solely of one's own ego and desires.

—Pope Benedict XVI*

The need to confront the "dictatorship of relativism" should not be underestimated, for as we shall see, it is leading not only to a decline in transcendence, faith, morality, and purpose in life, but also to an underestimation of the true dignity and destiny of every person, and ultimately to a decline in civility and civilization itself. In an interview with Peter Seewald, Pope Benedict nuanced this point further:

A large proportion of contemporary philosophies, in fact, consist of saying that man is not capable of truth. But viewed in that way, man would not be capable of ethical values, either. Then he would have no standards. Then he would only have to consider how he arranged things reasonably for himself, and then at any rate the opinion of the majority would be the only criterion that counted. History, however, has sufficiently demonstrated how destructive majorities can be, for instance, in systems such as Nazism and Marxism, all of which also stood against truth in particular.[1]

---

* Mass *Pro Eligendo Romano Pontifice* [for the election of the Roman Pontiff], Homily of His Eminence Joseph Cardinal Ratzinger, Dean of the College of Cardinals (April 18, 2005), http://www.vatican.va/gpII/documents/homily-pro-eligendo-pontifice_20050418_en.html.

[1] Benedict XVI, *Light of the World: The Pope, the Church, and the Signs of the Times; A Conversation with Peter Seewald*, trans. Michael J. Miller and Adrian J. Walker (San Francisco: Ignatius Press, 2010), p. 50.

Could the contemporary world degenerate into a culture of narcissism or worse? Might it affect not only individuals and cultures, but also religions and social institutions? Even a remote possibility of this scenario bodes ill for civilization and all mankind. Yet Jesus Christ has called us out of darkness and has given us the light of the Holy Spirit in the Church and her rich moral, spiritual, and intellectual wisdom. This Trilogy attempts to summarize the Church's moral wisdom. In so doing, it complements my previously written Quartet—*Happiness, Suffering, and Transcendence*, which summarizes her intellectual and spiritual wisdom. For the moment, suffice it to say that the more we know about the moral teaching of Jesus and the Church, the more we will understand ourselves, our true dignity, and our destiny—and the more we understand this, the more we can act to restore the true freedom of Christ within the dictatorship of moral relativism.

I approach this work with great trepidation because I do not want to imply that I have achieved even a high state of moral conversion or perfection—for I have not. As anyone who knows me can tell you, I have a long way to go on my moral journey. Nevertheless, I have come a considerable way because of the grace of Jesus Christ, the Holy Spirit, and the Catholic Church, and the insights of the spiritual and moral masters presented in this Trilogy—particularly Saint Ignatius of Loyola, Saint John of the Cross, and Saint Teresa of Avila. Throughout the years, I have learned a great deal about spiritual and moral conversion—and because I started out fairly low on the moral totem pole, struggled with many of the deadly sins, and resisted deeper moral conversion even in the midst of spiritual conversion, I thought I could provide some very helpful insights to people like myself—insights into the reality of spiritual evil and how it works, the "deadliness" of the deadly sins, and most importantly, insights on how to fight temptation and grow in virtue. Though I am no saint, I have gleaned some important practical insights to help egocentric and obdurate personalities—like myself—to follow Christ out of the darkness into the light. If I implied that I have arrived, I beg the reader's forgiveness, because that would be both false and hypocritical.

Despite all this, I am making small progressive steps out of the darkness and have learned much about the power of grace—and how to submit to it through suffering, faith, and prayer. I hope the insights, most of which are borrowed from truly great saints, will be useful to people struggling with spiritual darkness and evil through the light and grace of Jesus Christ.

I. How the Quartet Connects to the Trilogy:
Three Dimensions of Conversion

The combination of my previously written Quartet (*Happiness, Suffering, and Transcendence*) and this Trilogy (*Called Out of Darkness: Contending with Evil through the Church, Virtue, and Prayer*) is intended to help Christians negotiate the challenges of conversion in the contemporary world. Some of these challenges are the following:

- Being immersed in a culture of Level One (sensual and materialistic) and Level Two (ego-comparative) happiness and purpose
- Being confronted by skepticism about God, the soul, and Jesus
- Being discouraged by suffering and God's seeming involvement in it
- Being undermined by the culture's critique of the Church and her moral teachings
- Being inundated with violence and pornography on the Internet
- Being pushed into the egocentric and often narcissistic world of social media
- Being drawn into a permissive and often hypersexualized social milieu
- Being desensitized to ethical principles and the promptings of conscience

Given these extraordinary challenges, it should come as no surprise that many Christians have grown weak and apathetic in their faith, and some have lost or forsaken it altogether.

Bernard Lonergan distinguished three dimensions of conversion: intellectual, religious/spiritual, and moral conversion[2]—all of which

---

[2] See Bernard Lonergan, *Method in Theology*, ed. Robert M. Doran and John D. Dadosky, vol. 14 of *The Collected Works of Bernard Lonergan*, ed. Frederick E. Crowe and Robert M. Doran (Toronto: University of Toronto Press, 1990), pp. 144–45, 153–54, 204–5, 220–39.

are challenged by the above problems in our culture. Though these challenges can be more than met with an abundance of evidence and methods that have recently come to light through science, medicine, philosophy of mind, and scriptural exegesis, we need to develop willing disciples of evangelization to point to these methods and sources of evidence, to help those gripped and even daunted by the above challenges. Though we are not prepared to discuss this now, we will do so in the conclusion to this Trilogy. For the moment, let us return to the three dimensions of conversion—intellectual, religious/spiritual, and moral conversion.

Let us begin with *intellectual conversion*, which we might define as rational conviction about the truth of God, the soul, and the transcendent life, as well as Jesus Christ and His teachings. Such rational conviction can be obtained through a variety of means: empirical evidence, verifiable reported evidence, logical proof, scientific evidence, and combinations of these methods. Since the evidence indicating the reality of transcendence is abundant, it is not necessary to rely on only one or two kinds of evidence or methods. It is best to assemble a large number of sources of evidence that are mutually complementary and corroborative. As explained in the conclusion to this Trilogy, we have provided this evidence for the reality of God, the soul, and Jesus in Volume II (*The Soul's Upward Yearning*) and Volume III (*God So Loved the World*) of the Quartet. The evidence includes contemporary philosophical proofs of God's existence as well as contemporary scientific evidence for an intelligent Creator from the Borde-Vilenkin-Guth proof; entropy; and fine-tuning for life in the initial conditions and constants of the universe. It also includes evidence of a transphysical soul capable of surviving bodily death from peer-reviewed medical studies of near-death experiences; studies of terminal lucidity; and the implications of our five transcendental desires, Gödel's proof, and contemporary studies of self-consciousness. With respect to Jesus, the evidence includes scientific studies of the Shroud of Turin and the Sudarium (face cloth) of Oviedo, N. T. Wright's arguments for the historicity of the Resurrection, and contemporary scientifically validated miracles. In all, there are about twenty different sources of evidence for transcendence covering the five major methods mentioned above—empirical data, verifiable reports of events after clinical death, logical proofs, scientific conclusions, and validated historical testimony as well as different combinations of these. These kinds of evidence have considerable probative value on their own, which increases when they are seen within their mutual corroboration and complementarity.

In our culture, a large number of young people will have to have pursued *intellectual* conversion successfully (through examining the above evidence for God, a transcendent soul, and Jesus) before they will be able to engage in spiritual and moral conversion, because belief in these three fundamental realities provides the foundation for pursuing a source of revelation and a church community (integral to spiritual conversion). Stated plainly, if analytically oriented students are apathetic or doubtful about God, the soul, and Jesus, they will not seriously participate in a church community or feel obligated to adhere to its moral teachings.

In my view, it is a huge oversight to offer middle school and high school catechesis courses that do not explore the evidence for God, the soul, and Jesus. As noted in the conclusion to this Trilogy, this oversight has led more than 40 percent of our young people not only to abandon the Church, but also to detach from faith in God altogether.[3] Young people identify the principal reason for their unbelief as a contradiction between faith and science—or faith and logical evidence.[4] For this reason, I would recommend that young people be acquainted with the evidence given in Volumes II and III of the Quartet before presenting them with the need for spiritual and moral conversion given in this Trilogy. (The Magis Center has prepared free and accessible summary presentations of this evidence

---

[3] See Michael Lipka, "Millennials Increasingly Are Driving Growth of 'Nones'", Pew Research Center, May 12, 2015, http://www.pewresearch.org/fact-tank/2015/05/12/millennials-increasingly-are-driving-growth-of-nones/.

[4] See Michael Lipka, "Why America's 'Nones' Left Religion Behind", Pew Research Center, August 24, 2016, http://www.pewresearch.org/fact-tank/2016/08/24/why-americas-nones-left-religion-behind/.

for young people in its 7 *Essential Modules*[5] and the *Credible Catholic Little Book*[6].)

We may now proceed to *spiritual conversion*, which Lonergan frequently calls "religious conversion".[7] It begins with our awareness of our inability to be satisfied without a relationship with a transcendent (divine) Being. Volume I of the Quartet (*Finding True Happiness*) describes this as Level Four happiness, within the movement from Level One (external-pleasure-material) and Level Two (ego-comparative) to Level Three (contributive-empathetic) and Level Four (transcendent) happiness and purpose.[8] This transition arises out of self-discovery similar to what Saint Augustine describes in his *Confessions*. As we move through the stages on life's way, we begin to notice the supersophistication of our nature by the emptiness and alienation we feel when we are devoid of interpersonal relationships with others and God. We also notice that we cannot be satisfied by the truth, love, fairness, goodness, beauty, and "home" offered by this world alone, and that we will be satisfied ultimately only by *perfect* truth, love, fairness-goodness, beauty, and "home".

Frequently enough, this sense that our true fulfillment and home lies beyond us is accompanied by what I have called "cosmic emptiness", "cosmic alienation", and "cosmic loneliness" (on the negative

[5] The 7 *Essential Modules* (ninety minutes each) resource is a "voice-over" PowerPoint that can be used not only for individual viewing, but by catechetical and Confirmation teachers who are trying to "inoculate" middle school and high school students from cultural challenges to their faith. It includes modules on the evidence of a soul from near-death experiences and terminal lucidity (Module 1); evidence for God from science and philosophy (Modules 2 and 3, respectively); evidence of Jesus' Passion and Resurrection from the Shroud of Turin (Module 4); evidence of the Church from contemporary scientifically validated miracles, emphasizing why one should be Catholic (Module 5); the four levels of happiness (Module 6); and why God allows suffering (Module 7). Free of charge, you can stream or download all seven modules for seventh grade and above (ages twelve and up) and tenth grade and above (ages fifteen and up). Spanish translations are also available. To access this resource, go to www.crediblecatholic.com and click on the big red button that says "7 Essential Modules", or simply click on this site: https://www.crediblecatholic.com/programs/.

[6] To access this resource, go to www.crediblecatholic.com and click on "Little Book" then on Volumes 1, 2, 3, 4, 6, 13, and 19. A much larger free resource called the *Credible Catholic Big Book* features much fuller explanations, original sources, and a full bibliography, which can be accessed by clicking on "Big Book" on the homepage.

[7] See Lonergan, *Method in Theology*, pp. 144–45, 153–54, 204–5, and 220–39.

[8] See Robert Spitzer, *Finding True Happiness: Satisfying our Restless Hearts* (San Francisco: Ignatius Press, 2015), Chapters 1–5.

side),[9] as well as the numinous experience and intuition of the sacred (on the positive side)[10]—all of which impels us to search for the God who at once seems to be present yet hidden, the question and the answer. Since He wants us to acknowledge our need for Him—not only for fulfillment and a response to our radical incompleteness and loneliness, but also to rescue us from our awareness that there is spiritual darkness around and within us—He waits for us to make our decision. God will not make the choice for us, but waits for us to open ourselves to His numinous and sacred presence we feel within us. This response is what we have called "a little leap of faith".[11] When we make this little leap, we complete the first of four steps of spiritual conversion. There is a thorough summary of this first step in Volume II (Appendix I)—the movement from Levels One and Two. There is an explanation of the move to Levels Three and Four in Volume II (Chapter 4, Section I).

The little leap of faith helps us attain a sense of peace, extricating us partially from our sense of cosmic emptiness, alienation, loneliness, and guilt. Yet, we still sense incompleteness and the need for the Sacred One to rescue us from the darkness we sense around and within us. Very frequently, this opens us to the need for a religious community having legitimate religious authority, and a real conduit to the sacred. This might take us to the Church of our childhood or might open upon yet another search for a true source of God's self-revelation and the Church, through which that revelation best occurs. In Volume III of the Quartet (*God So Loved the World*), we discussed how Jesus' revelation of love as the meaning of life holds out the key to His self-identity as the ultimate source of revelation (Emmanuel—"God with us"). The acceptance of this truth in our hearts—and our desire to live according to it—constitutes the second step in Christian conversion. Once we have accepted Jesus as the ultimate source of God's self-revelation in our *hearts*, we can then attend to the evidence of the mind (intellectual conversion) once again. Chapter 4 of Volume III of the Quartet examines the evidence for the historical reality of Jesus' glorified Resurrection (through the

---

[9] See ibid., Chapter 5.

[10] See Spitzer, *The Soul's Upward Yearning: Clues to Our Transcendent Nature from Experience and Reason* (San Francisco: Ignatius Press, 2015), Chapters 1 and 2, respectively.

[11] See Spitzer, *Finding True Happiness*, Chapter 6, Section I.

Shroud of Turin, N. T. Wright's arguments for its historicity, and the witness value of the apostolic preaching); Chapter 5 examines the evidence for Jesus' miracles as well as the presence of the Holy Spirit then and now; and Chapter 6 examines Jesus' self-revelation in the light of His mission to give Himself totally to mankind in an act of unconditional love (His Passion).

If we respond to Jesus by opening ourselves to Him in our hearts and acknowledging His reality in our minds (through the evidence He left for us), we can then proceed to the third step in spiritual conversion—choosing a church community. In Chapter 1 of Volume II of the Trilogy, we detail the substantial evidence for Jesus' initiation of His Church under the leadership of Saint Peter and his successors who are promised the Holy Spirit to help them maintain fidelity to Jesus' truth. In the appendix of this volume, we examine the contemporary, scientifically validated miracles that point to the continued presence of Jesus within the Catholic Church—through His Mother (in Marian apparitions), His saints, and His Holy Eucharist. Though this evidence is significant, it still requires a movement of the heart, as in all dimensions of spiritual conversion. As noted later in this Trilogy (Volume II, Chapters 2 and 3), this confirmation of the heart is best obtained by participating in Mass, devotions, prayer, and pilgrimages, as well as reading the lives of saints and other spiritual writings. If one proceeds into the Catholic Church through Baptism, profession of the faith, and Confirmation, then it is time to move toward the fourth and final step of spiritual conversion, which is the deepening of our faith through participation in the Church. This is covered in detail later in this Trilogy (Volume II, Chapters 1–3).

II. Moral Conversion—the Reason for This Trilogy

By now it will be apparent that the Quartet is devoted to *intellectual conversion* (Volumes II and III) and *spiritual conversion* (Volumes I and IV), while this Trilogy is devoted mostly to *moral conversion* (which completes the conversion process). Moral conversion is often the final dimension of the conversion process—not only because it is difficult, but also because it requires the conviction of intellectual conversion and the grace of spiritual conversion to make progress.

There are three major dimensions of moral conversion corresponding to the three volumes of this Trilogy:

> Volume I, *Christ versus Satan in Our Daily Lives: The Cosmic Struggle between Good and Evil.* The first dimension of moral conversion is to acknowledge the darkness within us and around us—from human beings and from spiritual realities who have chosen to act against God and Jesus. We also need to understand how evil works—both the evil coming from our hearts as well as the tactics of Satan and other evil spirits.
>
> Volume II, *The Way Out of Darkness: The Church, Spiritual Conversion, and Moral Conversion.* The second dimension of moral conversion is interior purification that begins with the grace and resolve of spiritual conversion and proceeds to what Saint Paul calls the transition from the "old man" to the "new man" (Eph 4:22, 24; Col 3:9–11; cf. Rom 6:6; Eph 2:15). We give techniques to assist this process of moving from the "lower self" to the "higher self", and then show how to use this transition effectively to resist temptation and to grow in virtue.
>
> Volume III, *The Moral Wisdom of the Catholic Church: A Defense of Her Controversial Moral Teachings.* The third dimension of moral conversion is the formation of our consciences through principles of personal and social ethics. We begin by explaining the critical and hermeneutical assumptions needed to assent to Jesus' and the Church's teaching on moral principles and methods, and then proceed to the principles themselves, giving special emphasis to the sin of adultery (in personal ethics) and Catholic social teaching (in social ethics).

Though moral conversion takes a lifetime, the continued practice of its three dimensions draws us closer to the heart and light of Jesus Christ, which opens the way to a life of sanctity and effective evangelization. This Trilogy concludes with a discussion of Christian evangelization—that is, on how to help others move through intellectual, spiritual, and moral conversion.

Just as spiritual conversion integrates aspects of intellectual conversion (e.g., the evidence for Jesus) in its ongoing process, so also moral conversion integrates aspects of spiritual conversion into its ongoing process. So we should not be surprised to learn that part of Volume II of this Trilogy is devoted to spiritual conversion (Chapters 1–3). We may now proceed to an overview of the three volumes of this Trilogy that explains the three dimensions of moral conversion.

A. Volume I—The Recognition of Spiritual Evil and Its Tactics

Volume I (*Christ versus Satan in Our Daily Lives: The Cosmic Struggle between Good and Evil*) introduces the supernatural dynamic in which our life (particularly our eternal life) is embedded—the struggle between the Trinity (and their representatives) and Satan (and his representatives). The reader may be wondering why the process of moral conversion includes an explanation of the reality of spiritual evil. Shouldn't this be obvious? Unfortunately, it is not obvious to the young and most vulnerable in our culture. We seem to be caught between two extremes concerning the reality of spiritual evil. One group, which probably fashions itself as enlightened or intellectual, views any allusion to spiritual evil, such as Satan or demonic spirits, as mere mythology, figments of the imagination, and the regrettable remnants of a bygone age—while another group has become fascinated by the occult, witchcraft, and Satanism.[12]

---

[12] Matt Baglio gives statistics for this marked increase in the occult, Satanism, and Wicca, both nationally and internationally. See Matt Baglio, *The Rite: The Making of a Modern Exorcist* (New York: Doubleday, 2010), pp. 6–7.

The Catholic Church has become quite concerned about this increase in Satanism and occultism, which has led to a substantial increase in demonic possession and hauntings throughout the world. In 2011, the Vatican held a special conference for priests and other officials at the Pontifical Athenaeum Regina Apostolorum (a university in Rome) to address this issue. Since that time, an annual course in possession and exorcism has been held at the same university—and Pope Francis has asked that each diocese throughout the world appoint an exorcist with appropriate knowledge of demonic possession and the Catholic ritual of exorcism. Much of the increase in occult practice has come from the Internet and appeals specifically to young people who are either psychologically fragile or seeking thrills from supernatural power. They are apparently unaware of the dangerous world into which they are entering, which can lead to both demonic possession and haunting. See Ann Schneible, "Practical Help for the Demon-Possessed: Vatican Rolls out New Exorcism Course", *Catholic News Agency*, April 10, 2015, http://www.catholicnewsagency.com/news/practical-help -for-the-demon-possessed-vatican-rolls-out-new-exorcism-course-36248/; Yasmine Hafiz, "Exorcism Conference at Vatican Addresses the Need for More Demon-Fighting Priests",

Evidence suggests strongly that both groups are in error. The first group has made an error of omission by ignoring the substantial evidence for spiritual evil (and the negative influence it can have over our lives), while the second group has made a spiritual and moral error by believing that the power and promises of evil can provide a supernatural benefit without causing self-destruction, destruction of others, darkness, emptiness, and pain. Both errors can lead to the most negative imaginable decisions about life, purpose, and identity. Therefore, it is necessary to explain the reality of spiritual evil in a balanced Christian way that requires four clarifications.

Firstly, in Chapter 1, we explain the *reality and presence of spiritual good*—the Trinity and their representatives: the angels, the Blessed Virgin Mary, and the saints. This includes public apparitions of the Blessed Virgin Mary and miracles through the intercession of the Blessed Virgin Mary and saints, as well as the divine presence within us—for example, the numinous experience, the actions of the Holy Spirit in our lives, personal visions or revelations, and mystical experiences. Personal experiences of the divine are quite common but, because they are frequently subtle, can be overlooked if we are not attuned to them. Readers should not proceed to Chapter 3 ("The Devil Is Real", the reality of spiritual evil) without first being aware of the power and presence of God (and His representatives). We do not confront spiritual evil by ourselves, but with the immense power and assistance of God.

Secondly, in Chapter 2, we consider *Jesus' definitive defeat of Satan and his demonic spirits*. Though Satan continues to exercise power in the world (in the lives of individuals and the direction of culture), he cannot be ultimately victorious—nor can he be victorious in any particular battle in which the affected individuals have put their faith in Jesus Christ and called upon Him for help. The evidence for this in the New Testament and throughout Church history shows

Huffington Post, May 13, 2014, http://www.huffingtonpost.com/2014/05/13/exorcism -conference-rome-priests_n_5316749.html; Nick Squires, "Surge in Satanism Sparks Rise in Demand for Exorcists, Says Catholic Church", *Telegraph*, March 30, 2011, http://www .telegraph.co.uk/news/religion/8416104/Surge-in-Satanism-sparks-rise-in-demand-for -exorcists-says-Catholic-Church.html; and Baglio, *Rite*, pp. 9–38.

the power of the Holy Spirit through Jesus' name and the ultimate demise of Satan.

Thirdly, in Chapter 3, we proceed to the *reality of spiritual evil*. Though some readers may object to presenting details from the exorcisms of Julia (a recent case reported by psychiatrist Richard Gallagher) and Robbie Mannheim (based on the diary of the Jesuits who performed the exorcism on which the book and film *The Exorcist* was based), I could think of no better way of calling readers' attention to the reality, presence, and malicious intent of Satan and his followers (demonic spirits). Why present this evidence in such an explicit and "scary" way? Because Satan is exceedingly crafty and disguised, preferring to remain hidden in the lives of ordinary people so that his schemes to bring darkness to the world will go unrecognized. Virtually every spiritual work, beginning with the Gospels' accounts of words spoken by Jesus[13] and the writings by Saint Paul,[14] has acknowledged this. If a brief examination of the evidence for Satan can alert believers to his presence, then they can learn how to resist him.

Fourthly, in Chapter 4, we discuss the *sources of evil in our lives*, from malevolent spirits—or our evil intentions. Most of the time, these two sources of evil interact with each other, compounding their effects. Evil spirits exert their influence in a hidden way most of the time—through temptations, deceptions, and, above all, despair. Evil also arises out of the human heart through what the Catholic tradition has called either "the seven deadly sins" or "the eight deadly sins" (I prefer the latter).[15] I examine the tactics of Satan in Chapter 4 and then the "sins of our hearts" (the deadly sins) in Chapters 5 and 6. Let us begin with the tactics of Satan (Chapter 4).

Satan's most frequent approach is to use temptations and deception. Temptation normally arises through images and suggestions directly conveyed to our conscious and/or subconscious psyches. Satan's objective is to keep our self-consciousness focused on our

---

[13] E.g., "You are of your father the devil, and your will is to do your father's desires.... He is a liar and the father of lies" (Jn 8:44).

[14] E.g., "And no wonder, for even Satan disguises himself as an angel of light" (2 Cor 11:14).

[15] The history of the Catholic tradition regarding the deadly sins will be discussed in detail in the introduction to Chapter 5 below.

"lower self" (described below), which is the seat of our lower desires for sensual pleasures and ego-comparative satisfaction. His plan is to keep us perennially mired in these lower desires so that they will take our minds off of God, as well as off of Jesus and His teaching. This opens the way to superficial and self-destructive lives that will negatively affect the people and culture around us. Temptations can be resisted by virtue, the sacraments, and prayer, as well as special techniques designed to make the higher self the dominant self-image in the subconscious mind (see Volume II, Chapters 5–6). Deceptions can be exposed and resisted by making recourse to the rules for the discernment of spirits, particularly those written by Saint Ignatius of Loyola. Satan can also deceive a whole culture—even radically—by a variety of deceptions and temptations. However, these too can be countered by reestablishing the third and fourth levels of happiness/purpose in life, and the teachings of Jesus within the culture.

In Chapters 5 and 6, we proceed to the *eight deadly sins*—the interior attitudes that open the way to evil within our hearts. Throughout the first five centuries of Christian reflection on Jesus' moral teaching in the New Testament, the Church Fathers discerned eight interior attitudes (that can become habitual) from which sinful and unloving behaviors can spring. Chapter 5 explores five of these attitudes—gluttony, greed, sloth, lust, and vanity, many of which are common today. Though the theological literature about these sins is substantial, I thought that younger audiences might appreciate looking at the impressive examples of them from the vantage point of literary classics and history. Great works of Ovid, Virgil, Shakespeare, Dickens, Dostoyevsky, Tolstoy, Spenser, and Milton, as well as modern literature and films, provide significant examples of how alluring and entrapping these sinful attitudes can be and teach of their incredible destructive power to self and others. The lesson is clear: keep these attitudes at arm's length——not only for the sake of your soul, but for the sake of family, friends, colleagues, and community.

In Chapter 6, we explain the three deadliest and most destructive sins—anger, envy, and pride. Using the above classics (particularly Shakespeare's *Hamlet*, *Othello*, and *Macbeth*) as well as stories from the Old Testament and twentieth-century history, we examine the addictive nature and destructive power of anger, envy, and pride. Though it is common opinion that anger and pride are "not that harmful" because everybody engages in them, nothing could be further from the truth because they are explosive and almost limitless in the hatred and contempt they can generate. Iago characterizes his envious plot (in *Othello*) as follows:

> I have't. It is engender'd. Hell and night
> Must bring this monstrous birth to the world's light.[16]

Again, the point for all readers is clear: no matter how innocuous these three sins may seem, they are to be avoided by all possible means—prayer, virtue, and the sacraments. Hopefully, after Chapter 6, readers will no longer "be in the dark" about the destructive power of either Satan or the deadly sins he instigates. This may provide the incentive to delve seriously into Volume II of the Trilogy—engagement in moral conversion itself.

B. Volume II—Engagement in Spiritual and Moral Conversion

Volume II of the Trilogy (*The Way Out of Darkness: The Church, Spiritual Conversion, and Moral Conversion*) begins with an explanation of how to deepen spiritual/religious conversion to provide a foundation for moral conversion. It starts with affirming the Catholic Church as the original and true Church of Jesus Christ under the supreme teaching authority of Saint Peter and his successors. It then proceeds to exploring religious/spiritual conversion through the guidance of the Church, the supreme gift of the Holy Eucharist, the sacramental life, and the inner gifts coming from integration into the Mystical Body of Christ. This leads to the development of contemplative and devotional life that prepares the way for moral conversion. It then explores moral conversion itself through affirmation of the virtues of faith and love (particularly manifest in the Beatitudes), and the use of spiritual and psychological techniques for resisting temptations and developing the higher self (what Saint Paul called "the new man", as mentioned above). We will examine each of these stages in turn.

---

[16] William Shakespeare, *Othello: The Moor of Venice* (Project Gutenberg, 2019), act 1, scene 3, www.gutenberg.org/files/1531/1531-h/1531-h.htm#sceneI_3.

Stage One—Affirmation of the Catholic Church as the Original and True Church of Jesus Christ. In Chapter 1, we closely examine the need for a Church, particularly a Church with a supreme teaching and sacramental authority and power—to avoid problems of disunity and misinterpretations of Jesus' words, which would undermine spiritual and moral conversion. We explore the scriptural references in the Gospels concerning Jesus' intention to start a church that would be unified through His risen body and last until the end of time. We also examine the exegetical evidence for Jesus' commissioning of Peter and his successors as the supreme teaching authority of the Church in Matthew 16:17–19, John 21:15–19, and Galatians 2:9. We then look into Peter's supreme role in the Acts of the Apostles, particularly at the Council of Jerusalem. This leads to an investigation of how the first popes, bishops, and Church Fathers understood the role of Saint Peter's successors (as the Bishop of Rome). This evidence is complemented by nine contemporary scientifically validated miracles connected with three doctrinal proclamations of the Catholic Church—the Blessed Mother, the saints, and the Real Presence of Jesus in the Eucharist (in the appendix to Volume I).

Stage Two—The Development of Religious/Spiritual Conversion. In Chapters 2 and 3, we examine how religious/spiritual conversion is deepened through the guidance of the Magisterium, the graces of the sacraments, and the interior spiritual gifts given through integration into the Mystical Body of Christ. We address how to receive the sacraments and how to engage in and deepen our contemplative lives, particularly through contemplation on the Word of God, contemplative prayer practice, and devotion to Mary and the saints.

Stage Three—From Spiritual Conversion to Moral Conversion. In Chapters 4 through 6, we explore how to develop the major virtues of faith and love and then how to resist temptation by using spiritual techniques (such as the Examen Prayer) and psychological techniques (such as those developed by Dr. Albert Bandura). We then turn our attention to the development of the higher self (the "new man"), which habitualizes (makes second nature) our moral conversion.

The term "self" is somewhat technical, referring to a persona or identity that self-consciousness can assume. In view of this, we offer a method to make the higher self as the dominant persona-identity, not only in our conscious mind, but also in our subconscious mind. Using techniques from Dr. Bandura, and others, we show how we can accomplish this effectively. When these psychological techniques are combined with the power of grace (from contemplative prayer, the Examen Prayer, and spontaneous prayers), significant self-transformation can take place expeditiously.

In Chapter 7, we look into the vehicles for Christ's merciful love in the Sacrament of Reconciliation and spontaneous prayers of forgiveness. Even if we should make real progress in self-transformation and moral conversion, we will still need reconciliation and healing from moral failures in the past, present, and future. Saint Paul makes clear that the road to moral conversion is filled with obstacles, weaknesses, and failings (see Rom 7:15–25). We cannot save ourselves, and we cannot rely on ourselves to be perfected in love. As Jesus tells us, we are all in deep need of a Savior to forgive us, heal us, lead us, and protect us—a Savior who would not spare anything to save us and who would give his very life for us and for the life of the world:

> For God so loved the world that he gave his only-begotten Son, that whoever believes in him should not perish but have eternal life. For God sent the Son into the world, not to condemn the world, but that the world might be saved through him. (Jn 3:16–17)

Jesus left us with so many assurances of His unconditional love, forgiveness, and healing grace that we should be confident to put our faith in Him. His Parable of the Prodigal Son, in which the father shows unconditional forgiving love to his son who has betrayed him in every imaginable way, is a revelation of the very nature of His Heavenly Father (see Lk 15:11–32). Likewise, His assurance to the good thief on the cross, who turned to Him after a lifetime of crime— "Truly, I say to you, today you will be with me in Paradise"—shows us His unconditional mercy even at the last minute (Lk 23:43). Furthermore, the many instances of His love and forgiveness of sinners, and His desire to be with them and seek them out, tells us of His compassion for us even at the worst of times. Above all, His Passion and death for the sake of our salvation, explained so beautifully in His Eucharistic words, reveal that He would do absolutely anything to bring us into His Kingdom. If we find ourselves doubting His love and mercy for us when we have failed badly, all we need do is look at a crucifix and recall His words to the good thief. This should assure us that our faith in His love is warranted, and that He can rescue us from even the darkest of circumstances.

If we have this faith in Jesus, then the remarkable Sacrament of Reconciliation, which He left to us through His apostles, will bring not only His unconditional forgiveness of our sins, but also His healing grace and the power of His Spirit to renew us again.

The road to moral conversion is not smooth, and even Saint Paul was tormented by his failings after twenty years, crying out, "I do not do the good I want, but the evil I do not want is what I do" (Rom 7:19). He knew well what he had to do because he could not save himself—he had to call upon the Lord's mercy, knowing that He would save him from his very self; and so he concludes, "Wretched man that I am! Who will deliver me from this body of death? Thanks be to God through Jesus Christ our Lord!" (Rom 7:24–25). We should accept his good counsel and do the same—otherwise, moral conversion will be impossible.

C. Volume III—Formation of Conscience through the Teaching of Christ and the Church

In Volume II we addressed the foundational dimension of moral conversion—interior purification—particularly moving from the lower self to the higher self (what Saint Paul calls the "old man" to the "new man"). This process not only helps us to resist temptation effectively, but also to live in the light of Christ's love and virtue, which empowers our conscience. Yet it is not enough for our conscience to be empowered by love and grace; we also need to *form* our conscience—that is, to conform it to the principles of personal and social ethics taught by Jesus and the Church. This is the objective of Volume III of this Trilogy—*The Moral Wisdom of the Catholic Church: A Defense of Her Controversial Moral Teachings*—which brings the process of moral conversion to completion. These principles inform and then conform our conscience so that it will alert us to behaviors we want to avoid (with feelings of alienation and guilt) and behaviors we want to pursue (with feelings of peace and nobility). Once conscience has been formed to alert us to the presence of good or evil, our process of self-transformation (in Volume II) can come to full effect, for we can now apply the power of conscience to our nuanced set of principles to refine our moral conversion. We articulate these principles in two major areas:

1. Personal ethics (Chapters 1–5)
2. Social ethics (Chapters 6–7)

Let us begin with *personal ethics*. In Chapter 1, we explain three major conditions of trusting discipleship necessary for understanding and following Jesus' and the Church's moral teaching in our hearts. Without this openness of the heart, it will be exceedingly difficult to assent and adhere to these principles with love and reverence, which will likely cause resistance and interior conflict.

So what are these three conditions?

1. Deepening our trust in the Lord.
2. Deepening our relationship with the Lord through gratitude and love.
3. Cultivating the freedom to lovingly follow the precepts of Christ and the Church.

If we do not grow in trusting discipleship, we will never be able to assent and adhere fully to the precepts of Christ and the Church. We will always be standing outside Jesus' and the Church's perspective, trying futilely to understand why they hold these principles to be true, good, and consistent with God's will.

Chapters 2 through 5 focus on the six major principles of Christian *personal* ethics themselves—the six commandments articulated by Jesus in Mark 10:19:

Do not kill, Do not commit adultery, Do not steal, Do not bear false witness, Do not defraud, Honor your father and mother.

In the current day, these commandments take on considerable sophistication, nuance, and complexity corresponding to the sophistication of education, technology, and communication within the culture. In Chapters 2 and 3, special consideration is given to the prohibition of adultery because the sexual revolution has caused a reinterpretation of sexuality that has undermined the proper nature of sexuality within marriage as well as marital commitment itself. Jesus' view of sexuality promotes and enhances marriage, exclusive permanent commitment, and intimacy and generativity in marriage, all of which impact the security and well-being of children and the family—not to mention the culture and society formed by sound families. In light of Jesus' and the Church's teaching about love and sexuality, we give special consideration to why Jesus and the Church teach against extramarital sexuality, premarital sexuality (including cohabitation), and homosexuality. Chapter 3 examines the negative effects of pornography and gender change as well as the positive effects of natural family planning and the myth of overpopulation.

In Chapter 4, special consideration is given to the prohibition of killing. We first examine the evidence for the intrinsic dignity and transcendental nature of every human being, and then give special attention to abortion, eugenic infanticide, in vitro fertilization, euthanasia, and physician assisted suicide. In Chapter 5, we give consideration to stealing, lying, and cheating, arising out of new issues raised by medicine, science, business, academia, mass media, and social media. The chapter concludes with an important section on creating our own personal code of ethics, which is vital to the process of personally appropriating the principles mentioned above.

We then proceed to the area of *social* ethics, which has become increasingly more important throughout the course of the industrial revolution, two world wars, and economic globalization. Social ethics is the responsibility of the culture, society, and state, so no individual can be completely responsible for its successful practice. Nevertheless, every individual can do his best to inform and influence the culture and society (through media, church, and educational efforts), and the state (through political engagement), to move ever more closely to the ideal of justice and charity articulated by Jesus and the Church. We begin this discussion in Chapter 6 with a consideration of the world-transforming influence of Jesus and His teaching in four important respects:

- The Golden Rule (see Mt 7:12), which moved society from ethical minimalism (the Silver Rule) to ethical maximalism.
- The equal intrinsic transcendental dignity of every human being ("As you did to one of the least of these my brethren, you did to me" [Mt 25:40]).
- The positive law, which is subordinate to the intrinsic transcendental dignity of every human being ("The sabbath was made for man, not man for the sabbath" [Mk 2:27]).
- The responsibility of all Christians to assist those in need, a proclamation that enabled the early Church community to evolve into the largest provider of public healthcare, welfare, and education in the world today.

The effects of these teachings led to four major principles that ultimately evolved into the doctrine of the inalienable rights of all human beings to life, liberty, happiness, and property. This occurred mostly through Saint Augustine ("An unjust law is no law at all"); Saint Paul and Saint Thomas Aquinas (the natural law); Father Bartolomé de Las Casas, O.P. (the doctrine of universal personhood); and Father Francisco Suarez, S.J. (the doctrine of the inalienable rights of all human beings). These Christian reflections on social ethics provided the foundation not only for the Church's teaching on slavery, the life issues, and socioeconomic rights (Catholic social teaching), but also for Locke's *Treatise on Government*, the United States Declaration of Independence, and the United Nations Universal Declaration of Human Rights.

Chapters 6 and 7 provide a brief, but comprehensive, explanation of the major declarations on Catholic social ethics. Chapter 6 addresses the rationale for the prohibition of slavery, abortion, and assisted suicide, based upon the principles of social ethics described in the chapter. These principles form the basis of *individual* natural rights, but social ethics goes much further—to the domains of social institutions, business organizations, political communities, and the international communities. The need for ethical guidance in these critical social areas moved the Church to write a comprehensive set of guidelines over the last one hundred years called "Catholic social teaching" (beginning in 1891 with Pope Leo XIII's famous encyclical *Rerum Novarum*).

In Chapter 7, we discuss the six major principles of Catholic social ethical analysis:

1. The intrinsic transcendent dignity of every human being
2. The principle of the common good
3. The universal destination of goods
4. The principle of subsidiarity
5. Participation in democracy
6. The principle of solidarity

We then apply these principles to the Church's reflection on seven major areas of socio-political and economic ethics—the family, the working environment, the economic/business community, the political community, the international community, the environment, and the pursuit of peace.[17] As we shall see, Catholic social teaching is incredibly extensive, giving guidance to our individual and collective minds on just about every topic of ethical relevance to the modern world.

After completing Volume III, readers should have a strong foundation on which to form their consciences to make progress in moral conversion. Moral conversion is a lifetime project, but continued progress brings gradual closure to the conversion process.

III. Conclusion

After completing this Trilogy, the reader will have journeyed through the deep and wide Catholic traditional and contemporary reflection on intellectual conversion, spiritual conversion, and moral conversion. The contents of this reflection draw on a vast array of evidence not only from theology and scriptural exegesis, but also from philosophy, the natural sciences, medicine, history, psychology, sociology,

---

[17] The Pontifical Council for Justice and Peace has prepared an excellent consolidation and summary of the major Catholic social encyclicals and documents called *Compendium of the Social Doctrine of the Church* (2004; repr., Washington, D.C.: Libreria Editrice Vaticana—United States Conference of Catholic Bishops, 2005), which is free of charge on the following website: http://www.vatican.va/roman_curia/pontifical_councils/justpeace/documents/rc_pc_justpeace_doc_20060526_compendio-dott-soc_en.html.

political theory, and economic theory, as well as spirituality, mysticism, and world literature. To plumb the depths of this evidence is to get a glimpse into the mind and heart of God as He reveals Himself to our transcendent souls. As we do this, entering more deeply into the conversion process, we feel the call of the Lord to bring the good news of His unconditional love and salvation to the world. We recognize at once that we are truly made in the image and likeness of God, that we are called to eternal joy and love with Him and one another in His Kingdom, and that He lavishly gives grace, power, and love to us through His Son, Jesus Christ; the Holy Spirit; and the Catholic Church. Yet we also recognize that there is something dark and aberrant in this world that belongs neither to God or His Kingdom—something that wills us to embrace hatred, egocentricity, domination, and self-worship, leading ultimately to our demise. We see in the teaching of Jesus that this power is Satan, who sows the seeds of discontent, stokes the fires of passion, entices us to self-idolatry, and tries to separate us from the Lord of love. We might at first be overwhelmed by the recognition of this foe described so aptly in the Letter to the Ephesians:

> We are not contending against flesh and blood, but against the principalities, against the powers, against the world rulers of this present darkness, against the spiritual hosts of wickedness in the heavenly places. Therefore take the whole armor of God, that you may be able to withstand in the evil day, and having done all, to stand. Stand therefore, having fastened the belt of truth around your waist, and having put on the breastplate of righteousness, and having shod your feet with the equipment of the gospel of peace; besides all these, taking the shield of faith, with which you can quench all the flaming darts of the Evil One. And take the helmet of salvation, and the sword of the Spirit, which is the word of God. (6:12–17)

As the Pauline author states, Jesus Christ has not left us alone with our enemy, but has prepared and equipped us for this battle by the gifts of His Holy Spirit, His Word, and His Church, as well as virtue and prayer. Yet even with these supernatural gifts, we have one more exceedingly important grace to rely on beyond our natural powers—the unconditional love and mercy of Jesus Christ. Thus, even if we should fail miserably again and again, we are not on our own to "win" entrance into the Kingdom of God, for in our weakness, Christ comes, forgives, heals, and sanctifies. This mystery is so remarkable and beautiful that it astounds Saint Paul, who found himself still struggling with "the flesh" (certain deadly sins) after twenty years. As noted above, his exasperation at his continued weakness and failure is worth repeating, for it shows us what we ourselves must do when faced with the same challenge:

> I do not understand my own actions. For I do not do what I want, but I do the very thing I hate.... I can will what is right, but I cannot do it. For I do not do the good I want, but the evil I do not want is what I do. Now if I do what I do not want, it is no longer I that do it, but sin which dwells within me. So I find it to be a law that when I want to do right, evil lies close at hand.... Wretched man that I am! Who will deliver me from this body of death? Thanks be to God through Jesus Christ our Lord! (Rom 7:15, 18–21, 24–25)

If we bear Saint Paul's good counsel in mind, while firmly aiming at continued self-transformation and formation of conscience, we will make progress. This has certainly been my own life experience, and I assume, with my many imperfections, that I am not very different from the rest of humanity. Notwithstanding this, progress in moral conversion brings us ever more deeply into the truth, love, goodness, beauty, and home of the Lord we seek—or perhaps better, the Lord who seeks us. As we draw closer to the Lord, we touch ever more deeply the joy and peace He offers—even if we are beset by temptations and other interference from our spiritual enemy. This is true happiness, the most sublime happiness arising out of what we have termed "Level Four purpose in life". The more we taste it, the more we are drawn like Christian mystics into the Lord's living flame of love.

So where do we go from here? As the great commentator on Christian mysticism Evelyn Underhill implies, no Christian mystic stays in the highest heavens, but always returns to Christ's flock to share the goodness and love of Christ he has experienced.[18] Thus, all Christians—particularly those living in the highest dimensions of

---

[18] See Evelyn Underhill, *Mysticism: A Study in the Nature and Development of Spiritual Consciousness* (New York: Renaissance Classics, 2012), pp. 15–17.

Level Four—are called by the unconditionally loving Lord to the mission of evangelization; and so our Trilogy concludes with a detailed summary of the need for evangelization within our culture, and how to use the information and tools of evangelization presented in the four volumes of the Quartet and the three volumes of this Trilogy. This enables us to say the prayer of the Pauline author to the Ephesians for every person who is open to the words of evangelization we bring in Christ Jesus:

I bow my knees before the Father, from whom every family in heaven and on earth is named, that according to the riches of his glory he may grant you to be strengthened with might through his Spirit in the inner man, and that Christ may dwell in your hearts through faith; that you, being rooted and grounded in love, may have power to comprehend with all the saints what is the breadth and length and height and depth, and to know the love of Christ which surpasses knowledge, that you may be filled with all the fulness of God. (3:14–19)

PART ONE

The Reality of Divine Goodness
and Spiritual Evil

INTRODUCTION TO PART ONE

In Volume II of the Quartet (*The Soul's Upward Yearning*), we described our unconscious awareness of a cosmic struggle between good and evil—manifest in our dreams (through unconscious archetypes) and in the literature of contemporary myths such as J.R.R. Tolkien's *Lord of the Rings*, J.K. Rowling's *Harry Potter*, and George Lucas' *Star Wars*. We further noted that the reason these contemporary myths are at the top of all-time literary and film sales is that they resonate within the deepest dimensions of our psyche—almost as if the myth and its symbols were present to the psyche itself before we had any capacity to learn about them. Carl Jung validated the presence of these archetypal symbols in the unconscious psyche of children as revealed by their dreams.[1]

Yet we must ask ourselves the questions, is the cosmic struggle between good and evil only an archetypal myth within our unconscious psyches, or does it represent the reality in which we live? Are we immersed in a supernatural reality transcending and imbuing the worldly reality accessible to our senses? Are the powers of cosmic good—the Triune God, Mary, the saints and angels—present in the world? And do our thoughts and actions interact with them? Do our actions have significance within the cosmic struggle between good and evil? Are there really dark forces—Satan and other demons—who are attempting to affect our identity and destiny? Do they hope to seduce us into their plan to turn the world into a place of domination, hatred, self-idolatry, and despair—instead of love, community, joy, and worship of the true God? Do they hope to seduce us into eternal ruin in addition to assisting their plan to bring ruin to the world? If so, how do we interact with these powers of good and evil?

---

[1] C.J. Jung, *Children's Dreams: Notes from the Seminar Given in 1936–1940*, ed. Lorenz Jung and Maria Meyer-Grass, trans. Ernst Falzeder (Princeton, N.J.: Princeton University Press, 2010), Chapter 1.

How do we protect ourselves from spiritual evil—and how do we contribute to the victory of spiritual good over spiritual evil?

At first glance, the modern mind might think that this "*Lord of the Rings* interpretation" of life and the world is a mere medieval fantasy—a mere projection of our unconscious archetypal myth; but before submitting to this unfounded interpretation, I would ask the reader to consider the evidence for the reality of God, a transphysical soul, and the Resurrection of Jesus given in the Quartet (Volumes II and III) as well as the evidence elucidated in the following three chapters:

Chapter 1, which describes the reality of spiritual good and its presence in the world

Chapter 2, which describes Jesus' defeat of Satan

Chapter 3, which describes the reality of spiritual evil and its presence in the world

Chapter One

The God of Love Is with Us

Introduction

We have already given considerable evidence for the presence of the Triune God within our psyche, human history, and the present moment throughout Volumes II and III of the Quartet—for example, the numinous experience, the intuition of the sacred, the divine source of conscience, and the unconscious awareness of the cosmic struggle between good and evil (Volume II, Chapters 1 and 2). Additionally, we considered the evidence of an intelligent Creator from contemporary physics (see Volume II, Appendix I), and the evidence for a transphysical soul surviving bodily death (and its encounter with a loving white light and Jesus in a heavenly domain) from peer-reviewed medical studies of near-death experiences (Volume II, Chapter 5). Finally, we explored the evidence for the incarnate presence of the Son of God in Jesus Christ, who came to save us and redeem us through an unconditional act of love (Volume III), and Jesus' gift of the Holy Spirit to the Church and to each baptized individual, the Spirit who is almost as interiorly and charismatically active today as in apostolic times (Volume III, Chapter 5).

Evidently the Triune God is exceedingly active in the world and involved in the cosmic struggle between good and evil. Yet the reader may have noticed a glaring omission in the elucidation of previous evidence for God's presence and action. When we spoke of God's interior presence to us, we spoke only of His presence to *all* of us throughout the world—the numinous experience, the intuition of the sacred, conscience, and the subconscious awareness of the cosmic struggle between good and evil. However, we did not address the inspiration, power, and guidance of the Holy Spirit; heightened visions and revelations to specially chosen individuals; or Christian mysticism (with its special states of purification, guidance, and ecstasy). Therefore, we will devote this first chapter to these three special ways in which God makes His presence, guidance, and inspiration felt. In Section I, we will address the power, guidance, and inspiration of the Holy Spirit; in Section II, we will address heightened visions and revelations; and in Section III, we will address Christian mysticism. We also address God's presence in public apparitions of Mary and contemporary scientifically validated miracles concerned with Mary, the saints, and the Holy Eucharist in the appendix to this volume.

I. The Guidance, Power, and Inspiration of the Holy Spirit

The Lord has given us a most remarkable gift: the gift of His Spirit, who is filled with peace, love, protection, unity, inspiration, truth, and life. Jesus told us He would send the Paraclete who would remind us of everything He said and would give us a wisdom that would confound our enemies. Saint Paul tells us that the Holy Spirit knows the mind and heart of God, and when he dwells in us through Baptism, he imparts the love and inspiration of the Father and Jesus to us:

> As it is written, "What no eye has seen, nor ear heard, nor the heart of man conceived, what God has prepared for those who love him," God has revealed to us through the Spirit. For the Spirit searches everything, even the depths of God. For what person knows a man's thoughts except the spirit of the man which is in him? So also no one comprehends the thoughts of God except the Spirit of God. Now we have received not the spirit of the world, but the Spirit which is from God, that we might understand the gifts bestowed on us by God. And we impart this in words not taught by human wisdom but taught by the Spirit, interpreting spiritual truths to those who possess the Spirit. (1 Cor 2:9–13)

As we try to live out our lives as Catholics/Christians, we need to be aware of how our greatest advocate, consoler, protector, inspirer, transformer, and guide works in our lives and how we might be able

to work in tandem with His wisdom and love. I will present four
general points about the Spirit's workings and how we might coor-
dinate our efforts toward love, the common good, and the Kingdom
of God:

  1. A Peace beyond All Understanding (Section I.A)
  2. Inspiration and Guidance (Section I.B)
  3. Transformation in the Heart of Christ (Section I.C)
  4. Working with the Holy Spirit (Section I.D)

There are other dimensions of the guidance, inspiration, and
power of the Holy Spirit that we will take up elsewhere:

  The Holy Spirit's engagement in our struggle with evil spirits (see
    the section of discernment of spirits in Chapter 4, Section V, of
    this volume)
  The Holy Spirit's power and activity in our spiritual conversion
    (see Volume II, Chapter 3, of this Trilogy)
  The Holy Spirit's activity and inspiration in the Church's Magiste-
    rium and in the inspiration of the saints (Volume II, Chapters 1
    and 3, of this Trilogy)

We may now proceed to the activities of the Holy Spirit to guide,
inspire, and protect us in our relationship with the Lord and our
struggle with evil.

A. A Peace beyond All Understanding

The peace coming from the Holy Spirit is more than relief from suffering, a sense of well-being, or a sense of equanimity. It is rooted in
a deep sense of home, home amid the cosmos (which we who have
faith know is being at home with God). Its opposite is alienation, a
sense of not being at home in or "being out of kilter with" the totality. The signature of the Holy Spirit is the sense of having a place in
the totality, of "fitting in", of being bathed in joy or light (even when
one is aware of sadness and darkness)—that is, of being in unity with
the Creator and principle of all being: the Trinity.

As Catholics/Christians, we very likely view this "being at home in the totality", this "freedom from being alone in the totality" as "being part of the Mystical Body of Christ". Being part of Christ's Mystical Body through the Holy Spirit is an experience of home, holiness, unity, joy, and peace as seen through the eyes of thousands of saints who have embraced a life of holiness throughout history.

I have had several explicit experiences of being "at home" in the Mystical Body. They occurred while hearing a bird, hearing truths about the Kingdom of God, walking in a thirteenth-century monastery, and celebrating the Holy Eucharist. These experiences are termed "affective consolations" (see Chapter 4, Section V.A) and point to the essence of Paul's "peace beyond all understanding". There are multiple fruits of this peace. I will address only three:

1. Peace in Times of Suffering (Section I.A.1)
2. Peace in Times of Persecution (Section I.A.2)
3. The Peace Necessary for Good Judgment (Section I.A.3)

1. Peace in Times of Suffering

Have you ever had the experience of being immersed in a tragedy or a troubling or threatening series of events, and in the midst of these troubles, experiencing a deep sense of calm and assurance that everything is going to be alright? When I was younger I had such experiences of the peace of the Holy Spirit, but I actually tried to talk myself out of them. I remember hearing the news of my father's death, and having this deep and abiding peace and sense that everything was going to be fine. I thought to myself, "I should not be feeling this; this is really tragic; my father was only fifty-nine years old; and furthermore, my mother is probably frantic; and furthermore, my sister is not finished with college; and furthermore ..." The more the Holy Spirit attempted to intervene with peace, the more I "guilted myself" out of it. I later came to find, through multiple experiences of this "peace in the midst of troubles", that the Spirit was genuinely present, working within my life and the lives of people around me to bring good out of what seemed so negative. My advice is to "take the peace and follow the lead of the Spirit who assures us that everything is going to be alright." Doing this will give the Holy Spirit room to maneuver through your free will to bring about optimal goodness and love for you, others, the community, and the Kingdom of God.

2. Peace in Times of Persecution

Have you ever had the experience of being marginalized, embarrassed, or even threatened because of your faith or your loyalty to Christ or the Church? If you're anything like me, when these situations occur, you might feel a deep dejection, emptiness, or even a sense of fore-boding or evil. These feelings may debilitate you for a few moments or even cause disturbance of sleep. These feelings can be mitigated by praying the prayer "Thy loving will be done." The more I surrender to God through this most efficacious prayer, the more I sense God's guidance, and the more I know that the persecution occurring will result in a better condition for others, my organization, my commu-nity, and yes, even me.

This sense of confidence about the redeeming love of God is not a sense that God is going to bail me out of the bad situation and the bad feelings that accompany it. Rather, it is a sense of what is promised in the Gospels:

> When they bring you to trial and deliver you up, do not be anxious beforehand about what you are to say; but say whatever is given you in that hour, for it is not you who speak, but the Holy Spirit. (Mk 13:11; cf. Mt 10:19; Lk 21:12)

The Holy Spirit grants us serenity through surrender, and then guides and inspires. I frequently wake up at three o'clock in the morning, and the words I need to say are given to me, and these words (or arguments) are more than sufficient to introduce truth in the midst of trickery, deception, and outright falsity. Most of the time these words are convincing, but even when they fail to per-suade opponents, they have a way of letting light into the world. When one thinks about the Cross of Christ, one can see that His words did not convince His opponents, but they did, through the Holy Spirit, let the light of the Father shine before all. As a result, those words let the light of the Holy Spirit, the Church, the sacra-ments, the Sacred Scriptures, the Liturgy, and the actions of *agapē* flood into the world. In the end, the Holy Spirit will be victorious, even if we, as human instruments, are somewhat baffled as to how and when it will occur.

The interesting aspect of this is the confidence we feel in times of persecution. It is not a confidence derived from our thoughts or planning, for frequently our thoughts leave us bereft of confidence. Neither is it a confidence derived from our natural feelings, for they are filled with foreboding and bewilderment. The source of the confidence? It is the peace beyond all understanding, the grace of the Holy Spirit, who comforts, protects, guides, and ultimately allows the loving will of God, indeed, the very Kingdom of God, to be victorious. It is lovely indeed to have experienced this grace, to have been honored to be an instrument, even if it comes at the cost of persecution. This is why Christ says: "Blessed [happy] are you when men revile you and persecute you" (Mt 5:11).

3. The Peace Necessary for Good Judgment

Good judgment is needed because many of our decisions cannot be resolved by mathematical or analytical processes. They require an intuition about the right thing to do, which is developed over the course of hundreds of experiences and relationships. Without peace of mind, this intuition (this essential power of judgment) could be led astray. When it is so led, it could harm people, organizations, and even communities.

If you are anything like me, then you will need the peace of the Holy Spirit to overcome the concerns of egocentricity. Countless have been the number of times when I have gone on an ego trip to the detriment of my good judgment. I recall once being given excellent advice by a subordinate who did not, in my view, adequately acknowledge my "superior intellect". He was simply asserting his opinion as better than my own! This really upset me. Indeed, I found it deeply disturbing. This led to a reflection about how others had similarly mistreated me. I immediately began to make mountains out of little ego molehills, and the next thing I knew, I could not concern myself with the big decisions of the day or the common good of the organization. I had to allow my psyche to be fully occupied with blame and outrage toward these contemptuous underlings.

The Holy Spirit began to weave His wonderful grace into my heart, but at first I would not listen. It was as if the Holy Spirit was telling me, "Bob, move over and let me drive for a minute," but I had to reply, "I'll get back to You as soon as possible. I need to drive this car into the wall first."

As the car approaches the wall, the Holy Spirit has a way of being more persistent, of calming me down, of gently but firmly guiding me to look at the silliness (or even the potential insanity) of my egoism. He frequently helps me to not only sense imminent tragedy and the embarrassment following from it; He helps me to overcome the embarrassment I feel just before the car hits the wall. For a fleeting moment, I have the peace of good judgment and can apply the brakes with proper apologies.

This experience points to a more subtle, fundamental truth—namely, that the peace of the Holy Spirit helps us to attain good judgment in our decisions, great and small. If we ask for and attend to His peace, which is even embedded in our most egocentric moments, good judgment can return, and that good judgment, under the influence of the Holy Spirit, will lead to the common good, indeed, the optimal good, the good of the Kingdom, within the world.

B. Inspiration and Guidance

The Holy Spirit not only provides peace, but also inspiration and guidance. I will consider three aspects of this inspiration, which is by no means exhaustive:

1. Words of Help and Edification (Section I.B.1)
2. The *Sensus Fidei* (Section I.B.2)
3. Guidance on Our Way (Section I.B.3)

1. Words of Help and Edification

I might begin with the passage cited above: "Do not be anxious beforehand about what you are to say; but say whatever is given you . . . for it is not you who speak, but the Holy Spirit" (Mk 13:11). The Holy Spirit "gives words" not only in times of persecution, but also for the building of the Kingdom and the edification of listeners. Many have been the times when I was inspired to write about a topic, but I could not quite conceive of what to say. I would start writing one simple thesis statement that reflected the direction I wanted to go. Suddenly, words began to come to me. I began to think of additional points that bolstered the thesis statement, additional distinctions that clarified it, stories that animated it, and then good advice that could be drawn from it.

You might immediately conjecture, "Well, that is the normal muse of an author. Why call it 'inspiration of the Holy Spirit'?" I certainly agree that this process does represent an ordinary muse of authorship, but when I read back what I just said, and actually derive benefit from it because my writing was more profound than anything I had consciously thought of previously, I must admit I am truly given pause. I find myself asking, "Who said that?" For it really doesn't sound like something I would say. It doesn't sound like my style, and the content seems to have exceeded my limited powers of perception and wisdom. One might say, "Well, your subconscious mind was tacitly aware of all of this, but your conscious mind was not. That is why your conscious mind was genuinely surprised at the depth of content and the beauty of style." Hmmmm. If my subconscious mind is so smart, how come it doesn't speak more often to my conscious mind so that I might derive benefit from it every day outside the context of preaching, writing, or helping others? Why is it that when I am not trying to help someone, I am almost befuddled by my musings and confused by my subconscious mind? Just curious.

This gives us a clue about how the Holy Spirit of love operates. The usual context is when we're trying to help or edify another person. The Spirit does not blast thoughts into our heads, but rather gives us a thesis statement with a sense of drawing us to something deeper. Now we, in our freedom, must follow this sense of being drawn. If we do, then our desire to help, and our effort to formulate, combine with this sense of following Wisdom, and words begin to tumble out. They may be prosaic or poetic, ordinary or beautiful to behold, plain and straightforward or filled with metaphor and imagination, but whatever the case, they have the capacity to reach into the hearts of deeply empathetic individuals, moving them to new depths and directions of love. Our job is to follow this sense of being drawn, and to exert the effort to put words into what our hearts already seem to know. The Holy Spirit will take care of the rest.

2. The Sensus Fidei

The Second Vatican Council's Dogmatic Constitution on the Church, *Lumen Gentium*, declares:

> The holy people of God shares also in Christ's prophetic office; it spreads abroad a living witness to Him (cf. Heb. 13:15).... The entire body of the faithful, anointed as they are by the Holy One (cf. Jn. 2:20, 27), cannot err in matters of belief. They manifest this special property by means of the whole peoples' supernatural discernment in matters of faith when "from the Bishops down to the last of the lay faithful" (cf. S. Augustinus, D Praed. Sanct. 14, 27: PL 44, 980) they show universal agreement in matters of faith [sense of faith] and morals. That discernment in matters of faith is aroused and sustained by the Spirit of truth. It is exercised under the guidance of the sacred teaching authority, in faithful and respectful obedience to which the people of God accepts that which is not just the word of men but truly the word of God (cf. 1 Thess. 2:13).[1]

What the Council Fathers acknowledge is that when we loyally defer to the teaching authority of the Church, the Holy Spirit grants us deep insight into the truth of faith, which has the capacity to move, transform, and deepen our love and life. Have you ever had the experience of reading a book or listening to a lecture, and as you were reading or listening, you began to think, "I don't know why this is wrong, but this sounds wrong." You may have gone to the lecture without any suspicion or any knowledge that would have evoked such a thought, yet you feel that there is something wrong, and even disquieting or disturbing. You may have left the lecture preferring not to follow the lecturer's advice and to leave the entire matter aside. Then, five years later you read an article where this precise idea is shown to be contrary to Church teaching or to the love of Christ. You might have thought, "Hey! I knew that five years

[1] Second Vatican Council, Dogmatic Constitution on the Church, *Lumen Gentium* (November 21, 1964), no. 12, http://www.vatican.va/archive/hist_councils/ii_vatican_council /documents/vat-ii_const_19641121_lumen-gentium_en.html.

ago, but I just didn't know why." I believe this sense of disquiet or disturbance is the Holy Spirit, protecting us from what could lead to disruption of life and love.

It might be retorted, "Well, maybe all your reading in theology that has congealed in your subconscious mind led you to the discovery of the potential for aberrancy or error. Why call it the Holy Spirit?" I might find this explanation tempting were it not for the fact that I had such experiences prior to doing any significant reading in theology. When I was in high school, I had some fine catechism teachers, but they did not equip me for the ideas I was to confront in college. Yet, I *knew* that there was something wrong with "situation ethics", even though I first found it rather noble and attractive. I wanted to believe that all I needed to do was "seek the greatest amount of neighbor welfare for the greatest number of people" and not have to worry about principles, rules, or anything like that. Yet, I felt a deep disquiet amid the feelings of nobility and simplicity, and I began to sense an error of omission that was not yet clear to my discursive power. It led me to research, then to Christian ethicist Paul Ramsey,[2] and then to the revelation that one needs principles and rules to assess the *means* to even the most noble ends. Without such rules, the end could easily be thought to justify an evil means.

How does one know what one does not know? How does one know *that* one does not know? How does one have the foreknowledge about an error of omission when one does not know all the possibilities? How does one feel deep disquiet while feeling a great sense of nobility? I am not certain of the answer to this, but I have a sneaking suspicion that it is not the efficacy of my subconscious mind. Perhaps the Holy Spirit?

Conversely, have you ever had the experience of reading a book by a spiritual writer and finding yourself absolutely captivated?[3] I have. When I was in college, a friend gave me a used copy of the *Summa* and indicated that I should at least read part of the first part. Though I found the style incomprehensible (with all the counterarguments and the responses to the counterarguments), I felt inspired by these passages. I recall three feelings in particular. First, I felt a genuine sense of

---

[2] See the main work of Paul Ramsey in *Deeds and Rules in Christian Ethics* (Lanham, Md.: University of America Press, 1967).

[3] E.g., Saint Thomas Aquinas, *Summa Theologica* I, q. 2, a. 3.

being at home with God. I also had a sense of Saint Thomas' holiness and a desire to be involved in it myself. Thirdly, I felt not so much an awareness that particular propositions were true, but that I was in the presence of Truth itself. At the time, I was not able to articulate these feelings, but I knew that Saint Thomas' writings were not only true but also life-changing. As I read through the unusual style and difficult prose, I felt fed, at home, and desirous of more. Again, given my ignorance at the time, I hesitate to attribute these desires, thoughts, and feelings to some mysterious certitude within my subconscious. Quite frankly, I believe that the Holy Spirit was there inspiring, cajoling, guiding, and filling me with light, delight, and home.

The Holy Spirit will not leave anyone bereft of the disquiet of falsity, or the inspiration of truth. All we need do to experience this deeper, life-changing, efficacious, and loving insight is to defer to the teaching authority of the Church, as the Second Vatican Council suggests, and follow the sense of light, home, holiness, and peace that brings not only joy to the soul, but a wisdom and love quite beyond our natural ability. As usual, the Holy Spirit takes care of the rest.

3. Guidance on Our Way

The Acts of the Apostles is filled with instances of guidance by the Holy Spirit. As one reads the multiple testimonies of Peter, Paul, and the other disciples about how the Spirit guided them to and from specific towns and circumstances, one gets the feeling that the direct experience of the Holy Spirit guiding the Church was almost commonplace (see Acts 8:28–30; 10:18–20; 11:12; 13:4; 16:5–7; 19:6–8, 20–22; 20:21–23; 21:3–5).

I suppose most people have had the experience of making a prudential judgment and then feeling a deep sense of disquiet. As one begins to follow through on the prudential judgment, the disquiet becomes disturbance of soul and even foreboding, and eventually, one begins to see that the prudential judgment was not prudential at all. The continuous movement from disquiet to discord to disturbance to foreboding can *sometimes* be indicative of the Spirit's guidance. Needless to say, one cannot equate disturbance of soul with the guidance of the Holy Spirit, for there could be many natural reasons for this—for example, insecurity, natural fear, anxiety about associating with certain people, and anxiety about the unknown. Furthermore, the Evil One can use disturbance of soul to dissuade us from a course of action that is good and holy (see Chapter 4). This is why we need rules for the discernment of spirits (see Chapter 4, Section V).

How, then, do we know when disquiet is from the Holy Spirit? By following the best light of our reason and prudential judgment, while keeping attuned to *possible* problems indicated by the sense of spiritual disturbance. If problems arise and become truly precarious, then one might want, not necessarily to reverse one's course of action, but to redirect or redesign it. The objective is to keep both lights (i.e., the light of reason and the light of the Holy Spirit's peace) in conformity with one another. If one neglects the light of reason, one could easily be paralyzed by negative emotions. Conversely, if one neglects the light of the Holy Spirit, one can be deceived by rationalization and unforeseen consequences. It is important to note that the Holy Spirit does not in any way want us to ignore the light of reason and prudence, for reason and prudence are also inspired and guided by that same Spirit.

The Holy Spirit can also move one *toward* action through peace, excitement, and zeal. The Holy Spirit can draw one into an opportunity, then open doors into that opportunity, then draw one further into the opportunity through a sense of peace, excitement, and zeal, and then open more doors, and so forth. This favorite "approach" of the Holy Spirit can happen so quickly that one can find oneself in a whole new dimension of life, marking out whole sections of one's calendar, starting whole new institutes, and writing whole new books before one has had the opportunity to ask how one got oneself into this new state of life in the first place.

I am not suggesting that all manifestations of this approach are the action of the Holy Spirit, for sometimes one can be *naturally* drawn toward an opportunity, and by *natural* happenstance have doors open, and be drawn into an opportunity further by *natural* feelings of peace, zeal, and excitement. But one can see the "fingerprints" of the Holy Spirit when one finds oneself doing what one was previously disinclined to do, doing it well, and producing considerable spiritual fruit beyond one's highest expectations. Hmmmm. Could this aggregate of improbable events be more than mere coincidence?

The Holy Spirit also guides us in our long-term plans, vocations, and elections in life. Saint Ignatius tried to show how we might best discern the Spirit's guidance in this regard through his "Rules for the

Discernment of Spirits" in his *Spiritual Exercises*. These will be taken up in Chapter 4, Section V.

C. Transformation in the Heart of Christ

By now, it is probably clear that the grace of the Holy Spirit is personally transforming. The Spirit's power does not simply *help* us in times of suffering; it *transforms* us as well. The Spirit not only gives us words of faith in times of persecution, but also transforms our capacity for love through that persecution. The Spirit does not merely guide us to opportunities for the Kingdom or opportunities to edify, but helps us through zeal, love of the Kingdom, and service to grow in faith, wisdom, and love. Thus, the Spirit always has a twofold agenda:

1. the advancement of the human community (in peace, justice, love, the common good, and the Kingdom of God), and
2. the personal growth and transformation of the individuals involved in advancing the Kingdom.

How can we cooperate with this twofold agenda of the Spirit? By attending to His "game plan" for bringing personal transformation out of life's successes and sufferings. This is frequently marked by a six-part cycle:

Greater vision and capacity for following
opportunities presented by the Spirit

6. Greater sense of peace and home in the God of Unconditional Love

5. Increase in *agapē* (ends virtue), detachment, humility, and other means virtues through grace in suffering

1. Following the opportunities provided by the Spirit

2. Sense of inspiration, enthusiasm, zeal, contribution, and love

3. Increase in confidence, trust, and faith in the Spirit

4. Reliance upon the Spirit in times of suffering

When I follow the opportunities provided by the Spirit and notice some good for the Kingdom emerging out of this joint effort (no. 1 in the above chart), I cannot help but feel inspired and filled with zeal (no. 2). It is not merely the sense of contribution, the sense of making a difference to something of ultimate significance, but also a sense of "doing something beautiful for the one I love". This inspiration/enthusiasm/zeal/sense of contribution/love makes the promise of Jesus in the parables (e.g., the parables of the talents [Mt 25:14–30; Lk 19:11–27] and the mustard seed [Mt 13:31–32; Mk 4:30–32; Lk 13:18–19]) come alive. If we use our faith and act on the opportunities given us to build the Kingdom, it will generally lead to an increase in trust (that is, faith [no. 3]). The sense of inspiration/enthusiasm constitutes a history of working well with the Spirit, which leads to an inner confidence that the Spirit really is working with me. This inner confidence, in turn, translates into trust in the providence promised by Jesus Christ.

This trust (built on a history of partnership with the Holy Spirit in building the Kingdom) will become a conduit of grace in times of suffering and persecution (no. 4). To the extent that I trust in the Spirit, I will also be able to believe in His providential action working in and through suffering. This trust enables me to bear patiently with suffering when I do not yet see its ultimate meaning or goodness. I genuinely believe that there is meaning and goodness in the suffering, and that if I cooperate with the Lord in prayer, He will affect this goodness in His own time and way. When He does this, it will generally produce goodness (for me, the community, and the Kingdom) far beyond my highest expectations.

Grace in suffering leads to *personal* transformation. In my experience, the Spirit has brought personal transformation out of suffering in four ways that are directly related to my ability to live the life of the Beatitudes:

1. Leveraging pain to break the spell of bad habits
2. Leveraging pain to give deeper perspective into others' needs, and therefore, deeper empathy
3. Leveraging pain to produce greater humility (detachment from ego) so that I might live more deeply the life of the Beatitudes (see 2 Cor 12:7)
4. Leveraging pain to increase my dependence on and trust in Christ (see 2 Cor 12:8–10)

These points are taken up in detail in Volume IV of the Quartet (*The Light Shines on in the Darkness*, Chapters 7 and 10). Though suffering is unpleasant, it can produce the fruits of *agapē* in ways that no other life experience can. Suffering contains the magic ingredient of "pain leading to new habits". If I cooperate with the Spirit in times of suffering, I can break old habits and form new habits with an incredible freedom. This freedom for "new habits of the heart" leads toward the life of the Beatitudes (no. 5).

For example, with respect to leveraging pain to break bad habits, I can identify several instances in my life where I was being carried along by a momentum that was destructive to both myself and others (e.g., self-justified outbursts that no one else thought were justified and intellectual elitism). I had two strikes against me when the bad habits were strong—namely, I believed them to be justifiable, and their momentum was so strong that they prevented me from reflecting on their destructive character.

The wonder of abject pain is its capacity to break down the structure of previously existing beliefs. I am really not a masochist; indeed, I hate pain. Yet, I know that some of the more painful experiences of my life have caused me to doubt thoroughly entrenched destructive belief systems. If I cooperate with the Holy Spirit in this moment of doubt, He can rush in with a new belief system (patterned along the lines of the Beatitudes). The "trick" is for me to be responsive. When I perceive wisdom (particularly the wisdom of the Beatitudes) in ways that I never saw before, I need to be responsive—that is, to embrace the wisdom that will bring me beyond my previous "blindness of convenience and past habit".

However, this is not enough, for I cannot rely on pain (a negative motivator) alone to break the bad habit. Indeed, I really don't want to, because it hurts too much! I then must cooperate with the Spirit to reinforce the good habit through *prayer*. I need to allow the beauty of God's wisdom manifest in my contemplative life to move the good habit into a position of dominance in my psyche. Here, the Holy Spirit uses the sense of peace, beauty, awe, love, and home intrinsic to prayer and contemplation to infuse the goodness, beauty, and wisdom of the Beatitudes within my psyche (no. 6).

The above example is really like a dialogue between the Holy Spirit and the suffering person. The Holy Spirit does not cause pain. Pain generally happens through natural causation or human agency.

When it does, it is up to the suffering person not to turn inward, but to look for the grace of the Spirit operating through the pain. This grace can normally be found by looking for destructive belief systems that are being called into question by the pain (and by the Holy Spirit). The job of the suffering person is then threefold:

1. Not to become bitter, self-pitying, and closed off, but rather, to remain open to an adventure of grace
2. To look for the "self-justified", destructive belief system that is being challenged
3. To allow oneself to doubt that self-justified, destructive belief system seriously and deeply

The Holy Spirit will then present the wisdom of the counter-position (the position of the Beatitudes). When the Spirit does this, one will be struck by the rightness and goodness of what was previously thought to be virtually unintelligible. One should not be surprised to hear oneself exclaiming, "I finally understand what is meant by 'the poor in spirit' (i.e., the humble-hearted). I'm beginning to see why the poor in spirit are truly blessed. I'm beginning to understand what Jesus was up to and how serious He was about the Beatitudes. They were not intended in a merely idealistic way; they really are the meaning of life and are truly *beautiful*." One might even come to the remarkable conclusion (as I have over multiple occasions) that God really is unconditional love, and Jesus really is the Son of God. It was not that I didn't believe this tenet of faith *in my mind* previously, for I had strong intellectual convictions and beliefs. But I really did not understand this truth in my heart of hearts; I did not understand it from the vantage point of love (*agapē*). The job of the suffering person at this point in the dialogue is to say, "This is really the meaning of life." These points are discussed thoroughly in Volume IV of the Quartet, *The Light Shines on in the Darkness* (Chapters 3, 7, and 9).

The final stage of the dialogue is to replace negative motivations with positive ones. The main positive motivation for me comes through prayer. When I begin to deepen my belief in and living of the Beatitudes, I see them more deeply in the reading of Scripture and in my loving of the Lord in prayer. When I say, "I love You, and

I know You love me," or "I love the beauty of Your ways and the beauty of Your heart," or "I want to imitate You in Your love," I understand it, believe it, and intend it in a way that is filled not only with the appreciation of lessons learned through pain, but also with a deep sense of the grace of prayer, which is filled with a serenity, peace, love, and above all home that is woven into the experience of contemplation by the Holy Spirit (no. 6 in the abovementioned cycle). An explanation of contemplation is given in Chapter 1 (Section III) of this volume. This becomes the foundation for beginning the cycle anew with even greater opportunities for advancing the common good and the Kingdom of God, and greater opportunities for embarking on the adventure of personal transformation, contemplation, and *agapē*.

D. Working with the Holy Spirit

By now it might be clear that the Holy Spirit works through a conspiracy of grace. The Spirit gives peace, home, and perspective, even in the midst of suffering and persecution; gives inspiration and guidance when our natural insight and logic seem to fail; gives a sense of faith and transcendent knowledge through our deference to Church teaching; and brings deep personal transformation out of suffering and zeal for the Kingdom. But the Spirit does not stop there. He works in the hearts of others to cultivate faith, hope, and love; He inspires zeal within our *community*, blows open doors of spiritual opportunity, and creates a *collective* "field of grace" that grows in direct proportion to our cooperation with Him. How can we cooperate with the grace of the Holy Spirit? By remembering two simple thoughts:

1. Follow the opportunity manifest in the inspiration of the Spirit.
2. Pray "Come Holy Spirit, enter the hearts of Your faithful and enkindle in them the fire of Your wisdom and love."

The content of this prayer is self-evident, but the first point merits brief attention. Recall from Section III.B that the Holy Spirit's preferred method is to draw us into an opportunity, then open doors into that opportunity, then draw us further into the opportunity through a sense of peace, excitement, and zeal, and then open more doors, and so forth. When you feel inspired (through peace, excitement, and zeal), when you feel the energy of an opportunity that you might be able to accommodate, when you feel the opportunity to "help build the Kingdom of God" and to participate in a little piece of this eternal legacy, follow it. If doors keep blowing open in front of you, and you sense that you can accommodate it without doing damage to your other commitments, then keep following. If people start joining in and a "conspiracy of grace" seems to form around your initiative, and you are not required to undermine previous commitments, keep following it.

However, if you find that following the opportunity is undermining previous commitments, or causing interior disturbance (over the medium- to long-term), or that doors are not opening, you might reconsider the so-called opportunistic prospect. I have had multiple experiences of following "false leads" in my life. Generally two or more of the above negative signs manifest themselves, and enough doors slam so that I know within about three months that the effort is probably not worth my time, or is meant for somebody else, or is meant to be initiated in the future.

There are many reasons why false leads manifest themselves. Sometimes it is attributable to *me* wanting an initiative to succeed because it's appealing, or it (egotistically) adds to my list of accomplishments, or it's a great idea whose time has not yet come, or it requires a gathering of additional people. Unfortunately, I find that half the time, false leads are attributable to my egotistical motivations. The Holy Spirit tries to warn me, but my ego cannot let go. Nevertheless, the Holy Spirit prevails and protects me (even if this should hurt a lot and result in abject failure). I have become better at detecting ego-driven initiatives (through the school of hard knocks, God's grace, and the contemplative life), but it is still a challenge, because opportunity-seeking is always a two-sided coin. Whatever is done for the greater glory of God can also be done for the "greater glory of me" when I try to replace God at the center of my universe or when I just plain and simple want to get another ego hit from another entry on my list of accomplishments. In any case, you can be sure that the Holy Spirit will try to ward off the bad effects of "ego gone mad" and will try to replace it with gentle peace, a love of the Beatitudes, and a sense of who one really is through the Eucharist, through the contemplative life, and, if need be, through the school of failed endeavors.

If, through our spiritual life, we allow the Lord to infuse purity of heart (a desire that He be in the center that motivates a desire for *His* Kingdom and will), we may be reasonably certain that the open doors following upon excitement/peace/zeal will be "our opportunity" (with the Holy Spirit) to be engaged in the noble enterprise of doing our little part to build the eternal Kingdom. What could be better than this?

II. Visions and Revelations—and Their Distinction from Psychologically Induced Phenomena

We might begin with a few distinctions. First, public apparitions are distinct from private visions, because the former occur before many witnesses and have additional miraculous dimensions (such as instantaneous healings of late-term diseases) that are scientifically validatable. Private visions do not have this corroborative quality. The appendix to this volume presents three public apparitions with accompanying miracles concerned with Mary (Lourdes, Fatima, and Guadalupe), the saints (healings associated with the beatification or canonization of Pope Saint John Paul II, Saint Padre Pio, and Blessed Fulton J. Sheen), and the remarkable Eucharistic miracle overseen by Archbishop Bergoglio (now Pope Francis).

Despite the fact that private visions are generally not susceptible to scientific validation, they are nonetheless real, and many of the saints have experienced them. Though the faithful do not have to believe any private revelation, they have provided devotional methods and contemplative death for many. Yet we must be very careful about accepting the validity of someone's claim to have an authentic private vision or revelation, because some of them can be hoaxes perpetrated for the self-aggrandizement of the "visionary" and because many are not visions from God at all, but manifestations of psychological disorders such as schizophrenia. Nevertheless, if God really does manifest Himself through private revelations to people living genuinely holy and humble lives, how can we have some assurance that their "visions" really did come from God, and did not arise out of a psychological disorder?

How might we generally distinguish between heightened visions and revelations versus psychological illness? Dr. Craig Isaacs, a clinical psychologist and Anglican priest who has studied these phenomena extensively, responds:

> The range of human functioning referred to [between psychosis on the one hand and mystical experience on the other] can also be conceptualized as the level of differentiation in the ability to consciously observe reality, to distinguish between self and other, between subject and object, and this is related to the proportionate integrity of the ego. At one end of the scope of ego functioning there is very limited differentiation between subject and object while at the other end there is a transcendent integration of subject and object, with various intervening levels of discrimination.[4]

If the ego is functioning well, the subject will be able to distinguish easily between himself and others, subject and object, and real versus merely imaginary objects. However, if the ego is not functioning well, there will be a blurring of these ordinary distinctions. This blurring is precisely what characterizes psychological disorders. The most serious disorder that is tantamount to an eclipse of ego functioning is psychosis where there appears to be a loss of the ability to distinguish between self and others, subject and object, and real objects versus merely imaginary ones. Personality disorders (ranging from paranoid, schizoid, borderline, antisocial, and histrionic to narcissistic, avoidant, dependent, and obsessive-compulsive personality) have varying degrees of ego disengagement, but not complete disengagement. Thus, in personality disorders, the subject has partial ability to distinguish between self and others, subject and object, and real versus imaginary objects.

Much less serious than psychological disorders is the imaginary playmate of children. Evidently there is a suspension of ego engagement by the child, but there also appears to be awareness on the part

---

[4] Craig Isaacs, *Revelations and Possession: Distinguishing Spiritual from Psychological Experiences* (Kearney, Neb.: Morris Publishing, 2009), p. 62.

of the child that the imaginary playmate is not completely real. As the child grows, ego functioning becomes clearer and stronger, making it difficult for the child to suspend ego functioning. When the imaginary playmate no longer seems real, the child loses interest in it.

Let us now turn to the opposite end of the spectrum—that is, the mystic or the recipient of an authentic revelation from God (e.g., a vision, or a voice).[5] One indication that the vision, voice, or mystical experience is authentic is that the subject has clear and strong ego functioning and therefore discriminates clearly and strongly between self and others, and between subject and object. This enables him to distinguish clearly between real versus imaginary objects.[6] The subject is also aware that the vision or voice is extraordinary, that it is not part of ordinary experience. His ego functioning with respect to ordinary experience is acute, which makes the extraordinary experience stand out—as extraordinary. Frequently, subjects of authentic revelation say nothing to family or friends because they know that their friends will not be able to relate to their extraordinary experiences. Thus they are not only able to distinguish between self and others; they realize what others can and cannot be expected to understand.

Additionally, recipients of an authentic revelation are able to distinguish the transcendental and sacred nature of the "wholly Other" appearing to them in the midst of profane and immanent ordinary experience.[7] This sacred transcendental feature is not merely an authoritative voice, a divine vision, or a heightened experience—it is a voice, vision, or experience filled with mystery, majesty, glory, and sacredness, inducing awe, reverence, and worship. Thus, the recipient of authentic revelation or mystical experience is able to make ordinary distinctions not only between self and others, subject and object, and real and imaginary objects, but also between the ordinary and the extraordinary—the transcendent and the immanent, and the sacred and the profane.

---

[5] See Adolphe Tanquerey, *The Spiritual Life: A Treatise on Ascetical and Mystical Theology*, trans. Herman Branderis (1930; repub., Rockford, Ill.: Tan Books, 2000), pp. 701–8.

[6] See Isaacs, *Revelations and Possession*, pp. 61–64. See also Tanquerey, *Spiritual Life*, pp. 11–14.

[7] See Evelyn Underhill, *Mysticism: A Study in the Nature and Development of Spiritual Consciousness* (Mineola, N.Y.: Dover Publications, 2002), pp. 9–13, 46–67, 78–81, 99–105, and 152–62.

Moreover, recipients of authentic revelation do not have the compulsiveness, confusion, fear, and agitation that oftentimes accompanies psychosis and personality disorders[8]—quite the opposite. They have an overwhelming sense of peace, fulfillment, enchantment, love, joy, and even ecstasy.[9] For these individuals, not only the ego, but the soul (explained in Volume II of the Quartet) is fully engaged. Thus the soul's awareness of perfect truth, goodness, and love; the sacredness of the "wholly Other"; and the call to authenticity of self (in light of its awareness of perfect truth, goodness, and love) enables the recipient of authentic revelation to be aware of and strive for his most authentic self, which leads to a conviction about the truth of his experience. Isaacs describes it as a "deep, calming, ego-syntonic conviction that what has been experienced is truly real".[10] This awareness leads the recipient of authentic revelation to a sense of humble and holy unworthiness—as he experiences perfectly good, loving, and holy "Worthiness Itself". This inclines the subject toward surrender to the Holy One—and in the case of the mystic, to complete surrender to the absolutely holy.[11]

This stands in direct contrast to psychosis in which the subject's loss of ego consciousness causes him to inflate his ego and construct what Isaacs calls "a defiant, proud, judgmental attitude with an unrealistic elevation of self-worth".[12] This unfounded extreme ego inflation appears to be a defensive reaction to the fear, confusion, and agitation the psychotic experiences in his hallucinatory state.[13] Furthermore, the voices of a psychotic (or those suffering from serious personality disorder) are not encouraging, peaceful, and clear in direction and guidance. Rather, as Isaacs notes, "[The psychotic's] voices are often confusing, harsh, and destructive. The psychotic may experience hearing voices which savagely criticize the self or command him or her to die."[14] Finally, instead of gaining a heightened sense of one's authentic self (in the light of the divine authentic self),

---

[8] See Isaacs, *Revelations and Possession*, pp. 84–85.
[9] See Underhill, *Mysticism*, pp. 18–24, 37–42, 74–77, 86–92, 129–33, 153–56, and 208–19.
[10] See Isaacs, *Revelations and Possession*, p. 86.
[11] See ibid., p. 96.
[12] Ibid., p. 85.
[13] See ibid.
[14] Ibid.

the psychotic loses his sense of self-continuity, causing an inability to differentiate clearly between subject and object.[15]

Isaacs gives a case study of a newly ordained Anglican priest who began to have a severe doubt in his vocation. Instructed by his bishop to go to a retreat house in England, he was praying before the tabernacle to gain clarity on what the Lord wanted from him. Isaacs describes his experience as follows:

> There, while kneeling and praying in the chapel, it happened to him. Out of the tabernacle placed above the altar appeared Jesus, arrayed in the robes and crown of the King of Kings. There was a glow to the otherwise seemingly corporeal image that stood before him. As Jesus emerged from the tabernacle he proceeded down the center aisle of the chapel until he stood beside this searching priest. As he approached, the priest had an increasing sense of awe, to such an extent that he was immobilized, and as Jesus came to his side he swooned. When he returned to normal consciousness his doubt and depression were gone, and he experienced the phenomenon known as the Baptism of the Holy Spirit.[16]

Did this priest have an authentic experience of Jesus—or was it merely an intrapsychic projection to a wounded, and therefore undifferentiated, ego? Isaacs indicates that before the experience itself is analyzed, it is best to look at the history and current status of the subject, particularly to determine whether a physical or circumstantial cause might have induced the vision. With respect to physiological causes, was the subject taking medications that could have induced a hallucination? Are there tumors or abnormal functioning of the thyroid? If no physiological factors can be found, then Isaacs recommends that the next step be to rule out psychiatric, social, and familial factors. Does the subject have a history of hospitalization? Do his family members have such a history? Does the subject belong to a coercive cult or other group that might induce an intrapsychic projection or hallucination?[17] If not, then Isaacs recommends judging the specific qualities of the experience itself.

[15] See ibid.
[16] Ibid., p. 67
[17] See ibid, pp. 68–69.

Isaacs delineates five criteria for judging an authentic revelation or mystical experience that closely resemble the analysis given above as well as that of Evelyn Underhill[18] and Adolphe Tanquerey:[19]

> The subject experiences a vision or voice as coming from outside himself from a Wholly Other (a transcendent, spiritual or divine Other). This quality must be present in the experience itself—and not merely thought to have been present after subsequent reflection on the experience.
>
> The experience is numinous—filled with sacredness, mysteriousness, majesty, glory, and perfect goodness.
>
> The numinous dimension of the experience induces reverence, rapt attention, worship, and awe—even to the point of being overwhelmed or fainting.
>
> There is an immediate awareness of a message or a truth—of which the subject has exceedingly clear and immediate cognizance. This cognizance of truth does not come from subsequent reflection upon the experience or any process of reasoning.
>
> When the vision is supernatural—if it is divine in origin, it will be accompanied by a beautiful light—and if it is evil in origin, by a "shadowy darkness."[20]

After investigating potential physiological, psychiatric, social, and familial causes of the abovementioned newly ordained Anglican priest, Isaacs determined that the experience should be judged on the basis of its qualities. There can be little doubt that the subject experienced Jesus as a transcendent or divine wholly Other. Moreover, the experience was definitely numinous— filled with sacredness, majesty, and divine power that caused the subject to be in a state of rapt attention, filled with reverence and outright awe, to the point of swooning. During the experience, the subject not only had a sense of himself, as distinct from others and objects, but also an intense awareness of humble and holy unworthiness before the holiness of Jesus. Yet instead of diminishing him, this experience dignified him and gave him a clear and strong indication not only

---

[18] See Underhill, *Mysticism*, pp. 170–209.
[19] See Tanquerey, *Spiritual Life*, pp. 700–710.
[20] For all five criteria, see Isaacs, *Revelations and Possession*, p. 70.

of his vocation, but also of his belovedness by Jesus. The effects of the revelation remained with him.

Was the subject's experience an authentic revelation? There were no public miraculous phenomena accompanying the subject's apparition, such as the multiple medically verified miraculous healings at Lourdes,[21] the miracle of the sun at Fatima,[22] or the apparitions seen by Padre Pio, accompanied by his stigmata and many public miracles.[23] However, since close scrutiny of the subject's physiological condition, history, family, and social milieu did not indicate a propensity toward low ego functioning or psychological illness, and since his experience was of the numinous wholly Other manifesting beauty and glory (inspiring rapt attention and awe), which gave an immediate clear cognizance of God's will for him, it seems likely that he received an authentic revelation.

Some may believe that such revelations occur only in the lives of saints. Though many saints do in fact receive authentic revelations from God (particularly mystical experiences and sometimes apparitions), they are not altogether infrequent in the lives of individuals with committed faith and virtue. Much of the time these more ordinary individuals are genuinely surprised by these extraordinary experiences—and keep them hidden from friends and family. C. S. Lewis called his mystical experiences "surprises" or "stabs of joy".[24] Saint Ignatius of Loyola called these experiences "consolation without previous cause", implying that they come quite surprisingly from God without any seeming natural cause.[25] When such surprising and

---

[21] For a list of miraculous healings recognized by the Church at this time compiled by the Lourdes Medical Bureau, whose physicians investigate and catalogue miracles, see "Miraculous Healings", Lourdes Sanctuaire (website), accessed April 20, 2020, https://www.lourdes -france.org/en/miraculous-healings/. See also Ruth Cranston, *The Miracle of Lourdes* (New York: McGraw Hill, 1955).

[22] See Stanley Jaki, *God and the Sun at Fatima* (Fraser, Mich.: Real View Books, 1999).

[23] See Renzo Allegri, *Padre Pio: Man of Hope* (Ann Arbor, Mich.: Charis Books, 2000).

[24] See C. S. Lewis, *Surprised by Joy: The Shape of My Early Life* (New York: Harcourt, 1955), pp. 72, 78, and 130.

[25] In the "Rules for the Discernment of Spirits" in his *Spiritual Exercises*, Saint Ignatius of Loyola indicates that ordinary people can experience a high degree of affective and spiritual consolation from God—without any "previous cause"—that is, without natural thoughts, preparation, or circumstance. Such surprising and intense consolation is caused by God alone. See Saint Ignatius, *The Spiritual Exercises of Saint Ignatius*, trans. Anthony Mottola (New York: Image-Doubleday, 1989), p. 133.

intense consolation occurs, Ignatius indicates that it may point to God's confirmation of a way of life, such as a religious vocation[26] (as in the case of the abovementioned newly ordained Anglican priest). Whether this be the case or not, these experiences are a call from God to a deeper commitment to prayer and service to His Kingdom.

III. Christian Mysticism

The Lord calls some people to a special life of contemplation that frequently includes mystical encounters with Him. Much of the time this takes the form of a call to monastic life, though not necessarily. Such a life requires great humility, discipline, and commitment to prayer, and in many cases, such as those of Saint Teresa of Avila[27] and Saint John of the Cross,[28] it is a call to mystical surrender. The

---

[26] See ibid., pp. 83–85.

[27] Saint Teresa of Avila was a sixteenth-century Carmelite mystic responsible for the reform of the Carmelite order. She was a spiritual colleague of Saint John of the Cross and wrote extensively about the spiritual and mystical life, though in simpler and more autobiographical terms than he. Her most influential book that describes the stages toward mystical surrender-perfection-union is *Interior Castle*. In it, she describes seven mansions, the first three of which concern the stages of preparation from prayer and meditation to humility, openness to God's will, and the repudiation of sin in all its forms. The final four mansions describe perfection in the spiritual and mystical life, giving guidance on how to proceed from the purgative to the illuminative and unitive stages of prayer. Her emphasis on the beauty, transformative power, and ecstasy of divine love is among the most lucid in the history of spiritual writing. Her autobiography is a remarkably humble and captivating story about her call to the Carmelites and her personal progression through the seven mansions detailed in the *Interior Castle*. Novices may want to begin with the autobiography, and then proceed to the *Interior Castle*, which is a more didactic approach to the seven stages of spiritual development. See Saint Teresa of Avila, "The Book of Her Life", in *The Collected Works of St. Teresa of Avila*, trans. Kieran Kavanaugh and Otilio Rodriguez (Washington, D.C.: ICS Publications, 1976), 1:31–308.

[28] The well-known sixteenth-century Carmelite mystic Saint John of the Cross writes in a more poetic style, making recourse to scholastic philosophy and the Church Fathers. Though more difficult to comprehend than Saint Teresa of Avila on initial readings, his works are at once practical, analytical, poetic, literary—and of course, deeply biblical and spiritual. He gives a systematic progression from the purgative to the illuminative and to the unitive stage of mystical surrender (perfection) in his classic work *The Ascent of Mount Carmel*. In other works he concentrates on the illuminative and unitive way—for example, *The Spiritual Canticle* and "The Living Flame of Love". He also spends considerable time on an intermediary stage, the dark night of the soul, which occurs before final union-surrender-perfection in a work by the same name. See Saint John of the Cross, *The Collected Works of St. John of the Cross*, trans. Kieran Kavanaugh, O.C.D., and Otilio Rodriguez, O.C.D. (1979; repr., Washington, D.C.: ICS Publications, 2000). Subsequent citations are to the 1979 edition.

three major stages of mystical life—the purgative, illuminative, and unitive—are described in detail by these two authors as well as contemporary mystics and scholars of mystical life.[29]

If one is called to a life of mystical union (i.e., mystical surrender to the unconditionally loving Absolute Being), it will entail dedicating several hours per day to contemplative prayer. This generally involves joining a contemplative monastery[30] or living in a hermitage.[31] In this setting of silence and separation, a person in a state of grace makes a long-term interior journey with the Lord through three "states of the soul":[32]

1. The purgative state, in which the person begins building habits of charity,[33] enabling him to resist sin and vice[34]
2. The illuminative state, in which a person has sufficient habits of charity and virtue to resist major temptations, enabling the Lord

[29] See Underhill, *Mysticism*; Benedict Groeschel, *Spiritual Passages: The Psychology of Spiritual Development* (Valley, N.Y.: Crossroads Publishing, 1984); and Bernard McGinn, *The Essential Writings of Christian Mysticism* (New York: Random House/Modern Library, 2006).

[30] These would include men's and women's monasteries in the following religious orders: the Cistercians, Trappists, Carthusians, and Discalced Carmelites. There are additional monasteries of religious women beyond those mentioned above, such as the Colettine Poor Clares, the Capuchin Poor Clares, and other monastic branches of women's religious orders.

[31] Some hermitages welcome long-term visitors such as the Camaldolese Hermitage in Big Sur, California; the Mt. Carmel Hermitage in Christoval, Texas; the Franciscan Contemplative Sisters in Toronto, Ohio; and the Benedictine Transfiguration Hermitage in Thorndike, Maine. There are many other contemplative hermitages throughout the United States and Canada that can be located by a web search. Those seeking a long-term stay at a hermitage must speak directly with the superior of the house. Serious commitment to this kind of life may best be accomplished by joining a specific cloistered contemplative religious order.

[32] These three states were initially articulated by Pseudo-Dionysius the Areopagite in A.D. 525 (see his *Divine Names* 1, 2; 4, 12–13; 7, 13; and *Mystical Theology* 1, 3; 2). Saint Thomas Aquinas commented on these states of surrender/perfection (*Summa Theologica* II-II, q. 183, a. 4). Since that time these states of perfection have been used by mystical theologians to articulate the journey to complete union with God (see the citations from Saint Teresa of Avila and Saint John of the Cross above).

[33] *Caritas* is the Latin translation for *agapē*, the distinctive word selected by early Christians to refer to Jesus' unique notion of "self-sacrificial love for the good of the unique intrinsically lovable other". This love is defined by Jesus Himself in the Beatitudes: poor in spirit (humble-hearted), meek (gentle-hearted), hunger for righteousness (zealous for salvation of self and others), mercy (which includes both forgiveness of others and compassion for the neglected and marginalized), purity of heart, those who mourn, being a peacemaker, and sacrificing oneself for the faith (see Mt 5:3–11). An extensive definition of this is given in Robert Spitzer, *God So Loved the World* (San Francisco: Ignatius Press, 2016), Chapter 1.

[34] See the extensive treatment of the seven deadly sins in Chapters 5 and 6 of this volume.

to come to him with significant beauty, grace, and affective consolation

3. The unitive state, in which, after a period of final detachment from self—called "the dark night" (that enables near-perfect charity and purity of heart; see below)—a person enters into the fullness of divine love, causing a state of unsurpassed ecstasy and union with the Absolute

Saint Teresa of Avila describes the last state, the unitive state, as follows:

> The loving exchange that takes place between the soul and God is so sweet that I beg Him in His goodness to give a taste of this love to anyone who thinks I am lying. On the days this lasted I went about as though stupefied. I desired neither to see nor to speak.... It seems the Lord carries the soul away and places it in ecstasy; thus there is no room for pain or suffering, because joy soon enters in.[35]

The mystical life is a special call to dedicated contemplation given to individuals seeking near-perfect authenticity, purity of heart, and charity through surrender to the unconditionally loving God. The mystic identifies true freedom—that is, the freedom of authentic love—with surrender to the heart of God. In a secular context, freedom is rarely identified with surrender, but in the spiritual or mystical life, it is—for the only way we can reach near-perfect authenticity and love is through the guidance and influence of the unconditionally loving Lord.

Most of us living active lives (away from a monastery or hermitage) experience our purification process by meeting the challenges of the world around us, trying to maintain the teachings of Christ with our spouses, children, colleagues and supervisors at work, and even our best friends and fellow church members. Though contemplatives certainly work in the monastery, they have a different kind of purification that occurs sometimes in community and work life, but also in times of contemplation and prayer. The contemplative is sensitive to states and feelings of consolation and desolation that occur both

---

[35] Saint Teresa of Avila, "Book of Her Life", p. 194.

inside and outside of prayer (see Chapter 4, Section V.A),[36] and the Lord uses these consolations and desolations to guide the contemplative on the journey to near-perfect authenticity and charity. Though the end of the journey is the life of ecstasy (recounted above by Saint Teresa of Avila), the journey itself is punctuated by desolation, unfulfilled desire, and darkness. These painful experiences are not punishments from God, but instruments of God to guide the contemplative to greater detachment from self and "things of the world", which leads to greater authenticity, greater freedom to love, and greater freedom to surrender ultimately to Him in spiritual union.

In his lucid and poetic work *The Spiritual Canticle*,[37] Saint John of the Cross describes the consolations and desolations involved in the purgative state, the illuminative state, the dark night of the soul, the dark night of the spirit, and the unitive state. This work is autobiographical, and so it describes the states of the soul in terms of Saint John's progressively developing relationship with the Lord, who is at times drawing him, leaving him, leading him, and fulfilling him. He uses the terms "the soul", "the Bride", and "she" to refer to the contemplative on his interior journey with the Lord, and he uses the terms "the beloved", "the Bridegroom", and "He" to refer to Christ—the Son of the unconditionally loving Lord who lies at the interior of the soul, guiding, enticing, and influencing it toward discovery, surrender, perfection in love, union, beauty, and ecstasy.

Saint John does not speak about the states of soul as achievements of an individual (which would be a solitary venture and a stoic victory). Rather, he sees it as a relationship between an individual and the Lord, which as it progresses in intimacy and union with the beloved, transforms the soul in authenticity and the capacity for charity (*agapē*). For Saint John, we do not bring ourselves to the higher states of soul; rather, the Lord leads us by consolations and desolations, love and absence, and light and darkness to the state of perfection commensurate with union with Him. Yes, we must exert

---

[36] See Robert Spitzer, *Finding True Happiness: Satisfying Our Restless Hearts* (San Francisco: Ignatius Press, 2015), Chapter 8, Section II.

[37] Using the imagery of the biblical book Canticle of Canticles (Song of Songs), Saint John of the Cross describes the major states of the soul in an allegory about the changing and progressive relationship between the soul ("the bride") and the Lord ("the Bridegroom"). See Saint John of the Cross, *The Spiritual Canticle*, in *Collected Works*, pp. 405–65.

our will—and be disciplined, trusting, and persistent—to follow the Bridegroom's lead; but in the end, it is not we who conquer ourselves, but the Lord who leads us into a love that is self-perfecting. We may now look at some of the poetic descriptions that Saint John uses to describe progressive growth in love—which is at once perfection and surrender—in the stages along the contemplative's way.

A. The Purgative Stage of Contemplative Life

The first or purgative stage (stanzas 1–21 in the poem and commentary of *The Spiritual Canticle*) is not the beginning of a life of faith. It assumes that an individual already has a vibrant faith life and is trying to purify the capacity for authenticity and charity by contending with the seven deadly sins—gluttony/drunkenness, sloth, lust, greed, anger, envy, and pride. Notice that these "sins" do not describe behaviors but rather interior attitudes that undermine authenticity and charity—thereby undermining progress in faith and relationship with the Lord. Thus an individual in the purgative state must already have a living faith, a desire to love and serve the Lord more deeply, and a commitment to resist the attitudes (deadly sins) that undermine this faith and desire.

In a word, an individual in the purgative state must already be on the road to salvation through virtue, faith, and prayer. This is precisely what allows the relationship between him and the Beloved (Christ) to develop and flourish in progressive states of surrender and perfection.

The Lord calls some individuals in this state to an intense longing for Him in the innermost depth of their spirits. This leads to a search for Him. He sees glimmers of the Beloved in the natural world (e.g., the majesty of mountains, sea, and forests) as well as signs of His love in the littlest of things (e.g., leaves, birds, and other creatures). When the contemplative walks through a forest or a garden, he does not simply see trees and leaves—he does not simply hear birds and the wind. The Lord makes his presence known, in these natural objects, and when the contemplative's soul becomes attuned to the presence of his Beloved in natural beauty and the voice of his Beloved in wind and birds—his desire is awakened even more intensely. He is so filled with love that he speaks poetically—even without this literary capacity. It is almost as if the poetry that comes from him is assisted by the One whom he loves. In such states, his heart is filled with the awareness of being loved, and he cannot help himself—he loves the One who has loved him first, out of sheer excitement, fulfillment, and gratitude.[38] After this intense experience, the Beloved fades away, and the contemplative is once again filled with desire and longing for the Beloved.

The purgative way may last for years, with the contemplative trying to remain vigilant in virtue, faith, and prayer despite temptations coming from the senses, egocentricity, and even the devil. Inasmuch as the contemplative perseveres in his deepening of virtue, faith, and prayer, he is gradually purified of the desire to give into temptations, which enkindles his desire to experience the love of his Beloved (Christ). If the Beloved does not respond with at least momentary glimmers of loving consolation, the absence is acutely felt, which causes spiritual heartache. Yet if he perseveres in trust, hope, and love—perseveres on the path to deeper virtue, faith, and prayer—this heartache will have the effect of even deeper purification.

We might specify the dimensions of the purgative way, using Saint John's vocabulary and concepts, as follows. When a contemplative enters the purgative way, he has already decided to dedicate himself to the pursuit of holiness in order to make himself a perfect offering to the One he loves—the unconditionally loving Lord who has loved him first. He is filled with an awareness that his true dignity, fulfillment, and destiny are to be found in this loving God, and he is grateful for all that God has given him—not only family, talents, his immortal soul, and many blessings throughout life, but also for being led to faith, awareness, and understanding of Jesus Christ and His Father. Moved by this need for and gratitude to God, the contemplative embarks on the path to greater holiness—authenticity and purity of love through the pursuit of virtue and the purification of the senses, the imagination, and the mind.

This pursuit of deeper holiness and purification includes what John calls "dark nights". There are four dark nights—the active dark night of the senses and the passive dark night of the senses, then the active dark night of the spirit and the passive dark night of the spirit. The

---

[38] Ibid., pp. 432–37. This corresponds to the commentary on stanzas 4–6 of the poem.

first two (the active and passive dark nights of the *senses*) are part of the purgative way that prepare the contemplative to move to the illuminative way,[39] while the second two (the active and passive dark nights of the *spirit*) are part of the illuminative way—preparing the contemplative to move toward the unitive way.[40] We will restrict ourselves to the first two dark nights here, and then address the others when we explain the illuminative way below.

An active dark night is one that is actively pursued by the contemplative seeking greater holiness, while a passive dark night is one that God initiates by withdrawing consolations, depriving the soul or the spirit of even the ordinary sense of divine love, peace, and beauty.

In the purgative way, the contemplative, moved by need, gratitude, and love, pursues the path of virtue, first, by a purification of the senses. This entails greatly simplifying life, restricting food, drink, and "creature comforts". He also significantly limits television, radio, other forms of media, and even convivial, but unnecessary talking. He does this not because there is anything wrong with them per se, but because they distract him from his true intention, which is to open himself to the love of God alone, and to discipline himself in simplicity and modesty, putting prayer, study, and spiritual work before comfort. The objective is to become detached or free from desires of the senses, particularly excesses leading toward the deadly sins of gluttony/drunkenness, lust, and sloth.

Though Saint John indicates that he wrote *The Ascent of Mount Carmel* for some of his Carmelite brothers and sisters—tailoring many of his suggestions for them and other contemplatives—he states explicitly that he intends to give others important advice on how to pursue perfectly loving union with the Lord. This does not mean that all noncontemplatives seeking mystical union with God in this life should follow

---

[39] These dark nights are described in detail—with instructions for moving through them—in *The Ascent of Mount Carmel*. See Saint John of the Cross, *The Ascent of Mount Carmel*, in *Collected Works*, pp. 73–292.

[40] Saint John speaks of the active and passive dark night of the spirit particularly in *The Dark Night of the Soul*, which is an extension of *The Ascent of Mount Carmel*. Most scholars believe that the two books should be considered a single work with two parts: the first part, *The Ascent of Mount Carmel*, which emphasizes the purification of the senses; the second, *The Dark Night of the Soul*, which emphasizes the purification of the spirit (the mind, memory, and will). See Saint John of the Cross, *The Dark Night of the Soul*, in *Collected Works*, pp. 293–389.

all of his suggestions, but only those that they can reasonably accomplish with the responsibilities they have in life. The main point John is trying to make for all of us is that simplicity of life (e.g., simplicity of goods and sensory stimulation, and the discipline necessary to restrain the desires for them) is necessary for detachment or freedom from creature comforts; and detachment or freedom from creature comforts is necessary to open oneself ever more deeply to loving union with the Lord. Thus, if we really desire deeply consoling and loving union with God through prayer, we will have to detach ourselves from creature comforts, and this, in turn, requires simplicity, self-discipline, and even voluntary deprivation from these stimuli.[41]

The active night of the senses is also concerned with resistance to three deadly sins of the body (gluttony/drunkenness, lust, and sloth) and the cultivation of virtues (good habits of the will) to oppose these deadly sins and the temptations actively that initiate them in the long term. Saint John recommends a threefold process to do this:

1. By training the mind to recognize when temptation toward the three deadly bodily sins is beginning to occur (originating either from within the self or from the devil), and then training the will to "nip them in the bud", we conscientiously choose the love of God before the temptation begins to gain momentum.

2. By recalling the peace, consolation, and love experienced from the Divine Beloved, causing true gratitude for His blessings, and by giving more time to contemplative prayer, our desire for union with God becomes more intense, which can be compared to and levered against our aberrant desires for sins of the body (gluttony/drunkenness, sloth, and lust).

3. By repeatedly nipping aberrant desires in the bud (self-discipline), by recalling the consolations of the Lord, and by intensifying our contemplative prayer, we conscientiously cultivate virtues opposed to the three deadly sins of the body—temperance to oppose gluttony/drunkenness, fortitude to oppose sloth, and chastity (viewed through the examples of Jesus and Mary) to oppose lust.

---

[41] Saint Ignatius of Loyola sets this same principle up for more active people in the very first part of his *Spiritual Exercises* called "The First Principle and Foundation".

This pursuit is not pure asceticism because God rewards the contemplative with an increased sense of His presence, peace, consolation, and joy. Though this increased sense of peace, love, consolation, and joy is not continuously present, the Lord provides it frequently during times of prayer and also unexpectedly throughout the day.

Though the active dark night of the senses brings peace, consolation, and confidence—as well as an alleviation of guilt—the contemplative may begin to develop a sense of pride (e.g., "*I* have really accomplished so much in the spiritual life") or vanity ("*I* am making greater progress than Joe and Tom") or a belief that he has reached the objective of the spiritual life because God has given him a sense of peace, consolation, and confidence. At this juncture, for the contemplative's own good, the Lord begins to withdraw the above consolations and spiritual gifts, causing the contemplative to feel a sense of aridity (dryness), spiritual emptiness, or even a renewed sense of guilt. The contemplative may believe that he has done something wrong, and as a result intensify his efforts at restraining his senses. However, this is frequently not the problem—or the solution. A good spiritual director will help him to see that the Lord is withholding His consolation and felt presence to prevent him from falling into spiritual problems; and so the true solution is to become more *humble* about spiritual progress, more respectful of others' relationship with the Lord, and more desirous of being in union with God (instead of desiring the consolation of God). These last points concern the transition from the dark night of the senses (in the purgative way) to the dark night of the spirit (in the illuminative way).

B. The Illuminative Stage of Contemplative Life

As the contemplative moves from the purgative way into the illuminative way—having purified his senses in a spirit of humility, respect for others, and desire for the Divine Beloved Himself—he will experience freedom from the deadly sins of gluttony/drunkenness, lust, and sloth and detachment from the sensorial world in order to be open to the Divine Beloved. The Lord rewards him with the fruits of this freedom and detachment with abundant consolation and intense joy. Saint John describes this consolation in *The Spiritual Canticle*, using metaphor and poetic language. Recall that "she" and "the bride" refer to the contemplative, and that "he" and "the Beloved" refer to the Lord of Love (Christ):

> Since she desires the divine eyes with such yearnings, the Beloved reveals to her some rays of His grandeur and divinity, which cause her to go out of herself in rapture and ecstasy.
>   This flight in which the soul is placed after much spiritual activity is called spiritual espousal. God communicates great things about Himself, beautifies her and adorns her with gifts and virtues. Her vehement longings and complaints of love cease, and a state of peace, delight, and gentleness of love commences.[42]

The contemplative then pursues the active dark night of the spirit in which he moves beyond the purification of his senses and imagination, to the purification of his spirit. For Saint John, the spirit is the domain in which God connects directly with the contemplative. Thus, it is the psychic domain through which we become aware of God Himself as well as His perfection in truth, love, goodness, and beauty; it is also the ground of mind, memory, and will. The mind is not the imagination (picture-thinking), but rather the agency through which conceptual ideas, abstraction, and syntactically meaningful language occurs. The memory is the ability to remember and recall, and the will is the capacity to choose between egocentricity or love, self-aggrandizement or self-surrender, self-idolatry or worship of God, domination or respect—to choose between two fundamental directions: "toward the self" or "away from the self toward God and others".

When we spoke of the purification of the senses, we addressed freedom from gluttony/drunkenness, lust, and sloth. Now as we address the purification of the spirit, we are concerned with freedom from the other four deadly sins—greed, anger, envy, and pride—which are sins of the spirit in which egocentricity and self-aggrandizement are emphasized above the love of God and neighbor. The contemplative, who has moved from the purgative way, is not in danger of overtly and directly choosing himself over God and

---

[42] Saint John of the Cross, *Spiritual Canticle*, in *Collected Works*, p. 406.

others, but he is in danger of implicitly, indirectly, and subtly doing so. There are many subtle and "rationalizable" ways of placing the self above God and others through greed, anger, envy, and pride (which includes both vanity and the lust for power); as the contemplative moves into the illuminative way, he finds himself besieged and hindered by them—and so he pursues the purification of his spirit in the active dark night of the spirit.

To do this, the contemplative focuses his mental activity on the single purpose of being united with God. Bolstered by the peace and consolations of God, he pursues virtue and prayer to purify his mind, memory, and will from the temptation toward greed, anger, envy, and pride (including vanity and the lust for power). Once again, a contemplative can implement the three techniques discussed above concerning the active night of the senses. This time, he takes the emphasis off of the sins of the senses and puts it on the sins of the spirit—greed, envy, anger, and pride.

Training the mind to recognize when temptation toward egocentricity and its four deadly sins (originating either from within the self or from the devil) is starting to occur, and then training the will to "nip them in the bud", we conscientiously choose God and/or others above the self before these temptations begin to gain momentum. This is a difficult and long road, but continued practice builds virtue.

By recalling the peace, consolation, and love experienced from the Divine Beloved, causing deep gratitude to Him, and by giving more time to contemplative prayer, our desire for union with God becomes more intense, which can be compared to and levered against our desires for egocentric, dominating, self-aggrandizing and self-idolatrous desires (the aberrant desires of the spirit).

By repeatedly nipping aberrant desires in the bud (self-discipline), by recalling the consolations of the Lord, and by intensifying our contemplative prayer, we conscientiously cultivate virtues opposed to the four sins of the spirit—generosity to oppose greed; gentle-heartedness and forgiveness to oppose anger; gratitude to oppose envy; and humility and charity to oppose pride, vanity, and lust for power.

As the contemplative continues in his efforts to discipline the sins of the spirit—as well as continued temptations to the sins of the senses—he will once again find himself experiencing increased peace, sacredness, love, and joy. These experiences will lead him gradually to shift from meditation to contemplation. Meditation, for Saint John, uses imagination and reason to move into prayer—reflecting on a particular passage of Scripture, thinking about a theological truth, meditating on the mysteries of the Rosary, reflecting on the Beatitudes, or reflecting on the imitation of Christ. Contemplation is passive from the vantage point of the contemplative, because God is responsible for the action. As the contemplative opens himself to the Lord in prayer, the Lord brings consolation—peace, joy, unity, sacredness, and love—to the contemplative. In order to do this, the contemplative must stop meditating, stop actively reflecting, imagining, and reasoning, so that his soul will be clear to receive the consolations that the Lord is waiting to bestow on him.[43]

C. The Lord's Presence and Consolation in Contemplative Life

A brief consideration of active thought versus passive thought may help to clarify the Lord's presence and consolation in contemplative life. There is no mystery about "active thought" (referred to as reason, or in Latin, *ratio*), because it is what we do every day—reflecting on the many disciplines of the arts and sciences (active *theoretical* thought) and studying and planning for practical activities we are about to perform (active *practical* thought). However, passive thought (contemplation, or in Latin, *intellectus*) is much more mysterious for contemporary culture.[44] So what is passive thought? It is not assembling data, logically analyzing it, and anticipating results (the domain of active thoughts). Rather, it is opening oneself to the Divine Presence—first in the beauty of the natural world, then in the goodness and love of human beings (made in the image of God), then in the contemplation of Jesus Christ (the incarnate Son of God), and then in the mystical presence of the Divine Beloved in prayer. The point of passive thought is not to gain an insight or to

---

[43] Saint John of the Cross elucidates the signs that mark when a contemplative should stop meditating to clear his mind for the coming of the Lord in contemplation. See *Ascent of Mount Carmel*, bk. 2, Chapter 13.

[44] Josef Pieper has written an excellent treatise on passive thought (*intellectus*) and its decline in modern culture in his essay *Leisure: The Basis of Culture*, trans. Gerald Malsbary (South Bend, Ind.: St. Augustine Press, 1998).

increase worldly knowledge, but rather to behold, appreciate, and be filled with the divine presence, beauty, goodness, and love offered by the Divine Beloved—and to respond naturally to Him with an outpouring of love. As one progresses in the beholding, appreciating, and being filled with the presence, beauty, and love of God in nature, in human beings, in Jesus Christ, and in the Divine Beloved Himself, one is simultaneously filled with a sense of joy, sacredness, and unity.

Contemplation can have an even purer form that goes beyond our openness and appreciation of the presence of God in nature, human beings, and Jesus Christ—it can be completely initiated by God Himself. This can occur by surprise, when God simply comes to the contemplative who is not praying or catching "sight" of Him in nature, people, or Jesus, or when the contemplative who is in the illuminative way (or progressing through the purgative way) enters into prayer with very little active thought. When the Lord comes in this purer form, He overwhelms the contemplative with His loving, sacred, unifying, consoling presence and places him in a state of what Saint Teresa of Avila calls "ecstasy". The contemplative, as Saint John notes above, loses the sense of time and worldly concern and is caught up in a state of loving rapture.

This loving, joy-filled, unifying, and sacred consolation is in no way produced by the human psyche. It is not simply a feeling; it includes a profound awareness of another loving consciousness who is unmistakable—indeed more present than any human being could be (except, of course, that there is not a sensory image accompanying the empathetic, interpersonal awareness of the other). Moreover, this hyperpresent consciousness is clearly transcendent and overwhelming in its love and beauty. It is not simply the wholly Other—it is also the wholly *loving and glorious* Other, at once completely beyond the contemplative and intimately present to him. Thus the Divine Beloved is not only hyperpresent, but also hyperloving, hyperbeautiful, and hyperintimate. When He ceases to be present, the heart is left longing—nay, yearning—for Him to return, which moves the contemplative to seek Him with even greater simplicity, discipline, and self-sacrifice.

Thus, the illuminative way is marked by consolations of many kinds—from little appearances of the Divine Beloved in nature, people, and Jesus to profound appearances of the Divine Beloved, causing the contemplative to be filled with an overwhelming sense of His sacred, loving, consoling presence. Yet, the illuminative way is only spiritual espousal, the way of proficiency; it is not yet "marriage", unity, or perfection. Thus, the contemplative must work hard on the active night of the spirit—and contend with renewed temptations of the senses. As he actively disciplines himself, reflects on God's goodness and gratitude, and gives himself to contemplative prayer, God graces him not only with the capacity and gift of virtue (to replace the deadly sins), but also the light of consolation to assure him of His presence and love.

D. The Passive Dark Night of the Spirit ("The Dark Night of the Soul")

There is still one more stage of purification required for the contemplative to move from the illuminative way to the unitive way, perhaps the most difficult purification of all—the passive dark night of the spirit. As can be seen, the illuminative way is marked by profound consolation coming from the loving presence of God, which can lead the contemplative to fix his desire and attention on this loving consolation. Yet the Lord desires the contemplative to fix his desire on Him, on His *self-sacrificial* love and His complete *gift of self*. This has often been described as refocusing the contemplative from the consolations of God to the God of all consolation. The final dimension of falling in love with God is to share in His self-sacrificial Spirit—His Son's complete gift of self in His Passion and death, for the final triumph of love over evil. In order to give the contemplative the same opportunity to purify his love so that it becomes as pure as that of Jesus Christ, the Lord calls the contemplative to a period of self-sacrifice—a period of true death to self and gift of self, requiring total trust in Him. Here, God withdraws His loving presence from the contemplative who has formerly experienced it with profound consolation—and the contemplative finds himself wandering not just in a desert, but in a wasteland of emptiness, loneliness, and alienation filled with anxiety and even the darkness of depression. As the contemplative enters into this passive dark night of the spirit (oftentimes generically referred to as "the dark night of the soul"), God removes not only His *extraordinary* consolations, which He has lavished on the contemplative, but also His ordinary consolation that keeps all of us aware of God.

Most people of faith do not even notice what might be termed "ordinary consolation" because it is so omnipresent. When we turn to the Lord in faith, He gives us a sense of His presence, which alleviates our feelings of cosmic emptiness, alienation, and loneliness (see Volume II, Chapter 4, of this Trilogy), and this ordinary consolation continues unabated unless we begin to move off of our faith journey to a life of overt sin or unbelief. When we first begin our faith journey, the movement from cosmic emptiness, alienation, and loneliness to one of peace, hope, and awareness of God's presence can be quite palpable, and if we maintain our faith commitment, it can become so "normal" that it is like a radio playing in the background of a household where it is turned on incessantly. After a while, the only time the residents notice it is when it is switched off. As noted above, God can "switch off" ordinary consolation when we are moving out of a life of faith toward a life of darkness, and He uses the resultant feelings of cosmic emptiness, alienation, and loneliness as a sort of warning to alert us to our self-destructive course of action. However, He does not need to do this for a contemplative who is in the illuminative way—who has reached a state of proficiency in virtue and the spiritual life.

The contemplative has need of only one thing—the final purification of his love into the completely self-sacrificial love of Christ Himself, a self-sacrificial love that can be joined to Jesus' and offered up for the salvation of all souls and the good of His Mystical Body, the Church. Since the contemplative has already experienced the ardor, rapture, and ecstasy of God's sacred and loving presence, the removal of ordinary consolation is incredibly painful, tantamount to a kind of slow torture—a passion in and of itself. Yet the contemplative will be aware of why the Lord is doing this—at least mentally—and will know that the Lord is completing his process of purification and offering the opportunity to join Him on the Cross for the salvation of the world. Though the contemplative is aware of this and tries to place his trust completely in the Lord, it is incredibly painful and lonely and empty; he is besieged with temptations to doubt the Lord—and even to doubt in His very presence. He cannot help but cry out in anguish and ask the Lord for relief; but in the end, the Lord will challenge him to be like Himself, to trust that He is there even if the contemplative cannot feel Him; to trust that the emptiness and sacrifice will be joined to His sacrifice even though he cannot sense it; to trust that his sacrifice will lead to the salvation of the world even though he cannot see how; and to trust that he will be brought into the full purification of His love and into a state of loving perfection so great that it is only exceeded by the beatific vision that is to come—the unitive way, the state of perfection.

E. The Unitive Stage of Contemplative Life

Saint John of the Cross, Saint Teresa of Avila, Saint Paul of the Cross, Saint Thérèse of Lisieux, and Saint Teresa of Calcutta are but a few of the saints who underwent this dark night and came out to the other side in ecstasy. Saint Thérèse of Lisieux and Saint Teresa of Calcutta experienced this state of ecstasy for a very short time before proceeding to the beatific vision, but Saint Teresa of Avila, Saint John of the Cross, and Saint Paul of the Cross, among others, lived long enough to speak and write extensively about it.

Saint John summarizes the freedom from passions and the devil and the blessings of being in unity with the Lord that occur when the Lord leads the soul into spiritual marriage:

> The bride knows that now her will's desire is detached from all things and attached to her God in most intimate love; that the sensory part of her soul, with all its strengths, faculties, and appetites, is in harmony with the spirit, and its rebelliousness brought into subjection; that the devil is now conquered and far withdrawn as a result of her varied and prolonged spiritual activity and combat; that her soul is united and transformed with an abundance of heavenly riches and gifts; and that consequently she is now well prepared, disposed, and strong, leaning on her Beloved, so as to come up from the desert of death, flowing with delights, to the glorious thrones of her Bridegroom.[45]

---

[45] Saint John of the Cross, *Spiritual Canticle*, in *Collected Works*, p. 628.

In "The Living Flame of Love", Saint John gives a brief glimpse of what it is like to come up from the desert of death with spiritual delights to the throne of the Bridegroom:

> And in your sweet breathing, Filled with good and glory, How tenderly you swell my heart with love! I do not desire to speak of this spiration, filled for the soul with good and glory and delicate love of God, for I am aware of being incapable of doing so; and were I to try, it might seem less than it is. It is a spiration that God produces in the soul, in which, by that awakening of lofty knowledge of the Godhead, he breathes the Holy Spirit in it in the same proportion as its knowledge and understanding of him, absorbing it most profoundly in the Holy Spirit, rousing its love with a divine exquisite quality and delicacy according to what it beholds in him. Since the breathing is filled with good and glory, the Holy Spirit, through this breathing, filled the soul with good and glory in which he enkindled it in love of himself, indescribably and incomprehensibly, in the depths of God, to whom be honor and glory forever and ever. Amen.[46]

Evelyn Underhill, who compiled one of the most deep and comprehensive studies of mysticism, elaborates this final state of unity or communion with the Lord, and the ecstasy and rapture that accompanies it:

> Since the object of all contemplation is the production of that state of intimate communion in which the mystics declare that the self is "in God and God is in her," it might be supposed that the orison of union represented the end of mystical activity, in so far as it is concerned with the attainment of a transitory but exalted consciousness of "oneness with the Absolute." Nearly all the great contemplatives, however, describe as a distinct, and regard as a more advanced phase of the spiritual consciousness, the group of definitely ecstatic states in which the concentration of interest on the Transcendent is so complete, the gathering up and pouring out of life on this one point so intense, that the subject is more or less entranced, and becomes, for the time of the ecstasy, unconscious of the external world.[47]

---

[46] Saint John of the Cross, "The Living Flame of Love", stanza 17.
[47] Evelyn Underhill, *Mysticism* (London: Methuen, 1930), p. 427.

It must be reiterated that these are not mere *feelings* of rapture and ecstasy, but rather an awareness of the consciousness of the Absolute into whom the mystic is absorbed. Ecstasy and rapture accompany this relational state with the Absolute, but they are only the result of being filled by the one who is loving them—the One who is perfect and unconditional love, goodness, beauty, and being. This union with absolute love is the culmination of mystical life, and it anticipates only one greater state—the beatific vision in Heaven.

IV. Conclusion

As can be seen, the Lord is quite manifest in our lives. He is present in the numinous experience and the intuition of the sacred, which draws all human beings into a life of religious practice and prayer. He is also present to us in scientifically, validatable public apparitions as well as private visions and revelations. For Christians, He is present in the Holy Spirit dwelling within us, imparting peace beyond all understanding, inspiration, guidance (particularly during times of suffering), and in His conspiracy of providence, all of which protects us, helps us, and fills us with His presence and love. He is also present in the ordinary and extraordinary consolations, which not only tell us of His love for us, but also help us to purify our senses and spirit. Finally, He is present in the life of contemplatives and mystics who through their journeys arrive at a unitive stage filled with His absolute loving subjectivity, giving rise to ardor and ecstasy.

The Lord will not appear in a way that will undermine our freedom or force us to submit to Him out of fear. He will always appear in a way that will respect and engage our freedom to respond to Him, and will guide us ever so carefully to the purification of our souls, the rejection of evil, and the embracing of His unconditionally loving heart, made manifest through the Incarnation of His Son.

There are many other ways in which the Lord is present, protecting us from evil, and leading us through purification to salvation— through the crucified and risen Body and Blood of Jesus (in the Holy Eucharist) and the grace of the sacramental life (see Volume II, Chapter 2); in His interior guidance through consolations and desolations (see the discernment of spirits in this volume, Chapter 4, Section V);

through the contemplative life, in which we are joined more closely to Him in love (see Volume II, Chapter 3); through the Holy Spirit in the magisterial action of the Church (see Volume II, Chapter 1); and through the countless recognized and unrecognized miracles occurring in our ordinary lives. However, we will not discuss these additional manifestations of the Lord at this juncture. For now, it is sufficient to know that the Lord is present in all of our lives and that He loves us, protects us from evil, and is leading us toward salvation. If we place our trust in Him, try to follow His teaching, and avail ourselves of His mercy, the darkness will never be able to overcome us, for He has overcome the darkness (see Jn 16:33).

Chapter Two

Jesus' Victory over Satan

Introduction

The Old Testament mentions the power of evil in a variety of different ways—"the sons of God" who commingled with the "daughters of men" (see Gen 6:1–6); the serpent who tempted Eve, leading to the fall (Gen 3:1–24); Satan as the accuser of men in Job (Job 1:6–12); and various references to the demonic in Psalms, Isaiah, and Wisdom literature; however, the idea of Satan as a fallen angel who becomes head of other fallen angels (demons) comes later, mostly in Jewish apocalyptic literature written during the intertestamental period—200 B.C.–A.D. 50 (see below, Sections I, II, and IV). Jesus was aware of these apocalyptic traditions, but brings a new perspective and an extraordinary clarity to the view that the world is immersed in a cosmic struggle between God (and His angels) and Satan (and his fallen angels)—a struggle that Satan seemed to be winning because of the free choices of human beings. Jesus sees Himself as the Divine Son and Messiah who has come into the world not only to bring God's Kingdom, but also to defeat Satan and rescue humanity from his seductive, malicious, and dominating intentions.

Satan's increasing power was evident not only in the large number of possessed individuals, but also in the decadence of some of the religious authorities, and in the terrible cruelties of the Roman Empire that had conquered not only Jerusalem, but much of the Mediterranean world.

For Jesus, bringing the Kingdom meant not only opening the way to heavenly glory in the Father's love, but also revealing this unconditional love in Himself and His Father. Yet even the gift of the Resurrection and the revelation of His and the Father's unconditional love was not enough. Jesus had to defeat the increasing power that had been gained by Satan and his demons, because they had as their foremost intention the frustration and prevention of people from choosing and entering the divine Kingdom.

At the time of His baptism (Mt 3:13–17; Mk 1:9–11; Lk 3:21–22; Jn 1:31–34), Jesus planned to bring salvation to mankind in three ways: bringing the divine Kingdom, revealing the unconditional love of God, and defeating Satan and his forces. He knew He was the One called by His Father to defeat the enemy of goodness, love, and life; so, after His baptism, He follows the Holy Spirit into the desert in order to do battle with Satan in what is characterized as "the temptations in the desert". Even before the temptations He had formulated a fivefold plan to defeat Satan:

1. Engage him in spiritual battle in the desert where He knew that Satan would tempt Him to choose satisfaction of His desires and spiritual pride over obedience to and love of His Father; by refusing to submit to Satan, Jesus would establish His authority over him, effectively causing Satan to submit to His authority (Section II)

2. Defeat Satan's demons in a widespread ministry of exorcisms in which Jesus not only banishes Satan from certain individuals, but demonstrates His authority over Satan for the world to see (Section III)

3. Teach His disciples about Satan's tactics (Section IV)

4. Impart the power to exorcise demons to His disciples (the power of the Holy Spirit) for their missionary journeys in anticipation of the time when they would become responsible for perpetuating the Church and His Kingdom (Section V)

5. Defeat Satan definitively by an unconditional act of self-sacrificial love, capable of redeeming not only the weaknesses of human beings, but also the darkness and evil brought by Satan (Section VI)

Jesus' Resurrection and gift of the Spirit enable the fruits of His fivefold plan to come to fruition in the Church—particularly in the lives and works of the saints. Each of the above five points requires further explanation. However, before explaining Jesus' fivefold plan, it will be helpful to address some general topics about Satan and demons in the Old and New Testaments.

I. Satan and Demons in the Old and New Testaments

As implied above, the Old Testament treats Satan and spiritual evil in a somewhat peripheral way, though occasionally, images of Satan, such as the serpent in the narrative on Adam and Eve (Gen 3:1–24), are presented as prominent.[1] This stands in stark contrast to the Gospels, in which Jesus' battle with Satan[2] is central to each Gospel, because it is central to Jesus' mission of bringing the Kingdom of God to the world to redeem us and bring us to His eternal salvation of love and joy. To do this, Jesus realizes that He has to defeat Satan, who presents a huge obstacle to our choosing Jesus' teaching and His salvation. Satan had gained power throughout the centuries and would stop at nothing to tempt, deceive, and prevent us from choosing the eternal fulfillment and destiny prepared for us by God from the beginning of time.[3]

The period between the Old Testament and the writing of the New Testament (200 B.C. to A.D. 50), the intertestamental period, falls at the end of the most vicious persecution of Judaism by Assyrian-Greek occupiers, particularly Antiochus Epiphanes, who outlawed circumcision and the reading of the law, desecrated the Temple, and tortured and killed those who resisted his official sacrileges.[4] During

---

[1] See Sydney Page, *Powers of Evil: A Biblical Study of Satan and Demons* (Grand Rapids, Mich.: Baker Books, 1995), p. 87.

[2] There is only one word used for "Satan" in the Old Testament: שָׂטָן, which is pronounced like the English "Satan". In contrast, besides the word "Satan" (Mt 4:10; 12:26; 16:23; Mk 1:13; 3:23, 26; 4:15; 8:33; Lk 10:18; 11:18; 13:16; 22:3, 31; Jn 13:27), the Gospels alone use seven additional expressions: "the devil" (Mt 4:1, 5, 7, 11; 13:39; 25:41; Lk 4:2–3, 5, 13; 8:12; Jn 8:44; 13:2), "the tempter" (Mt 4:3), "the Evil One" (Mt 5:37; 13:18, 38; Jn 17:15); "the enemy" (Mt 13:39; Lk 10:19); "Beelzebul" (Mt 10:25; 12:24, 27; Mk 3:22; Lk 11:15, 19); "the prince of demons" (Mt 9:34; 12:24; Mk 3:22; Lk 11:15); and "the ruler of this world" (Jn 12:31; 14:30; 16:11). The proliferation of names clearly indicates the importance of this figure in Jesus' ministry, as well as the theological development that Jesus gives to the power of evil and His vanquishing of it.

[3] See Page, *Powers of Evil*, p. 87.

[4] See ibid., p. 88.

this time, what had been a peripheral consideration of Satan and demons became more and more central to Judaism, with apocalyptic literature reflecting a central role of Satan along with the formulation of rites of exorcism.[5] Jesus was well aware of these apocalyptic traditions, but places a whole new level of emphasis on the reign of Satan and the obstacle that Satan presents to His mission to bring redemption and salvation to all. After His baptism, it is clear that Jesus sees Satan as His major opponent and the defeat of Satan as central to His mission and ministry. For without a definitive defeat of Satan, we would be vulnerable to rejecting His salvation in favor of Satan's temptations, deceits, and power. Hence, He proceeds after His baptism into the desert fully aware that Satan would come to tempt Him because He intends to subject Satan to judgment and defeat him by resisting him through obedience to His Father's will.

II. Jesus' Defeat of Satan in the Temptations in the Desert

There is little reason to doubt the historicity of the temptation accounts in Mark, Matthew, and Luke, because Mark borrows from a completely different tradition than Matthew and Luke, who very probably borrow from Q[6] (referring to Quelle, meaning "source" in German). Q is an early collection of Jesus' sayings translated into Greek.[7] Mark's tradition emphasizes Jesus' companionship with the "wild beasts" (Mk 1:13)—showing Him to be the new Adam

---

[5] See Genesis 6:1–6, where "the sons of God" are viewed as angels who come down from Heaven to have relations with human women and as a result fall from God's favor. See also the following Jewish pseudepigraphal works: 1 Enoch 6—9 (dating to 300 B.C.), about the angelic descent to earth, and 2 Enoch 29:3 (dating to the early first century), where Satan and his angels are hurled to earth. This kind of apocalyptic belief influenced the interpretation of Daniel 7 (the four beasts) as a cosmic or heavenly struggle and also influenced the interpretation of Isaiah 14:12 (the fall of the "Day Star, son of Dawn") as the fall of the angel Lucifer. See David S. Russell, The Method and Message of Jewish Apocalyptic, Old Testament Library (Philadelphia: Westminster, 1964), pp. 235–62. See also Page, Powers of Evil, pp. 87–88.

[6] See Joseph Fitzmyer, Luke the Theologian: Aspects of His Teaching (New York: Paulist Press, 1989), pp. 154–55.

[7] Most scholars believe that Q is a single written source, though some hold that it is a plurality of sources. We do not know who the editor or editors were.

(redeeming the consequences of the fallen Adam)—while the Q tradition emphasizes the battle with Satan that results in a definitive victory by Jesus, and Jesus' power over Satan and all his demons (Mt 4:1–11; Lk 4:1–13).[8]

All three accounts indicate that the Holy Spirit either sent or led Jesus into the desert immediately after His baptism to be tempted by Satan. This indicates that the temptation of Jesus is part of the divine plan to redeem the world. Evidently, Jesus' Father could have prevented these temptations, because Satan is in His control, but He not only allows Satan to tempt His Son; He seems to provoke the confrontation—confident that His Son, in His human nature, will freely reject the temptations of the devil and obey His Father. This free choice of the incarnate Son of God to obey His Father lovingly—and to reject decisively the egocentricity, power, self-worship, and domination that caused Satan to fall from Heaven—is the first part of the Father's divine plan communicated by the Holy Spirit to Jesus. Jesus not only accepts the plan, but also freely chooses to obey His Father (over against the dark and egocentric desires of Satan), which shifts the balance of control within the world toward God's love and goodness—and away from Satan's self-idolatry and evil.

Though there are many similarities between Jesus' temptations and those of other human beings, they are also quite distinctive because of His incarnate divine nature. Two of the three temptations begin with "if you are the Son of God" (Mt 4:3, 6; Lk 4:3, 9), showing that the devil is trying to tempt Jesus to misuse His divine nature and origin for selfish ends instead of the self-sacrificial messianic ends to which He is called by His Father for the redemption of the world. When He overcomes these special temptations—designed for the "Son of God"—He wins a *cosmic* victory over Satan, which overcomes the angelic free act of Satan that led to the origins of evil not only on the earth, but also in the angelic heavens.[9] This is why the

---

[8] See Page, *Powers of Evil*, p. 89.

[9] It should not be thought that the idea of a fall from the angelic heavens by Satan originated with the Christians. It is already in Jewish apocalyptic literature. It is quite likely that Jesus was familiar with this apocalyptic literature and already sensed it deeply within His own divinely human nature. Hence, He was aware of the cosmic or heavenly struggle that was integral to the temptations in the desert. See Genesis 6:1–6; see also 1 Enoch 6—9; 2 Enoch 29:3. See Russell, *Method and Message*, pp. 235–62.

Father confidently sends His Son into the desert to be subjected to Satan's temptation—He knows that His Son will freely choose the right thing: self-sacrificial messiahship over misuse of divine prerogative for selfish purposes. At the moment the devil leaves, Jesus, the God-man, has complete power and authority over Satan and as such has won a victory both in the heavens and on the earth, a victory that will not only enable Him to exorcise Satan and his demons by His very presence, but also to give that same power to other men and women—His disciples—who will carry on His ministry until Satan is completely banished from the earth and heavens to his separate domain, reserved only for his demonic minions and those who have freely chosen him in this world.

Each of the three temptations indicates how Jesus was tempted, and we must suppose that this tradition originates with Jesus Himself.[10] If, as most scholars contend, Matthew's ordering of the temptations is more original than Luke's (i.e., the Q ordering), then we can clearly see the deceit and cunning of Satan in the progression of his temptations. Satan wants only one thing—for Jesus to be disobedient to His Father in order to gain some egocentric or worldly advantage. If successful, he (Satan) would win the cosmic struggle between good and evil. The stakes are so high that Satan makes this bold move even though he is well aware of Jesus' identity as the Son of God. His attempt to bring God's Son down to his level (to commit the same sin of disobedience as he did) is particularly bold because he knows that if he loses in this first confrontation, he will also lose the cosmic or heavenly struggle between God and himself; and in so doing, he will give the incarnate Son of God—and anyone to whom the Son grants the power of the Holy Spirit—power and authority over him. He will be a progressively greater loser until the end of time, when he is banished completely to his own domain of darkness and evil.

So Satan begins with a twofold temptation where Jesus seems to be quite vulnerable—first, to satisfy his earthly appetites above Jesus' awareness of His Father's will to keep His fast, and second, a challenge to misuse His divine power in an act of disobedience to God. There is another subtle temptation—Satan implies that Jesus' divine power is for Him alone to use as He wishes: "*If you really* are the Son

---

[10] See Page, *Powers of Evil*, pp. 88–89.

of God, then you should be able to do this.... Go ahead, ... I'm watching ... impress me."

We might begin by asking why the Father's will is for Jesus to keep His fast for more than forty days. The probable answer is that Jesus' fasting will redeem the sins of Israel, who grumbled against God during their forty-year sojourn in the desert (Deut 8:1–3). Jesus quotes Deuteronomy 8:3 in response to the devil: "It is written, 'Man shall not live by bread alone, but by every word that proceeds from the mouth of God'" (Mt 4:4; cf. Lk 4:4). This indicates that He will not commit the same sin of disobedience as the Israelites, but instead will redeem their sin by His own obedience.

Satan then moves to the second temptation,[11] in which he uses a visionary component. He immerses Jesus in a vision of the Temple and places Him at the highest parapet of it, asking Him to throw Himself down from there to fulfill the prophecy in Psalm 91:11–12: "'He will give his angels charge of you,' and 'On their hands they will bear you up, lest you strike your foot against a stone'" (Mt 4:6; cf. Lk 4:10–11). The beginning of the temptation is important here, for it is concerned with Jesus' proving to Himself, Satan, and perhaps others that He truly is the Son of God. This is why Satan repeats the challenge: "If you are the Son of God, throw yourself down" (Mt 4:6; Lk 4:9). Again, Satan tries to tempt Jesus to commit a similar sin to one that the Israelites committed in the desert—putting the Lord to the test by asking Him for a miracle to bring water out of the rock (Ex 17:1–7). Jesus refuses to be disobedient in this way, which redeems Israel's sin. In His refusal, He quotes Deuteronomy 6:16: "'You shall not tempt the Lord your God'" (Mt 4:7; Lk 4:12). We see in this passage the deceit and cunning of the devil—his ability to quote Scripture and to make disobedience seem like adherence to the prophecy in Psalm 91 (appearing, as Saint Paul warns, "like an angel of light" [2 Cor 11:14]). Jesus does not fall for any of it, because He has only one thing in His mind and heart: loving obedience to His Father.

We might pause for a moment here to consider what "obedience" means to Jesus—and ultimately to us in our resistance to temptation. We sometimes think that obedience comes from being in an enslaved

---

[11] Note that the Gospel of Luke describes this as the third temptation, not the second.

condition—like a slave obeying the capricious whims of his domineering master. But this is precisely the opposite way in which Jesus views obedience—the way we too should view obedience. For Him, obedience is not slavish subjugation to the will of a dominating other out of fear, but rather the loving surrender of His will to His Beloved, whom He loves even more than Himself. Obedience, in this sense, is built on the recognition of another's love for us, and our desire—in appreciation and friendship—to respond to the other with the same kind of love that we have been given.

Jesus views love as "gift of self",[12] and as such, His loving obedience is a gift of Himself to His Father—a surrender and a sacrifice to Him. Thus when He confronts Satan, He sees Satan's temptation in direct contrast to His deep and unconditional love of His Father—a love for which He is willing to make complete self-surrender and self-sacrifice. There are many analogies to this in human love—the self-surrender of two married individuals for the sake of one another and the children and the surrender of a religious celibate to God in a life of obediential love for the sake of the Kingdom and His people. The point is that obedience is not "servile obedience" or "fearful obedience", but rather loving self-surrender out of love for the Beloved, who has loved us first—as well as for His Kingdom and His people.

There can be no greater shield against temptation than truly loving obedience—the desire to be lovingly obedient in the same way Jesus was; for the desire to surrender ourselves to the Beloved out of love reorients all our desires away from ourselves toward the Divine Beloved. Such reorientation of desires moves us to great loyalty and to great resistance to egocentric sins of the flesh, power, greed, and pride. The simple prayer "Help me to be your lovingly obedient son" not only moves our whole being toward God, but reveals Satan's deceitful and cunning temptations to be mere darkness, emptiness, and separation from God—a true horror.

Satan is emboldened to use this temptation against Jesus because he thinks it just might work; and the reason he thinks it just might work

---

[12] This is explicitized in John's Gospel: "Greater love has no man than this, that a man lay down his life for his friends" (Jn 15:13). This is the intent of Jesus in His Eucharistic words when He declares, "Drink of it, all of you; for this is my blood of the covenant, which is poured out for many for the forgiveness of sins" (Mt 26:27–28).

is because he has no recognition of true love—no recognition of a desire to respond to another's love and self-surrender with a similar love and commitment. It is completely beyond his purview. The idea of loving obedience for him is, at best, a laughable confusion; he cannot see it as the fulfillment of his personhood and life, because his fulfillment comes only from himself and his power. Jesus' recognition of the Father's love for Him—and His corresponding self-surrendering love to His Father—is so obvious that the temptation to be disobedient in an act of spiritual vanity and pride must have almost seemed silly; so, He dispenses with it: "Again it is written, 'You shall not tempt the Lord your God'" (Mt 4:7; cf. Lk 4:12).

When Satan proceeds to the third temptation,[13] he no longer attempts to cloak his deception in deceit and cunning, but rather proceeds to a temptation to pure power. Once again using a visionary component, he brings Jesus to the top of a mountain where all the kingdoms can be seen in their so-called glory (Mt 4:8; cf. Lk 4:5). He claims that this authority has been given to him (Lk 4:6; cf. Mt 4:9), which Jesus would have undoubtedly recognized to be a lie, knowing that all authority comes from His Father, and that His Father would never have relinquished even worldly kingdoms into the hands of His adversary.

Though some scholars have contended that the Father allowed Satan to have such power after the fall of Adam, it is highly unlikely that God would have given up *His* sovereignty to Satan because of *human* sinfulness. Moreover, the Father reserved His sovereignty over the world to give to His Son not only after the Resurrection (Mt 28:18), but after Jesus' victory over Satan in the temptations. When Jesus emerges victorious over Satan, He has power over him to command him to leave—"Be gone, Satan!" (Mt 4:10)—and then to exorcise him at will by His mere presence until His final victory over him by His completely obediential, loving, self-surrender in the Passion.

Let us now return to the third temptation. Though Satan justifies the temptation by a claim of authority over the world, he unmasks his intention unqualifiably—he wants Jesus to worship him (Mt 4:9; Lk 4:7), and in so doing, to disobey His Father. He claims that he is willing to give everything he has over to Jesus, including the kingdoms of

---

[13] Note that the Gospel of Luke describes this as the second temptation, not the third.

the world, which he has falsely claimed as his own. Jesus would have undoubtedly recognized the second lie in this offer—that Satan would willingly give over anything that belongs to him to anyone for any reason. Jesus knows that he would never do this—not even to gain the worship of the Son of God, and certainly not out of an act of love. Jesus reacts quickly by recognizing that the Father is the only one in the juxtaposition who is faithful to His promises and willing to give of Himself—and so He responds, once again quoting Deuteronomy, "Be gone, Satan! for it is written, 'You shall worship the Lord your God and him only shall you serve'" (Mt 4:10, quoting Deut 6:16).

Satan obeys Jesus and leaves Him, revealing Jesus' victory over him as well as the victory of loving obedience over the lies, seductions, empty promises, and narcissistic dominance of evil. The first part of Jesus' plan—the plan of the Father—is actualized, and now it remains for Him to solidify it and finalize it in His Passion.

It is important to note that there is absolutely no precedent in all of Jewish literature—from the Old Testament Midrash or Qumran— that mentions a vanquishing of Satan. It is completely unique to Jesus. Joachim Jeremias concluded the following from an exhaustive study of contemporary Jewish literature in the intertestamental and New Testament periods:

> There is no analogy to these statements [about definitively defeating Satan] in contemporary Judaism; neither the synagogue nor Qumran knows anything of a vanquishing of Satan that is already beginning in the present.[14]

When Jesus completes the first part of His plan—the initial vanquishing of Satan in the desert—He proceeds to the second part: His ministry of exorcisms.

III. Jesus' Prolific Ministry of Exorcism

Though Jesus does battle with Satan, who is the clear enemy of Him and His Father, the Gospels indicate that He casts out "demons".

---

[14]Joachim Jeremias, *New Testament Theology* (London: SCM Press, 1971), 1:95.

Who are these demons? Throughout the Synoptic Gospels, Satan is portrayed as the prince of demons—implying that the demons are lesser evil spirits than Satan, who has authority over them. Matthew reveals that these lesser evil spirits are angelic beings in the phrase "the devil and his angels" (Mt 25:41). These demonic angelic spirits are referred to as "demons", "unclean spirits", and "evil spirits".[15]

There is considerable evidence for the historicity of Jesus' exorcisms (and other miracles). The most striking evidence comes from His adversaries during His ministry who did not challenge the fact that he worked miracles, but attributed them instead to the devil or sorcery.[16] N. T. Wright notes in this regard:

> We must be clear that Jesus' contemporaries, both those who became his followers and those who were determined not to become his followers, certainly regarded him as possessed of remarkable powers. The church did not invent the charge that Jesus was in league with Beelzebul; but charges like that are not advanced unless they are needed as an explanation for some quite remarkable phenomena.[17]

The Gospel reports about this charge are highly credible, because it cannot be imagined that Mark (or the other Evangelists for that matter) would have dared to mention that Jesus was in league with the devil or was doing exorcisms and other miracles by the power of the devil, unless they believed it was needed to respond to a charge that was *really* being leveled against Jesus. Hence, Jesus' harshest critics really did accuse Him of exorcising (and performing other miracles) by the power of Beelzebul (Satan)—in which case, they testified that Jesus was in fact successfully exorcising demons and performing miracles. It can hardly be thought that Jesus' harshest critics would concede to His having supernatural power unless there was wide contemporaneous acknowledgment that Jesus was doing exorcisms and healings—and they had to explain them away

---

[15] Page, *Powers of Evil*, pp. 137–38.

[16] As Raymond Brown notes: "[Jesus' enemies] attributed [His extraordinary deeds] to evil origins, either to the devil (Mark 3:22–30) or in 2d-century polemic to magic (Irenaeus, *Adversus Haereses* 2.32.3–5)." Raymond Brown, *An Introduction to New Testament Christology* (New York: Paulist Press, 1994), pp. 62–63.

[17] N. T. Wright, *Jesus and the Victory of God* (Minneapolis: Fortress Press, 1996), p. 187.

by attributing them to Jesus' cooperation with evil. Therefore, Jesus' prolific ministry of exorcisms and other miracles is almost certainly historical.

In addition to the above testimony of Jesus' critics, there is significant multiple attestation to Jesus' exorcisms in four out of five independent sources—Mark, Q, M (special Matthew), and L (special Luke).[18] According to John P. Meier,[19] there are seven nonoverlapping accounts of exorcisms in the Synoptic Gospels:

1. The possessed boy (Mk 9:14–29)
2. A passing reference to the exorcism of Mary Magdalene (Lk 8:2)
3. The Gerasene demoniac (demon-possessed person) (Mk 5:1–20)
4. The demoniac in the Capernaum synagogue (Mk 1:23–28)
5. The mute and blind demoniac in the Q tradition (Mt 12:22–24; Lk 11:14–15)
6. The mute demoniac (Mt 9:32–33)
7. The Syrophoenician/Canaanite woman's demoniac daughter (Mk 7:24–30; Mt 15:21–28)

These seven distinct instances are complemented by many *sayings* (about exorcisms) as well as references to exorcisms within *summary texts*. From this we can adduce fourfold multiple attestation of sources:

1. Mark, who was responsible for most of the exorcism narratives (which Matthew and Luke used in their narratives)
2. L (special Luke), which gives a passing reference to the exorcism of Mary Magdalene, who was among "some women who had been healed of evil spirits and infirmities, from whom seven demons had gone out" (Lk 8:2).
3. Q, which has one narrative—the mute and blind demoniac (Mt 12:22–24; Lk 11:14–15)
4. M (special Matthew), which recounts one narrative—Jesus exorcises a mute demoniac (Mt 9:32–33).

---

[18] The fifth independent source is J (the Johnnine tradition).

[19] John P. Meier has written the most comprehensive analytical and literary study of Jesus' miracles to date in *A Marginal Jew: Rethinking the Historical Jesus*, vol. 2, *Mentor, Message, and Miracles* (New York: Doubleday, 1994).

When we combine the Marcan narratives and the Q *sayings* with the above sources, we see a strong confluence of attestation, which Meier summarizes as follows:

> Q sayings join Marcan sayings and Marcan narratives in providing multiple attestation for the existence of exorcisms in the ministry of the historical Jesus ... that there should be seven individual "specimens" of a very specific type of miracle [coming from four independent sources], namely, exorcism, supports the view that exorcisms loomed large in Jesus' ministry.[20]

Jesus begins the second part of His plan almost immediately after His victory over Satan during the temptations in the desert. Mark gives only one narrative between the temptations and the first of Jesus' exorcisms—the calling of four apostles (1:16–20). After the call of Peter, Andrew, James, and John, Jesus encounters His first demoniac (demon-possessed person) in a synagogue in Capernaum (1:23–28). Before examining this narrative in more detail, it is important to recognize the centrality of Jesus' ministry of exorcisms as portrayed in Mark—as well as the other Synoptic Gospels. First, Mark presents exorcisms as the first miracle in his Gospel and makes them the most prevalent. He includes them in every summary statement of Jesus' ministry and implies that they are an everyday occurrence. Generally, demoniacs are brought to Jesus, and Jesus exorcises the demon by His own authority—and therefore does not ask for divine power to intervene. He uses no words of incantation, special formulae, or religious objects (such as oils, holy water, or symbols). He simply commands the spirit by His own *divine* authority to be silent and to get out of the person—with which the demons immediately comply. For Mark, Jesus' exorcisms are central to His bringing the Kingdom of God to the world, because each exorcism not only frees each victim from his bondage to demons but also weakens the grip of Satan and his angels in the cosmic order.

As Jesus exorcises each victim, He is literally driving out Satan from the world and the whole cosmic order. This is the second part of His plan, to free the world from the grip of Satan and to replace it

---

[20] Ibid., p. 648.

with His Spirit and the Church (through the ministry of the apostles and their successors), His teaching, and ultimately through the full realization of His eternal Kingdom.

Let us now return to the first exorcism story in the Gospel of Mark, the demoniac in the synagogue at Capernaum:

> And immediately there was in their synagogue a man with an unclean spirit; and he cried out, "What have you to do with us, Jesus of Nazareth? Have you come to destroy us? I know who you are, the Holy One of God." But Jesus rebuked him, saying, "Be silent, and come out of him!" And the unclean spirit, convulsing him and crying with a loud voice, came out of him. And they were all amazed, so that they questioned among themselves, saying, "What is this? A new teaching! With authority he commands even the unclean spirits, and they obey him." And at once his fame spread everywhere throughout all the surrounding region of Galilee. (1:23–28; cf. Lk 4:33–37)

We might split this passage into nine parts, all of which typify extended exorcism narratives in the Gospels. These parts will help us to differentiate exorcisms from healings of physical maladies in the minds of the writers of the Gospel traditions:

1. Jesus confronts the demoniac in the synagogue.
2. The unclean spirit in the man cries out, "What have you to do with us, Jesus of Nazareth?"
3. The demon poses a second question: "Have you come to destroy us?"
4. Then the demon identifies Jesus: "I know who you are, the Holy One of God."
5. Jesus rebukes the spirit with the first command to be silent.
6. He follows this with a second command (by His own authority) to get out of the man.
7. The demon cannot resist Him, and so begins his exit from the man by convulsing him.
8. The demon cries out in a loud voice when exiting from him.
9. Everyone in the crowd recognizes Jesus' authority, and combines it with His "new teaching".

The above nine parts require some explanation. Firstly, the man who is possessed is not confronting Jesus and speaking to Him; rather, it is the unclean spirit. This is evident from the second question that is asked: "Have you come to destroy us?" This is a question asked out of fear of Jesus—a fear induced by the awareness that Jesus has ultimate power and authority over demons, which has come from His victory over Satan (their leader) in the desert. The possessed man couldn't possibly have had this knowledge, but the demons—being angelic subordinates to their master, Satan—would certainly have had this knowledge. Furthermore, the demoniac knows Jesus' real identity: "the Holy One of God", which is a parallel of "the Son of God". Once again, the possessed man could not possibly have known of Jesus' true identity, for this would have required supernatural knowledge of which the demons would have been aware.

Secondly, the term "us" is not a reference to multiple demons within the possessed man. This conflicts with the demon's later statement in which he uses the first person singular to identify Jesus: "*I* know who you are." So, to what does "us" refer? Very probably it means demons (evil spirits) as a class.[21] Apparently, the demon possessing the man is aware of Jesus' plan and mission to destroy them and their father, Satan; so, he asks the confrontational question: "What would you have to do with us, Jesus of Nazareth?" He then manifests his fear with another question: "Have you come to destroy us?"—that is, has He come to destroy all of the evil spirits?

Thirdly, the demon reveals to Jesus that he knows who He is. As noted above, this requires supernatural knowledge, revealing the identity of the speaker. But it must be asked, "Why did the demon tell Jesus that he knew His true identity?" The probable answer lies in the fact that knowledge and use of a person's name gave one power—for good or evil—over him. The demon recognizes Jesus' power over him, but makes a last-minute desperate effort to exert some control in the situation. It obviously does not succeed, because Jesus is completely unphased by the revelation and simply orders him to be silent, whereupon He gives a second command to get out of the man, to which the demon is forced to comply. He is powerless to do anything except make the man suffer—by convulsing him violently—upon his imminent exit. At this juncture, the man is set free, and the implication is that Jesus has won a victory, not just for the individual man, but within the cosmic struggle between good and evil.

---

[21] See Page, *Powers of Evil*, p. 141.

It should not be thought that demonic possession was mistakenly attributed to serious physical illnesses, seizures, epilepsy, and the like by an ignorant and superstitious Semitic population. The New Testament Gospel writers—who were given authority by Jesus over unclean spirits and were well aware of His teaching about them— were careful to differentiate exorcisms from healings of physical illnesses. Though demon possession could have accompanying physical debilitations resembling epilepsy, grand mal seizures, and the like, they are not reducible to them for one very obvious reason: there is another personality manifesting itself in a demonic possession who has supernatural knowledge, about which a possessed man could not possibly be aware. Jesus is aware of this difference, and so are the Gospel writers; they are careful to point to it in the major exorcism narratives. There are many minor differences as well. Firstly, people with only physical illnesses do not cry out confrontationally when they encounter Jesus—"What would you have to do with us, Jesus of Nazareth?"—they or their loved ones simply request a healing from Jesus.

Secondly, those requesting a physical healing are not afraid of Jesus, pleading with Him not to destroy or torment them—they simply want relief from their physical maladies. Thirdly, those with physical maladies are not aware of Jesus' divine identity and certainly do not try to use it as a means of deflecting His power or distracting Him. Fourthly, Jesus does not use the commands "Be silent, and come out of him" in physical healings, but rather, he commands by addressing the physical healing alone—for example, "Rise" (Mt 9:6, the healing of the paralytic), "Be [made] clean" (Mk 1:42, the cleansing of the leper), or "Be opened" (Mk 7:34, the healing of the deaf man). Finally, when physical illnesses are cured, the sick person simply (and immediately) regains his physical health—he does not convulse violently and show signs of being knocked unconscious (as in exorcisms). These differences should be sufficient to redress the contention that first-century Semitic audiences were incapable of distinguishing a demon-possessed person from a person with merely physical illnesses. Indeed, as we shall see in the next chapter, these differences are present in contemporary exorcisms that are diagnosed medically and psychiatrically by competent professionals (see the cases of Julia and of Robbie Mannheim in Chapter 3, Section III).

No doubt, there are some exorcism narratives—short ones—that do not clearly differentiate between a demon possession and a physical illness; but all the extended narratives do make the above distinctions, revealing that they are a different class of miracles—those that are directed to the destruction of Satan and his angelic subordinates, who are intent on preventing human beings from choosing the salvation and Kingdom that Jesus was bringing into the world. Satan's grip had to be broken—and Jesus does this with each exorcism until He accomplishes the final victory over him through His Passion and death (see below, Section VI).

One might wonder why Jesus allows the evil spirits to continue their work in the world after He has broken Satan's dominance over them. In brief, the answer concerns human freedom as explained below in Chapter 4, Section III. We must choose between good and evil—between love and unlove—if our good and loving deeds are to be our own. If we don't have any real choice to do evil, then we don't have any real choice to do good either. If the only actions we can do are *good* ones, then they do not spring from our power, but rather from programming by a power beyond our own. Therefore, God has to allow us to choose evil in order to choose good truly—to choose unloving deeds in order to choose loving deeds. Our goodness and love cannot originate from within us—cannot be our own—if we do not have any choice other than goodness or love. Not only that—God has to allow us to be exposed to evil from others exercising the free use of their will, and even the evil of spiritual powers exerting influence on us through temptation and deceit.

God can also influence our desires for the good through the numinous experience, the intuition of the sacred, and the felt awareness of conscience (see the Quartet, Volume II, Chapters 1 and 2) as well as the influence of His Holy Spirit and direct appearance in public apparitions, private visions, and mystical experience (see Chapter 1 above). This counterbalances the influence of the evil spirits on our desires through temptation and deceit.

This counterbalancing of influences by both God and Satan is present from the very creation of the human soul within our first parents (see Section I above). No doubt, there was a tempter, like a serpent, present to "help" our first parents to disobey the sacred mandate of God—and rationalize the foul deed as something "good". According to Jesus, the time between the fall and His coming manifested a temporary victory of sorts for Satan, who seems to have gained considerable control, not only over individual human beings, but also civilization, cultic religion, and even some aspects of the Jewish faith (particularly the Temple administration and some religious teachers during Jesus' time). Jesus reveals that He came into the world to redress this imbalance within the cosmic struggle between good and evil and to move it permanently in favor of God, goodness, and love through the breaking of Satan's power—by His victory over him in the desert, His ministry of exorcism, His Passion and death, and the conveyance of His power to exorcise to His apostles and the Church.

Yes—Jesus allowed Satan and his demons to continue to influence the desires of human beings in order protect human freedom. However, He provided the means to guarantee His sovereignty over evil for all who want to choose freely this unconditionally good and loving sovereignty, and to bring everyone who desires to live in the light of that sovereignty—even imperfectly—into the fullness of His Kingdom. Jesus truly was and is, as N. T. Wright puts it, "the victory of God".[22]

IV. Jesus' Teachings about Satan and His Power

There are two central passages concerned specifically with Jesus and His mission to defeat Satan: the passage about the Beelzebul accusation and the passage about Satan's fall from Heaven. Jesus' other teachings about Satan concern how Satan will interact and interfere with the apostles in their spiritual and apostolic lives. We will first consider the passages concerned with Jesus' conflict with Satan, then proceed to the teachings about Satan's opposition to the apostles.

A. The Beelzebul Controversy
(Mt 12:22–32; Mk 3:22–29; Lk 11:14–23)

Let us begin with the passage about the Beelzebul accusation. We have already considered this passage as a testimony to the efficacy

---

[22] The title and theme of Wright's book *Jesus and the Victory of God.*

of Jesus' prolific ministry of exorcisms by His adversaries. Yet, the passage contains much more than this, giving us an insight into the absolute opposition between the two parties. Matthew's rendition of the passage follows:

> Then a blind and dumb demoniac was brought to him, and he healed him, so that the dumb man spoke and saw. And all the people were amazed, and said, "Can this be the Son of David?" But when the Pharisees heard it they said, "It is only by Beelzebul, the prince of demons, that this man casts out demons." Knowing their thoughts, he said to them, "Every kingdom divided against itself is laid waste, and no city or house divided against itself will stand; and if Satan casts out Satan, he is divided against himself; how then will his kingdom stand? And if I cast out demons by Beelzebul, by whom do your sons cast them out? Therefore they shall be your judges. But if it is by the Spirit of God that I cast out demons, then the kingdom of God has come upon you. Or how can one enter a strong man's house and plunder his goods, unless he first binds the strong man? Then indeed he may plunder his house. He who is not with me is against me, and he who does not gather with me scatters. Therefore I tell you, every sin and blasphemy will be forgiven men, but the blasphemy against the Spirit will not be forgiven. And whoever says a word against the Son of man will be forgiven; but whoever speaks against the Holy Spirit will not be forgiven, either in this age or in the age to come." (Mt 12:22–32)

Matthew's text borrows from both Mark and Q, and so it is the most instructive with respect to Jesus' teaching and the earliest traditions about it. So what does this passage tell us? Prior to Jesus' time, demons were thought to be "independent agents" of evil and misfortune. However, in this passage, the Pharisees indicate that Beelzebul (i.e., Satan) is "the prince of demons". There can be little doubt that Jesus subscribed to this contention—and taught His apostles that demons were in fact a unified force under their supreme leader, Satan.[23] This implies that the powers of evil are far more organized and insidious than was communicated by the Old Testament.[24] Moreover, it implies that the demons that Jesus exorcized were agents

---

[23] See Page, *Powers of Evil*, pp. 101–2.
[24] See ibid.

of Satan—even though Satan is not mentioned in the exorcism narratives. Thus, for Jesus every exorcism of a demon (an agent of Satan) was a "loosening of the grip" of Satan himself over mankind.[25]

The first argument that Jesus uses to prove the logical inconsistency and hypocrisy of His opponents states what seems to be the obvious: if Jesus is using the power of Satan to cast out Satan's minions, then how can His Kingdom stand? Satan would ultimately undermine himself. Jesus' argument is logically rigorous, but it does assume that the demons that Jesus is exorcising are the minions of Satan himself. Jesus does not try to prove this, because he thinks it is virtually self-evident. Recall that Satan is not present in any of Jesus' exorcisms—only demons. Hence, Jesus' association of the demons with Satan himself indicates that the demons are a unified force under Satan. The demons are characterized as tormentors, while Satan is characterized as a tempter, deceiver, and cunning leader of the demonic forces.

The second argument ("Then by whom do your sons [followers] cast them out?") seems to be an ad hominem used by Jesus to show that the same illogical argument can be used against Jewish exorcists in the similar arbitrary way it was used against Him. We might rephrase the argument as follows: "If you can claim illogically and without any evidence that I am casting out Satan's minions by the power of Satan, then what is to prevent me from saying the same thing about your exorcists? Nothing—arbitrarily asserted, arbitrarily denied."

It should not be thought that Jesus is equating the effectiveness and significance of His exorcisms with those done by Jewish authorities—indeed, the next argument shows conclusively that he does not believe this. Rather, Jesus believes that His exorcisms are initiating the Kingdom of God in the world. Evidently, Jesus not only believes that His exorcisms are superior to those of the Jewish authorities; He believes that they have eschatological significance—that they are literally ushering in the Kingdom of God that will save humanity from the powers of evil and bring them into the fullness of eternal light, goodness, love, and joy. This is a mission that can be accomplished only by a divine messiah, by one who comes from the Father and possesses the Father's Holy Spirit. Jesus does not make this claim

---

[25] See ibid.

directly, but places it within a conditional statement that allows His Jewish opponents to draw their own conclusion: "But if it is by the Spirit of God that I cast out demons, then the kingdom of God has come upon you" (Mt 12:28).

Why did Jesus believe that His exorcisms were so much more significant than those of the Jewish authorities? The fourth argument gives us His answer: "How can one enter a strong man's house and plunder his goods, unless he first binds the strong man? Then indeed he may plunder his house" (Mt 12:29). What does Jesus mean by this phrase? Clearly, the strong man is Satan, and Jesus believes that He is the one who has bound him, thus enabling him to plunder his goods. When did Jesus bind Satan? As the reader may by now infer, He did so when He overcame Satan's temptations in the desert (see Section II above). Jesus understood His victorious battle with Satan in the desert to have cosmic and eschatological significance. He was the one and only divine man to overcome Satan definitely, which loosened the grip of Satan not only in the world, but also in the heavens, an event that would immediately bring the Kingdom of God in Jesus' Person into the world to replace Satan's position and power. Since He had won this cosmic and eschatological victory, every exorcism He worked would lead not only to the liberation of an individual person, but also to the plundering of Satan's position and power ("his goods"). Jesus' exorcisms alone would be able to undermine the power and grip of Satan in the world and the heavens. The Jewish exorcists could not do anything like this, because they had not tied up Satan, giving them access to the whole of his dominion.

We can now see why Jesus is so vigorous in His ministry of exorcism. He believes that each and every one of his exorcisms is plundering and undermining Satan's dominion, weakening him for the final defeat that will occur at His Passion and death (see below, Section VI). We can now see the significance too of Jesus' preaching about the unforgiveable sin of blaspheming the Holy Spirit (Mt 12:32). What does "blaspheming the Holy Spirit mean"? The context of the passage makes it clear: it is to claim that the Holy Spirit is Satan. Why does Jesus consider this to be unforgiveable? Because the Holy Spirit is the Spirit of God Himself. Thus to equate the Holy Spirit with Satan is the same as equating God with Satan. If one *knowingly* and *intentionally* does this, it can only mean one of two things: either you worship

Satan as your God or you subject God (your Savior and Redeemer) to the most reviling of insults—calling Him Satan (the father of evil, lies, darkness), the enemy of our human nature. The first meaning makes a person a Satan worshipper; the second heaps the most horrible insult imaginable upon the Creator and Redeemer—the act of perfect ingratitude.

Does Jesus mean that this sin is literally unforgiveable? There is considerable debate about this because there are other passages in the New Testament indicating that if we repent for our sins, God will forgive us.[26] Would this then mean that the sin of blaspheming the Holy Spirit would be unforgiveable if we sincerely repented after doing it? Though Jesus seems to be quite adamant about the unforgiveable nature of the sin, even in the life to come, it is difficult to say definitively that God would deny forgiveness to anyone who was sincerely contrite for sin—even this one. Perhaps it is best to say that Jesus views this sin as the very worst sin anyone can commit, because one is either declaring that Satan is his god or that God the Creator and Redeemer is Satan. Hence, He is warning us, with the sternest admonition possible, never to do this knowingly and intentionally— not even to go anywhere near this, for it literally risks an entrance into the domain of Satan himself.

B. "I Saw Satan Fall Like Lightning" (Lk 10:18)

"I saw Satan fall like lightning" (Lk 10:18) is unique to Luke's Gospel and probably comes from one of his special sources. It is said in the context of another passage unique to Luke—the missionary journey of the seventy-two (see below, Section V). The disciples of Jesus returned from their missionary journey, rejoicing that even the demons are subject to them in Jesus' name, to which Jesus responds, "I saw Satan fall like lightning from heaven." To what does this "fall" refer?

---

[26] See 1 Jn 1:9: "If we confess our sins, he is faithful and just, and will forgive our sins and cleanse us from all unrighteousness"; Acts 3:19: "Repent therefore, and turn again [to God], that your sins may be blotted out"; and implicitly, Lk 15:11–32 (the Parable of the Prodigal Son); Lk 18:9–14 (the Parable of the Tax Collector and the Pharisee); Mt 6:14–15; 18:21–22; Eph 1:7; 4:32; Col 1:13–14.

Though some scholars advocate that it refers to Satan's initial fall from Heaven after committing his sin of disobedience, most scholars believe that it refers to a vision that Jesus had after defeating Satan in the desert.[27] The reason for this is that Jesus is responding to the disciples' announcement that they have authority over evil spirits in *Jesus'* name. Thus the passage apparently refers to *Jesus'* defeat of Satan in the desert (the real source of the disciples' authority over unclean spirits) and not to Satan's fall, because of *his* sin. Evidently, Satan's sin did not give the disciples authority over unclean spirits in Jesus' name.[28]

It is difficult to determine whether Jesus was speaking about a vision He had of Satan falling like lightning or was simply speaking figuratively, because the verb *theōreō* allows either interpretation. In light of the apocalyptic dimensions of the battle with Satan in the desert, and the other visionary components in it (being brought to the parapet of the Temple and to the top of a mountain), it is not out of the question that Jesus could have had a vision of Satan's defeat like "lightning falling from heaven".

Whatever the case, it seems that Jesus had some kind of incisive confirmation of His defeat of Satan after overcoming his temptations in the desert, a defeat that subjected Satan to His authority and power—and even to the power of His name. This is why Jesus can say with confidence (in response to the Beelzebul accusation) that He has bound Satan until the end of time when Satan's banishment from the earth into his dark domain will be complete. Jesus' binding of Satan also allows His disciples to have the authority over evil spirits in Jesus' name. Satan has been permanently weakened and injured, and he cannot prevent Jesus' disciples from defeating his minions through the use of Jesus' name. The stage has been set—Jesus has bound Satan, begun His ministry of exorcism, shared His authority with His disciples, and given His life in loving self-sacrifice to guarantee the ultimate defeat and banishment of Satan. This allows the disciples and their successors to continue this ministry until that final victory and banishment occurs. So long as disciples continue to take up this ministry of Jesus, Satan cannot possibly win

[27] See Page, *Powers of Evil*, pp. 109–10.
[28] See ibid.

the ultimate victory, for Satan will be defeated by Jesus' gift of Himself guaranteeing His ultimate victory.

The above two passages reveal how Jesus saw Himself within His conflict with Satan—His victory in the desert, His binding of Satan, the weakening of Satan's grip, the subjugation of demonic forces, the gift of authority over demons to His disciples, and the ultimate victory He would win in His Passion, death, and Resurrection. It also reveals His intention to bestow the Holy Spirit permanently on His disciples, not only for the purpose of subjugating Satan, but also for building the Church and supporting the Kingdom that Jesus has brought to earth so that as many as possible may experience the fullness of His eternal salvation. We will now look at four other passages concerned with Satan and spiritual evil that focus on teaching the disciples about these evil forces, rather than the revelation of Jesus' victory over Satan.

C. The Sermon on the Mount

The Sermon on the Mount has two probable references to Satan: the first with respect to the prohibition of oaths—"Let what you say be simply 'Yes' or 'No'; anything more than this comes from the Evil One" (Mt 5:37). The second one is familiar to all Christians, coming from the final petition of the Our Father—"But deliver us from the evil one" (Mt 6:13, NIV). Some may have heard these passages translated with the indefinite "evil" instead of the personal "evil one", which would evidently refer to Satan. Why would we prefer the latter to the former when the former seems to be the more common translation? First, when Matthew uses the adjective *ponēros* (evil) like a noun (which he does in the above two cases), he generally uses it to refer to a person.[29] Second, in the final petition of the Our Father, "deliver" is followed by the preposition *apo* (which generally refers to persons) instead of *ek*, which generally refers to things (and the abstract) instead of persons.[30] Hence, the translators of the New International Version prefer the rendering

[29] See ibid, p. 112.
[30] See ibid.

"the evil one". If this translation is correct, it might also reveal a connection between the final petition of the Our Father and Jesus' priestly prayer in John's Gospel: He asks God to protect the apostles "from the evil one" (17:15).

If this interpretation is correct, then Jesus anticipated that the apostles and their followers would be subject to temptations and direct conflicts with Satan and his demons; so, Jesus urges them to pray constantly for deliverance from him, his temptations, and his power.

What about the prohibition of oaths? Once again *ponēros* is used substantively (like a noun), indicating a probable reference to a person: the Evil One. Why bring up Satan in this context? Because Satan was seen by Jesus and the apostolic Church as the "father of lies" (Jn 8:44), the great deceiver. The prohibition against oaths is not simply against oaths; it is against small and large falsehoods—it is about using oaths to substantiate everything from misleading statements to exaggerations to outright lies. For Jesus, the temptation to use oaths to substantiate a statement is only necessary if we are not known to be scrupulously honest about what we are saying. Hence, Jesus is saying that we should be scrupulously honest about what we say. If we are, we will have a reputation of being so, and we would not have to use oaths to substantiate our statements; anything else is from the Evil One—the father of lies, the great deceiver.

D. Three Parables—
"The Sower" (Mt 13:1–23; Mk 4:1–20; Lk 8:4–15),
"The Weeds" (Mt 13:24–30, 36–43), and
"The Sheep and Goats" (Mt 25:31–46)

The Parable of the Sower (Mt 13:1–23; Mk 4:1–20; Lk 8:4–15) speaks about Satan in the interpretive section. Jesus indicates that the sower represents Himself, that the seed is the Word of God—the message about the Kingdom—and that the birds are Satan. When the seed is planted within the human heart, Satan is said to approach immediately like a bird who swoops down to consume the seed as it is taking root in the heart. For Jesus, Satan's primary objective is to prevent His word from affecting the human heart, as soon as possible after planting. He does this by causing doubts, distracting people with false views of happiness, dignity, and fulfillment, and causing discontent rather than gratitude. By doing this, he hopes the power, hope, and grace of the Word will simply diminish before it can have real effects. How can he have such power? Because God will protect the free will of every human being for the reasons mentioned above (Section III). Thus God will not supersede the power of the human will even to help His Word to become effective within our souls. By allowing us to accept or reject His Word freely, He also allows the temptations of the Evil One to distract us from it—even to the point of forgetting our initial awareness of it. Notice that it is not the devil who steals it from us before it is implanted, but rather the devil who distracts us from it after it is implanted to the point where we simply forget about it, preferring instead the empty pleasures and promises given to us by Satan.

Thus Jesus instructs His disciples on the power with which God has endowed our free choice and will, showing them how careful they must be with new converts—to warn them about the tactics and empty promises of the devil, which are sure to tempt and distract them at the very beginning of their conversion process until the Word has begun to take root and grow sufficiently. The devil can also tempt us after we have grown in faith, but this is a much more difficult and complex process for him, because now he must battle the power of Jesus' Word and the gifts of the Holy Spirit that come with growth in faith. All things being equal, implies Jesus, Satan would prefer nipping faith in the bud from its beginning, than battling His word and the power of the Holy Spirit after it takes root. Thus converts must be hyperaware of being distracted and must fight those distractions by committing themselves to learning more about His Word, greater participation in Church and prayers, and sharing the faith with others. If they do this, the Word will grow more powerfully in them, and they will present opposition to the devil not only within themselves, but with respect to all those with whom they share their faith.

The Parable of the Weeds (Mt 13:24–30) with accompanying interpretation (Mt 13:36–43) is unique to the Gospel of Matthew; Satan is compared to an enemy of Jesus who stealthfully sows weeds at night into a field of wheat (representing the followers of Jesus). The weeds are called "sons of the evil one" (Mt 13:38), implying that they are committed to undermining and weakening the follow-ers of Christ. The point of the parable is that God does not separate the wheat from the weeds immediately, but allows both to grow up together, at which point He makes the separation permanent—the wheat to Heaven and the weeds to the domain of their master, Satan.

The parable responds to the question of why God allows peo-ple who are committed to undermining His Word to have such a destructive effect on His followers (e.g., persecuting them, under-mining their attempts at evangelization, and even trying to seduce those who are mature in their faith). Jesus responds by saying that it will be too dangerous for the Father to do so because the wheat might get harmed in the process. Therefore, He prefers to delay the separation for the welfare of the wheat: the followers of Christ. However, this will require that the wheat face opposition, resis-tance, and intentional seduction to the world. They will have to be strong in their faith, committed to Church and prayer, and fore-armed to contend with attacks from others that will be both painful and challenging. Nevertheless, if they remain faithful to the end in the midst of challenge, they will be taken to Heaven and separated permanently from those who have actively opposed and harmed them. We should not try to read additional meanings into this par-able beyond the question it is trying to answer. For example, Jesus is not trying to answer the question of whether the weeds (the sons of evil) might repent and be saved; nor is He trying to answer the question of why the sons of evil are so adamantly opposed to Jesus. Again, He is not trying to answer the question why it is more dan-gerous to have a premature separation of the wheat from the weeds than a later separation, for example. The parable simply makes clear that for the sake of the followers of Jesus (the wheat) the Father prefers to delay the separation of the wheat from the weeds until the end of the world—hence, the followers of Jesus must be prepared for temptation, ridicule, opposition, seduction, and every kind of resistance to evangelization. But in the end, a separation will occur that will be permanent.

This leads us to one final question: Are the "sons of evil" demons or are they men or both? Given Jesus' other teachings about Satan and demons, the "sons of evil" must include demons, spiritual beings who are actively committed to the destruction of the followers of Christ. Yet human beings cannot be excluded from this group because Jesus anticipates that some will give their allegiance freely to the rule of Satan, for the empty promises of power, egocentric fulfillment, domination of others, and self-idolatry (the seven deadly sins; see Chapters 5 and 6 below). Though even these individuals could freely repent of their sins before dying, they will very likely (because of their alignment with the empty promises of Satan) actively oppose, seduce, resist, and persecute the followers of Christ—just like the demons. The separation of the followers of Jesus from the followers of Satan will occur at death for each individual; the ultimate separation will occur at the end of time, when even the demons will be subject to final separation from the followers of Jesus, and consigned to the domain of their "father", Satan.

The Parable of the Sheep and Goats (Mt 25:31–46) is also unique to Matthew; it follows the same lines as the Parable of the Weeds with respect to the ultimate judgment of the unrighteous, but it adds several details not included in the previous parable. The definition of the "unrighteous" is expanded from those who are committed to opposing Jesus to include those who lack compassion for the unfortunate. Jesus asserts that every person has incalculable dignity, and so He equates one's dignity with His own. He then urges His disciples to recognize that dignity and to take compassion on those who are unfortunate in the world. He then implies that those who have no compassion for the unfortunate—those who are heartless—are not His followers, but the followers of another master who likewise has no heart for anyone in any unfortunate circumstance. This "hardness of heart" endangers salvation as much as actively opposing Jesus and the Holy Spirit.

The same theme is reinforced in the Parable of Lazarus and the Rich Man (unique to Luke [16:19–31]). The mandate in this parable must be combined with Paul's teaching about the diversity of gifts from the Holy Spirit. Thus, it is not necessary for everybody to serve every unfortunate person. We should concentrate on those people whom we know and encounter and serve them according to the gifts we have. All of us will encounter people on the streets who are genuinely in need of food or transportation, and we will want to help them. Some of us will have funds to help with various good works—for example, Catholic charities to help the poor, foundations to help children go to Catholic schools, or support for our parishes or other charities. Some of us actually will have gifts to serve in these mission areas; so those with a gift for teaching may want to dedicate themselves to this profession or volunteer time to teach catechism or religious education.

Those with the capacity to serve in corporal works of mercy may want to do so professionally or as a volunteer, for the Red Cross, Meals on Wheels, a healthcare institution, a homeless shelter, or a soup kitchen. Some who have the gift of evangelization may want to do outreach at parishes, high schools, or university campus ministries. Those with a gift for administration may want to volunteer time to the parish council, finance council, or diocesan council. Those with a background in education or ethics may want to join a school board or an ethics board; and those with a capacity for tutoring may want to help with boys or girls clubs, for example. When we incorporate this kind of service into our lives (without of course undermining the welfare of our families and the work responsibilities necessary to support them), we are participating in the mission of serving Christ's little ones who have the same dignity as Himself. Yet He warns us that if we do not have a heart to serve the needy we are capable of serving, we are not His followers, but rather the followers of "another master"—the one who has no heart.

Matthew identifies Satan's minions—called "demons" throughout the Gospels—with angelic beings. As noted above, this means that Satan must also be an angelic being since he cannot be less than the beings he leads and unites. As noted above, Jesus (and Matthew) would likely have been aware of Jewish apocalyptic traditions that associated demons with fallen angels. They would have also been aware of apocalyptic interpretations of Genesis 6:1–6, where the "sons of God" were identified with fallen angels. The idea of Satan and other demons as fallen angels and adversaries of God was quite well developed between 300 B.C. and Jesus' time in Jewish apocalyptic literature (see, for example, 1 Enoch 6—9, particularly Chapter 7). Evidently, Jesus affirmed this view, developed it, and perpetuated it.

The Parable of the Sheep and Goats is the only indication from the Gospels that Satan is to receive final judgment, banishment, and punishment in a separated domain at the end of time ("Then he will say to those at his left hand, 'Depart from me, you cursed, into the eternal fire prepared for the devil and his angels'" [Mt 25:41]). The Book of Revelation speaks about this final judgment, binding, and punishment of Satan in apocalyptic imagery:

> Then I saw an angel coming down from heaven, holding in his hand the key of the bottomless pit and a great chain. And he seized the dragon, that ancient serpent, who is the Devil and Satan, and bound him for a thousand years, and threw him into the pit, and shut it and sealed it over him, that he should deceive the nations no more, till the thousand years were ended.... When the thousand years are ended, Satan will be loosed from his prison and will come out to deceive the nations which are at the four corners of the earth, that is, Gog and Magog, to gather them for battle; their number is like the sand of the sea. And they marched up over the broad earth and surrounded the camp of the saints and the beloved city; but fire came down from heaven and consumed them, and the devil who had deceived them was thrown into the lake of fire and brimstone where the beast and the false prophet were, and they will be tormented day and night for ever and ever. (20:1–3, 7–10)

As implied above in the Parable of the Sower and the Parable of the Weeds, Satan and his minions will continue their destructive course of action—temptation, deception, and despair—until the end of time, because God intends to protect human freedom; and so He will not, in all cases, prevent us from being tempted or willingly influenced by Satan and his angels. Nevertheless, Jesus has won complete victory over Satan, and so he will never gain a dominant place in the world again. His attempt at dominion will continue to be frustrated by the Holy Spirit, the saints, and the Church ("And I tell you, you are Peter, and on this rock I will build my Church, and the gates of Hades shall not prevail against it" [Mt 16:18]). Then after years of conflict, there will be a final judgment of the world, at which point Satan and all his angels will be cast into the fiery domain prepared for them—and they will never be released throughout eternity.

We may now proceed to the fourth part of Jesus' plan—the initiation of the Church that will have the power to cast out Satan in the name of Jesus, to know and teach the truth of Jesus through inspiration of the Holy Spirit, and to bestow the protection of Jesus on the faithful.

V. The Church and the Ongoing Victory over Satan

Jesus' victorious conflict with Satan and his angels guarantees that Satan will not be able to move into a position of domination again. It will also lead ultimately to Satan's and his angels' final judgment, punishment, and banishment to a domain completely separated from Jesus and His followers. Yet Jesus was well aware that this final judgment and banishment of Satan would not come immediately (see the eschatological discourses: Mt 24; Mk 13; Lk 21); so He took steps to prepare His disciples for continued conflict with Satan and his angels throughout the course of history until the final age. He did this in two major substeps:

1. He gave power and authority to both His apostles and other disciples to cast out demons and to be protected from oppression by them.
2. He initiates the Church under Peter, to whom He gives the inspiration and power of the Holy Spirit to maintain His truth and the unity of His people, guaranteeing that the gates of Hades would not prevail against it.

Let us consider each of these substeps in Jesus' plan.

First, the Gospel of Luke tells us that Jesus prepared His apostles not only for missionary journeys, but also for Church-founding and Church-building activities. "And he called the Twelve together and gave them power and authority over all demons and to cure diseases, and he sent them out to preach the kingdom of God and to heal" (Lk 9:1–2). Luke follows Mark 6:7–13, indicating that Jesus gave His apostles authority over unclean spirits, to heal the sick, and to preach. Apparently, the apostles were successful in all three missionary activities, meaning that they shared effectively in Jesus' own ministry. Using this as a foundation, Luke indicates that Jesus went beyond his immediate circle of apostles to commission an additional seventy-two disciples with the same mission to expel demons, heal,

and preach. After sending them on mission with scarce resources—
to make them reliant upon divine providence—the seventy-two
returned amazed at how the demons were subject to them:

> The seventy returned with joy, saying, "Lord, even the demons are
> subject to us in your name!" And he said to them, "I saw Satan fall like
> lightning from heaven. Behold, I have given you authority to tread
> upon serpents and scorpions, and over all the power of the enemy;
> and nothing shall hurt you. Nevertheless do not rejoice in this, that
> the spirits are subject to you; but rejoice that your names are written
> in heaven." (Lk 10:17–20)

Luke viewed these missionary journeys as Jesus' preparation for the
apostles' ongoing ministry within the Church after His Resurrection
and exaltation.[31] Graham Twelftree sees this passage as a sanction and
encouragement for the apostolic Church to continue Jesus' ministry
of exorcism.[32]

As the passage indicates, the apostles cast out demons in the name
of Jesus; however, Jesus did not invoke God or His Father to cast
out demons, because He did so by His own authority and power
(see Section III above). The use of the name of Jesus in faith carries
His presence, and along with His presence, his power and authority.
Apparently the disciples enjoyed remarkable success in their ministry
of exorcism and report this to Jesus with great joy.

Nevertheless, Jesus admonishes them not to take so much joy in
having power over demons—for spiritual power is not the objective
of their ministry or lives. Rather, it is to be in relationship with Jesus,
be faithful to His word, and teach others to do likewise. The power
of exorcism is quite secondary to relationship, holiness, fidelity, and
evangelization. This is why He tells them to rejoice more that their
names are written in Heaven.

Though exorcism was important in continuing Jesus' struggle against
Satan, Jesus' de-emphasis of it seems to have caused the early Church
to relegate it to a second tier of ministries, which may be inferred
from the fact that it was dropped from all the major post-Resurrection

---

[31] See ibid, p. 170.
[32] See Graham Twelftree, *Christ Triumphant: Exorcism Then and Now* (Hodder & Stoughton, 1985), pp. 99–100.

commissionings—Matthew 28:18–20; Mark 16:14–16; Luke 24:46–49; John 20:21–23; 21:15–19; and Acts 1:8.[33]

The second substep in Jesus' plan to give His disciples ongoing power over demons is blended into His initiation of the Church to continue all of His ministries through the power of the Holy Spirit and the leadership of Peter and his successors. This will be discussed in considerable detail in Volume II, Chapter 1, of this Trilogy. Therefore, we need only summarize a few of the points relevant to this topic explained there. Let us begin with the commissioning logion in Matthew 16:17–19:

> Blessed are you, Simon Bar-Jona! For flesh and blood has not revealed this to you, but my Father who is in heaven. And I tell you, you are Peter [*Petros*], and on this rock [*petra*] I will build my Church, and the gates of Hades [the netherworld] shall not prevail against it. I will give you the keys of the kingdom of heaven, and whatever you bind on earth shall be bound in heaven, and whatever you loose on earth shall be loosed in heaven.

Let us now consider some summary points indicating the logion's origin in Jesus, the supreme power given to Peter and his successors, and Jesus' intention to start an office of supreme juridical and teaching authority for Peter and his successors.

The commissioning of Peter as head of the Church is not unique to the well-known commissioning in Matthew 16:18. There are four other indications of it in the New Testament: (1) There is a primitive Aramaic tradition (from which Matthew drew) that was known and used by Saint Paul in Galatians 1 and 2 (see Volume II, Chapter 1, Section IV). (2) There is a special commissioning of Peter as the chief shepherd in the Gospel of John (21:15–19). (3) The order of the Resurrection appearances in 1 Corinthians 15:5–6, which according to Reginald Fuller parallels the order of leadership in the new eschatological community,[34] sets Peter in first place, while using the Aramaic name he received from Jesus at his commissioning (*Cephas* [rock]).

---

[33] See Page, *Powers of Evil*, pp. 170–71.

[34] Reginald Fuller, *The Formation of the Resurrection Narratives* (Minneapolis, MN: Fortress Press, 1980), pp. 36–60.

(4) Though Luke does not have a special commissioning of Peter in his Gospel, he implies in the first part of Acts (1–10) that Peter is the head of the Church and shows him to be the universal spokesman of the Church, placing both James (head of the Church in Jerusalem) and Paul (the primary missionary to the Gentiles) in a subordinate place at the Council of Jerusalem (Acts 15:7–10).

There is considerable evidence for the abovementioned primitive Aramaic tradition underlying Jesus' commission to Peter in Matthew 16:17–19, Galatians 1, and John 1:42 that very probably originates with Jesus Himself (see Volume II, Chapter 1, Section IV).

Jesus' commissioning of Peter is not limited to him alone, but extends to his successors. Matthew's use of "keys of the kingdom" (16:19) very probably refers to an *office* similar to that of prime minister of Israel. This is indicated by the last line of the oracle of Isaiah against Shebna giving the authority of prime minister to Eliakim in his place (Is 22:18–22). This office entitles its holder to be the ultimate juridical authority of the nation in God's absence: "I will thrust [Shebna] from your *office*, and you will be cast down from your *station*.... And I will place on [Eliakim's] shoulder the key of the house of David; he shall open, and none shall shut; and he shall shut, and none shall open" (Is 22:19, 22; italics added).

This is quite similar to Jesus' phrasing of Peter's commission: "I will give you the keys of the kingdom of heaven, and whatever you bind on earth shall be bound in heaven, and whatever you loose on earth shall be loosed in heaven" (Mt 16:19). The use of "office" and "station" in Isaiah and the parallelism between Isaiah's oracle and Jesus' commissioning is so striking that it is difficult to believe that Isaiah's oracle was not at least implicitly in the mind of Jesus when he used his words of appointment to Peter. If it was, then the phrase "keys of the kingdom" along with its supreme juridical power to bind and loose very probably refer to an *office*, the highest juridical office in the Church. If this is the case, and Jesus was aware that Peter would die before the end of the Church (indicated by the eschatological discourses in all three Synoptic Gospels [see Volume II, Chapter 1, Section II]), then Jesus created an office of highest juridical power to be conferred not only upon Peter, but also upon his successors.

Within Peter's commissioning in Matthew 16:18, Jesus indicates that the gates of Hades will not prevail against the Church He intends to build on the foundation rock of Peter. The terms "gates" and "Hades" had specific meanings to a first-century Jewish audience. Albert Barnes has a particularly lucid synthesis of the layered meanings within this text:

> And the gates of hell ... —Ancient cities were surrounded by walls. In the gates by which they were entered were the principal places for holding court, transacting business, and deliberating on public matters.... The word "gates," therefore, is used for counsels, designs, machinations, evil purposes....
>
> "Hell" means, here, the place of departed spirits, particularly evil spirits; and the meaning of the passage is, that all the plots, stratagems, and machinations of the enemies of the church would not be able to overcome it a promise that has been remarkably fulfilled.[35]

Apparently, Jesus made an unconditional promise to Peter in His commissioning—namely, that he and his successors would be protected from all of the machinations and plottings of evil spirits and deceased souls. This promise extends not only to protection from evil spirits oppressing and possessing human beings, but also to protection against ultimate victory by Satan through his deceits, temptations, and destructive power.

The apostolic Church understood that though Jesus guaranteed protection against ultimate victory by Satan, she still had the responsibility of doing everything within her power, through the power of the Holy Spirit, to take all possible steps to remain holy, to understand the truth of Jesus, to evangelize all people, and to bring instruction, sacramental grace, and spiritual depth to them. Jesus had warned them that this would not be easy, and that Satan (and his demons) would do everything in their power to stop them.

The challenge to the apostles begins before Jesus' Passion, death, and Resurrection. Satan deceives Peter into believing that Jesus would not have to suffer and die (in complete self-sacrificial love) to bring the kingdom of love to the world. After Jesus solemnly proclaims that He will have to suffer and die, Peter stridently disagrees with Him,

---

[35] "Albert Barnes' Notes on the Whole Bible", 1870 commentary on Matthew 16:18, Study Light.org, accessed April 8, 2020, https://www.studylight.org/commentaries/bnb/matthew -16.html.

saying, "God forbid, Lord! This shall never happen to you" (Mt 16:22). Jesus rebukes him by saying, "Get behind me, Satan! You are a hindrance to me; for you are not on the side of God, but of men" (Mt 16:23). Jesus here is not saying that Peter is under the influence of Satan—after all, in the previous passage, He has just acknowledged that Peter was the recipient of divine inspiration in his confession of Jesus' messiahship. So what is He saying? Very probably, He means that Peter has been deceived by Satan and, as such, is presenting a temptation and obstacle to Jesus himself. Hence He is telling Peter that his challenge to Jesus' proclamation about the necessity of complete self-sacrifice comes from Satan himself—and it is meant not only to deceive Peter, but also to hinder Jesus in following the more difficult path of obediential self-sacrificial love.

Yet Satan's attacks would not stop there—he will tempt Judas to betray Jesus out of greed and other motives (Lk 22:3; Jn 13:2, 27); then tempt Peter to deny Jesus three times, as foretold by Jesus (Mt 26:34; Mk 14:30; Lk 22:34; Jn 13:38); and then tempt all the apostles to flee from Jesus after He has been betrayed (Mt 26:56; Mk 14:50; cf. Jn 16:32). We will discuss the temptation of Judas within the context of John's Gospel below. For the moment, we will examine only Luke's text of Jesus' declaration to Peter: "Simon, Simon, behold, Satan demanded to have you, that he might sift you like wheat, but I have prayed for you that your faith may not fail; and when you have turned again, strengthen your brethren" (Lk 22:31–32). Here, Jesus tells Peter that Satan has asked for permission of his Father to sift him—that is, to put him to a severe test. Jesus makes clear that Satan cannot do anything he wants to Peter; he can only present him with challenges that are within the scope of His Father's will. Jesus prays that Peter's severe trial will not end in failure—and implies that it won't because he predicts that Peter will return to strengthen his brothers.

What was Peter's severe trial? The enormous pressure that was put on him after Jesus was taken by the chief priests to protect himself by denying his association with Jesus. Peter was to fail not only once, but three times. Yet this was not to end in failure as Jesus predicted, but rather in Peter's restoration by the risen Jesus, leading to his becoming head of the apostles and chief shepherd of the Church. One might ask why Jesus' Father allowed Satan to put Peter to this severe trial. The answer seems to be that the Father knew that Jesus' prayer and Peter's faith would be sufficient to keep him from a complete failure of faith. This would allow the risen Jesus to restore him, which would in turn allow him to strengthen the other apostles with the gift of Jesus' unconditional forgiving love: "So that the genuineness of [their] faith, more precious than gold which though perishable is tested by fire, may redound to praise and glory and honor at the revelation of Jesus Christ" (1 Pet 1:7). Though Satan seeks the destruction of Peter, the Father planned to use this severe test, which He knew would not succeed in light of His Son's prayer and Peter's faith. He did this to strengthen Peter's faith and reliance on His Son to pave the way for an even greater defeat of Satan. This kind of test and trial would mark the lives of Peter, the other apostles, and their successors throughout the rest of Church history. These trials, in turn, would lead to the same strengthening of faith, like gold tested in fire, for all subsequent generations until the end of the world, when Satan's destruction would be complete.

In sum, the fourth step in Jesus' plan was to give His apostles the capacity to carry on His ministry of defeating Satan and his demons until the end of time. He did this in two major ways:

1. By giving the apostles the power to exorcise demons in His name
2. By establishing a Church on the foundation rock of Peter, against which the gates of Hell would not prevail

This Church and her leaders would have the Holy Spirit to discern the truth about Jesus' teaching and to resolve all juridical disputes, which could be definitively decided through the supreme power of binding and loosing that was given to Peter and his successors.

Nevertheless, this Church and her leaders would be subject to severe trials from Satan and his demons, but these trials would never end in ultimate failure and catastrophe; they would always lead to the strengthening of faith, increased reliance upon the mercy of Christ, and a heightened resolve to imitate Jesus in holiness and love. And so the Pauline author of the Letter to the Ephesians, filled with confidence in the hope and love of Jesus and the power of the Holy Spirit, warns all subsequent generations of the Church and her leaders to be vigilant in resisting Satan and his minions:

For we are not contending against flesh and blood, but against the principalities, against the powers, against the world rulers of this present darkness, against the spiritual hosts of wickedness in the heavenly places. Therefore take the whole armor of God, that you may be able to withstand in the evil day, and having done all, to stand. Stand therefore, having fastened the belt of truth around your waist, and having put on the breastplate of righteousness, and having shod your feet with the equipment of the gospel of peace; besides all these, taking the shield of faith, with which you can quench all the flaming darts of the Evil One. And take the helmet of salvation, and the sword of the Spirit, which is the word of God. Pray at all times in the Spirit, with all prayer and supplication. To that end keep alert with all perseverance. (6:12–18)

VI. Jesus' Passion and Death: The Ultimate Defeat of Satan

Jesus' fifth and final step in His plan to defeat Satan would be definitive—an act of total self-sacrificial love concretely actualized in history through His Passion and death; an unrestricted act of love that would outshine the whole of finite human evil; an act of love to be won at the cost of His death that would be completely counteracted by His Resurrection in divine glory. Satan's narcissistic, self-idolatrous, and domineering mindset would not allow him to see the unrestricted redemptive love in Jesus' plan; his darkened heart and limited awareness deceived him (ironically) into believing that he would be ultimately victorious in encouraging Judas' betrayal, Peter's denials, the authority's rejection, the apostles' abandonment, and Jesus' death. As Jesus approaches Jerusalem, Satan quickens his plan to effect a complete failure and destruction of Jesus, the apostles, and the Church that Jesus intends to initiate through them. The Gospel of John, perhaps more than the Synoptic Gospels, appreciates the depth of Satan's evil and plotting while recognizing Jesus' perspective of the ultimate glory and victory that would be His through the unrestricted love of complete self-sacrifice: "And I, when I am lifted up from the earth, will draw all men to myself" (12:32).

John indicates that Satan's defiant plan begins by tempting the religious authorities to murder Jesus. When Jesus confronts them about the malice in their hearts, He tells them that they are following the designs of their father, and then shows why their father is neither Abraham nor God because of their murderous plot (8:39–43), which leads to His final revelation that their father is Satan (8:44). He then explains that their murderous plot is consistent with their father's (Satan's) nature: "He was a murderer from the beginning", an allusion to Genesis 3:1–24, in which the serpent, whom Jesus interprets as Satan, brings death into the world through his lies. Jesus' confrontation with the Pharisees has no effect on them except to heighten their desire to murder him. Yet Jesus is aware that Satan's murderous plans will only lead to His ultimate victory through complete self-sacrificial love: "When you have lifted up the Son of man, then you will know that I am he, and that I do nothing on my own authority but speak thus as the Father taught me" (8:28).

Satan, completely unaware of Jesus' plan to set his plot on its head through an unrestricted act of love, picks up the pace when Jesus decides to go to Jerusalem for the feast of the Passover. It seems to him like an unbelievably felicitous twist of fate, and he has the perfect human protagonist in mind, an apostle of Jesus that he has been cultivating for years: Judas Iscariot. Jesus was aware of Judas' vulnerability and his later betrayal early in His Galilean ministry: "'Did I not choose you, the Twelve, and one of you is a devil?' He spoke of Judas the son of Simon Iscariot, for he, one of the Twelve, was to betray him" (Jn 6:70–71).

Judas plays a central role at the supper portrayed in John 13 (which closely resembles Luke's observation about Judas at the same Last Supper: "Satan entered into Judas called Iscariot, who was of the number of the Twelve" [Lk 22:3]). John states in 13:2 that "during supper ... the devil had already put it into the heart of Judas Iscariot, Simon's son, to betray him." Later during the supper he again notes:

> "[My betrayer] is he to whom I shall give this morsel when I have dipped it." So when he had dipped the morsel, he gave it to Judas, the son of Simon Iscariot. Then after the morsel, Satan entered into him. Jesus said to him, "What you are going to do, do quickly" (13:26–27).

This seeming contradiction between Satan entering Judas before the supper and then during the supper is probably attributable to the textual ambiguities in John 13:2. Scholars have been unable to adduce the most primitive manuscript tradition, and in light of this, Sydney Page proposes the following resolution:

> There is no reason why verse 2 cannot refer to Satan's role in the initial planning of the betrayal, and verse 27, to the final decision to execute the plan. The repetition simply emphasizes the satanic character of the betrayal, and the enormity of Judas's sin makes the focus on Satan's involvement entirely appropriate.[36]

John's portrayal of Satan's involvement in Jesus' Passion is clearly ironic: for on the one hand, he states that Satan (the prince of this world[37]) is catalyzing his human instruments—Judas, the religious authorities, and even the Roman occupiers—to bring Jesus to His humiliating public execution (12:31; 14:30; 16:11); yet on the other hand, he indicates that the Passion to which Satan is leading Jesus will not be the demise of Jesus, but the final defeat and judgment of Satan himself (12:31; 16:11). Jesus' plan is to give His whole self over to His enemies in unconditional self-sacrificial love, which He will offer to the Father as the perfect means to wipe out the finite sins and indiscretions of humanity. Anyone who wishes to be a recipient of this healing and forgiving love needs only to ask the Father in the name of Jesus. Hence, Jesus' Passion and death (His unconditional self-sacrificial love offered to the Father on behalf of humanity) is at once that by which Satan will be condemned (12:31; 16:11) and the power by which any individual who wants to avail himself of it can be forgiven and healed (3:16–17; 15:13).

Obviously, Satan is not aware of these self-destructive consequences of Jesus' Passion; otherwise, he would have avoided them. The problem is, he is completely blind to the intentions, actions, and outcomes of love, and so he cannot possibly see the true outcome of Jesus' self-sacrificial act until it has already come to pass, at which

---

[36] Page, *Powers of Evil*, p. 128.

[37] For John, Satan is prince of this world only in the sense that God allows him to be a prince for those who give themselves over to his influence and dominion. Inasmuch as some people's sinful actions bring them under Satan's domain, they are part of the world over which he is prince. The term "world" here does not mean the whole world of mankind, but only the world of those who are corrupted to the point of bringing themselves under Satan's domain. Jesus will definitively break this dominion with His unconditional self-sacrificial loving act: His Passion and death.

point all human beings have a chance to extricate themselves from their sinful actions, and he (Satan) is already condemned. Every step that Satan takes to advance what he considers to be the demise of Jesus is ironically leading to his own demise and the redemption of every human being who turns to Jesus in sincere repentance—his entrance into Judas, his influence over the religious authorities, his influence over the Roman occupiers, and even his temptation of Peter to deny Jesus.

The plan of unconditional redemptive love—which remains hidden to Satan, but is Jesus' glory—is set into motion by Satan's malicious intentions, but redeemed by the Father's and Jesus' unconditionally loving intentions. Satan tempts Peter to resist Jesus' way of the Cross—not because he sees Jesus' self-sacrificial love as redemptive, but because he wants Jesus to disobey what Jesus considers to be His Father's will. Satan has no idea *why* Jesus believes this to be His Father's will—that is, to bring an unrestricted act of redemptive love into the world through complete self-sacrifice; he only knows that Jesus believes *that* the way of the Cross is His Father's will. So, he aims at the evil he knows—to tempt Jesus (through Peter) to commit an act of disobedience. Evidently, his plan gives rise to catastrophic defeat—universal salvation for humanity, and his own condemnation.

The question now arises, if Satan is really condemned by his antipathy to Jesus' unrestricted, unconditional act of redemptive love (which he has decidedly and freely rejected), then why does he still have power to hinder and harm human beings and the Church after Jesus' Passion, death, and Resurrection? How can he be defeated if he is still present and active to this very day? We must suppose that prior to His Passion and Crucifixion, Jesus was aware that Satan would continue to be active in the world after His Passion and Resurrection—otherwise, the eschatological discourses in the three Synoptic Gospels would not make any sense, and neither, for that matter, would the priestly prayer of Jesus in the Gospel of John: "I do not pray that you should take them out of the world, but that you should keep them from the evil one" (17:15). Why would Jesus ask the Father to protect His disciples from the Evil One after His death and Resurrection if Satan was going to be completely defeated?

So, what was Jesus' understanding of the defeat of Satan that would occur when His Passion—His unrestricted act of self-sacrificial redemptive love—was complete? He seems to have had three effects in mind. Firstly, Satan would never be able to gain mastery as prince of this world over mankind again—Jesus' unrestricted act of love, the Holy Spirit, and the Church would prevent this from happening through the Father's providential will. Secondly, Satan would never be able to bring a person to ultimate demise even by seducing him into the most horrible crime—there would always be a chance for a person to turn back to God (even at the last minute) through Jesus' unrestricted redemption. This means that the last word would always be the Father's and Jesus'—not Satan's. Thirdly, Satan's categorical rejection of Jesus' unconditional redemptive love is his judgment and condemnation. His total malice—antithetical to and unmitigated by Jesus' redemptive love—is completely inconsistent with the heavenly Kingdom, the essence of which is the fullness of God's love, the fullness of joy. This means that Satan and his minions will have to be banished to a state or place that is completely separate from the Kingdom of Heaven—a state or place where he and his minions cannot have any further effect upon those who have freely chosen to live in God's truth and love.

This condemnation will not take effect immediately, because as has been said above, humanity must and will remain free until the end of the world—otherwise, human actions would not be self-defining, but only the result of a divine program. This means that human beings must be capable of initiating evil and unloving actions on their own, and capable of being tempted by Satan and his demons to do so. The Lord gives us grace to resist these temptations and self-initiated aberrant desires, and even forgives us for yielding to them in our weakness and egocentricity if we are sincerely repentant. However, He cannot prevent us from desiring, thinking about, being tempted by, or yielding to them—for if He did, we would no longer be free.

Therefore, He allows Satan and his minions to have limited, but nonetheless significant, influence in the world until the end of time. At that point, Satan and his minions will be banished to a domain completely separate from that of God, Jesus, and the blessed where they can act according to their chosen hearts' desire of tormenting and dominating one another throughout eternity.

It seems that John's interpretation of the condemnation and ultimate banishment of Satan has influenced the author of the Book of Revelation (particularly in Chapter 12). According to Yarbro Collins,

Chapter 12 has two distinct pre-Christian Jewish apocalyptic sources that the New Testament biblical author (influenced by John's Gospel) has edited and adapted to accommodate Jesus as the Messiah: (1) the narrative of a woman who gives birth to the Messiah and (2) the narrative of a combat in Heaven.[38] The author of Revelation identifies the woman in the myth first with Mary, the Mother of Jesus (in verses 1–6), and then after the combat in Heaven with Mary, Mother of the Church (verses 14–17). Her role as Mother of the Church is explicitized in verse 17: "Then the dragon was angry with the woman, and went off to make war on the rest of her offspring, on those who keep the commandments of God and bear testimony to Jesus."

How might we interpret this text that seems to be influenced by John's Gospel? The author of Revelation views Mary as having two roles: Mother of the Messiah and Mother of the offspring of the Messiah—the Church and her members. The opponent of the woman is clearly Satan. The author first identifies the dragon with the serpent in the Book of Genesis (3:1, 13–14), and then with Satan himself (Rev 12:9). He also calls Satan "the deceiver of the whole world" (12:9) and "the accuser" (12:10). Satan, at first, attempts to devour the child after His birth (12:4), but is unable to do so because "the child was caught up to God and to his throne" (12:5). We might infer from this that likewise Jesus' victory over Satan is symbolized by His being snatched up to Heaven to take His throne. After Jesus' Passion, death, Resurrection, and exultation in Heaven, the author of Revelation portrays Jesus' victory over Satan as having definitive eschatological significance. Saint Michael, who is part of the angelic hierarchy, is given power to banish Satan from the heavenly angelic domain to the earth (12:7–12). The author portrays Satan as being virtually imprisoned on the earth, although he has power to tempt and harass human beings, particularly the Church (the woman's other offspring), for a specific time—"a time, and times, and half a time" (12:14). The author then introduces a hymn referring to Job 1:9–11, where Satan is portrayed as an accuser of human beings before God, indicating that he has been defeated through "the blood of the lamb"—Jesus' Passion and death.

---

[38] Adela Yarbro Collins, "The Apocalypse", in *The New Jerome Biblical Commentary* (Englewood Cliffs, N.J.: Prentice-Hall, 1990), p. 1008.

The hymn is a song of liberation from bondage to Satan, evil, and sin—a liberation that will enable human beings to become part of the heavenly Kingdom:

> And I heard a loud voice in heaven, saying, "Now the salvation and the power and the kingdom of our God and the authority of his Christ have come, for the accuser of our brethren has been thrown down, who accuses them day and night before our God. And they have conquered him by the blood of the Lamb and by the word of their testimony, for they loved not their lives even unto death. Rejoice then, O heaven and you that dwell therein!" (12:10–12)

Satan's defeat is definitive—he is cast out from Heaven and can never return there again, because of his rejection and attempted destruction of the Son's redemptive love. He is banished to earth for a short time, where he is allowed to harass and persecute the Church. The author portrays this as Satan (the serpent) spewing water out of its mouth to try to destroy the Church (the woman and her off-spring) by a flood (12:15). However, God's grace protects the Church through His providence on earth, portrayed by the earth swallowing up the waters of the serpent (12:15). The Book of Revelation goes on to describe some of the harassments the Church will have to endure before the final banishment of Satan. Throughout Chapters 13—22, the author presents apocalyptic portrayals of Jesus' eschatological discourses showing times of great tumult before the end of the world. The Church's battle with Satan on earth—portrayed as superimposed within a heavenly battle—is ultimately victorious (though not easy). At the end of time, the faithful—redeemed by the blood of the Lamb and written in his Book of Life—are brought into His Kingdom, while Satan, his demons, and those people who have sided with him are banished to his dominion of emptiness and darkness, portrayed as a lake of fire (20:11–15). This is the final banishment of Satan, whose influence will come to an eternal end.

VII. Conclusion

Jesus' fivefold plan wrests control of the world and human history from Satan, and causes his ultimate defeat, which will lead to his final banishment with his minions in Hell (a domain completely separated from God and the blessed) at the end of time. Though Jesus (and the Church) will be ultimately victorious over him, the Lord allows him to remain active in the world in accordance with the requirements of human freedom. This means that we and the Church herself will have to struggle against Satan; but if we avail ourselves of the supernatural gifts with which Jesus has left us—the Holy Spirit, the Church, and the seven sacraments—and integrate them into our spiritual and moral conversion through lives of virtue and prayer, we will be saved by the Lord and brought with the saints into eternal bliss.

Before discussing these supernatural gifts and spiritual and moral conversion (in Volume II of this Trilogy), we must first examine the tactics used by Satan, particularly temptation, deceit, and despair (Chapter 4), as well as the eight deadly sins (Chapters 5 and 6). Even before we can discuss these tactics, we must discuss the reality of Satan's (and his minions') presence in the world (Chapter 3). Unfortunately, the reality of Satan, which seemed obvious to virtually every culture and generation prior to the twentieth century, has been reduced to a myth, a cartoon character, or a relic of "the dark ages". This obliges us to delve into Satan's manifest evil and darkness in contemporary validated cases of possession—the topic of our next chapter.

Chapter Three

The Devil Is Real

Introduction

I am sure that many members of the psychological and psychiatric profession—and many of my academic colleagues—believe that personified evil is a medieval superstition or the stuff of "folk spook stories" that have no place in contemporary scientific models. I don't think this viewpoint has been justified by any logical, empirical, or scientific method. In fact, I think there is considerable empirical evidence for the preternatural, not simply the existence of spirits of the deceased and poltergeists, but also angelic spirits—both benevolent and malevolent.

I. Evidence of the Preternatural, Supernatural, and Angelic Spirits

I present this evidence, not to scare people or engage in a counter-academic polemic, but rather to inform people about what they are *really* up against in what I have called "the cosmic struggle between good and evil". In Volume II, Chapter 2, of the Quartet, I summarized the thought of Carl Jung on the archetypes, and the archetypal hero myth, as well as the thought of contemporary "myth writers", such as J. R. R. Tolkien (*Lord of the Rings*), George Lucas (*Star Wars*), and J. K. Rowling (*Harry Potter*), on the cosmic struggle between good and evil. I suggested there that the reason why these contemporary myths enjoy such great popularity (greatest popularity next to the Bible and a few perennial classics in Western literature and filmmaking) is that they resonate with the archetypal myth of the cosmic struggle between good and evil in our unconscious psyche. I would further add at this juncture that these are not mere fantasies, but represent, in mythic language, a reality in the real spiritual world around us, a struggle between the good forces of divine providence and demonic forces that have rebelled against it—a struggle in which we are immersed. There is considerable evidence for the presence of these good and demonic forces that I will endeavor to present (quite briefly) throughout this chapter. The way we interact with this cosmic struggle can have a significant effect on our lives in this world and our eternal destiny.

My objective is not to convince a completely close-minded skeptic about the reality of spiritual evil, because no amount of evidence—such as levitation, objects flying through a room, use of unknown languages, and awareness of people's thoughts and discreet communication—will ever convince a "true skeptic", for he can always make recourse to implausible explanations such as mass hypnosis or mass hysteria among multiple psychologically balanced, even-tempered, rational witnesses. He can also claim fraud or conspiracy on the part of those witnesses, even when the proceedings of most exorcisms are kept secret and later leaked.

The same kinds of implausible explanations can be used to dismiss the tens of thousands of reports of spirits, hauntings, and poltergeists whose witnesses were previously skeptical about the preternatural. The evidence for the existence of such spirits is overwhelming in every country and culture throughout the world—particularly in the late twentieth and early twenty-first centuries.

The existence of the spirits of deceased human beings has been medically and scientifically studied in the veridical data of near-death experiences (which I have described in detail in Volume II, Chapter 5, of the Quartet). Principal among these are the studies of Dr. Samuel Parnia at Southampton University,[1] Dr. Pim van Lommel,[2] Dr. Kenneth Ring's study of near-death experiences (NDEs) of the

---

[1] See Samuel Parnia et al., "AWARE—AWAreness during REsuscitation—A Prospective Study", *Resuscitation*, October 6, 2014, pp. 1799–1805, http://www.resuscitationjournal.com /article/S0300-9572(14)00739-4/abstract.

[2] See Pim van Lommel et al., "Near-Death Experience in Survivors of Cardiac Arrest: A Prospective Study in the Netherlands", *The Lancet* 358, no. 9298 (2001): 2039–45.

blind,[3] and Dr. Janice Holden's analysis of veridical evidence in NDEs from thirty-nine independent studies.[4] These studies are amplified by many other researchers (e.g., Emily Kelly[5] and Bruce Greyson[6]) at the Division of Perceptual Studies in the Department of Psychiatry and Neurobehavioral Sciences at the University of Virginia School of Medicine.[7] These studies validate independently verified unique veridical data accurately reported by patients at the time of clinical death, as well as evidence that 80 percent of blind people have accurate visual perception at the time of clinical death. Thorough analysis of these reports by neuroscientists such as Mario Beauregard,[8] psychiatric neurobehavioral scientists such as Bruce Greyson,[9] and physicians such as Eben Alexander[10] and Pim van Lommel[11] indicates that physicalist explanations of these reports are inadequate. Hence, these data show the strong likelihood of the survival of human

[3] See Kenneth Ring, Sharon Cooper, and Charles Tart, *Mindsight: Near-Death and Out-of-Body Experiences in the Blind* (Palo Alto, Calif.: William James Center for Consciousness Studies at the Institute of Transpersonal Psychology, 1999). See also Kenneth Ring and Madelaine Lawrence, "Further Evidence for Veridical Perception during Near-Death Experiences", *Journal of Near-Death Studies* 11, no. 4 (Summer 1993): 223–29.

[4] See Janice Holden, *Handbook of Near Death Experiences: Thirty Years of Investigation* (Westport, Conn.: Praeger Press, 2009).

[5] See Emily Kelly, "Near-Death Experiences with Reports of Meeting Deceased People", *Death Studies* 25 (2001): 229–49, https://cpb-us-w2.wpmucdn.com/web.sas.upenn.edu/dist/b/160/files/2017/04/kel13_ndewithreports_of_meeting_deceased_people-wxfbls.pdf. See also E. W. Kelly, B. Greyson, and I. Stevenson, "Can Experiences Near Death Furnish Evidence of Life After Death?" *Omega: Journal of Death and Dying* 40 (2000): 39–45.

[6] See Bruce Greyson and C. P. Flynn, eds., *The Near-Death Experience: Problems, Prospects, Perspectives* (Springfield, Ill.: Charles C. Thomas, 1984). See also Bruce Greyson, "Seeing Dead People Not Known to Have Died: 'Peak in Darien' Experiences", *American Anthropological Association*, November 21, 2010, http://onlinelibrary.wiley.com/doi/10.1111/j.1548-1409.2010.01064.x/abstract.

[7] See the research area of near-death experiences on their website at https://med.virginia.edu/perceptual-studies/.

[8] See Mario Beauregard, *Brain Wars: The Scientific Battle over the Existence of the Mind and the Proof That Will Change the Way We Live* (New York: HarperOne, 2012).

[9] See the following, which Greyson coauthored: Edward F. Kelly et al., *Irreducible Mind: Toward a Psychology for the 21st Century* (New York: Rowman & Littlefield, 2007), which attempts to reconcile contemporary cognitive psychology and mainstream neuroscience with studies in parapsychology (e.g., near-death experiences and mystical states).

[10] See Eben Alexander, "My Experience in Coma", *Journal of Neurosurgery* 21, no. 2 (2012), http://www.ebenalexander.com/my-experience-in-coma/.

[11] Pim van Lommel, "Continuity of Consciousness", International Association for Near-Death Studies, last updated April 25, 2015, http://iands.org/research/nde-research/important-research-articles/43-dr-pim-van-lommel-md-continuity-of-consciousness.html.

consciousness after bodily death. Though many of these people move to a transphysical domain that is frequently described as "heavenly" (populated by other deceased persons and overseen by an intensely loving white light and/or Jesus), many remain in the physical world, where they might be able to make their existence known. When they do, they are frequently called "apparitions" or "ghosts" or "spirits".

Apparitions are another indication of the survival of human spirits after bodily death. These have been studied by various scientific groups, such as the Division of Perceptual Studies at the University of Virginia School of Medicine.[12] According to Ian Stevenson, these "apparitions" can be verified beyond simple visual apprehension of a spirit, which might be explained by hallucination or interpsychical suggestion. He gives three principle criteria for such verification:[13]

1. The same apparition was witnessed by multiple individuals who describe it similarly.
2. The witnesses were unaware of the death of that individual, because it occurred at a different place (e.g., a foreign country) and the witnesses had not yet been informed of the death.
3. The description of the person matched his state at the time that he died, not at the time that he was last seen by the witnesses (e.g., a deceased person had grown a beard overseas, which none of the witnesses had previously seen; yet, this is precisely how he appeared after his death).

After studying a large number of cases, Stevenson believes that only about two thousand cases qualify for this kind of validation over the course of a century. This does not mean that other witnessed reports of apparitions are false, but only that they did not qualify according to the three criteria required by Stevenson.

[12] For additional information, see their website: https://med.virginia.edu/perceptual-studies/.

[13] See Ian Stevenson, "The Contribution of Apparitions to the Evidence for Survival", *Journal of the American Society for Psychical Research* 76 (October 1982): 341–58. The article is available on the website of the Division of Perceptual Studies at https://med.virginia .edu/perceptual-studies/wp-content/uploads/sites/360/2017/09/The-Contributions-of -Apparitions-to-the-Evidence-for-Survival_-Ian-Stevenson-1982.pdf. The references given in this article are extensive and give detailed assessments of many of the cases examined by Stevenson. For additional contemporary studies, see Karlis Osis and Erlendur Haraldsson, *At the Hour of Death: A New Look at Evidence for Life After Death*, 3rd ed. (Norwalk, Conn.: Hastings House, 1997).

Additionally, there are literally thousands of anecdotal reports of hauntings and apparitions of both human and demonic spirits. Hundreds of these "paranormal phenomena" have been tested with varying degrees of scientific instrumentation, such as ambient temperature sensors, electromagnetic field sensors, and ultrasensitive motion detectors. The number of reports is so prolific that one cable channel has catalogued and videoed hundreds of hauntings by spirits of both human and demonic origin. Though the producers do not approach the subject in a scientific way, and the "experts" used to test the signs of paranormal phenomena are not research scientists, the hundreds of credible (and even previously skeptical) witnesses and the evidence of objects flying through a room, property being destroyed, and objects being moved from one place to another without known physical or human causation is hard to dismiss cavalierly. Additionally, dozens of books and websites have also been devoted to these phenomena cataloguing hundreds of accounts by witnesses, some of whom have great scientific and academic credibility.[14] Even if one discounts 95 percent of these accounts as the work of overactive imaginations, suggestive or gullible personalities, or religious fanaticism—which I do not believe to be the case—the remaining 5 percent reported by scientists, doctors, and other professionals should at least give one pause. As Peter Kreeft observed:

> Without our action or invitation, the dead often *do* appear to the living. There is enormous evidence of "ghosts" in all cultures.... We can distinguish three kinds of ghosts, I believe. First, the most familiar kind: the sad ones, the wispy ones. They seem to be working out some unfinished earthly business, or suffering some purgatorial purification until released from their earthly business.... Second, there are malicious and deceptive spirits—and since they *are* deceptive, they hardly ever *appear* malicious.... Third, there are the bright, happy spirits of dead friends and family, especially spouses, who appear unbidden, at God's will, not ours, with messages of hope and love.[15]

---

[14] For a Catholic explanation of these phenomena, see, for example, Tim Townsend, "Paranormal Activity: Do Catholics Believe in Ghosts?", *U.S. Catholic* 78, no. 10 (October 2013): 12 17, http://www.uscatholic.org/articles/201309/paranormal-activity-do-catholics-believe-ghosts-27887.

[15] Peter Kreeft, *Everything You Ever Wanted to Know about Heaven—But Never Dreamed of Asking* (San Francisco: Ignatius Press, 1990), pp. 33–34.

As noted above, my purpose here is not to convince the close-minded skeptic, because I believe, as G. K. Chesterton did, that such skeptics are, in reality, dogmatists who either disdain the common person or arbitrarily and aprioristically foreclose the possibility of the transphysical:

> The plain, popular course [of nonacademic "common folk"] is to trust the peasant's word about the ghost exactly as you trust the peasant's word about the landlord. Being a peasant he will probably have a great deal of healthy agnosticism about both. Still you could fill the British Museum with evidence uttered by the peasant, and given in favour of the ghost. If it comes to human testimony there is a choking cataract of human testimony in favour of the supernatural. If you reject it, you can only mean one of two things. You reject the peasant's story about the ghost either because the man is a peasant or because the story is a ghost story. That is, you either deny the main principle of democracy, or you affirm the main principle of materialism—the abstract impossibility of miracle. You have a perfect right to do so; but in that case you are the dogmatist. It is we Christians who accept all actual evidence—it is you rationalists who refuse actual evidence being constrained to do so by your creed.[16]

The individuals to whom I am writing are those who are open to the "enormous evidence" of ghosts, apparitions, and near-death experiences—that is, those who are not aprioristically and unjustifiably closed to the possibility of the transcendent, spiritual, preternatural, and/or supernatural.

Why write about such things? Can't a case against evil be made without making recourse to demons, ghosts, and malicious human spirits? Yes, a very convincing case can be made on the basis of natural law to do good and avoid evil, to pursue virtue and avoid vice, for the sake of oneself, others, culture, and the world.[17] Yet strong as the natural law and natural virtue case may be, it is only a small part of the story. We are living not only in the physical world, but also within a *spiritual* struggle between good and evil, which has effects

---

[16] G. K. Chesterton, *Orthodoxy* (1908; repr., Project Gutenberg, 2005), Chapter 9, https://archive.org/stream/orthodoxy16769gut/16769.txt. (The e-book is available for free.)

[17] See C. S. Lewis, *The Abolition of Man* (New York: HarperCollins, 1974).

on the human soul or spirit beyond the physical universe. It is this dimension of evil, the dimension with which Jesus was urgently concerned, that I intend to bring up in this book, precisely because it is frequently ignored or overlooked while having transcendent and eternal consequences. If we are open to the whole story (the transcendent and eternal story), then we will not be able to escape the spiritual dimension of good and evil—angels and demons as well as benevolent and malevolent human spirits—and the spiritual struggle between good and evil.

Why is the whole story so important? As every prudent person knows, "forewarned is forearmed." If there really is a calculating, dangerous, dark, destructive, and vicious evil force who intends us harm—even eternal harm—then we should want to know about it. If a terrorist is living in our neighborhood, wouldn't we want to swallow the bitter pill of knowing this fact so that we could do something about it, or would we rather pretend that he is not there until he goes away? The devil, like the terrorist, does not go away if we ignore him. Instead, he increases his influence, domain, destructiveness, and malevolent intent to seduce and goad "the unaware" into his eternal darkness. Putting our hands in front of our eyes and insisting, "You can't see me!" is a highly ineffective strategy for contending with a demon of remarkable intelligence and cruelty.

So, what kind of strategy is effective? One that recognizes the presence of spiritual evil, how it works, and most importantly, who and what prevents it from working. Though all the world's religions have rites and prayers to ward off and exorcise demons,[18] Christianity, particularly the Catholic Church, has the most extensive, nuanced, and deep articulation of the sources of evil, its workings, and the ways to protect ourselves from it.[19] It is not based on magical incantations and practices, which fall prey to the very evil it is trying to avoid; rather,

---

[18] See Stafford Betty, "The Growing Evidence for 'Demonic Possession': What Should Psychiatry's Response Be?", *Journal of Religion and Health* 44, no. 1 (Spring 2005): 13–30, http://www.ucs.mun.ca/~jporter/spiritualism/Stafford%20demonic%20possession.pdf.

[19] See Michael Freze, *The Rite of Exorcism: The Roman Ritual Rules, Procedures, Prayers of the Catholic Church* (self-pub., CreateSpace, 2016). For the prayers associated with the Rite of Exorcism, see "The Roman Ritual, Part 2", trans. Philip T. Weller, S.T.D., copyright 1964, EWTN.com, accessed April 9, 2020, https://www.ewtn.com/catholicism/library/roman-ritual-part-2-11883. For an explanation of the rite within the story of an exorcist, see Matt Baglio, *The Rite: The Making of a Modern Exorcist*, 1st ed. (New York: Doubleday, 2009).

it is based on the teachings, prayers, and redemptive actions of Jesus Christ—and faith in Him. As we have seen in the previous chapter, Jesus definitively defeated evil, which means that all free agents who trust and try to follow Him can never be *ultimately* subjugated by evil. Jesus will always have the last salvific word. If we throw ourselves upon His mercy while trying to follow His "way", His Holy Spirit will guide us through His Church to the heavenly Kingdom that He has prepared for us with His Father.

Nevertheless, spiritual evil can still tempt us, deceive us, attack us, and try to seduce us away from God into its lair of emptiness, coldness, darkness, and loneliness. To be sure, it disguises its dark reality with desirable objects that appear to be sources of true happiness— power, dominion, egocentricity, and all the seven deadly sins (see Chapters 5 and 6)—but eventually it will reveal glimpses of the darkness into which it is leading.

The purpose of this chapter is to show not only the reality of malevolent human spirits, but also the reality of demons—malevolent angelic beings, "fallen angels". By exploring the relatively rare phenomenon of demonic possession, I hope to show the reality of demonic angels and spirits whose activities are far more extensive than possessing people who are directly connected or associated with the occult. Though there is a growing number of people involved in satanic worship and occult practices (e.g., séances, conjurings, ouija boards, and even the new game "Charlie Charlie"), leading to an increased number of demonic possessions around the world,[20] the phenomenon of possession is still rare when compared with the other more disguised activities of Satan and other demonic spirits, such as temptation, deceit, and discouragement/despair (see the following chapter).

In a very serious, but humorously portrayed, book about the correspondence between a very mature and "wise" demon (Uncle

---

[20] Matt Baglio gives statistics for this marked increase in the occult, Satanism, and Wicca, both nationally and internationally. See Matt Baglio, *The Rite: The Making of a Modern Exorcist* (New York: Doubleday, 2010), pp. 6–7.

Recall from the Introduction to the Trilogy above in this volume that the Catholic Church has become quite concerned about this increase in Satanism and occultism, and that beginning in 2011, the Vatican holds a special conference for priests and other officials at the Pontifical Athenaeum Regina Apostolorum in Rome to address this issue. See footnote XX in Section II.A of the Introduction to the Trilogy for additional information and also a list of sources.

Screwtape) and his novice nephew (Wormwood), C. S. Lewis describes the strategy of Satan with respect to keeping his activities disguised:

> My dear Wormwood: I wonder you should ask me whether it is essential to keep the patient in ignorance of your own existence. That question, at least for the present phase of the struggle, has been answered for us by the High Command [Satan]. Our policy, for the moment, is to conceal ourselves. Of course this has not always been so. We are really faced with a cruel dilemma. When the humans disbelieve in our existence we lose all the pleasing results of direct terrorism and we make no magicians. On the other hand, when they believe in us, we cannot make them materialists and sceptics. At least, not yet. I have great hopes that we shall learn in due time how to emotionalise and mythologise their science to such an extent that what is, in effect, a belief in us, (though not under that name) will creep in while the human mind remains closed to belief in the Enemy [Jesus Christ and the Church]. The "Life Force", the worship of sex, and some aspects of Psychoanalysis, may here prove useful. If once we can produce our perfect work—the Materialist Magician, the man, not using, but veritably worshipping, what he vaguely calls "Forces" while denying the existence of "spirits"—then the end of the war will be in sight. But in the meantime we must obey our orders. I do not think you will have much difficulty in keeping the patient in the dark. The fact that "devils" are predominantly *comic* figures in the modern imagination will help you. If any faint suspicion of your existence begins to arise in his mind, suggest to him a picture of something in red tights, and persuade him that since he cannot believe in that (it is an old textbook method of confusing them) he therefore cannot believe in you.[21]

II. The Signs of Demonic Possession

My objective in this section is to give a brief description of the primary indications of demonic presence. When a large number of these indications are manifest in a single person, a reasonable inference of demonic possession or severe oppression can be made. The following

---

[21] C. S. Lewis, *The Screwtape Letters* (1941; repr., Quebec: Samizdat University Press, 2016), PDF e-book, p. 13 (italics in original), http://www.samizdat.qc.ca/arts/lit/PDFs/Screwtape Letters_CSL.pdf.

list of demonic manifestation was taken from Craig Isaacs' *Revelations and Possession: Distinguishing Spiritual from Psychological Experiences*,[22] and may also be found in Matt Baglio's *Rite*[23] and Father Jose Antonio Fortea's *Interview with an Exorcist*.[24]

In a possession, a demonic spirit (or spirits) inhabits a person's body (but not his soul). This spirit (or spirits) can choose to manifest its presence when it wants; when it does so, the victim goes into a trance (generally with the eyes rolled back) and begins to manifest a very dark, arrogant, and controlling personality. This sudden transition (called a "crisis") is frequently accompanied by knowledge of facts and languages with which the victim would have no acquaintance. Paranormal activity, sometimes on a significant level, often accompanies the manifestation of the demonic personality. After its manifestation, the demonic spirit retreats into the background, allowing the victim's personality to reemerge. Victims appear to have no recollection of the manifestation of the demonic personality within them. Those who witness the manifestation are confused and often terrified, but the victim—even long after a successful exorcism—has no recollection of it. When threatened with exorcism, a demon (or demons) will frequently move the victim into the trancelike state and confront the exorcist with its blasphemies, rages, and spiritual power. The demon's first tactic is to hide behind the victim's personality, making it appear that nothing is wrong; but when confronted by holy objects and the prayers of exorcism, it will generally emerge to confront the exorcist directly.

The following lists (given in Sections II.A–II.C) give three kinds of indications of demonic presence: paranormal indications, behavioral indications, and effects of demonic presence on other people. Notice that these indications of demonic presence are not restricted to a demonic possession, but can also occur in what is called "severe demonic oppression", where the demonic spirit attacks victims by pushing, hitting, scratching, or even levitating them. It also tries to influence or invade victims, temporarily overwhelming their personalities with feelings of hatred, arrogance, and violence. The key

---

[22] Craig Isaacs, *Revelations and Possession: Distinguishing Spiritual from Psychological Experiences* (Kearney, Neb.: Morris Publishing, 2009), pp. 114–26, 164–65.

[23] Baglio, *Rite* (2010), pp. 49–51.

[24] Father Jose Antonio Fortea, *Interview with an Exorcist* (Westchester, Pa.: Ascension Press, 2006), pp. 86–87.

difference between possession and severe oppression is that in the latter, the demon does not inhabit the victim with the intent to stay. It intends only to attack and invade victims for the purpose of intimidating and terrifying them and their loved ones.

As will be seen below (in Section IV), possession occurs when either a victim voluntarily cooperates with the occult or demonic forces, or when another person actively cooperating with demonic power brings it to bear on a victim—that is, according to Baglio, possession must originate either from a person opening the door to the devil or from being a victim of one who has opened that door.[25] In contrast, severe oppression can occur merely by being in a demonically infested house or being emotionally close to someone who is possessed. Oppression need not take place in the infested house— demons can follow victims outside the house and attack or invade them in remote places. Opening oneself to the demonic or being directly cursed by a demonically influenced person is not ingredient to demonic oppression (as it is for possession).

We now proceed to the three kinds of indications of demonic presence:

1. Paranormal indications (Section II.A)
2. Behavioral indications (Section II.B)
3. Effects of demonic possession on others (Section II.C)

Recall that the trancelike state (with the eyes generally rolled back into the head) and the emergence of an alternate personality, which is filled with hatred, arrogance, and violence, is almost always present in a possession along with other indications.

A. Paranormal Manifestations of Demonic Possession

There are eight common paranormal manifestations of a demonic spirit that have been observed in virtually every culture throughout the world:[26]

---

[25] Baglio, *Rite* (2009), p. 59.

[26] One of the most common beliefs among the world's diverse religions and cultures is the belief in demonic spirits and their capacity to haunt and possess, as well as the need for rituals

1. Poltergeist activity, such as the flying of objects and destruction of objects (without known physical cause), slamming of doors, loud footsteps, evidence of footprints, loud noises, and movement of furniture (without known physical cause)

2. Levitation, when the possessed person defies gravity and is elevated without known physical cause

3. Excessive weight of an individual when he can become so heavy that he is impossible to lift with several strong men, and when he sometimes collapses the beds or furniture on which he is reclining

4. Telepathy, the ability to read the mind and communicate with remote individuals, and even to effect phones and other information devices

5. Remote movement or destruction of religious objects

6. Understanding (and sometimes speaking) hitherto unknown foreign languages with proficiency (e.g., Latin, Greek, and Hebrew)

7. Knowledge of the personal secrets and sins of the exorcist and exorcism team members

8. Appearance of dark figures, animals, or insects, and other apparitions

Every possession is not the same, and some possessions have very few paranormal features; but the ones discussed in Section III below have virtually all of the above paranormal features seen by multiple witnesses. In view of this, a reasonable judgment of possession can be made.

---

of exorcism to free dwellings and people from their effects. See the accounts of possession and exorcism in China and India detailed in Betty, "Growing Evidence for 'Demonic Possession'".

There is belief in demonic spirits and rites of exorcism in other religions. For Judaism, see Rabbi David Wolpe, "Dybbuks, Demons and Exorcism in Judaism", *Jewish Journal*, June 27, 2012, http://www.jewishjournal.com/cover_story/article/dybbuks_demons_and _exorcism_in_judaism_20120627; for Islam, see the comprehensive link on exorcism in the Islam Universe website: http://www.islam-universe.com/Exorcism.html; for Buddhism, see Aromiekim, "Tibetan Buddhism: Ghosts, Demons, and Exorcisms", *Exorcise Me* (blog), January 28, 2015, https://exorciseme.wordpress.com/2015/01/28/tibetan-buddhism-ghosts -demons-and-exorcism/; for Taoism, see Jessica Orofino, "Taoist Exorcisms", in *China's Magical Creatures*, by Tineke D'Haeseleer, Open.Muhlenberg.Pub, 2020, Chapter 2, https:// open.muhlenberg.pub/chinasmagicalcreatures/chapter/taoist-exorcisms/.

B. Behavioral Manifestations

By "behavioral" manifestations, I am speaking only of *outward* manifestations of mental and emotional states, but not the actual interior mental or emotional states themselves. Some of these behavioral manifestations are less frequent than others, but in virtually every possession, trancelike states, violent and blasphemous reactions to religious or holy objects, and revulsion at the name of Jesus or holy objects are present. Additionally, trancelike states (often with the eyes rolled back) during an exorcism rite are frequently followed by blasphemous and violent outbursts, and many times there appear scratchings on the body (sometimes in words and *not* produced by the subject or others). The possessed will most often exhibit revulsion toward anything religious or holy—holy water can even cause pain—and being touched by religious artifacts can cause violent reactions. There is oftentimes fear or revulsion at the name of Jesus, and displays of hatred of religious objects sometimes including destruction of religious objects, and extreme secretions generally from vomiting (beyond normal bodily capacity). They can exhibit remarkable strength, far beyond the subject's normal capacity. Also too, a presence of another personality frequently appears manifesting a deep guttural voice—sometimes the voice or voices emerge when the jaw is clamped shut. It is usual also that the possessed will exhibit highly irregular changes in their facial features—sometimes manifesting "an evil face with an evil smile" and/or have extreme bodily contortions, sometimes into seemingly impossible positions.

C. Effects of the Possessed Person on Other People

In addition to witnessing paranormal phenomena (particularly poltergeist activities), team members or other witnesses at an exorcism may feel a significant drop in room temperature (without known physical cause) or a feeling of pressure on the chest; smell an acrid or putrid stench; or sense a dark or dangerous alien presence (not the subject) in the room.

Craig Isaacs gives a fuller explanation of all the above phenomena.[27] We are now in a position to examine two well-documented

[27] See Isaacs, *Revelations and Possession*, pp. 114–26.

cases of possession, after which we will address the difference between possession and mental illness as well as the causes of possession.

III. Two Documented Cases of Possession

There are many documented cases of exorcisms throughout the world, but the best documented ones (which include analysis from psychologists and psychiatrists) come from Catholic exorcism rites and Christian deliverance ministry in the United States and Europe.

The following two well-documented cases, both using a pseudonym—the case of "Julia" and that of "Robbie Mannheim" (underlying the movie *The Exorcist*)—are sufficient to show the reality of demonic spirits. They are based on multiple witnesses whose good reputation is indisputable, and they consist of paranormal phenomena of almost every sort and most of the other signs of demonic possession given above (Section II). They will be explained in detail below in Sections III.A (Julia) and III.B (Robbie Mannheim).

Readers interested in additional cases of exorcism will want to consult the two cases of exorcism detailed in Scott Peck's book *Glimpses of the Devil*, which were videotaped and had a team of psychological and religious experts present.[28] Readers may also want to consult the 2012 exorcism of Latoya Ammons and her three children, detailed in the *Indianapolis Star*, as well as a memorandum of the principal exorcist Father Michael Maginot.[29] In *The Rite*, Baglio details several

---

[28] Scott Peck, *Glimpses of the Devil* (New York: Simon & Schuster, 2005), pp. 15–132 (for case no. 1, Jersey), and pp. 133–70 (for case no. 2, Beccah).

[29] Marisa Kwiatkowski, the reporter from the *Indianapolis Star*, assessed eight hundred pages of documentation on the exorcism from psychologists, family members, and friends, as well as from Department of Child Protective Services case workers and the four officers from the Gary Police Department. See Marisa Kwiatkowski, "The Exorcisms of Latoya Ammons", *Indianapolis Star*, published January 25, 2014, updated October 31, 2019, http://www.indystar.com/story/news/2014/01/25/the-disposession-of-latoya-ammons/4892553/. Also, see the report of Father Michael Maginot, S.T.L., J.C.L., of the Diocese of Gary: "Report Seeking Permission of Bishop for Exorcism", DocumentCloud.org, May 21, 2012, https://www.documentcloud.org/documents/1005721-report-to-bishop.html; and the interview with Father Maginot in Patti Armstrong, "Parish Priest Aids Family in Fight against Demons", *National Catholic Register*, February 11, 2014, http://www.ncregister.com/daily-news/parish-priest-aids-family-in-fight-against-demons.

contemporary exorcisms witnessed and performed by Father Gary Thomas in the early twenty-first century.[30]

There are older well-documented cases of exorcisms, including the detailed narrative of the 1912 and 1928 exorcisms of Anna Ecklund by Father Carl Vogl entitled *Begone Satan!* (based on a diary by Father Theophilus Riesinger, the chief exorcist).[31] Another volume by Leon Cristiani, *Evidence of Satan in the Modern World*, details multiple exorcisms in France and Italy prior to 1940.[32]

A. The Case of "Julia" (2007)

We may now proceed to the case of the woman with the pseudonym "Julia", which took place in 2007. This case was witnessed and reported by psychiatrist Richard E. Gallagher and recounted in the *New Oxford Review*.[33] Gallagher is a board-certified psychiatrist in private practice in Hawthorne, New York, and associate professor of clinical psychiatry at New York Medical College. He is also on the faculties of the Columbia University Psychoanalytic Institute. He is a graduate of Princeton University and trained in psychiatry at the Yale University School of Medicine.

Dr. Gallagher agreed to anonymity, and so very little incidental material that could lead to the identification of "Julia" was provided.

[30] Baglio, *Rite* (2010). Baglio recounts seven exorcisms witnessed by or connected to Father Thomas: an unnamed woman in Rome in 2007 (pp. 2–5), Doug (pp. 235–42), Giovanna (pp. 180–85, 188), Maria (pp. 231–34), Silvia (pp. 192–93), Sister Janica (pp. 125–33, 146–47, 167, 174, 193), and Stephanie (pp. 223–29). Baglio also recounts several other exorcisms performed by Father Carmine DeFilippis, the instructor of Father Thomas (pp. 90–185).

[31] This detailed account of the two series of exorcisms of Anna (one in 1912 and the other in 1928, both of which were successful) shows many of the same paranormal and demonic activities mentioned in the case of Julia and that of Robbie Mannheim (given below). See Carl Vogl, *Begone Satan! A True Account of an Exorcism in Earling, Iowa, in 1928* (Charlotte, N.C.: Tan Books, 2010). The exorcism was also documented in newspapers at the time.

[32] Leon Cristiani, *Evidence of Satan in the Modern World* (Rockford, Ill.: Tan Books and Publishers, 1961); see pp. 74–91 (the case of Antoine Gay; 1837), pp. 92–95 (the case of a possessed woman exorcised by Saint John Vianney; 1850), pp. 96–104 (the case of Thiebaud and Joseph Burner; Illfurth, France; 1864–1869), pp. 104–7 (the case of Helene Poirier; Coullons, France; 1914), pp. 106–7 (Claire-Germaine Cele; Natal, Africa; 1906–1907), and pp. 109–23 (the bewitched woman of Piacenza, Italy; 1920). Cristiani relates other cases beyond these six, especially those performed by Saint Jean Vianney.

[33] Richard Gallagher, "A Case of Demonic Possession—among the Many Counterfeits", *New Oxford Review* 75, no. 3 (March 2008), https://www.newoxfordreview.org/documents/a-case-of-demonic-possession/#.

Given the date of the article (March 2008) and the fact that Dr. Gallagher is a board psychiatrist in New York, it might be inferred that the exorcism took place somewhere in New York in 2007, though this cannot be verified. Dr. Gallagher notes that the team members of the exorcism were credible, including several qualified mental-health personnel, at least four Catholic priests, a deacon and his wife, two nuns (both nurses, one psychiatric), and several lay volunteers.[34] The name of the Catholic exorcist is not mentioned for the same reason of anonymity.

Julia was a former Catholic who apparently disavowed her religion and became a prominent Satanist throughout "a long disturbing history of involvement with explicitly satanic groups".[35] Her satanic practice brought her extraordinary psychic powers, but also possession by a demonic spirit who would put her into trances in which the demon became the dominant personality. The presence of virtually all signs of demonic possession (see above, Section II) distinguished these states from dissociative identity disorder (what used to be called multiple personality disorder). When Julia was not in this trance state in which the demonic presence became dominant, she had no memory of what she said and did in the trance. Furthermore, she was logical, articulate, and friendly, and did not manifest any signs of psychosis. Nevertheless, she intuited the presence of the demon because of its oppressive manifestations, and so she very uncharacteristically sought the help of an exorcist in the Catholic Church.

The Catholic Church agreed to examine Julia, and retained Dr. Gallagher as a psychiatric consultant—at which point he became intimately familiar with the case. After psychiatric causes of Julia's condition had been ruled out because of the presence of paranormal activities, which have no causative basis in psychiatry or the known laws of physics, an exorcist was assigned to the case. Because of the complexity of the case, the many team members mentioned above, including Dr. Gallagher, were present at the rites of exorcism, along with the exorcist.

There were several manifestations of paranormal and demonic activity arising out of Julia, both during the times of trances and also between trance states. Julia went into a trancelike state during which another intelligent and evil personality would become manifest. This

34 Ibid.
35 Ibid.

personality exemplified hatred for God and an extreme reticence to leave Julia, cursing and threatening those who tried to do so. This is a universal sign of a possessed person when it is accompanied by paranormal activity, such as those recounted below. On one occasion in front of all the team members, Julia levitated one-half foot off her bed for thirty minutes. Psychokinetic activity (objects flying through the air without known physical cause) occurred several times, particularly when Julia was in a trancelike state. Julia was uttering intelligible phrases in both Latin and Spanish, languages with which she was completely unfamiliar. Julia was aware of the thoughts of various team members; when the demonic personality was dominant, she could recount facts about the clothes that team members were wearing away from the site of the exorcism, the characteristics as well as the place and time of death of team member's relatives and friends, and also unrevealed facts about team members' personal or family history.

On one occasion, Julia was aware of conference calls among the team members, to which she was not privy, and on one occasion actually inserted her demonic voice into one of those conference calls without the benefit of a phone. Julia displayed enormous strength beyond any natural capacity, which the nuns and other team members were frequently unable to resist or restrain. She had an extreme aversion to religious objects and was able to distinguish between holy water and unblessed water; when her demonic voice was dominant, she would curse and utter blasphemies. She would also groan, growl, and make other animal sounds, which most team members did not believe could be made by a human being.

As a psychiatrist who has acted as a consultant to other cases of demonic possession, Richard Gallagher is probably one of the world's best experts in distinguishing true demonic possession from psychiatric conditions that look like possession, but in reality are explicable through recognizable disorders in the *Diagnostic and Statistical Manual of Mental Disorders*.[36] Gallagher elucidates three kinds of psychological

---

[36] See Richard Gallagher, "True and False Possessions, Revisited—in a Strange and Confusing Realm", *New Oxford Review*, May 2015, https://www.newoxfordreview.org/documents/true-false-possessions-revisited/#. The psychiatric profession recognizes a standard set of mental disorders that are classified in the *Diagnostic and Statistical Manual of Mental Disorders*. The classification of these disorders changes from time to time, and so the manual has gone through five editions. The latest edition is American Psychiatric Association, *Diagnostic and Statistical Manual of Mental Disorders*, 5th ed. (Arlington, Va: American Psychiatric Publishing, 2013).

disorders that may be mistaken for demonic possession[37] (which will be discussed again in Section III.B):

1. *Chronic psychotic disorders* (such as schizophrenia and bipolar disorders) *or brief psychotic conditions or episodes.* These conditions are frequently accompanied by hallucinations—visual, auditory (voices) and gustatory—and frequently include a conviction of the presence of and possession by an angelic or demonic personality.
2. *Personality or character disorders in which patients believe themselves to have a strong interior disposition toward evil.* Sometimes this inner sense or feeling leads to the conviction that there is a devil or demonic spirit distinct from them, but present in them.
3. *Severely histrionic or dissociative individuals.* These conditions, particularly dissociative identity disorder (formerly called multiple personality disorder), give rise to alternate personalities, some of whom manifest aggressive, hateful, evil, and psychotic dimensions (as Mr. Hyde was to Dr. Jekyll). These alternate personalities can be so hateful and aggressive that they fool people into believing that a devil or demonic spirit is really present.

Dr. Gallagher ruled out all three of the psychiatric conditions for Julia, first because of the manifest paranormal and demonic activities, which cannot be explained whether by purely mental states or the known laws of physics. Furthermore, each of the above three psychiatric conditions has accompanying features that Julia did not possess when she was not in a trancelike state. Psychosis is a highly unlikely diagnosis for Julia because she manifested logic, prudence, good judgment, friendliness, and restrained behaviors between trances. This would not be the case for psychotics. Furthermore, Julia did not consistently manifest the full range of behaviors associated with personality disorders, character disorders, hysteria, or dissociative identity disorder. In view of this, it seems likely that Julia's other personality—that manifested itself with a low guttural voice accompanied by animal growls and sounds—was in fact a demonic spirit that had taken over her body and could at will induce a trancelike state in which its evil, dark, and blasphemous character could emerge.

[37] Gallagher, "True and False Possessions".

The cause of Julia's possession is quite clear: her frequent participation in satanic practices and rituals over many years. Dr. Gallagher later revealed that she was a high priestess in a satanic cult.[38] Though these practices apparently gave her great psychic capacities, they opened her to possession by a strong demonic spirit that ultimately scared her into asking for an exorcism from the Catholic Church. As progress was being made (and the demonic possession was weakening), Julia decided to discontinue after eight exorcisms without explanation. Gallagher believes she was conflicted, because she did not want to lose her preternatural power. One year later, she asked Gallagher if she could resume the exorcisms because she was dying of cancer. After Gallagher asked to interview her and her oncologist, she did not come back into contact with him. He and the exorcism team believe that she had died.

B. The Case of "Robbie Mannheim" (1949)

The case of the possession and exorcism of the young man with the pseudonym "Robbie Mannheim" (also known as "Roland Doe") took place in 1949. In early March, the first exorcism by a member of the Catholic clergy took place at Georgetown University Hospital, in Washington, D.C. Shortly thereafter, beginning March 16, a series of thirty exorcisms were performed by several members of the Catholic clergy; the exorcism was successfully completed on April 18 at the St. Alexius Hospital in St. Louis, Missouri. This second series of exorcisms formed the basis for the well-known fictional 1971 book and 1973 movie entitled *The Exorcist*, by William Peter Blatty. A much more accurate portrayal of the exorcism than Blatty's fictionalized account can be found in Thomas Allen's *Possessed: The True Story of an Exorcism*, the primary source used for the discussion below.[39] Allen's account of both the exorcism at Georgetown University Hospital and the second series of exorcisms is very well researched and documented; those interested in a much more detailed account of them, than the very brief one given here, will want to read this volume.

---

[38] See ibid.

[39] Thomas B. Allen, *Possessed: The True Story of an Exorcism* (Lincoln, Neb.: iUniverse.com, 2000).

The first exorcism, at Georgetown University Hospital, was performed by Father E. Albert Hughes, from Mount Rainier, Maryland—which did not end successfully. There are three sources for this exorcism that Thomas Allen was able to procure and summarize:

1. An interview by Allen with Father Frank Bober, Father Hughes' assistant pastor who was told about the exorcism by Father Hughes[40]
2. Notes taken by Father William Reppetti, S.J. (Georgetown University archivist) of a lecture given by Father Hughes at Georgetown University (in the Georgetown University archives)[41]
3. An interview with Father John J. Nicola, who had access to some of the secret archives, but was discreet about giving information on the Mannheim exorcism[42]

There are two primary sources for the facts surrounding the possession and second series of exorcisms: (1) a diary kept by Father Raymond J. Bishop, S.J., who first witnessed events of possession during an initial visit to the family home in St. Louis on March 9, 1949, and was present at events during the second series of exorcisms, assisting during the successful exorcism,[43] and (2) later testimony provided in an interview with Walter H. Halloran, S.J., who was a Jesuit seminarian at the time and who also assisted during the final exorcism; the interview was conducted by Allen for his book *Possessed*.

There are two other primary sources for the possession and exorcism, which are not available to the public:

1. A report given to the provincial of the Missouri province of the Jesuits (and to the Archdiocese of St. Louis) by Father William Bowdern, S.J., who was an associate pastor of College Church at Saint Louis University (a Jesuit university) and the lead exorcist for the second series of exorcisms

---

[40] Ibid., p. 302.
[41] Ibid., p. 309.
[42] Ibid., p. 302.
[43] The diary is available in an appendix to Allen's *Possessed*, pp. 243–91 (the diary itself begins on page 245 with the section entitled "Case Study"). This book is the most scholarly source of the contents of the diary and all of the events preceding those recounted in the diary.

2. Father Halloran's witness report, also given to the Missouri province of the Jesuits and to the Archdiocese of St. Louis

These reports have been read by officials who indicated to Allen that they cited forty witnesses to the possession and second series of exorcisms.[44] The diary itself mentions fourteen witnesses to them.[45]

There is an important secondary source concerned with distinguishing the paranormal and spiritual causes from the psychoanalytical and psychiatric causes of Robbie's behavior—Terry Cooper's and Cindy Epperson's *Evil: Satan, Sin, and Psychology*.[46]

The possession and exorcism of Robbie Mannheim is one of the most detailed accounts of a full possession available to the public. Though Richard Gallagher's account of Julia has the advantage of being witnessed by very credible psychiatrists and other scientific professionals, Gallagher's promise of confidentiality about Julia's case prevented him from relating the kinds of details explicitly mentioned in Father Bishop's diary and the other sources of Robbie's possession and two series of exorcisms, the latter of which included thirty recitations of the full Roman Ritual. There can be little doubt that the substantial paranormal and demonic phenomena—exhausting virtually every indicator of demonic possession mentioned in Section II above—indicates a demonic spiritual cause of Robbie's acute condition. The following brief summary will make this clear.

The description of the events surrounding Robbie Manheim's possession may be divided into two parts:

1. The paranormal and demonic phenomena manifested before the beginning of the second series of exorcisms (March 16, 1949). These include events that took place in Robbie's home in Cottage City, Maryland; at Georgetown University Hospital by Father Hughes, during the first failed exorcism; and after the family move to St. Louis, as well as the phenomena manifested in St. Louis at the homes of Robbie's Lutheran and Catholic relatives.

---

[44] Ibid., p. 300.

[45] See Bishop, "Case Study", in ibid., pp. 245–91.

[46] Terry Cooper and Cindy Epperson, *Evil: Satan, Sin, and Psychology* (Mahwah, N.J.: Paulist Press, 2008).

2. The series of thirty exorcisms beginning March 16, 1949, which includes events that took place at Robbie's relatives' home; the rectory of College Church at Saint Louis University; the family home in Maryland during a short stay; and the Alexian brothers' hospital in St. Louis, where the exorcism was successfully completed

Though most of the events described in part one (leading up to the exorcisms starting on March 16, 1949) are described in the first seven pages of Father Bishop's diary, I have relied heavily on Allen's book *Possessed*, which fills out the details of these events with material he gleaned from the four additional sources mentioned above. The material from part two (the exorcisms after March 16, 1949) is taken mostly from the diary kept by Father Bishop (pp. 7–29 of the original diary). It should be noted that though Father Bishop was the author of the diary, he referred to himself in the third person throughout it.

1. Paranormal and Demonic Phenomena Manifested in and around Robbie Mannheim prior to March 16, 1949

"Robbie Mannheim", born June 1, 1935, was the only child of a Lutheran couple residing in Cottage City, Maryland.[47] Robbie grew close to his aunt Harriet, who was a spiritualist and regularly tried to make contact with the dead through a ouija board and other occult means. Since Robbie was an only child who was not inclined toward sports and other activities outside the home, he associated regularly with his aunt who taught him how to use the ouija board during her frequent visits to the home. Robbie became proficient at using the ouija board and began to make contact with spirits on his own.

The ouija board is an occult tool used to communicate with spirits of the dead, but also can mediate demonic spirits. The objective of the people using the board is to make themselves mediums of these spirits, who would then enter the consciousness and body of the participants who placed their fingers on the board. The board has the letters of the alphabet, the numerals 0–9, and the words "yes" and "no" on it; the movement of a planchette spells words and responses to questions asked of the spirits conjured in the game.[48]

[47] Allen, *Possessed*, p. 9.
[48] Ibid., p. 11.

Though this may seem to be a harmless child's game, it is not. In order to play the "game", one must actively conjure spirits whose identities may be supposed, but are really unknown to the participants. Moreover, one must open oneself to being a medium for the spirits, which is an invitation to an elementary form of possession! Even if people use the ouija board as if they are playing a game, not even certain about the reality of spirits, they still open themselves up to this form of temporary possession, which could become, as we shall see, far worse.

There is good reason why the Bible prohibits the use of mediums, séances, and other means of conjuring spirits—if you want to make use of occult powers, you must also subject yourself to them! The Book of Deuteronomy makes this absolute prohibition clear:

> There shall not be found among you any one who burns his son or his daughter as an offering, any one who practices divination, a soothsayer, or an augur, or a sorcerer, or a charmer, or a medium, or a wizard, or a necromancer. For whoever does these things is an abomination to the LORD. (Deut 18:10–12)[49]

This prohibition is presumed by Jesus and the apostolic Church (see the previous chapter).

Countless numbers of house infestations, oppressions, and even rare cases of possession have begun by making recourse to these seemingly harmless unseen spiritual powers through occult means like the ouija board.[50] These games are not to be trifled with. Subjugation to dark or evil powers is dangerous not only to the individuals opening themselves to such powers, but also to the family, household, and friends of those individuals. Furthermore, it is an endangerment to one's eternal salvation and may even entail pledging allegiance to the dark lord—Satan himself. All forms of mediumship should be avoided, no matter how "harmless" their proponents make these practices seem. The proponents of them have already, wittingly or unwittingly, subjected themselves to the power of unknown spirits who can be deceitful and incredibly evil.

---

[49] See also the prohibition in Leviticus: "Do not turn to mediums or wizards; do not seek them out, to be defiled by them: I am the LORD your God" (19:31).

[50] See Baglio, *Rite* (2009), pp. 15–16, 59–60. See also Cristiani, *Evidence of Satan*, pp. 182–83.

The consequences of Robbie's and his aunt Harriet's use of the ouija board were worse than anyone could have imagined. They had released the power of an evil spirit within Robbie's house. On January 15, 1949 (when Robbie was thirteen years old), paranormal activity began to manifest itself in the Mannheim household. Dripping sounds could be heard without any known source. Scratching and tapping beneath the floorboards led Robbie's father to believe that there were rats in the house; yet none could be found. A picture of Jesus on the wall started shaking, almost as if the wall behind it were being pounded from the back, causing it to jump off the wall. The family was perplexed and was becoming alarmed.[51]

On January 26, 1949, Aunt Harriet died, devastating Robbie. In order to make contact with her, he used his ouija board, which caused the poltergeist activity to intensify. It also seems to have led to the spirit's (or spirits') initial invasion of Robbie's body. First, squeaky shoes could be heard walking and marching next to his bed; the furniture began moving on its own; then a Bible, a pear, and an orange flew through the air. One day in the midst of friends, Robbie's heavy living room chair rolled up on one side and tipped over, causing Robbie to fall out of it and tumble onto the floor. All the adults tried to imitate this but could not; and then a vase levitated and moved across the room, shattering against the wall.[52]

These phenomena were not limited to the Mannheim household. The spirit seemed to follow Robbie to school and elsewhere. Several times, Robbie's desk would "lurch into the aisle and begin skittering about, banging into other desks and causing schoolroom uproar".[53] Once when the family took a day off to visit with friends away from the infested home, the spirit again followed Robbie. During a conversation in the living room with family and friends, his rocking chair began to spin around like a top with his legs in the air, not propelled by any known physical force.[54] All these incidents, including the shaking and moving of Robbie's bed, caused his parents to consult their Lutheran minister, then a pediatrician and a psychiatrist at the

---

[51] See Allen, *Possessed*, pp. 11–15.
[52] Ibid., p. 18.
[53] Ibid., p. 16.
[54] Ibid., p. 18.

University of Maryland. Though their minister thought that something was highly unusual, he had difficulty believing that it could be a demonic spirit. The pediatrician and psychologist did not see the phenomena for themselves and flat out disbelieved any of the reports from Robbie and his parents. The psychiatrist declared Robbie to be "normal".[55]

The spirit then began to invade Robbie himself. At first it would cause his bed to shake and his dresser to move across the room, with all the drawers moving in and out. Robbie would go into a trance, cursing his parents and grandmother with incredible profanity—words they were sure he did not even know.[56] Scratches began to appear on Robbie's body, on his arms, legs, and chest—at first long scratches, but eventually, they began to spell out coherent words, like "Hell".

Finally out of desperation, Robbie's parents appealed once again to their minister, Reverend Luther Schulze, who decided he could help Robbie by inviting him into his house. This would enable him to see the phenomena for himself, and to determine what kind of treatment might help the disturbed boy. He slept in another bed next to Robbie's in a guest room. Soon Robbie's bed began to shake; so Schulze got up and offered Robbie a cup of cocoa, after which they returned to the room. Schulze had Robbie sit in a heavy chair instead of lying in bed; but the chair also began to shake, then moved across the floor to the wall and toppled over, throwing Robbie out of the chair onto the floor. Schulze tried to imitate the feat, but because of the chair's weight and low center of gravity, he was unable to do so. He then decided that Robbie should sleep on the floor on some blankets between the beds. At three o'clock in the morning, the blankets with Robbie on them, as one unit, began to glide across the floor. When the minister shouted, "Stop that!", Robbie and the blankets moved under the bed, then began to move up and down, propelling Robbie's head into the springs under the bed, causing him to be cut. At this juncture, Schulze began to think that Robbie's behavior was not nearly psychokinetic, but perhaps demonic possession.[57]

[55] Ibid.
[56] Ibid., pp. 21–22.
[57] See ibid., pp. 28–29.

Schulze had no acquaintance with demonic possession; he could think of only one church where Robbie might be able to get some relief, if indeed a demon was really present. He told Robbie's parents, "You have to see a Catholic priest. The Catholics know about things like this."[58] In late February, Robbie's father called St. James Parish in Mount Rainier, Maryland (a short distance from Washington, D.C.), and spoke with Father Hughes, who at that time was a young inexperienced priest with little knowledge of possession and exorcism. Robbie's father asked Hughes if he, Robbie, and his mother could come to the rectory as Protestants, and Hughes agreed to see them. According to Hughes, during the meeting the room turned cold, Robbie began to curse him, and the phone on Hughes' desk began to move. Hughes gave a bottle of holy water and two blessed candles to the Mannheims to take home with them for blessing and protection.[59] When the Mannheims returned home, Robbie's mother sprinkled the house with holy water and then lit one of the candles—at which point the flame shot up nearly hitting the ceiling, causing her to extinguish it before it set the house on fire. During the night, the holy water bottle was picked up, moved across the room, and smashed into the wall. Robbie's mother called Father Hughes, and while on the phone with him, the table under the phone lifted off the ground and smashed into a hundred pieces, at which point Father Hughes decided to come to the Mannheim home to see the phenomena for himself.[60]

Hughes visited the house, and according to one of his accounts, Robbie spoke fluent Latin to him (a language with which Robbie was not familiar), saying, "O sacerdos Christi, tu scis me ess diabolum. Cur me derogas?"—"O priest of Christ, you know that I am the devil. Why do you keep bothering me?"[61] As a result, Hughes decided to ask his superior, Archbishop Patrick O'Boyle, for permission to do an exorcism on Robbie.

O'Boyle granted permission to Hughes to do the exorcism, asking him to keep the details secret. Though Hughes had very little

[58] Ibid., p. 30.
[59] See ibid., pp. 34–35.
[60] See ibid., pp. 35–36.
[61] See ibid., p. 35.

knowledge of exorcism, he decided that it had to be done in a hospital where Robbie was under restraints. In March 1949, he and the Mannheim family entered Georgetown University Hospital, where Robbie was placed in a special room in a bed with restraints. As Hughes began the exorcism, the bed moved across the room on its own and slammed into the wall, in full view of the nuns who were present; scratchings began to appear on Robbie's body, and he began to curse Hughes. Hughes, kneeling down by the side of the bed, did not notice that Robbie had slipped one of his hands outside of the restraints down the side of the bed and unhinged a piece of the spring supporting the bed. As Hughes continued to pray, Robbie took the spring and slashed Hughes' arm from his shoulder to his wrist; his blood saturated the cassock and surplus.

Hughes discontinued the exorcism and required 140 stitches to close the wound in his arm. He suffered a breakdown, but then resumed pastoral duties—never fully regaining use of his arm.[62] The first exorcism of Robbie had ended disastrously.

When the Mannheims went back to their home, rumors abounded about Robbie, and the extraordinary phenomena at the house became well known, scaring the neighbors. Robbie's mother, who was from St. Louis, considered moving there to get away from the neighbors and to look into another course of action. Soon after, Robbie screamed out from his bedroom, and when they rushed in, they saw the word "Louis" scratched into his chest. So the Mannheims left Maryland and went to St. Louis.[63]

While in St. Louis, the Mannheims stayed at the home of Lutheran relatives who decided, along with the consent and participation of their Lutheran minister, to help Robbie by using a ouija board to connect with Aunt Harriet! They received the message that Aunt Harriet was present in Robbie and the home. This confirmation was followed by more shaking of the bed, loud rappings, and violent disturbances, to confirm Aunt Harriet's presence. These were witnessed by the Mannheim's relatives.

It should be noted here that evil spirits—particularly Satan, the head of all evil spirits—are deceivers. The idea that the family could make recourse to a ouija board (an occult practice open to the

---

[62] See ibid., pp. 42–43.
[63] See ibid., p. 45.

intervention of evil spirits) to find the truth could not possibly be more absurd. If it would behoove evil spirits to identify themselves falsely as Aunt Harriet, they would not hesitate to do so. Furthermore, the idea that one could appeal to the spirits tormenting Robbie to make a confirmation of "the truth" they found by using the ouija board doubles the absurdity. If evil spirits are willing to deceive the first time, then they are willing to deceive a second time. In any case, it seems that the Lutheran minister who participated in these activities became scared and surmised that he had taken the wrong path to finding "the truth". At that juncture, he recommended that the family see a Catholic priest.

The Mannheims then moved to the home of their Catholic relatives on March 8. While there, Robbie experienced some temporary peace, which caused his mother to think that the problem might be over. She discussed with her relatives the possibility of sending Robbie back to school—immediately after which, Robbie screamed out in pain and showed them his chest, which had the words "No school" scratched into it. That evening the Mannheims decided to put Robbie in a room with his cousin Marty (who was about the same age) because they got along so well. During the night, scratching noises could be heard in the mattress and throughout the room. The mattress began to flop violently, with both boys lying on it in a trance. This convinced the Mannheims that a priest should be consulted.[64]

Robbie had an older cousin, Elizabeth, who was attending Saint Louis University. She contacted her professor, Father Raymond Bishop (who kept the diary throughout the second set of thirty exorcisms), to talk about Robbie's condition. Bishop was the head of the department of education at Saint Louis University and a very logical, scientific, yet spiritually sensitive man. He heard Elizabeth's story and suspected demonic possession, though he wanted to verify it. He consulted broadly with the Jesuit community, who had several resources, and then questioned the Mannheim family about all of the incidents that occurred prior to contacting him. He asked about the number of witnesses for each of the paranormal events, which he indicated totaled fourteen witnesses.[65]

[64] See ibid., pp. 48–50.
[65] See ibid., pp. 55–59.

On March 9, Bishop then went to the Mannheim house to interview Robbie. During the interview, Robbie seemed to be normal; afterward, Bishop blessed all the rooms in the house, giving a special blessing to the room in which Robbie was staying. Robbie went to bed, and Bishop went down to consult with his parents. As he was about to leave, Robbie screamed, and he went back upstairs with the family members to see Robbie's mattress moving and scratches welling up from underneath his skin. At this juncture, he had seen for himself that Robbie's parents' account of the paranormal and demonic happenings were true.[66]

Father Bishop then enlisted the support of Father William Bowdern (described below). On March 11, Bowdern accompanied Bishop to the house to do a special blessing of Robbie with some relics from the College Church. Bowdern then became a witness to the paranormal phenomena. A relic of Saint Margaret Mary was launched from Robbie's pillow into a mirror in the room; scratches of a cross appeared on Robbie's arm; violent shaking began of the mattress, without any physical cause; a bookcase (weighing approximately fifty pounds) was turned around and moved into the entrance of Robbie's room; a bottle of Saint Ignatius holy water was thrown from a table two feet from Robbie's room. At this point, Father Bowdern was convinced—some kind of evil spiritual power was working in and around Robbie.[67]

On the following day, March 12, Fathers Bishop and Bowdern returned at 11:45 P.M. to the house. While there, the bookcase moved from the wall in an arc of about five feet toward the side of Robbie's bed. The priests stayed praying the Rosary until 3:00 A.M. Between March 12 and March 16, events at the house were relatively calm, with intermittent movement of the stool in Robbie's room, launching of the relic of Saint Margaret Mary, shaking of the bed, and some other paranormal phenomenon.

The priests of the Jesuit community believed that they were morally responsible for helping Robbie, and so petitioned their superior Archbishop Joseph Ritter for permission to begin an exorcism. Ritter granted the permission on March 15, selecting Father Bowdern to be

[66] See ibid., pp. 60–61.
[67] Bishop, "Case Study", in ibid., pp. 252–54.

the exorcist, because Bowdern seemed to be a very well-grounded, spiritual man. Prior to becoming pastor of Saint Louis University's College Church, Bowdern had been principal of three Jesuit high schools, and he was a remarkably strong, pastorally sensitive man. Father Bowdern was to be assisted by Father Bishop, Mr. Walter Halloran (a Jesuit seminarian at the time), and Father William Van Roo. Other Jesuits assisted Bowdern intermittently throughout the thirty exorcisms that concluded on April 18, around 10:45 P.M.[68]

2. The Thirty Exorcisms of Robbie Mannheim Commencing March 16, 1949

The following details of the exorcisms of Robbie Mannheim beginning on March 16—at the home of his relatives in St. Louis, Missouri—are taken directly from the diary of Father Bishop, in Allen's *Possessed*.[69] I reference other parts of Allen's *Possessed* occasionally when he presents material from sources other than the diary. Since much of the diary is repetitive, I summarized the events taking place in the four settings where the exorcisms took place:

1. Robbie's relatives' home in St. Louis
2. The rectory of College Church at Saint Louis University
3. The family home in Cottage City, Maryland (when Robbie and his family returned there temporarily)
4. The fifth floor of the St. Alexius Hospital in St. Louis (founded by the Alexian brothers)

Exorcism events at Robbie's relatives' home in St. Louis (commencing March 16)

On March 16 at Robbie's relatives' home in St. Louis, the exorcism began at 10:45 P.M. with Fathers Bowdern and Bishop as well as Mr. Halloran. Almost immediately paranormal activity began. Halloran describes it as follows:

The first night I was there I was kneeling at the bed on which the boy was lying and the bed started going up and down [eight inches] and

---

[68] See Allen, *Possessed*, pp. 58–63.
[69] See Bishop, "Case Study", in ibid., pp. 245–91.

then I just about got hit with a holy water bottle that was sitting on the dresser and came flying across the room and just missed me by an inch or two.[70]

Nevertheless, Father Bowdern helped Robbie examine his conscience and make an act of contrition. Other family members came up and made acts of faith, hope, love, and contrition. When Father Bowdern spoke the first *praecipio* (command or order to the demon to identify himself), there was immediate action. Scratch lines started forming all over Robbie's body, on his arms, legs, and chest—and then above his head, a red figure of the devil appeared, with arms stretched and webbed like a bat. The word "HELL" emerged on Robbie's chest, and everyone agreed that the figure of the devil and the word "HELL" could be no other word or figure. These scratch marks and brands hurt Robbie and were obviously not caused by him (he was in full view of the exorcists and the family). By the time he fell asleep, more than twenty-five different marks were made on his body, including the word "GO" above his groin.[71]

As the prayers continued, Robbie alternated between a state of fighting and wrestling (which he indicated was a fight with a large red demon who was holding him in a pit), and then breaking into song in a very high-pitched voice, when he seemed to relax. He alternated back and forth until he finally fell asleep. Over the next three days, Robbie went into combat with the devil. It took several men to hold him down. The liberal use of holy water and the presence of the Blessed Sacrament subdued the dark power within him. On Friday, March 18, Robbie stood up in bed and seemed to be lifting the darkness out of himself. He claimed that a dark cloud was leaving him, and in the cloud there was a black-hooded figure and other smaller demons. At one point he declared that the demon had left him. He was his old self again; he put on his bathrobe, spoke with the priests, and thanked them as they left. It was about 1:30 A.M. About 2:00 A.M., after the priests had left, Robbie began to scream out that

---

[70] Michael Brown, "An Interview with the Priest Involved in the Case behind *The Exorcist*", *Spirit Daily*, accessed April 11, 2020, https://www.spiritdaily.org/Halloran.htm.

[71] See Bishop, "Case Study", in Allen, *Possessed*, pp. 255–59.

the demons were coming back. The priests returned to the house about 3:00 A.M. and resumed the Rite of Exorcism. Events proceeded along the same line for the next few days. Every time the prayers of exorcism started, Robbie became exceedingly animated. As time progressed, he began to show real animosity toward the exorcists, screaming every imaginable obscenity at them. He would also break into song, showing a proficiency and knowledge of music that he did not have. In fact, Robbie was incapable of holding a tune, but he would sing the melody of the "Blue Danube" waltz and other classics perfectly. When awake, and out of his trance, he had no knowledge of the songs he was singing.[72]

Exorcism events at the rectory of College Church at Saint Louis University (commencing March 23) and subsequently at the relatives' house

Since the health of Robbie's mother was being affected, Father Bowdern decided to move the exorcism into the rectory of College Church (at Saint Louis University) on March 23. As the exorcisms continued, Robbie's violence increased significantly. He broke Mr. Halloran's nose, and gave Father Van Roo, another Jesuit who assisted, a bloody nose. His language became more foul and more deviantly sexual. He claimed to see some of the priests in Hell (eight years from the time of the exorcism); he barked and howled like a dog, then began to sing and then curse the exorcists. He would tear off his clothes and make obscene gestures, and then break into very uncharacteristic sarcastic expressions, for example, "You like to stay with me. Well, I like it too."[73]

After five days, Robbie was moved back to the relatives' house. Again Robbie would go into trances, tantrums, vulgarity, and snide remarks. Nevertheless, when he was out of his trances, another priest, Father Joseph McMahon, was giving him instruction in the Catholic faith (since March 23). Robbie seemed to be accepting this, but when the Rite of Exorcism would begin, he would go into his rages and obscenities.

[72] See ibid., pp. 260–64.
[73] Ibid., pp. 265–66.

Robbie began a curious new practice when he was in his trances. He would be reading from something like a blackboard that responded to information asked by the priests at earlier moments. He indicated that he (the devil) would leave in ten days and that his name was Satan himself. He also made threats concerning his salvation and that of the priests.[74]

Robbie asked to be baptized Catholic (when he was not in his trance), and his parents decided to let him be baptized in the religion of his choice. On April 1, as he was being driven by his relatives to College Church—where he was to be baptized and receive Holy Communion—Robbie fell into a trance and became unmanageable. He started by saying, "So, you are going to baptize me! Ha! Ha!—And you think you will drive me out with Holy Communion! Ha! Ha!" At this point Robbie's behavior became quite violent. He had to be held down by two men in the back seat, while his aunt drove. At one point, he leaped up and seized his aunt, who was driving. The struggle persisted so that it was impossible to bring him into the church. It was decided to bring him to the third floor of the rectory. He resisted so violently that the men were almost unable to get him there.

The Baptism was not an easy matter. Every time Robbie was asked to say the Creed, he would go into a trance. Father Bowdern found a short form of the Creed, and Robbie was able to say this at one point when he remained normal. When he was asked to renounce Satan, he would go into a trance. Finally, Father Bowdern found an opening of normalcy, to which Robbie stated, "I do renounce him." Prior to the Baptism proper, Robbie erupted with the greatest violence ever. Every time Bowdern began the rite—"Ego te baptizo in nomine Patris"—Robbie would fall into a trance; but eventually, Father Bowdern was able to accomplish it.

The priests resumed the Rite of Exorcism, to which Robbie responded with his usual violent rages and cursing.

On April 2, Robbie exhibited enough normalcy to go through a conditional confession, after which the priests decided to give him his first Holy Communion. A particle of the Host was placed on his

---

[74] See ibid., pp. 268–70.

tongue, but he spat it out five times, over two hours. Finally, they decided to pray a Rosary to Our Lady of Fatima, after which Robbie finally swallowed the particle of Holy Communion.[75]

Father Bowdern was now joined by another priest, Father John O'Flaherty—and they drove Robbie back to his relatives' home. Though there were three men in the back seat with Robbie, he was in a state of rage and fighting throughout the trip. Once home, Robbie came downstairs, and when asked to return to his room, he rushed toward the cross and reliquary, to do damage to them, but Father O'Flaherty caught him in time. The violence began again, and Robbie fell into a trance. Father Bowdern asked in Latin, "Dicas mihi nomen tuum, et horam exitus tui finalis." ("Tell me your name and the hour you will finally exit.") Robbie seemed to understand the Latin, and each time he was asked, he responded with the curse "No!" or by a laugh of ridicule.[76] Eventually, the word "GO" appeared above Robbie's groin, as it did on the first night of the exorcism. Then as Father Bowdern persisted, saying, "Tell me the time of your exit," three parallel scratches appeared on Robbie's right thigh, and then the words "at horam" ("at the hour") and then an "X" was branded.

The next day, Robbie had some intermittent moments of peace, but when he fell into a trance, his violent tantrums and cursing would continue, with attempts to destroy religious objects, the light in the room, and so forth. Since Robbie's father had missed so much work and the strain on Robbie's St. Louis relatives was becoming arduous, it was decided that the family would return to Maryland, along with Fathers Bowdern and Van Roo, to continue the Rite of Exorcism there. At this point in his diary, Father Bishop made special note of the nine Jesuits who were official witnesses to paranormal activity and Robbie's possession: Reverend George Bischofberger, Reverend Raymond J. Bishop, Reverend Joseph Boland, Reverend William S. Bowdern, Reverend Edmund Burke, Reverend John O'Flaherty, Reverend William Van Roo, Mr. Walter Halloran, and Brother Albert Schell.[77]

---

[75] See ibid., pp. 271–74.
[76] See ibid.
[77] See ibid., pp. 275–76.

Exorcism events at the family home in
Cottage City, Maryland (after April 4)

Robbie was normal on the train going to Maryland on April 4. When the group arrived the next day, Robbie returned to his family home in Maryland. Father Bowdern contacted Father Hughes (the priest who started to perform the failed first exorcism). He was willing to help Fathers Bowdern and Van Roo, but could not offer a place at St. James Church for the exorcism due to lack of space. Father Bowdern did not want to return to Robbie's home, and so contacted several hospitals, churches, and health institutes, but no one was willing to accept him, given the extenuating circumstances of the exorcism, so Robbie remained home.

After two days of relative peace, Robbie fell into a five-hour trance on April 7. Twenty scratch marks and branding appeared all over of Robbie's body—the number "4", a pitch fork, four scratch marks, and claw marks appeared on his belly and legs. Robbie went into violent tantrums with cursing and filthy talk about priests and nuns, and then would break into singing the "Ave Maria"—as if two personalities were fighting within him. This continued on the evening of April 8.

Father Bowdern and others decided to return to St. Louis because the Alexian brothers had graciously offered a place on the fifth floor of their hospital, where the exorcism could proceed. There were accommodations for violent psychiatric patients, in case Robbie should need them.

Exorcism events at the St. Alexius Hospital
in St. Louis (after April 9)

The train ride on April 9 from Maryland to St. Louis was quite peaceful, and so also was the check-in at the St. Alexius Hospital. Robbie was at peace throughout the remainder of April 9 and the following day. On the evening of April 10, Robbie received Holy Communion and sank back into his pillow in a state of peace. Robbie remained at peace throughout the day of April 11, but at about 9:00 P.M. he felt a sting on his chest. This was followed by a much sharper pain and a branding on Robbie's chest that spelled the word "EXIT". The same word reappeared three different times on Robbie's body, with an arrow pointing toward his groin. Robbie cried, suffering from very painful urination and severe pain in his kidneys.

At around midnight, the priests prepared Robbie to receive Holy Communion, but immediately Robbie resisted and the word "HELL" appeared on his chest and thigh. When the priest tried to give Robbie a particle of Holy Communion, he was taken off into a trance and Satan's voice said that he would not allow Robbie to receive it. The priest then tried to administer a spiritual communion (where a person who cannot receive the Holy Eucharist says, "Lord, I wish to receive you in Holy Communion"), but every time Robbie came to the word "Communion", he was stopped short and could not pronounce it. This led to more violent thrashing, cursing, and foul language throughout the whole night. Robbie would wake to relatively peaceful mornings, but launched into his barking, swearing, spitting, thrashing, and foul language in the evening. This continued for two days with the voice of Satan saying, "I will not let him receive Holy Communion."

These events led to Holy Week (Holy Thursday, April 14, through Holy Saturday, April 16). Robbie was quite peaceful during these days; he received Holy Communion and was able to watch the Easter services on the Catholic television channel.[78]

However, on Easter Sunday (April 17) events took a turn for the worse. When the hospital chaplain came to give Robbie Holy Communion, he would not receive it. He then leaped out of bed, grabbed one of the Alexian brother's breviary (liturgical book) and scapular (a monastic garment symbolizing the pledge to Christian life), and proceeded to trample the scapular underfoot in an Indian war dance. In the evening, Robbie again went into a trance and began to fight viciously. The devil tried to assert his power by showing he could make Robbie say various things. After the prayers of exorcism, Robbie calmed down, so the priests left.[79]

Easter Monday was to be the final day of Robbie's possession—his liberation from the demons who had occupied his body. When Robbie awoke, he was in a fighting mood. He would not receive

---

[78] See ibid., pp. 283–84.
[79] See ibid., pp. 284–85.

Communion—not even spiritual communion. Satan spoke from within him, saying that Robbie would have to receive spiritual communion nine times before he would leave, but he (Satan) would never allow him to do it—and would never allow Robbie to say the word "Communion", during the prayer for spiritual communion. Robbie then leaped out of bed, threw a bottle of holy water at the wall, threw a plate of chipped beef and other objects at the Alexian brothers, and also taunted the brothers.

Father Bowdern, Father Bishop, and Father O'Flaherty came in the evening and made some adjustments to the Rite of Exorcism. They decided to ask for the responses to be in English, then put a crucifix in Robbie's hands. As the exorcism proceeded, something very different began to happen. First, when Robbie came out of his trance states, he would revert immediately to prayer—and would recite the words for spiritual communion on his own. When he was forced back into a trance, he reported seeing light—as if at the end of a tunnel—as he went into the trance. With each later trance, Robbie reported seeing more light, and he became more reverent when he came out of the trance.

At 10:45 P.M., something truly extraordinary occurred. Robbie went into another seizure but remained calm. Father Bishop reported the following:

> In clear commanding tones, and with dignity, a voice broke into the prayers. The following is an accurate quotation: "Satan! Satan! I am Saint Michael, and I command you, Satan, and the other evil spirits to leave the body in the name of Dominus, immediately.—Now! NOW! N O W!" Then there were the most violent contortions of the entire period of exorcism, that is since March 16. Perhaps this was the fight to the finish.[80]

In a later interview with Father Halloran, the exit of the demon was quite forceful:

> I was taken off [of the case] five days before the conclusion, but from what I understand there was a very loud sound, a boom—sort of like

---

[80] Ibid., p. 289.

a sonic boom—and then the boy opened his eyes and said St. Michael came and that it was over. At the same time this took place there were about six or seven priests over in the college church saying their office, and there was a huge boom over there and the whole church was completely lit up. Father Bowdern, who was doing the exorcism, and the boy were at the rectory. There was a very, very bright light that lit up the whole church.[81]

The following day Robbie was perfectly normal. He participated in Mass for the first time since his possession (and also his conversion), received Holy Communion, and prayed ten Rosaries, in thanksgiving for his liberation from the devil. Several checks have been made by staff members of the exorcists, as well as Thomas Allen, who discovered that Robbie grew up to be a very healthy, responsible family man. He has no recollection of anything that happened to him from January 15, 1949, to April 18, 1949.

3. A Psychiatric Assessment of the Facts behind the Robbie Mannheim Case

Terry Cooper, Ph.D., a psychologist with doctorates from Vanderbilt University and Saint Louis University, and Cindy Epperson, a doctoral fellow at the University of Missouri, have done a thorough psychological review of the facts behind the Robbie Mannheim case and concluded that they cannot be explained by psychological interpretation alone.[82] Aside from the large number of paranormal activities—ranging from levitation, dozens of cases of psychokinesis, and the hundreds of scratches and brandings on Robbie's body, which have no known physical cause, to Robbie's awareness of Latin—Robbie's behavior does not fit any known psychological disorder. Several psychological explanations have been offered, but Cooper and Epperson rule them out for a variety of reasons.

The first psychological explanation offered is dissociative identity disorder (formerly known as multiple personality disorder [MPD]), where an individual splits into several different personalities, in order

---

[81] Brown, "Interview with Priest".
[82] See Cooper and Epperson, *Satan, Sin, and Psychology*.

to cope with a traumatic experience.[83] Cooper and Epperson discount this explanation for three reasons:

> The manifestation of Robbie's second satanic personality completely disappeared when the exorcism was complete. This does not occur in MPD where the only solution appears to be long and tedious therapy to reintegrate the personality and cope with the trauma.[84]

> MPD is linked to ongoing abuse during childhood. Investigation into Robbie's background indicates no such abuse.[85]

Prior to the possession beginning on January 16, 1949, there was no evidence of other personalities manifest in Robbie's life, which would have been expected if he had MPD.[86]

Another psychological explanation offered for Robbie's behavior is schizophrenia. As Cooper and Epperson indicate, schizophrenia is more of a shattered personality, instead of a split one. This shattering causes hallucinations, delusions, and other kinds of psychotic behavior. It is now thought to be a brain disorder that can be resolved by antipsychotic medication.[87] The important point, say Cooper and Epperson, is that schizophrenia cannot be resolved without antipsychotic medication; therapy alone will not resolve the disorder.[88]

There are three problems with diagnosing Robbie as a schizophrenic:

1. Robbie was thirteen years old—too young for the onset of schizophrenia, which occurs between seventeen and twenty-five.
2. When Robbie was not in a trance state, he remained coherent, indicating that he did not have a break with reality, which occurs during schizophrenia.
3. Robbie was completely cured on April 18, 1949 (after the exorcism) without antipsychotic drugs and/or psychotherapy.[89]

---

[83] Ibid., p. 28.
[84] See ibid.
[85] See ibid.
[86] See ibid., p. 29.
[87] See ibid.
[88] See ibid.
[89] See ibid., pp. 29–30.

A third psychological explanation suggested is to describe Robbie's behavior as Tourette's syndrome, a psychological disorder in which a person manifests a tic as well as outbursts, cursing, and other inappropriate expressions. This explanation is also inadequate for two reasons. Firstly, although Tourette's can explain Robbie's cursing and blasphemous outbursts, it cannot explain the violent rages, the repulsion to holy water and sacred objects, and the harmful acts done to those who participated in the exorcisms (e.g., acts done to Father Hughes, the Alexian brother, and Halloran). Secondly, it cannot explain the paranormal activity mentioned above. Tourette's syndrome does not simply go away; it is treated with counseling and medication.[90]

A fourth psychological explanation for Robbie's behavior is sexual abuse by Robbie's aunt Harriett. Aside from the fact that there is no evidence for this, Cooper and Epperson note, "Sexual abuse is unfortunately quite common in our society. How often do we see symptoms such as the ones displayed by Robbie?"[91]

A fifth psychological explanation for Robbie's behavior is group hysteria, but as Cooper and Epperson note, there were forty-eight witnesses to the paranormal activity and violent rages of Robbie who were spread out in many places in Maryland and St. Louis. Were all of these groups collectively hysterical?[92]

Other suggestions have been bipolar disorder and substance abuse disorder, but these suggestions do not describe Robbie's behaviors or frame of mind. In view of all this, it seems highly unlikely that Robbie's behavior, and the paranormal activity accompanying it, can be explained by psychological or psychiatric paradigms. In view of the paranormal activity and the evil manifest by the second personality, there is need to make recourse to a transphysical and transpsychological explanation such as an evil spirit or an evil demon.

Craig Isaacs has provided a general set of norms to distinguish psychologically explicable phenomena from phenomena requiring a transphysical and transpsychological explanation (i.e., a spiritual explanation).[93]

[90] See ibid., p. 30.
[91] Ibid.
[92] See ibid., p. 31.
[93] See Isaacs, *Revelations and Possession*.

IV. What Are the Causes of Possession and Why Does God Allow It?

There are two main causes of possession—either opening oneself to the demonic or being cursed by someone who has opened himself to the demonic. Let us take each cause in turn.

With respect to the first, how does one open one's soul to the demonic? By choosing to be in league with evil spirits or demonic powers (e.g., fallen angels), to obtain preternatural knowledge, power, and/or control of other people. With respect to preternatural knowledge, people may make use of a ouija board, séance, mediumship, divination, automatic writing, or a spiritualist, to obtain knowledge about the dead, future events, and others' thoughts. Sometimes these practices are nothing more than parlor games or fraudulent practices. However, if these practices really attempt to make contact with the dead or to conjure spirits or demons, and they are repeated, they can open the door to an evil spirit or a demon appearing in three ways:

1. In a place, which could cause a haunting or infestation
2. In the oppression of a person or a group of people
3. In a possession, where a demon (or demons) enters into a person's body for the purpose of tormenting him and the people around him

With respect to gaining preternatural (magical) power and control over other people, people may join satanic groups, engage in satanic rituals, sign a blood pact with the devil, and procure amulets and talismans from magicians for magical power.

The Christian Church does not distinguish between white and black magic, because consorting with spirits and preternatural powers for the purpose of gaining knowledge or power that God does not give us—or intend to give us—is dangerous. It leads us away from Him and toward the source of illicit knowledge and power—spiritual evil. We are given natural knowledge and power by God, and sometimes divinely inspired knowledge and power when God so ordains it, but when we try to obtain such knowledge and power on our own—independently of the will of God for the sake of aggrandizing ourselves and gaining control over others—we open ourselves to the demonic; for this is precisely what demonic beings do—seek power and knowledge independently of God, gain illicit dominion and power over others, and aggrandize themselves through means other than the ones given by God.

There is a price to pay for such illicit power and knowledge—one must subject oneself to the demonic power that bestows them. This is why all forms of magic and consorting with spirits who bestow magical power is unconditionally prohibited in the Bible (see Deut 18:10–12), quoted above in Section III.B.1.

The first case given above—Julia—fits the above profile perfectly. She voluntarily entered into satanic rituals for the sake of magical knowledge and power, which she used. She ultimately became possessed by the demons who bestowed these powers on her. The case of Robbie Mannheim is more difficult to understand because his aunt Harriet introduced him to the ouija board—and its magical powers. When she died, Robbie, almost innocently, used the ouija board to contact her. There can be no doubt that Robbie used occult means to gain knowledge from and connection to spirits of the dead— which opened the door to the demonic. But why did God allow an innocent use of this occult practice to take control over a thirteen-year-old boy? I will attempt to answer this after looking at the second cause of demonic possession—being cursed by someone who has opened himself to the demonic.

Several of the demonic possessions mentioned (but not fully described) above—for example, Latoya Ammons, Anna Ecklund, and some of the cases mentioned in Matt Baglio's *Rite*—were the result of being cursed by a person who consorted with spirits and demons. First, it should be mentioned that cursing an individual—or asking a witch or warlock to do so—opens the person asking for the curse to demonic oppression and even possession. The first to be cursed is the one who curses—or asks others to do so. All rituals used to make a curse invite demonic power into one's own life as well as the person who is cursed.

Yet it must be asked why God would allow a person to curse another person with demonic oppression or possession. After all, if God did not allow it, demonic oppression and possession would be impossible even for Satan. The simple answer is—free will. Inasmuch as God wants human beings to love one another voluntarily (not because of a predetermined program), He has to allow us to initiate actions that are unloving—even hateful and evil. Thus, God allowed Hitler and Stalin to cause incredible evil and suffering to millions of individuals—for without this possibility, we would never be able to love one another freely; our love would not come from our initiative or will, but only from God's. If we cannot choose to do anything other than love, our love is not our own.

The fact is, the price of love is the *possibility* of doing evil—not just individual evil, but mass murder, mass torture (e.g., the concentration camps), and, yes, cursing someone to be oppressed by an evil spirit. We can cause torments of similar magnitude by using purely natural means. Thus, the only difference between tormenting a person by natural means or cursing them with possession or oppression is that the latter uses spiritual (preternatural) power.

It is very important to note here that possession that comes from being cursed does not result in sin, because cursed persons are blameless for the evil cast upon them. Thus oppression and possession (coming from a curse) cannot endanger the soul of the victim. A demon can take possession of only a person's body—not his soul. It can manifest itself through that body and block the manifestation of a person's true soul and personality, but it cannot invade the soul, undermine it, or destroy it. Thus, cursing cannot affect the soul or the salvation of another any more than a whip or an instrument of torture.

It is also important to note here that when a demon is not manifest, the normal personality of the victim emerges—showing forth the same soul that was present prior to the possession. In virtually all cases of possession, the victim does not remember anything about what happened to him during the time the demon was manifest. For example, Robbie Mannheim remembered nothing about his long ordeal with the demon and the exorcism. He went on to develop into a mature adult, raised a family, and is now presumed to be living peacefully on his own. Similarly, the children of Latoya Ammons as well as many of the victims recounted in Matt Baglio's *Rite* and in Leon Cristiani's *Evidence of Satan in the Modern World* had virtually no recollection of what they had said and done when the demon manifested itself. Evidently, God protects the victims of possession and oppression from memories of the torments that they and their families had to endure.

So why does God allow a person to be possessed or oppressed through the curse of another? Because we have free will—and as such, we can misuse that free will to bring evil upon others by natural or spiritual means. This is the price we must pay for free will and true love.

We are transphysical (spiritual) beings through the grace of God, and as such we can be divinely inspired and led as well as make recourse to spiritual evil. If we choose the latter, we must remember that we subject ourselves to the evil we use to torment another. If a person opens himself to evil or even Satan in order to curse another, he is responsible for the evil done to himself and the other, and unlike the victim of the curse, his actions are sinful and gravely endanger his soul. If he becomes possessed, his exorcism will be more difficult than that of an innocent victim because he has cooperated with evil—while an innocent victim has not. Inasmuch as exorcists use the will of a victim to help break the spell of an evil spirit, an innocent victim will cooperate with the exorcist completely, while one who has cooperated with evil will have a mixed state of consciousness. This mixed state makes exorcism a more difficult and daunting endeavor.

Let us now return to the case of Robbie Mannheim, who seemingly became possessed by innocently following the lead of his aunt Harriet. Robbie's possession arose out of the free action of his aunt Harriet to teach him spiritualism. She herself must have felt the presence of evil and oppression in her spiritualistic practice, but persisted in it anyway—presumably because of the power and knowledge it gave her. When she taught Robbie how to conjure spiritual entities and use spiritual powers, she must have known that she would create a devotee of spiritualism, which would also subject him to its ominous and dark side. Why would she have done this? To have a companion in spiritualism? To have a companion after she died? It is hard to say. She may not have intended Robbie to be subjugated by a demonic power (to be cursed), but she initiated the possibility of this by introducing him to a practice that had this potentiality.

God created us as spiritual beings with free will. Inasmuch as we have free will and we are spiritual beings, God gives us the capacity to connect ourselves to either spiritual good or spiritual evil—and even to cause spiritual good or spiritual evil to others. Thus, He allows us to consort with evil so that we might freely choose Him. He allows us to dedicate ourselves to evil so that we might freely choose to dedicate ourselves to Him; He even allows us to curse another with evil so that we might freely choose to bless others with His grace. The price of choosing love, blessing, and goodness is allowing us to choose their opposites.

Even if a person tries to do *spiritual* harm to another through a curse, he cannot. God will not allow a demon to invade anyone's *soul*—only the body. Furthermore, after exorcism, God protects the victim by taking away recollection of what occurred during the possession. When a formerly possessed person dies—and even when a possessed person (whose possession was not his fault) dies—God will take that person to Himself if he calls upon the mercy of God with sincerity of heart.

Can any good come out of oppression and possession (beyond the necessary consequence of God creating us as spiritual beings with free will)? Absolutely. In the case of Robbie Mannheim, Robbie converted to Catholicism and became a fervent believer through his ordeal. Ultimately, so did his parents. The people around Robbie—including the two Lutheran ministers, Father Hughes, and the eight Jesuits—were challenged to deepen their faith to deal with Robbie's crisis. Finally, it must be acknowledged that the publication of the diary of the exorcism—and even William Peter Blatty's rendition of it in *The Exorcist* movie (though partially undermined by the Hollywood glitz)—has done some good. It has made people aware of the presence, nature, and tactics of spiritual evil, and has caused some of them, who are aware of the real incidents underlying Blatty's fictionalized account, to consider seriously the need for deeper prayer and virtue, to counsel others about the dangers of occultism, and to engage on the side of God against cosmic evil. There is an enormous good that comes out of oppression and possession. They always seem to galvanize individuals and groups to connect more closely with God and to join Him in creating a world of deeper and more authentic love that will endure throughout His unconditionally loving eternity.

V. How Does Possession Take Place?

We can now answer the remaining question: "Why can't a demon possess the soul of a human being?" In brief, a demonic spirit or angel cannot take possession of our transphysical soul because it is the domain in which God makes His home within us—the domain in which He makes His sacred presence felt. Recall from our discussion of the numinous experience (Volume II, Chapter 1, of the Quartet) that we experience this sacred presence as empathetic, mysterious, and inviting. We inferred from this that the soul is the domain in which God makes contact with us, the place where He resides within us. Hence, He will not allow any evil spirit to coexist with Him in His sacred place. Moreover, evil spirits would find His sacred place quite repulsive. The soul is a sacred sanctuary, and evil is prohibited from entering it by the mere fact of God's presence, goodness, and love.

Recall also from our discussion of consciousness (Volume II, Chapter 6, of the Quartet) that self-consciousness (ego) is intrinsic to our transphysical souls. Since demons are prevented from entering the soul, and self-consciousness is intrinsic to the soul, demons are also prevented from entering or possessing our self-consciousness (though they can block our self-consciousness temporarily when they manifest themselves). Furthermore, God protects our self-consciousness so that we might remain free to choose good or evil, love or unlove, worship of Him or worship of ourselves. Since this freedom is essential to our self-definition and eternal destiny, God protects its source—our self-consciousness.

So where does possession take place if it cannot occur in our souls or self-consciousness? It must take place in our bodies—that is, our physical brain and the sensorial systems to which it is attached. It can also take place in those areas of our psyche that are not directly affected by our souls or self-consciousness—the *unconscious* dimension of our psyche.

The psyche is the arena in which emotion, desire, and imagination interrelate. Some desires, and their associated feelings, are generated by the body (e.g., desires for food, shelter, procreation, and nurturing), while other desires, and their associated feelings, are generated within the transphysical soul by God (e.g., feelings of and desires for the transcendent, the spiritual, and the sacred, as well as for perfect truth, love, justice, goodness, beauty, and home).

The psyche has a conscious and an unconscious dimension. The conscious dimension is aware of being influenced by various desires, feelings, and images, but the unconscious dimension is not. Instead, the psyche assigns symbolic status to them (either learned symbols or innate archetypal symbols).[94] The unconscious psyche presents and projects these symbols and symbolic narratives to the conscious mind through nocturnal dreams, and sometimes daydreams.[95] These dreams can be interpreted by standard techniques of dream analysis.[96]

As noted above, demons cannot take possession of our self-consciousness—and therefore cannot take possession of the conscious part of our psyche. Hence, they can take only partial possession of the unconscious part of our psyche (as well as our bodies, our physical brains). This explains why the vast majority of possessed people go into deep trances when a demon manifests itself.

Demons can influence the unconscious part of the psyche through the desires and feelings generated by the body—and also through nonsacred symbols and archetypes (e.g., archetypes of the devil, the shadow, the monster, and the trickster—and other archetypes of domination, darkness and sexual power).[97]

In order to make the distinction between psychological illness and demonic possession, it will be useful to understand the source of psychological illness. It so happens that psychological illness also has its origins in the same domain as demonic temptation, suggestion, oppression, and possession. It comes from the brain, particularly from the images, desires, and feelings arising out of our embodiment—and also, from the unconscious part of our psyche, which makes use of bodily images, desires, and feelings, as well as innate archetypes, some of which are counterpoised to the sacred and the good (e.g., archetypes of the devil, the shadow, the monster, and the trickster).

For Isaacs, the ego (self-consciousness) and the special powers of the soul—that recognize truth, goodness, and love in their ideal form

---

[94] This archetypal theory, which is manifest by the use of a set of common archetypes and symbols by children throughout the world in their dreams and unconscious projections (e.g., imaginary playmates and boogey men), was first articulated by Carl Jung as a response to Freudian dream analysis. See C. G. Jung, *The Archetypes and the Collective Unconscious*, in *Collected Works of C. G. Jung*, vol. 9, pt. 1, trans. R. F. C. Hull (Princeton, N.J.: Princeton University Press, 1981).

[95] See Isaacs, *Revelations and Possession*, pp. 96–97.

[96] See Ann Faraday, *The Dream Game* (New York: Harper & Row, 1990), p. 3. See also Jean Dalby Clift and Wallace Clift, *Symbols of Transformation in Dreams* (New York: Crossroad Publishing, 1984).

[97] See Jung, *Archetypes and Collective Unconscious*.

from God—hold the key to distinguishing between psychological illness and demonic obsession and possession. They also hold the key to distinguishing between authentic revelations of God (say, from a mystic) and psychological illness. We have already discussed this above in Chapter 1, Section II.

VI. Conclusion

The power of spiritual evil is not the end of the story—indeed, it is not even the beginning of the story. It is an aberration of God's plan that poses a significant threat to us and our free will, but it is not an overwhelming threat. Let us return to our previous discussion in the Quartet and this Trilogy about some of the major ways in which God manifests Himself and acts in our lives:

God's *interior presence* to us in the numinous experience; the intuition of the sacred; conscience; and the five transcendental desires (Volume II, Chapters 1, 2, and 4, of the Quartet)

The *power, guidance, inspiration, and protection of the Holy Spirit*, given by Jesus to the Church and each baptized person (Chapter 1, Section I of this volume)

God's *extraordinary presence* to us in visions, mysticism, and acute consolations (Chapter 1, Sections II and III of this volume)

Public apparitions (with scientifically validatable miracles) concerned with Mary, the saints, and the Holy Eucharist (in the appendix to this volume)

Though spiritual evil can make itself felt, God also makes Himself felt within the constraints of our free will. He modulates His felt presence to conform to our needs, our free will, and His guidance and plans for us, and if we participate in the Church, engage in daily prayer, and try to follow His moral teaching, He will help and guide us through any influences, temptations, and deceits to which Satan (and his minions) can subject us. Furthermore, as explained in the previous chapter, Satan and his demons have been defeated by Jesus in the temptations in the desert, in His ministry of exorcisms, and in His Passion, death, and Resurrection.

Yes, Satan is still active, because God allows him to interact with us through our free will; and He will never prevent Satan from interacting with us because He leaves it to our free choice to pursue temptations and deadly sins, to reject them, or, if we fail, to turn back to Him by praying in trust for His mercy and compassion. The Lord will not allow Satan to overwhelm us. Even though He allows Satan to oppress or even possess some people who intentionally pursue him or the occult, He has provided His apostles and disciples with the power to cast him out, and to erase from our memories every trace of this possession. As noted above, Satan can never possess our souls, or our self-consciousness—he can try to block it only temporarily, because God will not allow it. Yet, even if he does subject people to this form of possession, he has no ultimate power to maintain it—for if the possessed person (or his family) desires it, even Satan himself can be exorcised from the most egregious Satanist. In the end, Satan will be completely banished from the world and the blessed will be protected from him in God's heavenly Kingdom for all eternity. Satan has no hope of winning, and no hope of overwhelming a person of faith.

This does not mean that we should not take the malicious intentions and actions of Satan seriously. He has considerable power and experience to tempt, seduce, deceive, and depress—and his best work is done when he combines all of these things. Thus, we will want to first familiarize ourselves with how he works—his temptations, seductions, deceptions, and discouragements (Chapter 4)—and then familiarize ourselves with the seven deadly sins that corrupt both our senses and our spirits (Chapters 5 and 6).[98] We can then proceed to a discussion of how to resist and defeat Satan through the grace of the Lord given to us by Jesus—the Holy Spirit, the Church, virtue, and prayer (Volume II of this Trilogy). All that remains after this is to refine our understanding of Jesus' moral teaching and integrate this into our conscience and moral practice (Volume III of this Trilogy).

---

[98] Note that an eighth sin, vanity, is discussed in Chapter 5, Section V.

PART TWO

Satan's Tactics:
From Temptation and Deception
to the Eight Deadly Sins

INTRODUCTION TO PART TWO

Though the reader at this point may be somewhat overwhelmed by the reality of evil, we must continue our presentation of the facts about the dark dimension of spiritual reality to complete the "bad news". Recall that forewarned is forearmed. So what does Scripture and the Church tradition teach us about the devil's tactics? We might summarize the many volumes written on these matters from two vantage points:

1. How the Evil One interacts with our psyche—through temptation, deceit, and discouragement (Chapter 4)
2. The eight major ways in which the Evil One seeks to undermine our freedom and corrupt us—called "the eight deadly sins"[1] (Chapters 5 and 6)

If we know how we are likely to be attacked, we will be better prepared to use the many gifts that Jesus has given us to defend ourselves, allowing us to engage in the process of spiritual and moral conversion (explained in Volume II of this Trilogy). This will enable us to heed the advice given by the Pauline author in Ephesians 6:12–18:

For we are not contending against flesh and blood, but against the principalities, against the powers, against the world rulers of this present darkness, against the spiritual hosts of wickedness in the heavenly places. Therefore take the whole armor of God, that you may be able to withstand in the evil day, and having done all, to stand. Stand therefore, having fastened the belt of truth around your waist, and having put on the breastplate of righteousness, and having shod your feet with the equipment of the gospel of peace; besides all these, taking the shield of faith, with which you can quench all the flaming darts

---

[1] Usually, the designation is "seven deadly sins". An eighth sin, vanity, is discussed in Part 2, Chapter 5, Section V.

of the Evil One. And take the helmet of salvation, and the sword of
the Spirit, which is the word of God. Pray at all times in the Spirit,
with all prayer and supplication. To that end keep alert with all perseverance, making supplication for all the saints.

Chapter Four

How the Devil Works

Introduction

As we begin this discussion, it must be remembered that though the Lord respects our freedom, we are not in this struggle alone. His unconditional love is always present to redeem us in our failings, and we always have His Holy Spirit, Church, and Word to guide us out of the darkness. We can help to facilitate His redeeming and guiding love by drawing close to the Church at Mass and in the sacraments—and by deepening our relationship with Him through virtue and prayer. We will give a detailed explanation of these protective graces and strategies in Volume II of this Trilogy.

I. Spiritual Maturity, the Cosmic Struggle, and the Lord's Loving Perspective

For those seeking a way to ultimate happiness, and a way out of cosmic emptiness, alienation, loneliness, and darkness, there comes a time when we must make a decision—first, about belief in God and in His unconditional love (Jesus Christ), and then how to follow His revelation about the path to eternal salvation. As we open ourselves to this path, we might find ourselves somewhat overwhelmed by the teachings of the Lord on how to pursue our moral and spiritual life. This is perfectly natural, and it shows that we have reached the first stage of spiritual and moral conversion: the sincere desire to follow the Lord more nearly, combined with an awareness that we are not quite up to the task. This sense of being overwhelmed should not lead to discouragement, because it is a realistic acknowledgment that we fall far short of the mark. Yet we do not have to reach the mark by ourselves; we have the unconditional love of the Lord, the guidance of the Holy Spirit, and the Church to help us ultimately reach that mark, amid a myriad of failings, in this life and/or the next (through the purification of Purgatory[1]). To abandon this hope is tantamount to disbelieving in the victory of Jesus. Remember, His victory is meant to assure salvation if we sincerely repent for our sins, remain close to the Church, and try as best we can to follow His Word through the Holy Spirit.

Recall also that we have an adversary—the Evil One—who wants nothing more than to discourage us from moving on our chosen path of spiritual and moral conversion, by abandoning hope in the victory of our Lord, Jesus Christ. His primary deception will be focused on *you*, trying to take your focus off of trust in Jesus, and putting it onto *your* shortcomings. As will be discussed in Section V below, he does this by playing the part of the accuser, saying something like, "*You* wretch, look at how far *you* are from living up to the words of Scripture—*your* past sins are so manifold and *your* sanctity so pathetic, *you* haven't got a chance. By the way, God is sick and tired of *you*—pretty ticked and pretty disgusted." Of course, what he fails to mention is that *you* don't have to make *yourself* spiritually and morally perfect; *Jesus* has already anticipated your failings and intends to redeem them all in His unconditional love, if you sincerely avail yourself of His mercy (particularly through the Sacrament of Reconciliation) and try to stay close to His Word through the sacramental life, virtue, and prayer. Your job is to *stay on the path* through trust in Him, participating in His Church, and *trying* to make the little improvements you can in prayer and virtue amid life's challenges. Saints are made, not born, and they are made not by themselves, but by trust in the Lord and reliance on His Spirit and participation in His Church.

The Evil One will try mightily to dissuade us from hoping in the Lord's love and redemptive grace. He comes to a person who is beginning a life of spiritual and moral maturity by disguising himself

---

[1] For an explanation of Purgatory, see Robert Spitzer, "Purgatory", in *Credible Catholic Big Book*, vol. 5, *Central Doctrines of the Catholic Church* (Magis Center, 2017), CredibleCatholic .com, Chapter 9, https://www.crediblecatholic.com/pdf/M5/BB5.pdf.

as an angel of light. He makes suggestions that seem right—for example, "You are very far from sanctity"—but "omits" telling you that Jesus has won the victory for you if you but stay on the path described above. This deceives the spiritual/moral novice into thinking that he will have to get there himself, and that the Lord, like a taskmaster, is commanding him, "Faster, better, harder, and more, more, more." If he persuades the novice that the Lord is this harsh taskmaster, the Evil One can talk the novice out of his newfound path quite quickly and discourage him in the process, unless he remembers that his hope for salvation, and even his hope for spiritual/moral conversion, is assured by Jesus Christ, if he but stays on the path to salvation described above. If we remember this one fundamental principle, stated over and over again in the New Testament, then we can proceed safely on the path to spiritual and moral conversion. We are then on a journey with the Lord, through His unconditional mercy, His Church, and His guidance, inspiration, and protection through the Holy Spirit.

As we proceed on the journey of spiritual and moral conversion, it becomes apparent that we are involved in a struggle between good and evil much bigger than ourselves. Of course this struggle involves our eternal souls, but also the good that we might be able to do for others as our conversion process deepens. There are many signs of this struggle—being overwhelmed by temptations just as we are trying to improve our lives, overwhelmed by deceptions that we later discover were intended to make us lose hope, and caught up in swings between self-righteousness on the one hand and feelings of overwhelming sinfulness on the other. When we look back on these initial stages of our journey, we can see in the extremes of these states another power or presence stoking and enhancing whatever proclivity we might have toward sinfulness or indolence in faith and prayer.

We might also discover inspirations toward love of God, gratitude, and wisdom, particularly the wisdom to know that despite our sinfulness, our job is not to save ourselves, but to stay on the path of salvation as best we can. We might also sense strong inspiration to participate more in the Church, build the Kingdom of God according to the gifts we have been given, and be compassionate to those in need. We might look back on these inspirations too and think to ourselves, "Where did I get all this from? I am not that holy or spiritually wise." Again, we might see another power or presence—this time a good one: the Holy Spirit—stoking and en-lightening whatever proclivities we might have toward staying on the path, building the Kingdom, and making our little improve-ments in prayer and virtue. It might occur to us that we are right in the midst of a spiritual struggle between the Evil One and the Holy Spirit, and may ask, "Why am I so important? Why is the strug-gle focused on me? Surely there must be someone more important for these supernatural forces to be focused on." These questions point to a truth—namely, that we are not the only ones in whom the struggle between spiritual good and evil is focused, because it is focused on *everyone*, particularly on those who are entering into spiritual and moral conversion and its path. The struggle, the battle, is taken to everyone, because each of us has an inestimable, eternal dignity that is completely worthy of fulfillment—or, in the viewpoint of the Evil One, completely worthy of His efforts to undermine and destroy. Yet as we move onto the path of spiritual and moral conversion, we present a much greater potential to help the Lord, and a much greater threat to the Evil One. Since we are at least ostensibly aware of these two supernatural powers, and the tactics they use, they will allow themselves to be manifest in more obvious ways, decloaking themselves and the struggle in which they are involved. At this point, we are drawn into the struggle our-selves, meaning that we will have to fight a little harder to stay on the path to resist temptation, and to contend wisely with deception.

In his *Lord of the Rings*, J. R. R. Tolkien portrays this figuratively and accurately in the ring that Frodo (a seemingly insignificant lit-tle creature, a hobbit) carries around his neck. As he proceeds on his journey (which may be considered an allegory of our journey of spiritual and moral conversion), the ring gets heavier, and when he approaches Mount Doom (the place where the ring and its evil maker, Sauron, can be put to death), it grows so burdensome that it almost overwhelms him. Yet through his desire to accomplish his mission, he always has enough capacity to proceed, with the help of Gandalf (the good wizard who represents, at once, a manifestation of the Holy Spirit and the Church) and his friends, to move closer to Mount Doom and ultimately to success in the mission. The closer Frodo gets to his goal, the more damage he can do to Sauron (the Evil One) and his king-dom, which causes the evil power of the ring to try harder to resist him. Nevertheless, Frodo grows stronger through his resilience on his spiritual journey and, with his friend Samwise Gamgee (who has also developed hugely in his spiritual maturity and strength through his journey with Frodo), manages to get to the top of Mount Doom; with the help of an unseen divine providence, he is able to avoid the last-minute attempt of Gollum (a pathetic creature seduced and corrupted by the ring's power) to stop him. Though Frodo's journey was difficult, the outcome was huge—not only for himself, but for the whole of Middle Earth.

Even though God is sometimes difficult to detect on our spiritual journey, we can know Him by His effects—inspiration beyond our capacity, guidance and protection beyond natural coincidence (revealing His unseen providence), and ever-increasing strength and wisdom in the spiritual and moral life through perseverance and resilience.

This last point merits closer inspection. Jesus speaks frequently about perseverance[2] because it is one of the most important dimensions of spiritual and moral conversion. Once we have reached spiritual and moral maturity and are on the path to spiritual and moral conversion, our progress in great part depends on this one virtue[3] (along with faith, hope, and love). Through six parables,[4] Jesus tells us that if perseverance fails, then all other virtues (with the exception of faith, hope, and love) on the spiritual journey will be virtually disempowered. The very process of staying on the journey resiliently will strengthen our perseverance (like physical exertion can strengthen a muscle) and will build up other virtues—most notably, wisdom, temperance, and faith. It will be worth it; for Jesus tells us that if we stay on the path despite challenges, temptations, criticism, exhaustion, confusion, and suffering, we will not only deepen our conversion, but also will be brought into His Kingdom of eternal love and joy. The point is never to give up on the journey; and if we fail, to turn back to the Lord again in trust and repentance, and get back onto the path as soon as possible—difficult as this may sometimes seem. In this regard, Winston Churchill's speech to the British people when facing

[2] See for example, Lk 8:4–15; 11:5–13; 12:35–40; 18:1–8.

[3] As will be made clear below, perseverance is integral to the virtue of fortitude, one of the four cardinal virtues, and includes not only commitment, "stick-to-itness", and resilience, but also courage and faith.

[4] See the Scripture references in note 2 above.

a seemingly overwhelming Nazi invasion and victory may prove to be edifying:

> Even though large tracts of Europe and many old and famous States have fallen or may fall into the grip of the Gestapo and all the odious apparatus of Nazi rule, we shall not flag or fail. We shall go on to the end, we shall fight in France, we shall fight on the seas and oceans, we shall fight with growing confidence and growing strength in the air, we shall defend our Island, whatever the cost may be, we shall fight on the beaches, we shall fight on the landing grounds, we shall fight in the fields and in the streets, we shall fight in the hills; we shall never surrender, and even if, which I do not for a moment believe, this Island or a large part of it were subjugated and starving, then our Empire beyond the seas, armed and guarded by the British Fleet, would carry on the struggle, until, in God's good time, the New World, with all its power and might, steps forth to the rescue and the liberation of the old.[5]

Though of course this speech was made during a time of world-changing significance, facing an enemy that threatened the entire free world, it shows what the human spirit is capable of when determined to defend itself and to reach its goal—both temporal and spiritual freedom.

Having said all this, we must now return to the three points mentioned above about the path to salvation:

1. Trust in and reliance on the unconditional love of God
2. Participation in the Church (particularly the sacramental life and the gifts of the Holy Spirit)
3. Sincere attempts to make improvements in prayer and virtue

Inasmuch as these three points constitute our role in the path to salvation, they also tell us the means and ends of our acts of perseverance. Recall that our role is not the only dimension of the path to salvation; the Lord is even more active than we are—initiating, complementing, guiding, protecting, supporting, forgiving, healing, inspiring, encouraging, edifying, loving, and fulfilling us on every

---

[5] Winston Churchill, "We Shall Fight on the Beaches", International Churchill Society, June 4, 1940, https://www.winstonchurchill.org/resources/speeches/1940-the-finest-hour /we-shall-fight-on-the-beaches.

level of our being. Thus, if we practice the three dimensions of the path, we unleash tremendous divine forces embedded in the providential conspiracy around us; we cannot help but grow in faith, hope, love, wisdom, and spiritual strength, bringing us ever closer to the eternal destiny promised us through the Incarnation, Passion, and Resurrection of Jesus and the unconditional love of God. Moreover, the more we progress on our path to salvation, the more we will be able to help others on their path to salvation. Let us now briefly consider each of the three dimensions of this path to salvation.

We have explained and developed the underpinnings of the first point—trust in and reliance on the unconditional love of God in Volume III, Chapters 1–3, of the Quartet. We noted there that Jesus changed the momentum of the history of religions by His unique definition of love (*agapē*) in the Beatitudes, the Good Samaritan, and other parables and sayings. Most importantly was His revelation of the Father as "Abba" and "the Father of the Prodigal Son". These teachings revealed not only the supremacy of love over all other virtues, but also the perfection of love in the Father's unconditionally and unrestrictedly compassionate and merciful heart. Yet Jesus did not stop at teaching the Father's unconditional love in words; He concretely proved it, as well as His divine Sonship, by an unconditional self-sacrificial act (His Passion and death). This complete self-sacrifice was not only a proof of the unconditional love of God; it gave birth to an unrestricted loving power or grace capable of outshining and healing human sinfulness. As He noted many times, the only condition necessary for us to receive fully from this infinite forgiving and compassionate love is to sincerely ask for it (see, for example, the prodigal son's petition in Luke 15:21; the petition of the good thief in Luke 23:42; the petition of the tax collector in the Temple in Luke 18:13—all of which resulted in immediate forgiveness and justification).

The Church teaches that in cases of mortal sin, we should avail ourselves of the Sacrament of Reconciliation for absolution. As we shall see, mortal sin has three conditions: grave matter, sufficient reflection, and full consent of the will (no impediments to the free use of the will).[6] Since there are many impediments to our free will,

---

[6] See *Catechism of the Catholic Church* (*CCC*), no. 1857; for a discussion regarding sin overall, see nos. 1850–76.

we must be careful about assuming that grave acts are mortally sinful. As the *Catechism of the Catholic Church* teaches:

> The promptings of feelings and passions can also diminish the voluntary and free character of the offense, as can external pressures or pathological disorders.[7]

This is taken up in detail in Volume II, Chapter 7, Section II.B.

With this proviso in mind, the point of Jesus' teaching is clear. If we sincerely repent for our sins (and avail ourselves of the Sacrament of Reconciliation, as in the case with mortal sins), He will not deny us, but will restore us back to the path of salvation—no matter how grievously we may have offended Him, as did the prodigal son, the good thief, and the tax collector. If we are to stay on the path to salvation, and be restored to it when we have failed, we will want to avail ourselves of this marvelous, beautiful, and grace-filled gift offered to us by our unconditionally loving Father. If we should let this gift slip from our minds for even a short time, we might begin to think that the path to salvation relies on us; but this would be catastrophic—for if we should fail, we would not be able to restore ourselves back to the grace of God by our merits alone. Bearing this always in mind, we proceed to the second point: participation in the Church.

In Volume II, Chapter 1, we will discuss in detail the scriptural and historical evidence validating Jesus' intention to start a Church founded on an ultimate juridical and teaching authority: Peter and his successors. Though some individuals within that Church have fallen into sin and scandal (beginning with Judas, one of Jesus' handpicked disciples), the Church's history testifies powerfully to how the Church maintained unity, developed a cohesive body of doctrine and a rich and varied spiritual tradition, overcame every historical challenge, and grew into the largest provider of healthcare, public welfare, and education in the world (with 1.2 billion adherents).[8]

So how do we participate intentionally in the Catholic faith? Minimally, we will want to find a parish that feeds us and participate in Mass on Sundays; avail ourselves of the Sacrament of Reconciliation

---

[7] *CCC*, no. 1860.

[8] For a complete explanation of this historical and current impact of Christianity, see Volume III, Chapter 5, of this Trilogy.

twice per year; receive the other sacraments; and if married, raise our children within the Church (or if called, to consider religious life and/ or ordination to the priesthood). Additionally, we will want to foster a life of prayer (for ourselves and our families); seek sufficient instruction to ground, defend, and spread our faith; participate in some form of Church service (e.g., teaching, evangelizing, social ministries, spiritual ministries, parish committees, or diocesan committees); and try to influence our community and culture to reflect the principles given by Jesus Christ.[9] These avenues of spiritual/religious conversion are discussed in detail in Volume II (Chapters 1–3) of this Trilogy. The more we participate in the Church and orient our families around her, the more we and our children will grow in faith, precisely as Jesus promises us in the parables of the mustard seed (Mt 13:31–32; Mk 4:30–32; Lk 13:18–19), the wheat and weeds (Mt 13:24–30), the yeast and the flour (Mt 13:33; Lk 13:20–21), and the talents (Mt 25:14–30; Lk 19:11–27). By doing this, we will not only progress on the path to salvation, but also help others to do so. Conversely, we must also take seriously Jesus' warning that if we wane in our participation in the Church, we will be like the man who buried his talent in the ground—we will lose what little faith we have and drift off the path to salvation. Practice does in fact make perfect—and failure to practice leads to continuous diminishment.

The third dimension of the path to salvation is our ongoing effort to make improvements in prayer and virtue, to purify the interior self so that we can more steadfastly resist the temptations and deceits of the Evil One, grow in love and faith, and enter more authentically into the cosmic struggle between good and evil. This is explained throughout the rest of this volume and in Volume II (Chapters 4–7) on moral conversion.

II. Two Common Defenses against Evil

In the last chapter we addressed the presence and power of spiritual evil that Jesus identified as Satan and his demons. We spoke there of

---

[9] There are many good parish programs to encourage this participation, e.g., Intentional Discipleship, Dynamic Catholic, Called and Gifted, and Amazing Parish—to mention but a few.

some of the more extraordinary manifestations of evil spirits, such as possession and oppression; but now it remains to explain the more common manifestations of spiritual evil, such as temptations, deceptions, and desolation. Recall from the previous chapter that Satan and his demons much prefer to remain almost invisible to the ordinary person so that they can introduce their malicious intentions into the sacred domain of human freedom, virtually unnoticed. This gives them considerable sway to plant perverted suggestions of every sort into the human psyche—some intended to seduce, some to deceive, and some to depress—before a person becomes aware of the perversion within the suggestion.

The Holy Spirit actively resists the suggestions of evil spirits, proposing counter-suggestions to those proposed by them. Recall that the Holy Spirit works through human freedom—and will not interfere with it to assure that it remains fully free. Evil spirits also work through human freedom—not because they want to preserve our capacity to choose God and His goodness, but because God forces them to accede to His will.

Before addressing specific dimensions of temptation, deceit, and despair, we should make one important observation—namely, that evil spirits have a much easier task of realizing their dark objectives if they can undermine two common defenses in any of their victims: that is, membership in a church and openness to the full range of rational evidence for a Supreme Being and human transcendence. If any person lacks these two common defenses, he makes himself subject to a large number of temptations, deceptions, and rationalizations that ultimately open upon desolation and despair. We will discuss each natural defense in turn.

Involvement in a church—particularly a Christian church (with the teachings of Jesus) and more particularly the Catholic Church (with its sacramental life and magisterial teaching)—is the first defense against evil spirits, for it allows the Holy Spirit to bring a variety of powerful suggestions to a person's mind and heart to counter the false, egocentric, and dominating suggestions of one's own making as well as those of evil spirits.

Evidently, evil spirits prefer to "work" with people who have no knowledge of either Christian or any other religious or moral teaching. Thus their ideal subjects are those who have no involvement in any church community. These individuals are virtually powerless to counter the suggestions of evil spirits on a conscious or discursive level, and they are left with only a vague sense of conscience (guilt and shame) to counter the suggestions of the enemy. Left to their own devices, they can be persuaded to deny their entire spiritual nature (reducing themselves to mere atoms and molecules), to be led to the extremes of hedonism and egocentricity (reducing themselves to mere pleasure impulses and ego satisfactions), to pursue monetary gain and economic power exclusively (reducing themselves to mere units of capital acquisition and retention), and to pursue political power and status (reducing themselves to mere units of social and political power). Interestingly, all these pursuits of self-reduction, self-limitation, and antitranscendence lead to an unquenchable and unmitigated desire for more power, domination, money, and glory—even to the point where some individuals are willing to deprive others of badly needed necessities, simply to aggrandize themselves with meaningless trophies of an unreflective and unfulfilling life.

For evil spirits, this produces a double "benefit"—the emptiness and despair of the churchless temptee as well as the misery and oppression of the people around him. It will not be easy for the Holy Spirit to urge a churchless temptee to look beyond his self-limitation lying at the root of his restless heart and his neighbor's oppression and misery. Since he lacks religious and moral teaching and community, he will open himself to complete deception—becoming convinced that his self-limitation is really true freedom, the denial of his spiritual nature is authentic realism, his tyrannical pursuit of academic, economic, political, and other status is the height of human meaning and purpose, and his indulgence in unmitigated sensorial pleasure is for fulfillment of his true nature. At this point, he is likely to fall into a state of confusion, meaninglessness, and desolation. As will be discussed below, nonreligiously affiliated individuals are much more likely than religiously affiliated individuals to experience meaninglessness, depression, impulsivity, aggressivity, substance abuse, and familial tensions, leading to increased suicides (according to the American Psychiatric Association's 2004 study[10]).

[10] See Kanita Dervic et al., "Religious Affiliation and Suicide Attempt", *American Journal of Psychiatry* 161, no. 12 (December 2004): 2303–8, http://ajp.psychiatryonline.org/doi/abs /10.1176/appi.ajp.161.12.2303.

If we try to persuade this convinced temptee that he is teetering on the brink of meaninglessness and despair because of false assumptions about his nature and freedom by presenting a few sage passages from Aristotle's *Nicomachean Ethics* or a few passages from the New Testament, he is likely to produce either a confused look or more probably a defensive reaction—"How dare you suggest that *my* life is somehow superficial, unreflective, self-limiting, and oppressive to others—you're just jealous of my successes. Who cares about those ancient Greek philosophers anyway; they didn't even have the Internet much less the latest apps."

If we are to penetrate this extensive superficial defensive bulwark, we will have to return to fundamental principles, reason, and logic so that we can show the preponderance of evidence in favor of God, a transphysical soul, and Jesus Christ. If we can establish the likelihood of these transcendent realities, the temptee may see his former position as superficial and self-limiting, inciting him to take the next step: the pursuit of a Christian church and a life of virtue.

This is precisely what we have attempted to do in Volumes I–III of the Quartet (on the rational and scientific evidence for God, a transcendent soul, and Jesus Christ, as well as the true fulfillment coming from transcendent happiness). Given the potential efficacy of using reason to establish the reality of transcendence and the need for a Christian church, we can expect that evil spirits will also try to undermine reason, suggesting that truth is impossible, logic is mere mental machination, and higher universal concepts are mere mental fictions. Since these suggestions are difficult for a reasonable-minded person to affirm, an evil spirit will likely use omissions of pertinent data (instead of outright factual errors or lies) to convince a temptee to abandon reason. Recall that there are far more errors of omission than commission.

Reason urges us not to ignore or categorically exclude *anything* that can be assessed by empirical, logical, or interior evidence, such as philosophical proofs of God, legitimate scientific evidence of a beginning, peer-reviewed medical studies of near-death experiences, contemporary scientifically validated miracles, scientifically validated elements of the Shroud of Turin, historical arguments for the veracity of the Resurrection, the thousands of cases of reported human and evil spirits, the religious experiences of mystics and the common man—or any other accessible piece of evidence. We do not need to have perfect access to or understanding of particular data to incorporate them into a holistic vision of reality. Indeed, ignoring such evidence because of imperfect access or understanding is very likely to result in a partial or imperfect view of ourselves, of ultimate reality, and of our true dignity and destiny.

Imagine what would have happened if Einstein said that he had an imperfect explanation of the Michelson-Morley experiment, and so excluded it from his worldview. We would have never moved from Newtonian physics to special general relativity. The same holds true for the evidence of such things as metaphysics, spiritual entities, post-mortem experiences, and interior religious experience. Imperfect understanding almost never equates to unreality.

We introduced C. S. Lewis' *Screwtape Letters* in the last chapter. Recall that "the patient" in the passage is a man who is considering conversion, and the "enemy" is the Holy Spirit and the Church. Uncle Screwtape, the experienced demon advising his nephew Wormwood, advises the following with respect to reason and science:

> The trouble about [reasonable] argument is that it moves the whole struggle onto the Enemy's [Holy Spirit's] own ground. He can argue too; whereas in really practical propaganda of the kind I am suggesting [focusing a person on a stream of consciousness or sensory data] He [the Holy Spirit] has been shown for centuries to be greatly the inferior of Our Father Below [Satan]. By the very act of arguing, you awake the patient's reason; and once it is awake, who can foresee the result? Even if a particular train of thought can be twisted so as to end in our favour, you will find that you have been strengthening in your patient the fatal habit of attending to universal issues and withdrawing his attention from the stream of immediate sense experiences. Your business is to fix his attention on the stream. Teach him to call it "real life" and don't let him ask what he means by "real".... Above all, do not attempt to use science (I mean, the real sciences) as a defence against Christianity. They will positively encourage him to think about realities he can't touch and see. There have been sad cases among the modern physicists. If he must dabble in science, keep him on economics and sociology; don't let him get away from that invaluable "real life". But the best of all is to let him read no science but to give him a grand general idea that he knows it all and that everything he happens to have picked up in casual talk and reading is "the results of modern investigation".[11]

[11] C. S. Lewis, *The Screwtape Letters* (New York: MacMillan, 1943), pp. 12–14.

In view of the above, it is essential for everyone who wishes to avoid the temptations, deceptions, and desolation coming from ourselves or evil spirits to seek out a Christian church, particularly the Catholic Church, and to affirm the efficacy of reason. Failure to do this will be tantamount to fighting a well-prepared enemy with both hands tied behind one's back.

We might begin with a brief explanation of a point made in the previous chapter—namely, that evil spirits must work within the confines of human freedom. They cannot overwhelm, suppress, or destroy human freedom, because this would make a human being into a robot incapable of being responsible for his actions. This would of course defeat Satan's plan to have us *choose* evil, darkness, and even Hell. Furthermore, God would not allow Satan to undermine His plan of creation and redemption. God created us in His own image and likeness, with self-reflectivity, conscience, spiritual awareness, and freedom, and He is not about to allow Satan to undermine these qualities on a grand scale. Furthermore, God anticipated our fall and our inclinations to pursue the empty pleasures, egocentricity, and self-worship promoted by Satan, and He has actualized His plan of redemption in the world through His Son. As such, He means to assure that human beings have the freedom to choose this redemption, and so will not allow Satan to undermine it.

III. A Brief Explanation of Human Freedom

Human freedom can be explained by the transphysical dimension of our self-consciousness' inner world enabling us not only to grasp ourselves, but to choose the powers and desires that will ultimately define the "self" we grasp. In Volume I (Chapters 1–5) of the Quartet, we explained how we are confronted from childhood by two fundamental options:

1. The option to aggrandize ourselves, and to possess others and the material world (Level One-Two happiness)
2. The option to pursue relationships with God and others, and to submit to the requirements of conscience and empathy/love (Level Three-Four happiness)

We make the choice of self-definition over the course of time, and we can change our minds along the stages of life's way. But through the course of choices and many changes, a preferred pattern begins to develop, and when it does, we begin to define ourselves, our essence—toward either the first option or the second. These choices and their cumulative effect on our self-definition is the most important dimension of our lives, for it will ultimately determine who we are and what we will become for an eternity.

Recall also (from Volume II of the Quartet) the substantial evidence for our transphysical souls from the medical studies of near-death experiences; the five transcendental desires; the phenomenon of self-consciousness, giving rise to David Chalmer's "hard problem of consciousness" (see Chapter 6); Gödel's Theorem; and the human capacity for syntactically meaningful language and conceptual ideas. This evidence reveals twelve capacities of the soul that are inaccessible to artificial and animal consciousness:

1. The capacity for conceptual ideas, allowing us to have abstract thoughts, syntactical control, and conceptual language
2. The desire for perfect truth, enabling us to recognize all imperfections in our knowledge and causing us to ask questions indefinitely until we reach perfect truth (the knowledge of everything about everything—complete intelligibility)
3. The recognition of the spiritual-sacred-numinous-transcendent reality (God), causing fascination, worship, awe, and obedience, which draws us into a deeper relationship with Him, bringing us to His transcendent, eternal, and sacred essence
4. The desire for perfect home, enabling us to recognize the imperfections of our worldly existence and causing us to pursue the sacred and its source until we have reached our perfect home
5. The capacity for empathy, which recognizes the unique goodness and lovability of the other and creating the desire to care about and care for the other even to the point of self-sacrificial love
6. The desire for *perfect* love, enabling us to recognize all imperfections in love and causing us to pursue deeper and more authentic love until we have reached perfect love

7. The capacity for moral reflection, originating from conscience, which is God's moral presence to our self-consciousness

8. The desire for perfect justice/goodness, enabling us to recognize all imperfections in justice/goodness (in groups, organizations, and community) and causing us to pursue more perfect forms of justice and the common good until we have reached perfect justice/goodness

9. The capacity to appreciate and be filled by the beautiful in nature, music, art, architecture, literature, intellectual ideas, love, and goodness and causing us to seek ever greater forms of beauty until we reach perfect beauty-majesty-splendor itself

10. The desire for *perfect* beauty, enabling us to recognize all imperfections in beauty and causing us to pursue ever greater beauty until we reach perfect beauty itself

11. The capacity for free will, self-consciousness' orientation toward either *itself* or toward others and God (in goodness and love)—explained below

12. The transphysical (transmaterial) dimension of the human soul, enabling us to survive bodily death (evidence from peer-reviewed medical studies of near-death experiences)

When these capacities are understood properly, there can be little doubt about the truth of the proclamation in Genesis that God has made us in His own image and likeness (1:27).

So how does free will operate? It arises out of a combination of several of the capacities of our transphysical soul and God's presence to it. At the center of free will is our capacity for self-consciousness enabling us to create our own inner world, indeed, to create our own moral essence. When God gave a transphysical soul to the first human beings, and to all subsequent human beings, He not only bestowed on them the capacity for self-awareness and self-definition; He also gave them the other capacities mentioned above. Key among these are empathy, conscience, and the awareness of Him (the spiritual-sacred-numinous-transcendent reality). This gave a *fundamental option* to human beings: to orient their thoughts and actions either toward *themselves*, their inner world (self-centeredness or egocentricity), *or* toward *Him* (in worship and prayer), *others* (through empathy and care), and the *good* (through conscience). Sometimes these two options are consistent with one another, but frequently they are opposed.

From the time we reach the age of syntactically significant language, we embark on a journey of increasing rational reflectivity, which, in turn, empowers our free will. As such, we become increasingly more aware of our two fundamental options: our desire for God, love (relationship with others), and goodness or our counter-desire for material comfort, ego satisfaction, and self-aggrandizement.

Our first parents succumbed to the temptations of Satan and chose the weaker self-referential option; and when they did, they fell and God withdrew some of His overwhelming presence to us, causing us to see Him "through[12] a glass darkly". In Christian theology, this is called "the fall" and "original sin".[13] The fall did not incapacitate us—for our desire for God, the good, and love is still slightly stronger than our desire for self-aggrandizement, domination, and possession. Nevertheless, the result of the fall was a significantly weakened state (that the Church calls concupiscence).[14]

Christ has overcome the effects of concupiscence, but we must still avail ourselves of the redemption He wrought by participating in the sacraments, the Church, praying, and cultivating virtues to counteract vice. The Holy Spirit will help us to do this, but the Evil One will do everything in his power, through temptation, deceit, and desolation, to prevent us from staying on this course of redemption.

Despite the fall, we are still free—free to choose lower goods (Levels One and Two) as well as the self-referential option, or higher goods (Levels Three and Four) of serving God, others, and the good. The following illustration may help to show how self-consciousness mediates between our desires for ego satisfaction, bodily pleasure, and material possession on the one hand, and our desires for the higher transcendental goods—perfect truth, love, goodness, beauty and home—on the other.

---

[12] See ibid.

[13] For an explanation of original sin in light of contemporary science and anthropology, see Robert Spitzer, "Free Will and Original Sin", in *Credible Catholic Big Book*, vol. 2, *Evidence of Our Transphysical Soul* (Magis Center, 2017), CredibleCatholic.com, Chapter 7, https://www.crediblecatholic.com/pdf/7E-P1/7E-BB2.pdf.

[14] For a contemporary view of concupiscence and its alleviation see ibid.

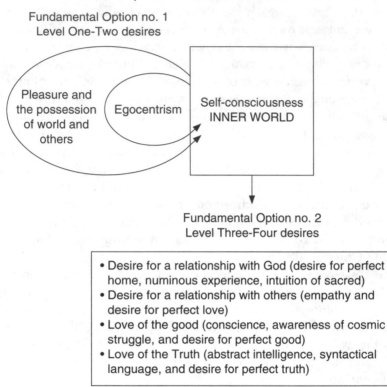

HUMAN FREEDOM
Which option and desires do I want more?

Fundamental Option no. 1
Level One-Two desires

Pleasure and the possession of world and others

Egocentrism

Self-consciousness
INNER WORLD

Fundamental Option no. 2
Level Three-Four desires

- Desire for a relationship with God (desire for perfect home, numinous experience, intuition of sacred)
- Desire for a relationship with others (empathy and desire for perfect love)
- Love of the good (conscience, awareness of cosmic struggle, and desire for perfect good)
- Love of the Truth (abstract intelligence, syntactical language, and desire for perfect truth)

IV. Temptation

Temptation can be viewed in a completely secular sense—the forsaking of higher long-term goals for the satisfaction of temporary strong urges (e.g., sensorial, libidinal, or egocentric urges). The classical virtues of temperance (self-control) and fortitude (committed and courageous drive toward long-term goals) counteract these kinds of temptations. Valid though this view is, we are looking at temptation in a decidedly spiritual way—through the lens of Jesus' teaching about Satan, his demons, and the cosmic struggle between good and evil. In this context, temptation has both a moral and spiritual significance as well as a significance for pursuing our highest long-term goals through virtue and prayer.

A. How Temptation Works

Temptations can originate from within ourselves, through demonic suggestion, or both. Frequently enough, we enter into situations that we know will present challenges, frequently called "the near occasion of sin"; it should not be surprising to us that these actions lead to the engagement of aberrant desires, which in turn can lead to a choice to satisfy them, giving rise to vice or sin. When we intentionally enter into situations that we know will engage aberrant desires, demonic influence is minimal. All that is required of them is to encourage the sinful action. Sometimes when we are consciously trying to avoid the near occasion of sin, we find ourselves besieged by dozens of images that seem to be drawing us into a sinful situation that we are not voluntarily pursuing. These images and thoughts are meant to engage our desire for one of the eight deadly sins: gluttony/drunkenness, lust, greed, anger, envy, sloth, vanity, and pride (see Chapters 5 and 6). The cause of this barrage of unwanted images and concepts is very likely a demonic spirit. Whether a temptation originates from within us alone or from an evil spirit, the process that occurs before we choose to act on it is generally the same. It includes four major steps:

1. A sensory or mental image capable of engaging an aberrant desire comes to our consciousness.
2. We let our desires be engaged by the aberrant sensory or mental image.
3. We entertain the aberrant desire over against the possibility of saying no to it.
4. Once the lower desire has gained momentum, we choose to act on it (instead of acting on higher desires).

All temptations begin with an image, a picture thought. These "picture thoughts" may come from a sensorial perception or the remembrance or reconstruction of a past picture thought (what we normally call "conceiving"). Whatever the origin, these picture thoughts stimulate (arouse) particular desires within us.

Most philosophers would agree that desire is one of the most difficult human characteristics to explain, for it is more complex than a stimulus-response mechanism. True enough—all of our desires have a fundamental receptivity to stimuli. When a stimulus is received, it creates an impulse or drive toward action, but it does not necessarily result in action. Every human desire can be contravened by a rational reflection process that determines that a particular action is good for us or bad for us—good in the long term or bad in the long term; good for our ultimate purpose and fulfillment or bad for our ultimate purpose and fulfillment; and so forth.

The recognition of the "good" does not come from a sensorial or imaginative stimulus, but rather from a reflection process that includes the movements of conscience, empathy, transcendental desires, and God, and compares them with other apparent goods from our senses, imagination, subconscious, and desire for ego fulfillment. If a potential action is self-destructive in the long term, it is conceptually judged as inferior, and for those who attend to their conscience and religious sensibilities, it is viewed as "bad" or "evil". Conversely, if a potential action is likely to bring about higher satisfaction, meaning, and fulfillment in the long term, it is judged to be superior, and if it is consistent with the movements of conscience and religious sensibility, it is viewed as "good".

What Aristotle called "rational desire" is more than the reflection process that determines the higher good. This reflection process is also connected to a desire to *do* the good. Thus, rational desire receives a stimulus from a practical reflection process (that determines the higher good) and produces an impulse to act on the higher good. This impulse from rational desire can contravene the impulse to move a lower desire into action. Alternatively, the lower impulse (from sensorial or ego desires) can contravene the rational desire for the higher good. When this occurs, our self-consciousness (ego) must choose between the lower desire (with its immediate and intense satisfactions) and the higher desire (with its less immediate and intense satisfaction, but greater meaning, fulfillment, and contribution).

There are other factors involved in this "battle of lower and higher desires" beyond the ones mentioned above. Some of them favor the lower desires, such as bad habits (to act on lower desires), stresses, fatigue, bad influences from peers, and psychological disorders (ranging from neurosis to psychosis, schizophrenia, bipolar disorder, multiple personality disorder, and so forth).

As we have seen, some factors favor higher goods, such as conscience, empathy, and the graces coming through faith. If we give emphasis to rational desire, conscience, empathy for others, virtue, and faith (through sacraments and prayer), we will likely resist spontaneously acting on lower or evil desires and will likely choose virtuous desires and higher goods.

Let us return for a moment to the four major steps in temptation, whether these come from self-initiation, an evil spirit, or both. How can we use our four higher powers (rational desire, conscience, empathy, and faith) to resist temptation and choose the higher good?

The reader may already have intuited part of the answer—namely, the earlier we bring our four higher powers to the process of fighting temptation, the more likely we are to resist it and to choose a higher good. So, for example, when an aberrant sensory or mental image comes to consciousness, we should engage our four higher powers before we engage our lower desire, the desire to which the sensory or mental image is oriented. If the combination of rational desire, conscience, empathy, and faith can take the center stage of our consciousness, they will effectively prevent engagement of the lower desire. However, if we are slow to engage our four higher powers, either because we ignore them or put them off, then we allow the image to engage our lower desire and we enter into temptation's enticement. This leads to entertaining the temptation, but we have another chance to bring the four powers to bear. Unfortunately, this time it will be harder to break the spell of temptation because we are already enticed. If we again ignore or put off our higher powers, and entertain the lower desire, we allow it to grow stronger and more powerful, leading to an almost inevitable path to action. We could, of course, bring our four higher powers to bear at the last minute, but it will be very difficult to break the spell of temptation because we have allowed the lower desire to grow into a Goliath.

B. Three Cardinal Virtues

The Church Fathers and medieval philosophers[15] recognized that three of the four cardinal virtues—prudence, temperance, and fortitude—could be brought to bear on the process of fighting temptation.[16]

---

[15] See Saint Augustine, *De Moribus Ecclesiae Catholica (The Morals of the Catholic Church)*, 1, 25, 46: PL 32, 1330–31; and Saint Thomas Aquinas, *Summa Theologica* II-II, q. 47, a. 2.

[16] See Saint Augustine, *De Moribus Ecclesiae Catholica*, ed. Philip Schaff, trans. Richard Stothert (self-pub., CreateSpace, 2015), 1, 25, 46: PL 32, 1330–31.

Prudence is first in importance because it enables us to differentiate between evil desires and good desires—and between lower goods and higher goods. We might say that the virtue of prudence guides our rational desires and our conscience to their proper ends—the higher or highest good. We will discuss how to make this practice a habit, a virtue, in Volume II (Chapters 4–6) of this Trilogy.

Temperance is the ability to say no to an evil or lower desire. As might be suspected, it is more than just saying no. It is the discipline of bringing our four higher powers (rational desire, conscience, empathy, and faith) to the forefront of consciousness as quickly as possible when we feel ourselves drawn into temptation by a particular sensorial or mental image. This requires that we be aware not only of our four higher powers, but also of how to use them to fight temptation. It also requires being alert to when a particular stimulus or condition is about to engage our lower desire and move us toward a regrettable action. Hence, we need to practice (to the point of creating a habit—a virtue) the following:

1. Recognizing lower stimuli that could lead to sin
2. Bringing our four higher powers to the forefront of consciousness to resist these lower stimuli
3. Disciplining ourselves to use our four higher powers as quickly as possible before the lower desire gains strength

Notice that the realization of these three dimensions of temperance is a free choice—and the continual practicing of them (to make them a habit) is also a free choice. Over the course of time, a habit (a virtue) will be formed that makes *choosing* the good easier and less consumptive of psychic energy, for we have made temperance "second nature" (i.e., a habit), allowing it to emerge *naturally* from our psyche when temptation occurs. We will discuss both spiritual and psychological techniques for encouraging this process (and habit) in Volume II (Chapters 5 and 6).

Fortitude is the commitment and courage to move toward the highest good in the pursuit of our ultimate and intermediate objectives. We might say that it goes in the opposite direction of temperance. Where temperance says no to evil and lower desires, fortitude is saying yes to good, Godly, and higher desires. As with temperance, fortitude is dependent on prudence—for we must be able to distinguish between evil and good desires (lower and higher) and to commit ourselves to the good and higher desires. Fortitude, like temperance, builds on our four higher powers, which moves us to avoid lower desires in favor of good, Godly, and higher ones. For example, rational desire takes reason's discernment of lower desires and brands it with a sense of "waste of my time", "underliving my life", and "beneath myself". It also takes reason's discernment of higher desires and brands it with a sense of "great use of my time", "optimizing my life's purpose", and "worthy of my time and energy". Similarly, the power of conscience brands evil actions with deep feelings of shame and guilt—while branding good actions with feelings of honor and nobility. Empathy brands actions that are hurtful to others with a sense of guilt, self-alienation, and regret—while branding actions that are good for others with a sense of bonding, higher purpose, and self-respect. Faith imbues evil actions with a sense of shame, regret for disobeying the loving Creator, and guilt—while imbuing good actions with feelings of being at home with the Creator and loving the Creator.

Philosophers have long noticed that feelings transform thoughts into actions. Thinking alone results in a conceptual judgment, but in order to transform this reasonable conceptual judgment into action, there must be an emotion—a feeling—that has the power to move us to action. Rational desire is imbued with the emotions to shun lower desires and love higher desires. Conscience not only recognizes the difference between evil and good actions; it also is imbued with feelings of guilt and shame toward evil actions, and feelings of honor and nobility toward good actions. The same holds true for empathy and faith. Thus our four higher powers not only conceptually recognize the difference between evil/lower desires and good/higher desires; they imbue those concepts with negative feelings to move us away from evil or lower desires, while imbuing good/higher concepts with positive feelings that move us toward the higher good. We might adduce from this that temperance cultivates and makes habitual the prompt use of negative feelings attached to evil or lower actions, while fortitude cultivates and makes habitual the prompt use of positive feelings attached to good or higher actions.

The more we grow in temperance (cultivating and making habitual the prompt use of negative feelings toward evil and lower desires), the more proficient we will become at resisting temptation, because we will be able to bring the feelings associated with the four higher powers strongly to bear on our decision process when an evil, destructive, or lower stimulus comes into our purview. We will have habitualized our aversion toward evil or lower desires before engagement takes place—or at the very least, before we begin to engage the desire.

The more we grow in fortitude (cultivating and making habitual the prompt use of positive feelings toward good and higher actions), the more we will empower consciousness to move committedly, resiliently, and courageously toward good and higher objectives— even in the most difficult of times. Though it seems like temperance is more important in resisting temptation than fortitude (because it mitigates evil or lower desires), subsequent reflection reveals that fortitude is just as important—because our love of the good drives us to our true end, which gives purpose to temperance's negative feelings. It is not enough to say no to evil or lower desires; we want to imbue our rejection of those lower desires with the noble reason and purpose for doing so—namely, to reach our highest meaning, dignity, and fulfillment. When we combine the negative feelings of temperance with the positive feelings of fortitude, we empower our rejection of the former with the rationale and purpose of the latter.

So what is the task that lies before us to help us resist temptation and pursue our ultimate and eternal purpose in the perfectly good and loving God? We will need to cultivate several disciplines, all of which will be discussed in Volume II (Chapters 4–6):

- To grow in *prudence*, which involves two steps:
  1. Understanding the difference between our lower and higher desires (Level One-Two happiness versus Level Three-Four happiness; see Volume II, Appendix I)
  2. Cultivating our four higher powers (rational desire, conscience, empathy, and faith) to grow in love of their effects (and the God who causes them)
- To grow in *temperance*, which involves cultivating and making habitual the prompt use of the negative feelings (intrinsic to our four higher powers) toward evil or lower desires

- To grow in *fortitude*, which involves cultivating the positive feelings and desires (intrinsic to our four higher powers) and habitualizing bringing these feelings and desires to bear quickly and strongly when temptation presents itself

As noted above, the detailed consideration of these three disciplines will be the subject of Volume II (Chapters 4–6). For the moment, suffice to say that the process of promptly recognizing and mitigating temptation (the enticement of evil or lower desires) can be greatly assisted by learning how to recognize and use our four higher powers (rational desire, conscience, empathy, and faith) in three distinct ways that philosophers past and present have identified as the virtues of prudence, temperance, and fortitude. This means that we will have to engage in long-term preparation to cultivate the above three virtues to hasten and strengthen our short-term response to temptation. Long-term concerted preparation leads to quick and effective short-term resistance to temptation.

C. How the Evil One Tailors Temptation for Each Individual

Satan does his homework—he seeks out the vices to which we are most prone, the virtues that are least developed, the times and conditions in which we are most vulnerable, and any deep resentments we might have toward God, the Church, or any moral authority such as parents and teachers. In his Fourteenth Rule (in the "Rules for Discernment of Spirits") in *The Spiritual Exercises*, Saint Ignatius of Loyola describes the tactics of the Evil One as follows:

[The Evil One] behaves as a chief bent on conquering and robbing what he desires: for, as a captain and chief of the army, pitching his camp, and looking at the forces or defenses of a stronghold, attacks it on the weakest side, in like manner the enemy of human nature, roaming about, looks in turn at all our virtues, theological, cardinal and moral; and where he finds us weakest and most in need for our eternal salvation, there he attacks us and aims at taking us.[17]

[17] Saint Ignatius of Loyola, *Spiritual Exercises*, trans. Elder Mullan, S.J. (New York: P.J. Kenedy & Sons, 1914), p. 90.

If we are to resist the temptations of Satan better, we will want to first study his techniques, and then with self-knowledge deduce his likely plan of attack for someone like us. The well-known military adage "Forewarned is forearmed" is applicable here. If we know how the Evil One is likely to attack us, we can prepare a strategy through virtue and prayer to resist him. As noted above, there are four major components that the Evil One considers when preparing his specific plan of attack for us:

1. The vices (eight deadly sins) to which we are most attracted
2. The virtues that are the weakest—or least developed
3. The times and conditions in which we are most vulnerable
4. The resentments we might hold toward God, the Church, or any moral authority (e.g., parents or teachers)

Let us consider each in turn. In Chapters 5 and 6, we will describe and explain each of the eight deadly sins—interior negative attitudes or vices—that undermine faith, hope, and love within us, and so impede our movement toward eternal salvation. They are gluttony, lust, sloth, greed, anger, envy, vanity, and pride.

It is not unusual for us to have propensities toward more than one deadly sin. Frequently, these stronger propensities are connected with our level of happiness/purpose in life (see Volume II, Appendix I, of this Trilogy). For example, if we are dominant Level One, we might expect that gluttony, sloth, greed, and to some extent lust would be our strongest vices (negative interior attitudes). If we are dominant Level Two, we might expect that anger, envy, vanity, pride, and to some extent lust would be our strongest vices. These propensities are frequently combined with perceived lacks or deficiencies during our childhood and adolescence. So, for example, if we negatively interpret, say, low economic status of our family during our youth, we will have a strong propensity toward greed. Similarly, if we negatively interpret our parents' dietary prescriptions during childhood, we may pursue a lifetime of compensation through gluttony. Again, if we negatively interpret our adolescence as being unattractive to the opposite gender, we may attempt to compensate for it by becoming romantically involved with everybody who shows an interest in us (lust). If we felt deprived of prestige and power, then we likely will pursue prestige and power—and so forth.

Another factor that is particularly relevant in this culture is the availability of stimuli in three of the deadly sins—gluttony, lust, and greed. The fact that these stimuli are easily available (e.g., fast food, free Internet pornography, and convenient online mail-order consumer goods), and that they help people with significant stresses and challenges to forget their problems, assures that many will avail themselves of them continuously. Hence, we have the cultural phenomenon that many have addictions not only to food, alcohol, and drugs, but also to pornography and shopping! These kinds of addictions seem to start as a type of self-medication for stressed, depressed, and bored dispositions, but they soon get out of hand because more and more stimuli is required to manage the same level of stress. This leads not only to distraction from higher desires and long-term contributive purpose, but also to craving for and obsession with the stimuli where one doesn't even recognize higher levels of desire and responsibilities beyond the self. As the obsession grows, families are undermined, work performance is diminished, personal growth is stunted, and conscience and empathetic connection are minimized.

The above three inducements—dominant Level One and Two happiness/purpose, perceived lack of fulfillment as children/adolescents, and easily accessible and addictive satisfaction of sensorial desire—are fertile ground for the Evil One. Anyone who has a combination of these susceptibilities to temptation can expect a barrage of imaginative suggestions and temptations from him. This is generally accomplished by suggesting past satisfactions through a particular vice, introducing new possibilities of the satisfaction of that vice, and then suggesting a myriad of ways that the vice can be satisfied quickly and easily—for example, "bring a cocktail to lunch", "just turn on your computer and search for the free stuff", "take some time after work to join friends at the bar", "a shopping trip to the mall will help you feel better."

As noted above, the Evil One can be greatly assisted by a lack of religious conviction, church membership, moral knowledge, and moral conviction. He can also be assisted by a dominant Level One-Two identity and considerable stress and challenge in one's work and family. Individuals with these characteristics are unlikely to be successful in resisting his temptations, because they have no moral or religious reason to resist them—and they need the satisfaction of these vices to fulfill their dominant Level One–Two desires, their perceived unfulfilled yearnings in the past, and their need for self-medication. This group might be considered "low-hanging fruit" for the Evil One, because they are easy "long-term converts" to his self-destructive way of life—and with very minor prompting, he can lead them to a lifetime addiction of selfishness, darkness, undermining of work and family, and in the end, resentment and despair.

As may now be evident, the above group is very susceptible to temptation, self-destruction, and the subversion of others; however, there are other groups that are likely to fare much better because of church membership, religious conviction, and development of the above three virtues *prudence, temperance,* and *fortitude.* We might begin our assessment of these other groups by offering the following principle: the stronger and more developed our religious conviction, our four higher powers, and our virtues of prudence, temperance, and fortitude, the more likely we will be to resist the temptations to the eight deadly sins and the destruction of self and others coming from them.

For Christians, this resistance to the deadly sins enables us to love more deeply, which in turn leads us to eternal salvation and helps us to lead others to their salvation. Thus, the life of church commitment, virtue, and prayer not only protects us from self-destruction and subversion of others in the short term; it also leads to our and others' salvation for all eternity.

We might here suggest a ranking of the path—from the least proficient to most proficient, to a positive and productive life in this world and ultimately to eternal salvation in the unconditional love of God:

- Lowest level—least proficient for reaching a positive, generative, nondestructive, loving life in this world and in the next. This is the group described above—no religious affiliation, little spiritual conviction, little awareness of the destructiveness (to self and others) of the deadly sins, little awareness of the four higher powers, and little development of the virtues of prudence, temperance, and fortitude. These individuals are likely to hit "rock bottom", forcing them to make a radical change in their lives or submit to emptiness, despair, and possibly self-destruction.

These individuals are described quite well by several protagonists in Shakespeare's tragedies: Macbeth, Iago, Richard III, and
King Lear (see Chapters 5 and 6).

- Low intermediate level—some possibility of resisting habitual attachment to one or more deadly sins, and the self-
  destructiveness and subversion of others coming from them.
  This group generally has a weak (underdeveloped) commitment
  to religious affiliation and may also have a vague awareness of
  the four higher powers and the destructiveness of the deadly sins
  as well as an elementary development of the above three cardinal
  virtues. This elementary development of virtue and prayer will
  prove vital to these individuals when the destructiveness of a life
  imbued with the deadly sins becomes painfully obvious. If they
  are to move beyond the destructiveness (to self and others) of
  the deadly sins, they will have to strengthen their commitment
  to virtue, which will probably entail a strengthening of religious
  affiliation and spiritual commitment.

- High intermediate level—reasonable likelihood of resisting
  habitual attachment to deadly sins, leading to a life of continuously improving virtue and love opening upon eternal salvation.
  This group has a high degree of commitment to God and religion, and as a consequence, they have an adequate awareness
  of the dangers of the deadly sins, a striving for more authentic
  love, and a basic awareness of the virtues and how to use them
  to resist temptation. These individuals are committed to God
  and interior moral conversion, but this conversion needs to be
  deepened; so they will not want to let their guard down and
  open themselves to temptation, rationalization, and submission
  to one or more deadly sins.

- The highest level—strong likelihood of resisting habitual attachment to deadly sins, leading to a life of continuously improving authentic love and virtue opening upon eternal salvation.
  This group not only has strong religious affiliation and spiritual commitment—they are also well aware of the dangers and
  destructiveness of the seven deadly sins; they have committed
  themselves to a life of virtue and prayer, leading to proficiency
  in prudence, temperance, and fortitude motivated by their faith,
  deep empathy for others, and a well-developed conscience.

The general path to moral conversion (awareness of the destructiveness of deadly sins and commitment to and proficiency in virtues for the sake of God, love, and others) frequently occurs through religious affiliation and commitment, which imparts at once an awareness of eternal and transcendental destiny, the spiritual world, the centrality of love, the destructiveness of the deadly sins, and the importance of virtues to mitigate those sins.[18]

Though religious conversion is frequently central to moral conversion, it need not always be so. There are many nonreligious individuals who take seriously Level Three contribution to others and experience deep empathy for those challenged and unfortunate. Evidently, they have deeply appropriated a Level Three purpose and identity (contribution and love), but not a Level Four purpose (faith and transcendence). The major reasons for not making the transition include the following:

- Growing up without any experience of religion or religious involvement
- Doubts about the rationality of God and transcendence (though these doubts, as Volumes II and III of the Quartet make clear, are unfounded)
- Growing up in a religious household that portrayed God as terrifying, angry, disgusted, or indifferent (which, as Volumes III and IV of the Quartet make clear, is not a proper conception of God according to Jesus Christ)
- Having the inability to reconcile suffering with a loving God (which is redressed in considerable detail in Volume IV of the Quartet)
- Having conviction that religion has caused more harm than good throughout history (which, as Volume III, Chapter 5, makes clear, is erroneous)

---

[18] According to Friedrich Heiler, the vast majority of religions promote some degree of all these good disciplines and habits. (The seven major positive dimensions of religions are summarized in Volume II, Chapter 1, Section I of the Quartet.)

See Friedrich Heiler, "The History of Religions as a Preparation for the Cooperation of Religions", in *The History of Religions*, ed. Mircea Eliade and J. Kitagawa (Chicago, Ill.: Chicago University Press, 1959), pp. 132–61.

Christian revelation, particularly within sacramental life of the Catholic Church, has the most highly developed conception and practice of these disciplines and habits (see Volume II, Chapter 1).

- Having a conviction that religion is naïve and mere wishful thinking (which is controverted by the scientific and rational evidence presented in Volumes II and III of the Quartet, as well as contemporary scientifically validated miracles described in the appendix to this volume and the interior presence of God to our consciousness discussed in Chapter 1)

As we have explained, it is impossible to disprove the existence of God by rational or scientific means, because it is methodologically impossible to do using empirical evidence, a priori evidence, scientific evidence, and logic.[19]

As noted above, those who do not have a religious and transcendent component in their lives can be deeply contributive and empathetic. Nevertheless, they are likely to feel cosmic emptiness, loneliness, and alienation, as well as the negative dimensions of nonreligious affiliation reported by the American Psychiatric Association in a study—increased meaninglessness, bouts of depression, suicides, impulsivity, aggressivity, substance abuse, and familial tensions.[20] Furthermore, they are unlikely to be aware of the reality of spiritual evil and the challenges it presents to the moral life. They are also unable to make recourse to prayer, grace, and theological teaching, to help them in their moral and ethical lives.[21] Finally, though these individuals can be deeply committed to the virtue of love, they frequently lack objective moral principles (conveyed by religion), tending instead to use emotivism and personalism as a foundation for ethics. This makes deeper moral conversion, beyond empathy and feeling, quite difficult.

These individuals constitute a subgroup within the second major group listed above, but they have no religious conversion and may have a deeper moral conviction than many in the second group. Since this Trilogy is directed to those open to faith (and who are willing to study the evidence in support of it) and to those who are able to

[19]See Robert Spitzer, *New Proofs for the Existence of God: Contributions of Contemporary Physics and Philosophy* (Grand Rapids, Mich.: Eerdmans, 2010), Chapter 6.

[20]See Dervic et al., "Religious Affiliation and Suicide Attempt".

[21]See the study in the following, showing that religious people are much less likely to act on an unethical impulse at the time that decisions are made: K. Praveen Parboteeah, Martin Hoegl, and John B. Cullen, "Ethics and Religion: An Empirical Test of a Multidimensional Model", *Journal of Business Ethics* 80, no. 2 (June 1, 2008): 387–98.

call upon faith, prayer, and the grace, guidance, and inspiration of
the Holy Spirit to support their moral lives and contend with the
Evil One, we will restrict our remarks only to the abovementioned
four groups, without making special mention of the nonreligious,
contributive/empathetic group. Helping these individuals to pursue
deeper moral conversion without recourse to religion, grace, prayer,
and religious teaching is beyond the scope of this book.

The Evil One uses different tactics to tempt and deceive each of
the above four groups,[22] and so it would be beneficial to examine
those tactics briefly for each group.

1. The First Group—No Religious or Moral Conversion

Since members of the first group have no spiritual or virtue defenses
against the deadly sins, the Evil One barrages them with multiple
suggestions toward multiple sins in the hopes of habitually attaching
them to a life of narcissism, domination, self-worship, self-indulgence,
and depravity. The Evil One's "hope" is to disguise the emptiness,
alienation, and loneliness arising out of this life of depravity by providing false consolations and "ego boosts" coming from sensuality, self-importance, and worldly status. He continues to do this as
long as possible to "secure the victim's allegiance", to prevent him
from repenting at the last minute, and to convince him ultimately to
choose Hell rather than Heaven (persuading him that Hell is where
he will find true happiness, and that Heaven is not worth the bother).

The victim will manifest behaviors and attitudes revealing his interior restlessness and discord, which others are likely to recognize long
before the victim. Many of these behaviors and attitudes are elucidated by the American Psychiatric Association's study mentioned
above.[23] Though the victim may recognize that something is missing
or wrong in his life (which may be manifest by severe emptiness,

---

[22] See the division between the first week and the second week in Saint Ignatius of Loyola's
"Rules for the Discernment of Spirits" in his *Spiritual Exercises*. The Evil One's tactics for the
first week (what we would call groups one and two) are direct and strong images and suggestions to continue in a life of habitual attachment to one or more of the deadly sins; however,
his tactics for those in the second week (what we would call groups three and four) are more
tricky—aimed at rationalization, deceit, and discouragement in times of suffering. See Saint
Ignatius of Loyola, *Spiritual Exercises*, pp. 84–94.

[23] See Dervic et al., "Religious Affiliation and Suicide Attempts".

nightmares, and free-floating anxiety), he does not associate the cause of these feelings with a lack of love, virtue, or communion with God. Instead, he treats his symptoms with increases in sensorial stimulation—both healthy (e.g., traveling, socializing, and nature) and unhealthy (e.g., alcohol, drugs, and trysts). He might pass by a church and feel compelled to go in (inspired by the Holy Spirit—which could have remarkable remedial effects), but the victim generally resists it. The longer the victim has given himself over to his life of habitual attachments to the deadly sins, the more he is likely to resist the Holy Spirit's inspirations to seek God and repentance. The Holy Spirit never stops providing inspirations and clues (e.g., from friends, colleagues, and television programs) to turn his life around, but in the end, the victim must *choose* to respond to these inspirations with an act of sorrow and a commitment to religious/spiritual affiliation. Evidently, the Evil One will do everything possible to convince the victim that the urgings and inspiration of the Holy Spirit are nonsense, weak, naïve, and likely to produce "unhappiness". As virtually every saint would say, this is a dangerous life that is superficial and meaningless, teetering on the brink of despair and the choice of eternal darkness.

2. The Second Group—Weak or Tepid Religious and Moral Conversion

The Evil One changes tactics for group two. Recall that even though this group has religious affiliation as well as an awareness of love and virtue, their religious affiliation is restricted and weak, and their awareness of love and virtue unrefined, inarticulate, and almost unconscious. The Evil One means to keep them precisely in this weakened and inarticulate condition. His first tactic is to "help" the victim to forget that commitment to a church (and its moral and spiritual life) is primarily concerned with relationship and communion with God, who has created him and called him to Himself. This causes the victim to shift his attention during church services from authentic communion with God (praying for his needs, expressing his sorrows, giving thanks, and giving praise) to "getting something out of it" or being "entertained". If the victim shifts his focus completely, he will leave church services complaining about boredom, poor preaching, and poor music (which may be the case); but he will be completely unaware of the fact that during the entire proceeding—including reception of the Holy Eucharist—he never once repented, expressed a need, or gave thanks or praise to his Creator and Redeemer. Church services were not about cultivating a relationship with God, but only about his regret and resentment for not having received enough. At this juncture, the victim may choose to search for another church where he can be better fed and connected with God—or he might give up worship altogether and settle for a Sunday morning filled with greater opportunities to obtain information and be entertained.

For group two, the Evil One focuses on rationalization, because their weakened spiritual state makes them susceptible to it. Rationalization can pave the way for a deep entrance into the darkness by justifying the satisfactions coming from the deadly sins. However, like all the protagonists in Shakespeare's tragedies, the former euphoric elation and satisfaction coming from the deadly sins turns into a departure from faith, authentic love, and integrity, which leads at once to emptiness, alienation, loneliness, and guilt as it undermines the lives of others and relationships with them. As we shall see, the deadly sins undermine faith and authentic love—no matter how innocent or satisfying they first appear to be; and when they do this, they destroy both self and others, undermining virtually every relationship.

When I was in a scriptural exegesis class at Harvard Divinity School, I sat next to a student who was thinking about going to seminary. I asked him where he went to church services, and he told me he no longer did so because the sermons were not very intelligent and the services were boring. He then went on to indicate that this led to an ongoing dilemma in his life—"Every Sunday morning, I get a Sunday edition of the *New York Times* on my doorstep, causing me to choose between it and church services; unfortunately, the *New York Times* always wins." I thought to myself that this was an incredibly brilliant tactic on the part of the Evil One. Here he had a victim who had enough religious affiliation to take theology classes at Harvard Divinity School, and even to aspire to the seminary and ministerial service. Instead of barraging him with temptations toward several deadly sins, he used the victim's egocentricity and intellectual pride—in combination with the culture's entitlement philosophy ("You have a right to be entertained and to obtain benefit from everything you do at all times")—to distract the victim from religious services and to weaken

his communion with God. Without this religious/spiritual commitment, the victim was left wide open to rationalize his way into two
deadly sins: spiritual sloth (acedia) and intellectual vanity (see Chapter 5) and pride (see Chapter 6). Acedia is a state wherein the victim
could care less that he does not care about the significance or ultimate
significance of his life, and so he simply follows the path of greatest
stimulation—either sensorial or intellectual—instead of directing his
path to his highest dignity, authenticity, fulfillment, and destiny.

Note here that the Evil One's tactic is not to regress a victim back
to the first group by compelling him to give up his weakened religious
and moral commitment. This could fill the victim with increased cosmic emptiness, loneliness, and alienation, alerting him to the fact that
there is something missing or wrong in his life. Instead, the Evil One
focuses first on keeping the victim in a weakened religious and moral
state by making him feel entitled, distracting him, and then inciting
him to rationalize his weak commitment. This keeps the victim in a
weakened moral state where he can be easily tempted to pursue a life
of egocentricity, intellectual vanity, and the pursuit of status and honors. The "ego boosts" from such a lifestyle are significant indeed and
can mesmerize the victim to such a great extent that he ultimately
forgets about God altogether—opening him to the suggestion that he
can be like "God" for himself and others (see Gen 3:5).

As with the first group, these victims will also experience cosmic
emptiness, loneliness, and alienation along with nightmares and the
other negative dimensions elucidated by the American Psychiatric
Association study—increased suicide thoughts, impulsivity, aggressivity, substance abuse, familial tensions, and bouts of depression.
However, when these negative interior dispositions manifest themselves, the Evil One uses the same three tactics with which he started
his deception—first, entitlement (e.g., "Church services and prayer
are to provide *you* with information and entertainment, not to enter
into relationship with God through prayers of need, forgiveness,
thanksgiving, and praise"); second, distraction (e.g., "There is something more important and more entertaining than prayer and church
services to which *you* will want to attend"); and third, rationalization
(e.g., "God really wants *you* to read the *New York Times* thoroughly
on Sunday because the more informed you are, the more you will be
able to help others").

Again, the Holy Spirit will counter the Evil One's tactic by calling the victim into a church or presenting him with a conversation or a book that makes God's reality and presence more palpable. If the victim has not fallen into spiritual acedia and other deadly sins, he might follow the Holy Spirit's inspiration and pursue an increased spiritual commitment followed by an increased moral commitment.

This was the path followed by Saint Augustine after his encounter with Saint Ambrose.[24] Though Augustine had broken free of Manichaeism and had begun to take Orthodox Christianity quite seriously (thanks to the teaching and example of Saint Ambrose), he had resisted a deepened moral conversion primarily because of his addiction to sexual gratification and his proclivity toward intellectual vanity. One day when he was anguishing about whether he should commit himself to chastity and humility, he heard a child in the next yard singing, "Take it and read it; take it and read it." He took out his Bible, opened it randomly, and read Saint Paul's words in Romans 13:13–14:

> Let us conduct ourselves becomingly as in the day, not in reveling and drunkenness, not in debauchery and licentiousness, not in quarreling and jealousy. But put on the Lord Jesus Christ, and make no provision for the flesh, to gratify its desires.

Immediately upon reading these words, Augustine had no doubt about his need for a deeper moral conversion and decided to be baptized in the Christian faith. After his Baptism on Easter A.D. 387, he not only committed himself to a life of prayer and virtue; he also pursued the priesthood and was ordained in A.D. 391. He was then elevated to bishop of Hippo a few years later.[25]

Notice how the Holy Spirit worked in the life of Saint Augustine. First, He inspired Augustine by Saint Ambrose's polished rhetoric, philosophical wisdom, and allegorical interpretation of Scripture, which moved him to study the Christian Scriptures more thoroughly (for he had formerly been quite disedified by the primitiveness of the Old Testament view of God that he thought contradicted the more

---

[24] See Saint Augustine, *Confessions* 8, 12.
[25] See ibid., 8–9.

mature and developed view of God in Manichean doctrine and the New Testament). As the obstacles to increased religious commitment were overcome by Ambrose's preaching, Augustine became more moved by his example, seeing in him a manifestation of authentic love, piety, and virtue. This brought him to the brink of decision, at which point the Holy Spirit moved him with a child's song and a random selection of Romans (13:13–14). At this point, Augustine had moved from group two to group four and was never to look back. It should be noted that the Holy Spirit never compelled Augustine to do anything. He used the words of Ambrose to redress the tactics and errors of the Evil One that kept Augustine in spirit abeyance. It was Augustine who received Ambrose's word with awe and delight, which inspired him to follow Ambrose into deepened spiritual and moral conversion.

The second group may also be subject to another dangerous rationalization: they may become convinced that they are morally sound without God or religion. No doubt, many people can live a fundamentally ethical life without being spiritually committed—that is, they can be authentically committed to the six general principles of ethical propriety: being fair, not harming others unnecessarily (personally, physically, psychologically, reputationally, or financially), not stealing, not cheating, not overtly lying, and avoiding marital infidelity. This is commendable indeed, but as Jesus pointed out, there is need for not only ethical *behaviors* in our relationships with others, but also *interior* conversion toward a heart of authentic love—away from egocentricity, anger, envy, vanity, and pride. Though it is theoretically possible for someone to achieve the interior conversion of, say, Socrates, we must remember that Socrates was not just a philosopher, but also a pious, religious man. Though he may not have benefitted from his religion in the same way that a Christian might benefit from the Holy Spirit in the process of moral conversion, his commitment to God and the sacred led to a remarkable humility that helped him to resist intellectual vanity, the pursuit of power and dominion, and obsession with envy and wealth.

I bring this rationalization up because I believe that the Evil One frequently suggests to group two individuals that they have attained a high state of personal and ethical development without a strong commitment to God and religion (because they believe in God and adhere to the six generally accepted principles of ethical behavior). The Evil One does not suggest giving up these commitments, but rather that they are *enough*, more than enough. Though God will no doubt look upon these individuals with great mercy for the commitments they have, we must remember the two dangers that lie beneath this rationalization. First, spiritual acedia is quite dangerous because it produces considerable apathy about one's ultimate purpose in life, not caring about one's ultimate meaning, significance, dignity, and destiny—and even not caring about not caring. This can lead to underliving one's life, underusing one's talents, and underactualizing one's potential for authentic love and transcendental dignity that might have been possible with increased spiritual commitment. Second, religious commitment almost invariably leads to greater humility (if for no other reason than our consciousness of being a creature). This in turn leads to greater authenticity of love (arising out of a nongodlike view of self) and a diminishment of most forms of vanity and pride. We are left in a precarious spiritual and moral position without this fundamental humility and striving for authentic love.

Once again, the Evil One's tactic proves brilliant because we will not strive for what we do not desire, and we will not desire what we are not aware of. Thus, we are better off following the inspiration of the Holy Spirit to greater religious/spiritual commitment that brings along with it the need for prayer, humility, authentic love, and virtues, to protect us from descending into the darkness of the deadly sins.

3. The Third Group—Striving toward Strong Religious and Moral Conversion

We may now move on to the third group—those who have a high degree of commitment to God and religion and, as a result, have a fundamental awareness of the dangers of the deadly sins, a striving for more authentic love, and a basic awareness of the virtues and how to use them to resist temptation. This group is committed to God and interior moral conversion, but they need to be vigilant about actualizing their moral conversion in the world. Commitment is excellent, but it must be followed by persistent action until we develop good habits and are transformed into our "higher selves"—what Saint

Paul calls "the new man" (Eph 4:22, 24; Col 3:9–11; cf. Rom 6:6; Eph 2:15; see Volume II, Chapters 5 and 6, of this Trilogy). Without vigilance and persistence, which Jesus addressed many times in the Gospels, they might let their guard down (or be tricked), opening themselves to temptation, rationalization, and submission to one or more deadly sins.

Though this group is well on their way to deepened spiritual and moral conversion, their use of prayer and the virtues to resist temptation is not yet proficient and habitual; hence, the Evil One can take them by surprise. If the believer begins to let his guard down, and becomes more complacent in his spiritual commitments and less vigilant in the practice of virtue to resist temptation, the Evil One will try to surprise him with several different kinds of stimuli and temptations. Recognizing that the believer may be alerted to the danger of these temptations (and the damage that they are likely to cause to himself or others), the Evil One suggests several opportune rationalizations to "help" the believer submit to the temptation: "So what if you have a few more drinks with your friends; you're not hurting anyone." "Go ahead and relax with a little bit of free Internet pornography—you're not harming yourself or anyone else." "It's alright to be angry and vengeful; the Old Testament is full of it!" "You're not being vain and proud; you're just being competitive in a competitive world." "Greed is good because it motivates people to take risks to build the means of production." Rationalizations need not be as blunt as the ones stated here—remember, the Evil One is a master at presenting them subtly.

If the believer has let his guard down, begins to engage in and even entertain a particular stimulus, and buys the rationalization, there is a good possibility he will submit to temptation. If he does, the Evil One will follow rapidly with false consolations and other rationalizations to cushion his fall and to minimize his perception of its effect. Though we can be quite certain that the Lord looks with unconditional mercy upon believers who fall into this situation, He will waste no time in trying to counter it before the believer descends more deeply into the deadly sins. Sometimes the Holy Spirit will present the believer with a sense of cosmic emptiness, loneliness, and alienation, which could scare the believer into getting back on track. However, if the believer has become smitten by the sin and has bought deeply into a rationalization for it, he might ignore his feelings of cosmic emptiness, loneliness, and alienation, and regress to a state of submission to temptation. At this point, the believer may sense three negative changes in his life—more intense feelings of emptiness, alienation, loneliness, and darkness; a decrease in trust, hope, love, and religious fervor; and a consequent loss of interest in religious and moral conversion. This should set off alarms in the heart of the believer; and if it does not, the Holy Spirit will intensify them, provoking the believer to reject the rationalizations that he has been using, express contrition for his sin, and turn away from his satisfaction from the sin before it takes more control over him, leading him progressively into its darkness.

Since group three believers have a strong commitment to God and a religious life, basic awareness of the dangers of the deadly sins, and the need to resist temptation out of love for God, protection of the soul, and adherence to conscience, there is a very good chance that the believer will reverse his regression into the deadly sins (along with his rationalizations) when faced with the negative consequences of his turn (dark and desolate feelings, confusion, and decrease in trust, hope, and love). This will normally result in deep contrition, a rejection of the rationalizations, and a rekindling of effort to resist the stimuli of temptations at their origin. When he does this, he will return to his former spiritual commitments and a renewed interest in deepening his moral conversion. As this occurs, he will become progressively more free from the enticements of sensorial stimulation, uncommitted sexual gratification, ego-comparative advantage, and vanity. This will lead to three important changes in disposition:

1. Awareness of authentic love and the freedom to follow Christ, our Lord, into it
2. Freedom to surrender to the Lord and His will before all else
3. A progression in the spiritual life that will fill him with affective consolation (feelings of love-sacredness-unity-joy-home, feelings of affective consolation that will be punctuated with affective desolation to help the believer in his final stages of purification)

Saint John of the Cross addresses four stages of desolation in this purification process: the active dark night of the senses, the passive dark night of the senses, the active dark night of the Spirit, and the passive dark night of the Spirit (all generically referred to as the "dark night of the soul"[26]).

As the believer (in the third group) becomes proficient at resisting temptation and draws closer to the Lord in prayer, the Evil One must shift his tactics from overt temptations (which have become less effective) to deception and discouragement. We will discuss these two tactics briefly here and discuss them more thoroughly below in Section V ("Deception, Discouragement, and Discernment").

With respect to deception, the Evil One will face many challenges in trying to tempt group three believers overtly. He will also have great difficulty convincing them of falsity in the area of faith and morals. Hence, he attempts to deceive them by appearing like an angel of light. This deception can be so devious that Saint Ignatius of Loyola had to devote a section of the *Spiritual Exercises* to what he called "discernment in the second week".[27] This will be taken up in detail below (Section V.C).

The Evil One also uses discouragement to undermine group three believers who are moving into group four. These believers are well aware of their shortcomings in charity, humility, and compassion— even though they have made great progress in resisting the deadly sins. The lives of the saints are filled with their recognition of inadequacy and past sin, which at first provokes discouragement, but later, consolation in the love, mercy, and grace of Jesus Christ. Saint Paul's plea in the Letter to the Romans is at first filled with excruciating frustration that ultimately leads to hope through Christ:

> I do not understand my own actions. For I do not do what I want, but I do the very thing I hate.... Wretched man that I am! Who will deliver me from this body of death? Thanks be to God through Jesus Christ our Lord! (7:15, 24–25)

Virtually everyone in group three will go through this kind of discouragement on multiple occasions, because attachments to certain

---

[26] As we noted in Chapter 1 (Section III), the dark night of the soul has these four stages. Saint John of the Cross explains these four stages of the dark night in his work *The Ascent of Mount Carmel*, which includes his well-known work *The Dark Night of the Soul*. See the references in Chapter 1, Section III.

[27] See Ignatius of Loyola, *Spiritual Exercises*, pp. 91–93.

dimensions of the deadly sins can be quite deep, and the Evil One will work overtime to prevent the believer from making progress. If he does make progress, then the Evil One takes on the role of the accuser (see Rev 12:10) by showing him his imperfections in the past and present, implying that he will never be able to attain the love of Christ in the future. He implies that this is what God really expects, and so God is not satisfied with either the believer or his progress. If the believer takes the "bait", the Evil One stresses his false doctrine that God looks only at the believer's imperfections, and in disgust, God rejects him and his "little" attempts to become better. This false doctrine can lead to complete discouragement and despair, causing the vulnerable believer to abandon his struggle for deeper moral conversion and even his striving to be united with God.

When Saint Ignatius of Loyola was in the throes of his religious and moral conversion in the caves of Manresa, and his view of God was not developed enough to recognize God's unconditional love, his recollection of his past sins and his present condition drove him to the point of complete discouragement and even self-destruction.[28] Fortunately, the Lord intervened and showed him that his discouragement was unwarranted—and the Evil One had caused his distress.[29] After that time, he was free from the discouragement of his past sins and present condition. What does this mean for us? Group three believers who are making progress in resisting temptation and appropriating the loving heart of Christ should expect that the Evil One (taking on the role of the accuser) will torment them with every form of discouragement about their past and present. The solution is to depend totally on the unconditional love of God preached by Jesus and demonstrated by His completely self-sacrificial Passion and death—and then to place themselves completely in His infinitely merciful arms, crying out with Saint Paul, "Wretched man that I am! Who will rescue me from this body of death? Thanks be to God through Jesus Christ our Lord!" (Rom 7:24–25).

---

[28] *The Autobiography of St. Ignatius*, ed. J.F.X. O'Conor, S.J. (New York: Benziger Brothers, 1900), pp. 45–51, https://books.google.com/books?id=T6dlAAAAMAAJ&q=man resa#v=snippet&q=manresa&f=false.

[29] Ibid., pp. 50–51.

As the group three believer continues on his journey, he will find himself moving into the fourth group (highest level of religious and moral conversion), in which he will be proficient at resisting temptation, free to love as Christ loved, and united with the Lord in prayer (union-home-love-ecstasy-sacredness).

4. The Fourth Group—Strong Religious and Moral Conversion

Those who become spiritually and morally proficient (entering into group four) can expect moral purification and sanctity, freedom for authentic love, and significant apostolic contribution. They are very likely to lead multitudes into faith and moral conversion by both example and works. They will likely experience periods of considerable affective and spiritual consolation (which may include extraordinary divine inspiration and even visions).

They can also expect to be confronted—rather than tempted—by Satan. This can happen in a variety of ways—for example, harassment where the Evil One will disturb their sleep with loud noises, pressure, and frightening images (as was the case for Saint John Vianney[30] and Saint Padre Pio[31]). They will also be challenged by the responsibilities that they have in their religious and apostolic lives. For example, the Evil One will attempt to use their willingness to do anything for the Lord, pushing them to go beyond even a state of exhaustion in the hopes of creating a mental collapse or discouragement (from exhaustion).

Additionally, individuals in this group may well be in the illuminative way—and so may be subject to the passive dark night of the spirit. (We discussed the challenges of this dark night in Chapter 1, Section III). These individuals, such as Saint Thérèse of Lisieux and Saint Teresa of Calcutta, are generally aware of the objective and ultimate result of this dark night (i.e., final purification, union with God,

---

[30] Leon Cristiani devotes about one-third of his text to the harassments of John Vianney (the Cure of Ars) and how he overcame them with trust in God, prayer, and humility. See Leon Cristiani, *Evidence of Satan in the Modern World* (Charlotte, N.C.: Tan Books and Publishers, 1977), pp. 5–40.

[31] Like Saint John Vianney, Padre Pio was often tormented and harassed by the devil throughout his life. He treated these harassments in much the same way as Vianney—with trust in God, prayer, humility, and patience. See Renzo Allegri, *Padre Pio: Man of Hope* (Ann Arbor, Mich.: Charis Books, 2000), pp. 35–45.

and mystic ecstasy). Hence, they are able to endure this purification patiently—painful as it is—with great trust in God. Saint Thérèse and Saint Teresa endured this purification until the end of their lives, but then the Lord came to them with the ecstasy and grace they confidently believed He would give. In the case of St. Thérèse, ecstasy came a few minutes before her death. One of her siblings, who was also a Carmelite sister, Mother Agnes of Jesus (Pauline Martin), gave the following testimony. Fixing her eyes on the crucifix, she slowly said:

> "Oh! ... I love him.... My ... God! ... I ... love ... You!" Having pronounced these words she fell back gently, her head a little to the right. Mother hastily summoned the community to return, and all were in time to witness her ecstasy. Her face, which had become purple and contorted during her agony, had returned to its pristine freshness and the lily-white colouring of healthier days, her eyes stared upwards, shining with peace and joy. A sister drew near with a torch to get a better look at this sublime gaze, and the light of the torch produced no movement of the eyelids. This ecstasy lasted for the space of a *Credo*. Then I saw her close her eyes; she sighed several times, and rendered her soul to God.[32]

Saint Teresa of Calcutta also experienced a long dark night of the soul, similar to that of the saint she longed to imitate (Saint Thérèse). Father Benedict Groeschel reports what happened to her in the last two weeks of her life:

> Toward the end of her life the darkness lifted. Fr. Brian records the sisters' observation when Mother Teresa returned to Calcutta shortly before her death: "After her return from Rome [and New York] ... Mother had been extremely happy, joyful, optimistic, and talkative. Her face was always radiant, full of fun. The Lord must have revealed to her the impending end of her life." Our readers may find it interesting to know that I personally observed this joyfulness the day before Mother returned to Calcutta. I was asked by her sisters to offer Mass for her. She was so weak that she could not stand, but attended

---

[32] "From the Testimony of Mother Agnes of Jesus [Pauline Martin] at the Diocesan Inquiry into the Life of St. Thérèse, Given as a Part of the Process for the Cause of Canonization", in *St. Thérèse of Lisieux by Those Who Knew Her*, ed. Christopher O'Mahony (Dublin: Pranstown House, 1989).

Mass lying on a cot. My confrere Fr. Andrew Apostoli and I were utterly astonished after Mass when she was "bubbly." She laughed and told us with great joy the number of sisters and convents they had throughout the world. Mother never spoke about this before, and she was not doing so in any boastful way. Rather, she was rejoicing "with triumphant exultation" at the great blessings God had been able to grant through the Missionaries of Charity.[33]

Notice that the dark night of the soul (particularly the fourth stage—the passive dark night of the Spirit initiated by God) is not ultimately vexing, though it may be frustrating and painful. Those who are spiritually and morally proficient generally have the faith, inspiration, virtues, and spiritual freedom to deal with it effectively. This leads to increased purification, freedom to love, and in the end, the ecstasy of eternal life.

D. The Evil One's Preparation for Effective Temptations

Since every individual, beginning with childhood, can begin the process of appropriating sufficient faith and virtue needed to resist temptations, the Evil One must plan to interrupt this process in childhood and beyond. We noted above how religious commitment, prudence, temperance, and fortitude help us to resist temptation; so we might expect that the Evil One will direct his efforts at undermining these four essential defenses against him. Inasmuch as religious commitment provides the spiritual and theological foundations for resisting temptation, we might expect that the Evil One will resist this commitment first and foremost. He will likely then turn his attention next to undermining prudence, because prudence guides temperance and fortitude. Finally, he will then turn his attention to temperance (the art and power of saying no) and finally fortitude (the art and power of committing ourselves to the highest good). Let us consider each of these four schemes in turn.

With respect to undermining religious commitment, the Evil One prefers to undermine all religious commitment. Therefore, he puts

[33] Benedict Groeschel, C.F.R., "Mother Teresa Remembered", First Things, September 11, 2007, https://www.firstthings.com/web-exclusives/2007/09/mother-teresa-remembered.

considerable effort into preventing people from attending church regularly—and if possible, to undermine faith in God and Jesus Christ. Much of the undermining of belief occurs through the media, the educational system, and the culture—particularly the false dichotomy between faith and science, the rejection of the soul (physicalist reductionism), and the rejection of Jesus as historical. (The evidence contravening these false claims is discussed in detail in Volumes II and III of the Quartet.) If the Evil One cannot undermine belief in God and Jesus, he will then try to undermine commitment to a particular religion, using the false claim that religion is superfluous and has been more harmful than helpful throughout history. He will suggest that it is good enough to be a spiritual and moral person; yet the insufficiency of this strategy is quite clear—those who do not belong to a church community are generally very weak in their religious commitment—and many abandon belief altogether. Furthermore, they lose the teaching guidance and the spiritual strength needed to resist temptation and pursue deeper degrees of authentic love. This explains why people without church membership find themselves in group one—not explicitly knowing right from wrong (trying to intuit the good from their feelings alone). Though emotivism can lead to considerable empathy and authenticity, it lacks principle and nuance in the development of virtue and ethics. Empathy alone is not enough to be virtuous and moral because feelings are so susceptible to rationalization (see above, IV.C.1 and IV.C.2).

If the Evil One fails to prevent a person from committing himself to a church community, he will then try to persuade them to commit to a church community that has no religious or moral nuance—a "spiritual church" that does not have doctrines or morals. He will suggest that these churches are very inclusive and open to everyone—so much better than churches that exclude people and restrict freedom. Of course he does not mention that the *truth* will set you free— not mere openness to everyone. He then skillfully uses the false idea that agreement is more important than truth—that pluralism is more important than doctrinal and moral nuance. He fills his victims with confidence that they are better than people who "ignorantly" belong to churches with strong doctrinal and moral commitments—"They are close-minded reactionaries whom you have wisely superceded." Though this strategy is not as ideal for the Evil One as preventing commitment to a church altogether, it achieves significant results for hindering religious and moral development, leaving the individual open to continued rationalization.

Those who have grown up in a church community will feel a loss of transcendental meaning and communion with God if they leave a church community. The horizon of these negative feelings can help individuals stay within a church community. Those who have not grown up in a church community are therefore at a disadvantage because they don't know what they are missing when they grow in unbelief. As a result, they will experience the negative feelings and states of mind set out by the American Psychiatric Association study referenced above. They may pass by a church and feel curious about or even inclined to go in, but talk themselves out of it. They may feel a radical incompleteness in meaning, nature, and destiny, and surmise that life would be better if God existed (as atheistic existentialists frequently do), but then talk themselves out of it by assuming that there is no evidence for God, the soul, and Jesus. Though the Holy Spirit calls them, the Evil One tries to prevent them from following their hearts or training their minds. Once again, C. S. Lewis' *Screwtape Letters* proves humorously instructive. The older devil, Uncle Screwtape, tries to show his nephew, Wormwood, that when the "patient" starts thinking about universals, metaphysics, and ideas that might present evidence for God, it is always best to distract him by something purely mundane, like lunch:

> I once had a patient, a sound atheist, who used to read in the British Museum. One day, as he sat reading, I saw a train of thought in his mind beginning to go the wrong way [toward universals, ultimate causes, etc]. The Enemy [the Holy Spirit], of course, was at his elbow in a moment. Before I knew where I was I saw my twenty years' work beginning to totter. If I had lost my head and begun to attempt a defence by argument I should have been undone. But I was not such a fool. I struck instantly at the part of the man which I had best under my control and suggested that it was just about time he had some lunch.... The Enemy presumably made the counter-suggestion (you know how one can never quite overhear What He says to them?) that this was more important than lunch. At least I think that must have been His line for when I said "Quite. In fact much too important to tackle it the end of a morning", the patient brightened up considerably;

and by the time I had added "Much better come back after lunch and
go into it with a fresh mind", he was already half way to the door.[34]

If an individual decides to follow his heart—either because of
encouragement from a friend or a stimulus from a book, television,
or the Internet—and if he finds the evidence needed to infer that
belonging to a church community is both reasonable and responsible, the Evil One will suffer a serious setback and lose significant
advantage. The individual will now belong to group two; and if he
commits himself to regular church services, he could break free from
Level One (pleasure/materialistic) and Level Two (ego-comparative)
happiness and meaning in life. He would now be a believer who
experiences a significant decline in cosmic emptiness, meaninglessness, loneliness, and alienation, and he will also experience the support and moral guidance of his church community. Hence he will
enter into the first stages of moral conversion, and the Evil One
would stand to lose the battle for his undivided attention and soul.
   At this juncture, the Evil One must shift from trying to undermine the religious commitment of the individual (which is always
his first priority) to undermining his *moral* commitment. Recall how
temptation works—and how prudence, temperance, and fortitude
mitigate it, helping the believer to mitigate and resist it. Normally,
the Evil One will try to undermine prudence first, because temperance and fortitude rely on the knowledge and guidance of prudence.
The Evil One's first tactic is to suggest to the believer that his feelings
are sufficient for good moral judgments—this will effectively keep
him away from a reflective and intelligent judgment. Failing this, the
Evil One might suggest that the believer is already well acquainted
with the Ten Commandments, and that there is no real need to go
any further—the eight deadly sins are simply a "repeat" of the Ten
Commandments. This is an excellent strategy because the believer
might say, "Well, I am not a thief, a murderer, an adulterer—I don't
bear false witness against my neighbor, and I have not coveted my
neighbor's wife or goods; so I am covered."
   What he doesn't realize is that the eight deadly sins are *interior
attitudes* that initiate a wide range of sins (unloving behaviors that
undermine the Kingdom of the loving God) beyond those explicitly

[34] Lewis, *Screwtape Letters*, p. 2.

prohibited by the Ten Commandments. If the believer begins reflecting on these interior attitudes that undermine love and the Kingdom of God—for example, gluttony, lust, sloth, greed, anger, envy, vanity, and pride (the need to dominate)—he will begin to sense the darkness and negativity of these attitudes, causing at least an initial impulse to resist them (and their destructiveness to self, others, and God's Kingdom). The Evil One does not want the believer under any circumstances to enter into this reflection process because it leads to the heart of moral conversion.

In view of this, the Evil One will first try to distract the believer from looking into these deadly sins, and failing this, to convince him that none of them really applies to him in any serious way. There are a variety of tactics he uses to do this—calling the deadly sins mere medieval anachronisms, suggesting that they induce unnecessary guilt that is psychologically unhealthy, or that they have been supplanted and superceded by new psychological ways of perfecting oneself. The "worst" turn of events for the Evil One would be the believer's fascination with the deadly sins, which causes him to see those sins within himself—to see them as undermining the Kingdom of God and "worst" of all to see the presence of the Evil One behind those sins. If the believer affirms these ideas—because of his religion and interior awareness of evil and darkness—he is in the midst of moral conversion, which again causes the Evil One to shift tactics.

Since the believer is at least partially repulsed by the evil, destructiveness, and interior darkness of the deadly sins, it is difficult for the Evil One to convince him to ignore them; so he will have to hide the three virtues (or their effectiveness) from the believer. As noted above, he will start with prudence and then move to temperance and fortitude. Recall that prudence is not simply knowledge of how the deadly sins undermine love and God's Kingdom; it includes the vital dimension of knowing how to use one's faith, empathy, and conscience to muster the feelings and desires to resist temptations to those deadly sins. Thus, prudence simultaneously recognizes the beauty and goodness of love (as defined by Jesus in the Beatitudes), the darkness, negativity, and destructiveness of the deadly sins, and *how* to use one's faith, empathy, and conscience to galvanize the emotion and desire to resist those sins. If prudence can be brought to bear against the temptations to the deadly sins, the spell of those temptations (appealing to our lower desires) has a reasonable chance of being broken. The Holy Spirit will reinforce this prudential knowledge and desire, but the Evil One will try to frustrate it by suggesting that obedience or surrender to God (faith) is not love, but enslavement, that empathy is weak and irrational, and that "conscience does make cowards of us all."[35] Using these and other related deceptions, the Evil One "hopes" to make the believer uneasy about using these essential transcendental gifts of God to the human spirit.

If the believer sees through the Evil One's deceptions and resolves to use his divine gifts of faith, empathy, and conscience in the pursuit of virtue and resistance to the deadly sins, the Evil One must make recourse to undermine temperance—that is, the habit of making swift recourse to faith, empathy, and conscience to resist the deadly sins. Though prudence knows how to use these three transcendental powers, the virtue of temperance activates them and applies them swiftly and boldly at the moment of temptation.

If a believer is aware of his three divine powers (faith, empathy, and conscience) and has become habituated to using them in times of temptation, he will ask for God's help in prayer, empathize with those he might offend, and listen to his conscience when temptation arises—and hence he will resist it.

In view of this, the Evil One will try to combat the believer's attempts to develop temperance. Normally, this takes the form of intensifying the temptation at the moment the believer begins to resist. His hope is to capture the imagination and desire of the believer so strongly that his will to pray, empathize, and listen to his conscience will be dulled or even overwhelmed. If the believer is practiced at temperance, he will summon his three divine powers to match the intensity of the temptation, but if he is not practiced, he may allow himself to be captured by the spell of his evil or lower desires. Practice makes perfect—and the Evil One will do everything he can to make sure that we do not practice being strong in our resolve to use our divine gifts.

If the believer becomes proficient at both prudence and temperance, then the Evil One is left with only one recourse—to dull the spirit of fortitude. Recall that fortitude is the resolve and commitment needed to actualize optimally good actions amid challenges,

---

[35] William Shakespeare, *Hamlet* (Project Gutenberg, 2019), act 3, scene 1, Hamlet's soliloquy, http://www.gutenberg.org/files/1524/1524-h/1524-h.htm.

difficult circumstances, resistance of others, and the need for great effort. It is the precise opposite of the deadly sin of sloth. If the Evil One does not succeed at quelling the believer's resistance to temptation (temperance), his only serious remaining tactic is to tempt the believer to sloth. This can be accomplished in a myriad of ways— through distraction, weakening the believer's resolve to push ahead amid hard times, inciting the believer to be less passionate or concerned about his good objectives, inciting him to pursue alcohol, drugs, and other ways to weaken his focus and higher desires. Above all, he will try to prevent the believer from asking for grace and help to reach his hard-won goal. This, too, can be accomplished in a myriad of ways: weakening the believer's resolve to pray, weakening his faith when times get rough, and suggesting that "rough times" indicate God's indifference.

Once again, the believer's best defense is the practiced habitual use of his three divine gifts of faith, empathy, and conscience when his pursuit of the optimal good is being seriously resisted. When the believer feels tempted to give up a noble pursuit because of resistance or problems, it is best to pray immediately for guidance, help, and protection—particularly by praying for God's loving will to be done. He will also be assisted by using his power of empathy, considering how many people he might be able to help—as well as how his actions will help the Church, the Kingdom of God, his local community, and the culture. He would also be well advised to listen to his conscience's aversion and repulsion to sloth. If the believer puts these gifts into use swiftly, concertedly, and repeatedly, he will build up an enormous resolve to push forward his agenda of optimal good, even amid the most daunting obstacles and temptations to give up. By using his three divine gifts, the believer will be able to enhance his pursuit of the optimal good, at which point he will be well on his way to the fourth group and, eventually, sainthood.

E. How the Evil One Works within the Culture to Promote Large-Scale Temptation

The Evil One's strategy is much broader than "working on" individuals. He also recognizes the efficacy of changing the culture. This allows thousands, if not millions, of individuals to be tempted, brought to their lower natures, and captivated by evil. These cultural changes are aimed at undermining faith, prudence, temperance, and fortitude so that people will be defenseless against the intense stimulation of lower desires from traditional media, social media, and other forms of social and digital networking. Though the Evil One's strategy is highly nuanced and everywhere pervasive in the Western world, we might break it down into four major prongs, which will assure that all affected individuals will remain ignorant of or reject a church community and the three divine gifts (faith/prayer, empathy, and conscience) to help them resist enslavement by lower and evil desires. As noted above, this enslavement leads to cosmic emptiness, alienation, and loneliness as well as the problems elucidated by the American Psychiatric Association study. These negative psychological and spiritual conditions can often incite an individual to pursue faith and virtue. However, we would be seriously remiss if we did not attempt in every way to help those individuals avert existential and psychological crisis by alerting them to the four ways in which the Evil One undermines culture—and to resist them. So what are these four prongs of the Evil One's strategy to corrupt cultures and the individuals within them?

1. Keep increasing the intensity of social and digital stimulation of lower desires
2. Keep undermining the truth and goodness of God, the soul, Jesus, happiness, love, virtue, and moral principles
3. Keep marginalizing and ridiculing churches, religious people, and religious commitment
4. Foster resentment of all moral and religious teachers who warn against reducing ourselves to mere material, sensual, and ego-comparative gratification

We will briefly discuss each prong in turn.

With respect to the first prong—intensifying the stimulation of lower desires—the development of the Internet and social media has provided an avalanche of intense stimuli on every imaginable level: chat rooms dedicated to seducing young people into immoral and even criminal conduct, free pornography, online shopping for every imaginable luxury, and websites devoted to unhealthy lifestyle changes. This is accompanied by a decline of social norms, making increased alcohol, drug use, sexual experimentation, and dangerous conduct not only socially acceptable, but sometimes even "laudable". Though the pressure among certain young people to succeed in high school and college has partially mitigated these stimuli, they can also force young people to sacrifice sleep and healthy social relationships in order to manage both contradictory poles.

Furthermore, social media has "amped up" ego-comparative gratification to extremely high levels. Young people spend hours working on their self-image through Facebook and Snapchat, sacrificing personal depth and real relationships for cool "selfies" and social façades. Self-image has become so important that it is replacing real empathy, principles, ideals, character, and friendships. One cannot help but think that young people are far more challenged today than they were ten to twenty years ago. They are continuously seduced by Level One desires (materialistic and sensual) and almost bullied into Level Two (ego-comparative) portrayals of themselves. This concentration on Level One and Level Two gratification is undermining several dimensions of Level Three (empathetic, ethical, and contributive) and Level Four (faith/transcendent) purpose in life. Indeed, young people who do not have a strong religious belief and practice from their families will have a very difficult time recognizing the importance of faith and transcendence in their lives. It seems that the Evil One has used important and positive technologies and prosperity to create a perfect storm of superficiality and egocentricity.

What can we do to retake the culture? First and foremost, parents must instill in their children the importance of commitment to God, Jesus, and a church community. If fathers go to church and reinforce the importance of religion in their lives, there is a strong likelihood (75 percent) that their children will also incorporate a religious commitment into their future lives and families.[36] Second,

---

[36] The following statistics from the Swiss demographic survey of 2000 were summarized by Robbie Low.

> The religious practice of the father of the family, above all, determines the future attendance at or absence from church of the children. If both father and mother attend regularly, 33 percent of their children will end up as regular churchgoers, and 41 percent will end up attending irregularly. Only a quarter of their children will end up

every elementary, intermediate, and secondary catechism class should include an extended component on the four levels of happiness, the comparison game, and cosmic emptiness, loneliness, and alienation (see Volume II, Appendix I, of this Trilogy). This presentation will help young people to see what they are missing when they ignore Level Three and Level Four and to recognize the negative and painful symptoms that are likely to arise because of this. This gives them a solution to these negative symptoms and a pathway to higher-level desires. Third, parents need to teach their children when they are young to be disciplined in the satisfaction of lower-level desires so that their higher-level desires and commitments can be achieved. This must include a component of limiting Internet use, the kinds of websites accessed, and the kind of Facebook content accessed and provided. It must also include monitoring of alcohol, drugs, and friends.

If adults (over the age of twenty) find themselves addicted to the Internet, social media, or unhealthy aspects of the Internet (e.g., pornography)—or find themselves addicted to other sensorial stimuli (e.g., alcohol or drugs), they will want to research the long-term effects of these behaviors, particularly if they have become addictive; and if they have become addictive, to consider seriously finding a group or some form of therapy to detach from the addiction before it becomes self-destructive and destructive of the family. Certain groups, such as Alcoholics Anonymous, emphasize the importance of prayer (Level Four), ethical responsibility, and mature, responsible friendships (Level Three) as fundamental aids for recovering addicts. Thus they can provide both a way out of addiction and a way toward higher-level contributive and transcendent commitment.

---

not practicing at all. If the father is irregular and mother regular, only 3 percent of the children will subsequently become regulars themselves, while a further 59 percent will become irregulars. Thirty-eight percent will be lost. If the father is non-practicing and mother regular, only 2 percent of children will become regular worshippers, and 37 percent will attend irregularly. Over 60 percent of their children will be lost completely to the church.

See Robbie Low, "The Truth about Men and Church", *Touchstone: A Journal of Mere Christianity,* June 2003, http://www.touchstonemag.com/archives/article.php?id=16-05 024 v #ixzz4RjWtmadF.

See also Werner Haug, Paul Compton, and Youssef Courbage, eds., *Population Studies No. 31,* vol. 2, *The Demographic Characteristics of National Minorities in Certain European States* (Strasbourg: Council of Europe Publishing, 2000).

With respect to the second prong of the Evil One's plan to undercut the culture—undermining the truth and goodness of God, the soul, Jesus, happiness, love, virtue, and moral principles—the Evil One has been working for more than one and a half centuries to undercut these vital dimensions of human contribution, ethical responsibility, empathy, faith, and transcendence. Exaggerated interpretations (beyond the evidence) of Darwinian evolutionary theory have led to biological reductionism, physicalistic socio-biology, social Darwinism, and elements of racism (all of which undercut human freedom, conscience, and transcendence). Exaggerated interpretations of Freudian psychological theory have also led to biological reductionism and a decidedly nontranscendent view of the human psyche.

Morally relativistic philosophies have led to the abandonment of objective principles, utilitarianism, and situationism (that tend to ignore conscience). Marxist dialectical materialism has led to the undermining of religion, the rise of the totalistic state, and the undermining of private enterprise. The influence of these mindsets and movements has led not only to the first and second world wars, but also to the secularized reshaping of culture in their aftermath. Today, traditional media, social media, the public education establishment, and the secularized juris prudence of the legal system have led to another perfect storm to undermine the above seven Level Three and Level Four realities and foundations—God, the soul, Jesus, Level Three-Four happiness, Level Three-Four love, virtue, and objective moral principles. If our young people and adults fail to recognize these realities and foundations, they will per force be relegated to Level One-Two purpose in life through ignorance and social pressure.

Though this superficial worldview and lifestyle is likely to result in the crisis of the comparison game, cosmic emptiness, loneliness, and alienation, as well as the negative psychological consequences of nonreligious affiliation, we would be exceedingly remiss in our social and cultural duty if we do not warn people of the difficulties and dangers of this mindset and lifestyle—and invite them to something better, something that will lead to their highest happiness, purpose, dignity, fulfillment, and destiny: contributive and transcendent fulfillment (Level Three and Level Four).

This duty lies at the core of my purpose for writing both the Quartet and this Trilogy. Everything in it is designed for a rational

and scientific mindset to restore credibility and understanding of the
above realities and foundations of Level Three-Four purpose in life:

1. The reality of God from science and philosophy—Volume II,
   Appendixes I and II, of the Quartet
2. Evidence for a transphysical soul that will survive bodily
   death—Volume II, Chapters 1–6, of the Quartet
3. Evidence of the reality and Resurrection of Jesus from outside the New Testament, particularly the Shroud of Turin—
   Volume III, Chapter 4, and Appendix I, of the Quartet
4. Evidence of Jesus' miracles, Passion, Eucharist, and ministry
   from historical criteriological evidence—Volume III, Chapters
   2–6, of the Quartet
5. Contemporary miracles that validate the Catholic interpretation of the Eucharist, the Blessed Virgin Mary, and the saints—
   the appendix to this volume
6. Historical evidence for Jesus' initiation of the Catholic Church
   through the supreme office given to Peter—Volume II, Chapter 1, of this Trilogy
7. The Four Levels of happiness/purpose in life—Volume I of
   the Quartet
8. Why an all-loving God would allow suffering, and Jesus'
   teaching on "suffering well"—Volume IV of the Quartet
9. The cosmic struggle between good and evil, and the reality of
   God and Satan in the world—Chapters 1–3 of this volume
10. The need for the Church, virtue, and prayer to contend with
    the deadly sins and the Evil One—Volume II of this Trilogy
11. The need for objective moral principles and how to use
    them—Volume III of this Trilogy

I started the Magis Center to disseminate the above evidence in
every way possible—through the Internet, social media, traditional
media, confirmation programs, high schools, university Catholic cen-
ters, adult education programs, and documentary films. The Magis
Center has two websites: MagisCenter.com and CredibleCatholic
.com. The latter is an integral part of this effort and the staging ground
for revitalizing the reality and significance of God, the soul, Jesus,
Level Three-Four happiness, virtue, and objective moral principles.

It has enough information to ground intellectual, religious, and moral conversion for both young people and adults, from basic levels[37] to advanced levels.[38]

With respect to the third prong of the Evil One's plan to undermine the culture—ridiculing and marginalizing churches, religious people, and religious commitment—the Evil One has already predisposed many institutions of culture (such as mass media, web media, the public education establishment, and the legal establishment) toward this perspective. Unfortunately, many of the leaders of these cultural institutions believe themselves to be justified in their antireligious viewpoint because of the Evil One's preparation work discussed above (e.g., undermining God, the soul, Jesus). This has led to their unjustified arrogance and imperiousness about being the official spokesmen for society and culture. They have declared themselves to be the new secular "priesthood", but their arguments are light on evidence, shallow in construction, and filled with culpable omissions of important evidence in favor of religion and morality.[39]

Unfortunately, these cultural institutions have remarkable influence on our young people. Thanks to the new "messianic message", our young people are worried about being thought naïve or stupid for their religious beliefs. If they are unfamiliar with the rational and scientific evidence for their position, they feel compelled to pretend they are secularistic, agnostic, morally relativistic, and unfettered by

[37] The 7 *Essential Modules* is a program designed for Catholic secondary students in confirmation and catechetical programs as well as high school theology classes. It is seven ninety-minute voiceover PowerPoints that can be shown by any teacher, and has a 97 percent rating as positive or very positive for responding to doubts and maintaining faith by students using them. It is free of charge and can be accessed along with the workbook by going to www.crediblecatholic.com, and then clicking on the big red button that says "7 Essential Modules", or simply click on this site: https://www.crediblecatholic.com/programs/. For a list of the information available for each module, see note 5 in Section I of the Introduction to the Trilogy in this volume.

[38] The *Credible Catholic Big Book* (two thousand pages of sourced materials) and the *Credible Catholic Little Book* (a "cliff notes" summary of the *Big Book*) provide the evidence for and explanation of the four major parts of the *Catechism of the Catholic Church*. To access go to www.crediblecatholic.com and click on "Big Book", and then select the topic you want in any volume or chapter.

[39] See Charles Taylor, *A Secular Age* (Cambridge, Mass.: Harvard University Press, 2007). See also Charles Taylor, *Sources of the Self: The Making of the Modern Identity* (New York: Cambridge University Press, 1992), and Charles Taylor, *Malaise of Modernity* (Concord, Ont.: House of Anansi Press, 1998).

norms and mores. They are also daunted by the accusation of being called simple-minded wishful thinkers who need a psychological crutch to get through life. These fears are exacerbated by the need to be cool in their social media portrayals, their collegiate gatherings, and the in-groups with which they associate.

So how do we push back on the Evil One's plan to persuade young people by their own fears and doubts to abandon religious and moral commitments? The solution is similar to the remedy mentioned above. We need to impart compelling, contemporary, scientific, rational evidence and justification for the religious and moral doctrines that have already been secularized—particularly the seven major realities mentioned above (God, the soul, Jesus, and so forth).[40]

Ridicule and marginalization of religion and morality is best refuted by rational evidence. Though this rational evidence is available—and is set out in detail at CredibleCatholic.com—we still must help our young people to discover and listen to it. This is a part of Jesus' universal call to evangelization. It is therefore incumbent upon those who are aware of this evidence to disseminate it in every way they can. We must help our young people to know the *whole* truth as well as the spirit of fair and rational discussion and debate.

At this juncture, we encounter one of the Evil One's premier strategies to influence our educational system—the overarching and unproven assumption that toleration is more important than the whole truth. Our young people are being taught that it is better to sacrifice the truth for the sake of being tolerant. Though they are willing to defend faith in God, the soul, and Jesus with rational evidence, they are frequently unwilling to do the same with respect to moral principles. Much of the time, they would rather "go along to get along" rather than cause discomfort by defending their moral principles. For this reason, it is important for them to have a sense of the darkness that surrounds the abandonment of virtue and moral principles. They may be uncomfortable with talking about Satan or evil spirits, but if they can summon the courage to say that they believe that abandoning the moral principles of Jesus leaves them *personally* in a state of emptiness, alienation, and darkness, they would have given a sterling testimony to the efficacy and beauty of morality.

---

[40] See the 7 *Essential Modules* for a complete voiceover program on these areas.

The fourth prong of the Evil One's plan to undermine culture—fostering resentment and hostility toward moral and religious authorities—arises out of what we call "the culture of entitlement". There seems to be a negative progression flowing from parental and societal indulgence of children—the more we hyperindulge ("spoil") a child, the more he expects to be hyperindulged, and the more he expects such indulgence, the more he bitterly resents being deprived of it, not only by his parents, but by anyone having the authority of a parent (e.g., teachers, religious authorities, or relatives). Coaches seem to be the only group capable of rejecting hyperindulgence and asking for self-sacrifice.

This entitlement culture dovetails perfectly with the intensification of Level One and Level Two stimuli (mentioned in the first prong above). A parent, teacher, or religious authority need not demand that an individual curtail Level One and Level Two indulgence to provoke resentment and hostility; they need only make a comment that such hyperindulgence is bad for the self and others to elicit a dismissal or resentful outburst. This has effectively led teachers, parents, and religious authorities to shy away from any kind of moral instruction, because they want to avoid being dismissed or rejected by the children.

The solution to this problem is a restoration of the virtue of *prudence*. Recall that prudence is not only a knowledge of what is most important, pervasive, enduring, and deep with respect to defining happiness, purpose, and identity; it is also a lived awareness of how to make the higher levels of happiness and purpose the most important ones in our daily lives and decisions. Thus it is having not simply a theoretical awareness of the four levels of happiness, but also a *decision* to prioritize one's life accordingly—and to strategize making these most important priorities the focus of one's goals, decisions, and daily actions.

It might be thought that teaching prudence to *young* people would be the first step in contending with this problem, but it seems that the virtue of prudence must be taught to *parents* first. As Aquinas intuited long ago, if parents are not aware of the four levels of happiness, or the practice of prudence, they will not be able to teach it to their children—and worse, they are likely to overindulge their children's Level One and Level Two desires. This is sure to create an entitlement expectation as well as resentment and hostility toward any authority who would advise, caution against, ask, or require self-control.

Thus, it is important that parents focus on learning the four levels of happiness and practicing it in their marriage and childrearing; it is also important that they find friends who are primarily Level Three and Level Four in their life's purpose. This will assure that the children are exposed to other parents and children with similar priorities. The earlier children are taught these priorities—and how to practice them through church, prayer, virtue, and respect—the less likely they will become entitled, resentful, and hostile toward religious and moral authority.

In conclusion, we must all take steps to reverse the Evil One's influence on the culture by first learning and then exposing our young people to the scientific and rational evidence for God, the soul, Jesus, and the Church, as well as the interior evidence of the darkness and emptiness of moral relativism and the light of Christ, which can replace it. Building on this foundation, we can then show young people how to put the four levels of happiness into practice through a church community and our three divine gifts of faith/ prayer, empathy, and conscience. If we do this concertedly with like-minded friends and use our influence within schools and cultural institutions, we will be able to play a part in healing the culture and helping our youth to resist the Evil One.

V. Deception, Discouragement, and Discernment

We have seen how the Evil One uses deception and discouragement in the process of temptation above. His attempt to undermine culture is a grand plan of deception—undermining belief in God, the soul, Jesus, happiness, love, virtue, and objective morality. It has been so successful that a large percentage of our young people have serious doubts about these most important realities and are incapable of seeing beyond Levels One and Two. We suggested several remedies to redress this grand deception. We also saw how the Evil One uses deception in his tailored plan for each individual—particularly distractions, rationalizations (to make evil look good), and false promises (to make evil and lower desires appear fulfilling). We have also looked at culturally pervasive deceptions, like the myths of entitlement, materialism, biological reductionism, and moral relativism. We noted some ways of detecting, challenging, and refuting these deceptions, particularly by studying the evidence for God, Jesus, transcendence, happiness, and ethics—and by practicing the virtue of prudence. In Volume III we will also discuss the importance of objective moral principles and Church doctrine as beacons or guidelines to prevent rationalizations and deceptions. It now remains to address two other kinds of deception:

1. Deception in the area of spiritual feelings
2. Deceptions from the Evil One disguised as an angel of light

Saint Ignatius of Loyola gives detailed instructions about how to deal with these two kinds of deception in his "Rules for the Discernment of Spirits" in the *Spiritual Exercises*. Before addressing them, we will have to clarify some pertinent terms used in discerning and redressing them—"affective consolation", "affective desolation", "spiritual consolation", and "spiritual desolation".

A. Consolation and Desolation

"*Affective* consolation and desolation" refers to our *feelings* of peace or discord while "*spiritual* consolation and desolation" refers to a state of *being* and relationship with God. We may now define all four terms specifically.

Affective consolation refers to a *feeling* or intuition of peace, joy, love, mystery, transcendence, sacredness, awe, glory, and ultimate home. Sometimes (in fact, most of the time) all of these dimensions are woven into a single experience. Thus, it connotes more than a *worldly* sense of peace, joy, and love, because it is filled with a sense of mystery, transcendence, sacredness, and ultimate home. These heightened feelings or experiences are gifts from the Lord and are not produced by us either consciously or unconsciously.[41] The Evil One can try to imitate these feelings to deceive us, but these

---

[41] We discussed this briefly in Chapter 1, Sections II and III.

deceptions can be detected by using some rules of discernment (see below in this section).

There are many kinds of affective consolation ranging from a rather subdued sense of divine peace, joy, and home to a more intense experience described by C. S. Lewis from his early life:

> It is difficult to find words strong enough for the sensation which came over me; Milton's "enormous bliss" of Eden (giving the full, ancient meaning to "enormous") comes somewhere near it. It was a sensation, of course, of desire; but desire for what? ... Before I knew what I desired, the desire itself was gone, the whole glimpse ... withdrawn, the world turned commonplace again, or only stirred by a longing for the longing that had just ceased.[42]

Affective consolations can be even more intense than the one described by C. S. Lewis. This is common to the experience of Catholic mystics in the illuminative and unitive stages of mystical life. Saint Teresa of Avila (the sixteenth-century Carmelite mystic and reformer) gives a brief description of her heightened state of ecstasy as follows:

> The *loving* exchange that takes place between the soul and God is so sweet that I beg Him in His goodness to give a taste of this love to anyone who thinks I am lying. On the days this lasted I went about as though stupefied. I desired neither to see nor to speak.... It seems the Lord carries the soul away and places it in *ecstasy*; thus there is no room for pain or suffering, because *joy* soon enters in.[43]

It is not uncommon for these experiences to happen in prayer or shortly thereafter. However, they can also occur quite spontaneously and surprisingly. Once when I was teaching an honors seminar in philosophy of physics at Seattle University, I was in the middle of an explanation of the Lorenz-Einstein transformation. I had the equations for the transformation on the board and was talking about length

---

[42] C. S. Lewis, *Surprised by Joy: The Shape of My Early Life* (New York: Harcourt, 1955), p. 66.

[43] Saint Teresa of Avila, "The Book of Her Life", in *The Collected Works of St. Teresa of Avila*, trans. Kieran Kavanaugh and Otilio Rodriguez (Washington, D.C.: ICS Publications, 1976), 1:194; italics added.

contraction and duration dilation. I heard a bird singing outside, and for a very short moment the bird song was much, much more. I felt like I was in unity with the whole of nature, which was so peaceful that it removed my alienation from self as well as others. This sense of unity with the sacred Totality was much more than a removal of alienation. It was a positive sense of being *at home* with everything. For a fleeting moment I experienced the joy and desire that C. S. Lewis spoke of in his "enormous bliss". And then I came back to reality. I couldn't begin to tell the students what had happened to me. They knew that I was interrupted in my train of thought; so I made an excuse, saying, "That's a beautiful birdsong." They probably thought I was a spacey professor.

Affective desolation is precisely the opposite; it is a feeling or experience of being alienated from the Divine or *not* being at home in the Totality. It often feels like we are in a cosmic darkness (without warmth)—as if we are profoundly alone. This can lead to confusion, emptiness, and even despondency.

Spiritual consolation is distinct from feelings of consolation and reflects our state of spiritual well-being. This is generally indicated by an *increase* in trust in God and hope in our salvation, as well as love (as defined, for example, in 1 Corinthians 13).

Spiritual desolation is the opposite—a decrease in trust, hope, and love in the long term.

Saint Ignatius notes that consolation and desolation have different meanings when applied to two groups—people of the first week and people of the second week. The term "week" refers to the week of the *Spiritual Exercises* most pertinent to that group. We can define this in terms of the four stages of religious and moral conversion mentioned above in Section IV.C:

1. Little or no religious and moral conversion
2. Weak or tepid religious and moral conversion
3. Striving toward strong religious and moral conversion
4. Strong religious and moral conversion

Saint Ignatius' "first week" refers to the first and second groups, while his "second week" refers to the third and fourth groups. As noted above, consolation and desolation have different meanings for those in the first week versus those in the second week.

Since the first group has no religious and moral conversion, Saint Ignatius indicates that they are heavily and directly influenced by the Evil One most of the time (though the Holy Spirit continually tries to intervene). Thus, the first group is generally in a state of spiritual desolation (little faith, hope, and capacity for self-sacrificial charity). The Evil One "lavishes" *feelings* of consolation, enthusiasm, and ego fulfillment on them (affective consolation) to support them in their lifestyle. Conversely, the Holy Spirit allows them to experience the cosmic emptiness, loneliness, alienation, and guilt that naturally flow from their separation from relationship with God, for which they were created. In order to move out of this condition, people in this group will have to pursue the following fourfold path:

1. Opening themselves to faith (particularly the evidence for God), the soul, Jesus, and the Church (see IV.D above)
2. Participating in a church community
3. Growing close to the Lord in prayer
4. Growing in virtue to resist temptation

The second group would also be considered part of Saint Ignatius' "first week", but they are in a less dangerous position. Since they have some (though weak) faith and acknowledgment of the need for moral conversion, they waiver between spiritual desolation and consolation. Thus, they are sometimes under the direct influence of the Evil One—and sometimes under the influence of the Holy Spirit. When they move toward deepening their religious and moral conversion, they open themselves to the Holy Spirit and move into a state of spiritual consolation (increasing in faith, hope, and love). When this group remains tepid in their commitment to God, the Evil One continues to support them with affective consolation, but the Holy Spirit allows them to experience the affective desolation that naturally follows from alienating themselves from God. When this group moves toward greater religious and moral conversion, the Holy Spirit supports them with affective consolation, while the Evil One fills them with doubts, confusion, nightmares, and yearnings for past sensual and ego gratification.

The third group (striving toward strong religious and moral conversion) is viewed by Saint Ignatius as belonging to the "second week". This time, the Holy Spirit has direct and strong influence over the believer (instead of the Evil One, who has the advantage for those in the "first week"). As such, these individuals are in spiritual consolation (increasing trust, hope, and love)—unless they grow tepid in their religious and moral commitments. Since the Holy Spirit has the advantage, He supports the believer with affective consolation—peace and certitude, as well as clarity about religious and moral truths and a sense of His loving presence.[44] Since the Evil One has been weakened significantly, he will be less successful with direct temptations and will have to make recourse to deception and discouragement. This he does by two methods—giving false consolations (see below, Section V.B) and disguising himself as an angel of light (see below, V.C).

Since the fourth group is strong in their religious and moral conversion, they are directly and strongly influenced by the Holy Spirit the vast majority of the time. It is highly unlikely that they will slip back into the first week, and they are familiar with the deceptions of the Evil One so that they are unlikely to fall prey to false consolations and the "angel of light". The Holy Spirit supports them with heightened affective consolation, certitude, clarity, and judgment. He may discontinue this affective consolation, but only for purposes of purification (the passive dark night of the senses and passive dark night of the spirit). Since this group is well aware of the deceptions of the Evil One (false consolations and the angel of light), he is compelled to make recourse to harassment and intimidation. The believer counters these harassments with trust in God and prayer, making his suffering an offering to the Father for the life of the world.

Our objective in the next two subsections (V.B and V.C) is to address the major deceptions of the Evil One for individuals *in the third group*. Since people in the first group are under the strong influence of the Evil One, they are subject to temptation and deceit most of the time—and the only way out of it is to move toward faith

---

[44] These feelings of affective consolation can be mitigated during times of purification—such as the passive dark night of the senses and the passive dark night of the spirit (see "Christian Mysticism", Chapter 1, Section III).

and moral conversion. Since people in the second group are under the influence of the Evil One as long as they remain tepid in their religious and moral conversion, they are also influenced by an evil spirit, though the Holy Spirit has more influence over them than the first group.

What are the special deceptions of the Evil One that are aimed at individuals in the *third group*? They fall into two categories:

1. Deception through spiritual feelings (Section V.B)
2. Deception through the Evil One posturing as an angel of light (Section V.C)

B. Rules for Discerning Deceptions in Our Spiritual Feelings

Assuming that the reader is in the third group, we will want to bear in mind two general rules offered by Saint Ignatius of Loyola to help us detect and redress the deceptions in our spiritual feelings:

1. Never make an important decision in times of affective desolation and/or spiritual desolation
2. Beware of false consolations induced by the Evil One

We will briefly discuss each of these two general rules and the deceptions they are designed to detect and redress.

1. Never Make a Major Decision in Times of Desolation

Let us begin with the first rule—never make an important decision in times of affective and/or spiritual desolation. Saint Ignatius recognized that both affective and spiritual desolation can fill our thoughts with confusion, darkness, and uncertainty. Moreover, they can obscure the movements of the Holy Spirit and our realistic perception of ourselves and the world. In these moods, black can appear white, and white can appear black, and we can be filled with apathy and melancholy—a sure recipe for making the wrong decision. Thus, whenever we are in a state of affective or spiritual desolation— whether this be caused by the Evil One or some other cause—Saint

Ignatius counsels us to put off the decision until affective and spiritual consolation return. If the decision is time-sensitive and we cannot delay it, we should seek the advice or oversight of a spiritual director, or good and wise spiritual friends.

As noted above, the Evil One is always responsible for *spiritual* desolation (a decrease in trust, hope, and love), while the Holy Spirit is always responsible for *spiritual* consolation (an increase in trust, hope, and love). Hence, if we remain strongly committed in the third or fourth group, and we have not been deceived by the Evil One posturing as an angel of light (see below), then we should be in a state of *spiritual consolation*. As such, we need only be concerned with *affective desolation*. As Saint Ignatius (and Saint John of the Cross and Saint Teresa of Avila) explain, *affective* desolation can occur within people of the "second week" (the third and fourth groups). This can happen for four reasons:

1. A person may be experiencing physical or natural causes that are creating difficulties (e.g., depression brought on by chemical imbalance, hormonal imbalance, trauma, or other psychological disorders). These difficulties should be resolved by redressing the natural or physical problems from which the depression arises; they are best addressed by a medical doctor, psychiatrist, or psychologist who has religious faith.

2. An individual in the third group who is contemplating serious sin or a regression into the second group is likely to experience incisive affective desolation—particularly in the form of cosmic emptiness, alienation, and loneliness. These feelings can be alleviated by returning to one's original commitment to religious and moral conversion—or if regression occurs, by sincere repentance and desire for amendment.

3. A person may be experiencing purification through the passive dark night of the senses or the passive dark night of the spirit, as noted in Chapter 1, Section III. The Lord will ask individuals of the third group to endure some periods of affective desolation—described as a spiritual desert or a dark night to wean them off their attachment to the *feelings* of security and love so that they can be strengthened in their commitment to the Divine Lovers Themselves (Father, Son, and Holy Spirit).

Normally, these "periods of the dark night" will come to an end in a reasonable time and, as Saint Ignatius indicates, are soon followed by periods of affective consolation once again.

4. An individual in the third or fourth group falls prey to the deception of the Evil One posturing as an angel of light. (This will be discussed below in Section V.C.) This *affective* desolation can be redressed by exposing the Evil One's deception and modifying any decisions made during the time of deception.

We might summarize by saying that people in the third and fourth groups should be in a state of *spiritual* consolation if they remain strong in their commitment to religious and moral conversion, and do not fall prey to the devil posturing as an angel of light. However, they can experience *affective* desolation for four reasons (described above). These sources of affective desolation can be redressed by the remedies mentioned above. When group three experiences affective desolation, Saint Ignatius advises that they make no serious decisions when they are in this state, and if their decisions are time-sensitive, to consult a wise spiritual director or spiritual friends.

2. False Consolations for Individuals in the Third Group

Saint Ignatius recognized well that feelings—even spiritual feelings like consolation and desolation—can be deceiving. Thus we might be in a state of affective consolation (see the feelings of consolation described in Section V.A above), but find ourselves declining in trust in God, hope in our salvation, and the desire and capacity to love (spiritual desolation). Though affective consolation and spiritual consolation frequently run hand in hand, this need not be so; the same holds true for affective desolation and spiritual desolation.

Normally, the Holy Spirit imparts affective consolation, and so it is not unusual to find that we experience spiritual consolation (an increase in trust, hope, and love) at the same time. However, the Evil One can try to deceive us by using feelings similar to those produced by the Holy Spirit. By doing this, he hopes to lead us to destructive decisions or on a destructive spiritual path. Typically, these false feelings of consolation subside and leave us dry and empty—and in the long term (over several months), they lead to a decrease in trust, hope, and love.

At the beginning of his spiritual journey, Saint Ignatius discovered how the Evil One used these feelings to distract and deceive him:

> Frequently on a clear moonlit night there appeared in the courtyard before him an indistinct shape which he could not see clearly enough to tell what it was. Yet it appeared so symmetrical and beautiful that his soul was filled with pleasure and joy as he gazed at it. It had something of the form of a serpent with glittering eyes, and yet they were not eyes. He felt an indescribable joy steal over him at the sight of this object. The more often he saw it, the greater was the consolation he derived from it, and when the vision left him, his soul was filled with sorrow and sadness.[45]

His final comment here is very important—"when the vision left him, his soul was filled with sorrow and sadness." This aftereffect stands in contrast to his experience of reading the life of Christ and the lives of the saints. These texts also filled his soul with joy and inspiration, but when he finished reading them, his soul continued to be inspired and edified. He concluded from this that the vision of the beautiful object induced a false consolation (from the Evil One), and therefore it should not be entertained or followed. Conversely, his reading of the lives of Christ and the saints produced true consolation from the Holy Spirit (because it endured long after he finished reading). He reasoned from this that it was safe to continue following this path of inspiration.

He also set out a second rule to discern false feelings of consolation— when feelings of consolation lead to spiritual desolation, they are false. As noted above, affective consolation is usually the work of the Holy Spirit unless it leads to spiritual desolation—that is, a *decrease*, rather than an increase, in trust in God, hope in salvation, or love (as defined in 1 Corinthians 13). He concluded from this that we should follow *affective* consolation unless it leaves us empty and/or causes *spiritual* desolation, in which case we should stop following the affective consolation, for it is very likely a false consolation induced by the Evil One. We should next make an examination of the decisions, attitudes, or actions that led to the false consolation. It is usually a good

---

[45] Saint Ignatius of Loyola, *Autobiography*, pp. 40–41.

idea to do this with a person (or persons) of spiritual experience and maturity. If there does not seem to be any reason for the false consolation other than a particular past decision or course of action, we will probably want to either tone down or reverse that decision or course of action altogether. If toning down or reversing our past decision causes an increase in *spiritual* consolation (trust, hope, and love), then we are probably correct in our adjustment of that past decision.

C. Beware of the Evil One Posturing as an Angel of Light

Recall that group three individuals are becoming gradually more proficient at detecting and redressing the Evil One's temptations. Hence, he must find other avenues to undermine the religious and moral conversion of these individuals. In addition to his tactic of false consolations, he also comes disguised as an angel of light (a good angel) to make a suggestion that seems good and pious, but in fact will lead to spiritual desolation (a decrease in trust, hope, and love) that he hopes will discourage, confuse, and depress the believer as well as undermining the believer's idea and confidence in God. Some illustrations may help to grasp his tactics.

Suppose you are in spiritual consolation. Your trust in God has increased, and along with this your hope in salvation and your appreciation of the Beatitudes. You are in a state of confidence, clarity, enthusiasm, and perhaps even fervor toward improving your spiritual life and your love of neighbor. In the midst of this fervor, you think to yourself, "If a half an hour of daily prayer is good, then three hours must be better." You begin your new discipline and find yourself growing progressively tired. You do not have enough time for your family and work, and even though the fruits of your prayer are good, you find yourself snapping at people and even thinking that *they* should be spending three hours in prayer (because you are making such a great sacrifice to do so). After a while you start believing that God really *expects* this of you; yet you feel like you cannot continue without dissolving emotionally and ruining your family. You begin to think, "God is asking too much of me, and He is not giving me the graces I need to continue this good and holy discipline." You begin to have a view of God as a stoic taskmaster, of your family as unappreciative spiritual "do-nothings", and your workplace supervisors as completely unfair. You keep thinking to yourself, "But I'm doing this for God!" When the collapse takes place (and it generally does), you find yourself frustrated, discouraged, cynical, and on the brink of despair. What happened? The Evil One came disguised as an angel of light and pushed you beyond your limits, beyond what was prudent, and, needless to say, beyond the guidance of the Holy Spirit.

There are many other common scenarios of the devil disguised as an angel of light. For example, when I am experiencing spiritual consolation, the thought may occur that I can get rid of the sin of pride tomorrow. "Indeed, I think I can get rid of all sinful inclinations tomorrow!" When I am in a state of consolation, it is quite easy to ward off temptation. However, as the consolation diminishes, I find myself slipping back into the old modes of conduct—for example, blaming others, pandering for praise or respect, seeking status as an end in itself. I am absolutely bewildered. "I thought I had it licked." Discouragement soon ensues, and along with it (as the Evil One hopes) cynicism and perhaps even despair.

You will probably notice that the tactic of the Evil One is to take something perfectly good and then *exaggerate* it to the point where it is either "over the top" or unaccomplishable. How do these exaggerations occur? In four major ways:

1. Inspiring you to do too many tasks of conversion or perfection— "I think I can tackle greed, lust, *and* pride within the next couple of months."
2. Inspiring you to decrease your timeline—"I think I can attain purity of heart *tomorrow*."
3. Inspiring you toward perfection on your own, as in the worst possible prayer—"Don't worry, God; *I* will get perfection taken care of any day now, and then You can come into my soul and be pleased with what *I* have accomplished."
4. Inspiring you to attribute stoic intentions to God when reading Scripture, doctrine, or tradition—"Spitzer, this is God speaking. Why haven't you become perfect as your Heavenly Father is perfect? It is set right out for you in Scripture; and by the way, why aren't you loving other people as I have loved you? You're slipping up so much that I'm getting tired of waiting.

And frankly, why were you distracted today in your meditation after Communion? ... And frankly ...". After several minutes of this reflection, you find yourself discouraged, giving up on the spiritual life, and running from God. Checkmate!

Another related (but seemingly opposite) tactic of the "angel of light" is discouragement arising out of increased awareness of ulterior motives. Seminaries are filled with good individuals who began their spiritual journeys with a genuine desire to serve God and others and to serve others for God. They were moved by zeal for God's Kingdom; they had a genuine love of Scripture, doctrine, and tradition; and their intentions were reinforced by affective and spiritual consolation. Then, some years after entering the seminary, they discover, in a remarkably lucid moment, that they had a variety of ulterior motives for entering ("I really didn't want to be a public accountant anyway. The breakup with my girlfriend was overwhelming; and after all, entering the seminary really did please my mother"). These motives could very well *have been* present, but might be irrelevant to the seminarian at the time when he is thinking about them. Nevertheless, the "angel of light" sees a fantastic opportunity that can lead, with a little push, to discouragement and perhaps even despondency. "You hypocrite. The *only* reason you entered was to escape from what you did not want to do, and to win favor with your family and friends. Your whole vocation is a sham. If you had any integrity or authenticity, you would drop this pretense and go back to public accounting."

Saint Ignatius gives sage advice to us in these situations. First, be very hesitant about giving up something that you *believe* you started for an authentic and good reason when the *only* things you can see clearly are your ulterior motives. When your vision is restricted to ulterior motives or to negative data (and you *believe* that this was not the case at the time you set out on your journey), then you are likely experiencing spiritual desolation. When you cannot remember consolation, it generally indicates that you are in desolation. Exaggerated negativity about yourself and your intentions (when you are deepening your spiritual commitment) is generally untrue, and therefore is a marker of spiritual desolation. You must go back to the first rule (given above) when this occurs—never make a life decision in times of desolation. The key word here is "*wait*". Until when? Until you can clearly remember and appreciate the thoughts and consolation that you *believe* you experienced at the time you made your decision.

As you can see, the Evil One can take just about any movement of spiritual consolation and push it just a little further than Divine Wisdom would prescribe in order to obtain his reward—the discouragement that leads to a decrease in trust, hope, and love, which, in its turn, will lead to cynicism and despair.

When we discover that good, holy, or pious intentions are (in the intermediate to long term) turning into spiritual desolation (a decrease in trust, hope, and love), then we will want to reexamine those thoughts, decisions, or resolutions as quickly as possible. As noted above, it is helpful to do this with a person of spiritual experience or maturity (preferably one who is educated and reasonable, following the advice of Saint Teresa of Avila). Why? Because we can be stubborn ("I thought this was a good idea last week, and so it still should be a good idea today, even though it's killing me"). Or we might think that everything we start with a pious intention must be God's will ("I believe the Holy Spirit inspired me to attain perfection by the end of the week; it must be God's will"). Or we told our friends about desires to deepen our conversion and spiritual lives (and they might think that we're hypocrites if we do not follow through—even though it's killing us).

If we find that our pious decision or resolution might be an exaggeration (a deception of the "angel of light"), then we ought to modify it. It is frequently not necessary to give up the pious intention, but only to "ratchet it down several notches" in order to make it correspond to our potential and to the Holy Spirit's will and timetable.

The above rules do not exhaust Saint Ignatius' writings (or the contemporary literature) on discernment of spirits. I give these three particular rules because they come up most frequently in my life and the lives of others with whom I am associated. Hopefully, they will provide a starting point for your own spiritual life.

VI. Conclusion

One might be thinking at this juncture that the Evil One's plan is so ingenious and extensive that it is virtually impossible to resist.

Though it is true that his plan is ingenious and extensive, it is *not* impossible to resist. Indeed, he has already been defeated by Jesus, and the Holy Spirit is exceedingly active in helping us move into the higher stages of the third group. If we keep to a simple plan of action—participation in our church community, continued study of our faith, and firm resolve to use our three divine gifts of faith/ prayer, empathy, and conscience to develop virtue and deepen moral conversion—we will be in a state of spiritual consolation, inspired by the Holy Spirit, and increasingly purified in our faith and love. Then all we need do is remain alert to false consolations, the devil posturing as an angel of light, and avoiding decisions during times of affective desolation. This will enable us to be true disciples of the Lord, following His lead into the Kingdom of eternal joy and using our gifts to help others to do the same. Yes, we must be alert, vigilant, and committed to progressing in religious and moral conversion, which has its complexities and challenges. But we must remember that if we follow the above path, we do not have to save ourselves; the unconditionally merciful God will use our open hearts and strivings to raise us to unimaginably authentic love—for to Him, all things are possible.

Chapter Five

The Deadly Sins—Part I

Gluttony, Greed, Lust, Sloth, and Vanity

Introduction

The deadly sins present one of the best paradigms for organizing and assessing the collective teaching on sin and virtue contained in the Bible, history, classical literature, and modern literature. This paradigm addresses not only principles, commandments, and sins, but also the interior attitudes that produce them, and the means and virtues to redress them. It contains the wisdom of not only the Old Testament—the Ten Commandments and the proclamations of the prophets—but also the New Testament, particularly the Sermon on the Mount. These sins are also present in extrabiblical literature in works by Virgil, Shakespeare, Dickens, Tolstoy, Dostoyevsky, and Fitzgerald—as the central theme of tragic dramas and narratives—and may be seen in the annals of great historians to explain the origins of war, crime, and corruption. It stands at the heart of Christian spiritual classics—from the earliest Fathers of the Church to contemporary spiritual autobiographies—and if psychologists are willing to admit it, at the origin of many psychological disorders. Whenever we see restless hearts, human discontent, bias, disrespect, marginalization, oppression, and every form of injustice and hatred, there we may also see the seeds of the deadly sins—the interior attitudes that form the heart of darkness and the antithesis to generosity, compassion, and self-sacrificial love.

Though the Old Testament as well as many classical philosophers, historians, and poets had great insights into the deadly sins,

Jesus provided the deepest and most comprehensive understanding
of them (though He did not use this phrase to describe them). There
are several lists of "sins" in the Old Testament and New Testament
that might be thought to be a precursor to the deadly sins—such as
Proverbs 6:16–19; Galatians 5:19–21; and Revelation 21:8—but these
contain lists of prohibited *actions*, whereas the deadly sins concern
interior attitudes that dispose a person to evil actions. The deadly sins
"lie at the heart" of *all* sinful actions. Jesus' Sermon on the Mount is
in good part concerned with them and provides the basis for Christianity's foundational moral catechism.

After Jesus, subsequent generations of Christian thinkers developed His moral teachings and eventually consolidated them into a
paradigm called "deadly" or "capital" or "cardinal" sins or vices. One
of the first paradigmatic presentations was developed by the fourth-
century ascetic monk Evagrius Ponticus (A.D. 345–399). He greatly
influenced Saint John Cassian (A.D. 360–435), who used the paradigm as the basis of his *Institutes* (particularly Books 5–12), which
addressed eight capital vices and how to redress them through virtue
and prayer. Pope Gregory I revised the list of John Cassian and gave
it his papal approval in A.D. 590. Gregory's revised list made its way
into the Western church and became the foundation for catechetical
preparation, confessional preparation, monastic manuals, and moral
tractates. It became a centerpiece of Christian art, which was used to
teach basic moral catechesis. In the thirteenth century, Saint Thomas
Aquinas defended and commented extensively on Gregory's list of
sins, enshrining it within the foundation of Christian moral teaching. He showed in the *Summa Theologica* that the deadly sins (what
he terms "the seven capital vices") lie at the heart of all sins, because
they are corrupt interior attitudes that orient human beings to false
ends (nonloving objectives of life). When we pursue these false ends,
thinking that they will make us happy, we are led into a myriad of
other sins (violations of commandments) in our pursuit of these false
ends. He notes in this regard:

> The capital vices are those which give rise to others, especially by way
> of final cause. Now this kind of origin may take place in two ways.
> First, on account of the condition of the sinner, who is disposed so
> as to have a strong inclination for one particular end, the result being

that he frequently goes forward to other sins. But this kind of origin does not come under the consideration of art, because man's particular dispositions are infinite in number. Secondly, on account of a natural relationship of the ends to one another: and it is in this way that most frequently one vice arises from another, so that this kind of origin can come under the consideration of art.[1]

The paradigm made its way into early European Christian literature, particularly Dante's *Inferno* and *Purgatorio*[2] and Chaucer's "The Parson's Tale".[3] Since that time, parts of the paradigm—either individual capital sins or combinations of them—have been integrated into every dimension of Western literature. We will consider but a few eras and authors below—English Renaissance literature (e.g., several tragedies of William Shakespeare and Edmund Spenser's *The Faerie Queen*), Victorian literature (e.g., Charles Dickens), nineteenth-century Russian literature (e.g., Fyodor Dostoyevsky and Leo Tolstoy), and twentieth-century American literature (e.g., F. Scott Fitzgerald).

Between the time of Evagrius Ponticus and Saint Thomas Aquinas, the list varied between eight and seven cardinal sins. We will use the list of eight because vanity (the disputed eighth sin) deserves treatment in its own right apart from pride. Thus, we will treat the following eight sins in our exposition below—in this chapter, gluttony, greed, lust, sloth, and vanity; in Chapter 6, anger, envy, and pride. Why this order of treatment? It corresponds best with

[1] Saint Thomas Aquinas, *Summa Theologica* I-II, q. 84, a. 4, trans. Fathers of the English Dominican Province (New York: Benziger Brothers, 1947), p. 965. Saint Thomas gives a detailed consideration of all the deadly sins in *Summa Theologica* I-II, q. 84.

[2] The *Purgatorio* is in great part organized around the deadly sins and uses one of the most imaginative symbolic explications of them, the harm they do, and the remedies for them. Interested readers may want to use an annotated version and a commentary to profit from it suitably.

[3] "The Parson's Tale", the last tale in Chaucer's *Canterbury Tales*, is not a fable, but a sermon devoted to penitence—to which Chaucer himself subscribes. The first part is about the three stages of repentance, and the second part is about the seven deadly sins and the virtues needed to remediate them. His seven deadly sins are pride, envy, wrath, sloth, greed, gluttony, and lust, and they are remedied by the virtues of humility, contentment, patience, fortitude, mercy, moderation, and chastity. Readers interested in this insightful sermon will want to use an annotated version of the text to help them through Chaucer's Middle English and rhetorical style.

our treatment of the four levels of happiness given in Volume I, Chapter 3, Section I, of the Quartet. How so? The first three capital sins (gluttony, greed, and lust) pertain in good part to Level One (though greed and lust can also pertain to Level Two). Sloth (which concerns apathy about life's meaning and purpose) results in its victim staying on Level One, because of sheer disinterest in making the most of life. Anger (which is concerned as much with unforgiveness and vengeance as with impatience or outbursts) is connected with ego concerns and ego offenses—and so we associate it with Level Two. Vanity (concerned with seeking the admiration and praise of others) is ego-comparative and again connected with Level Two. Envy (which not only resents a person for having more goods, talent, status, and beauty, but also covets these things and wishes ill on those who have them) is near the height of ego-comparative vice (Level Two) because it is so destructive to others and self. Finally, pride (which is a conviction of being intrinsically superior to others, leading to a belief that one is more worthy and deserves more power and dominion than others) is viewed as the height of Level Two vice, because it leads to all the other deadly sins and is most antithetical to love, and therefore salvation. Let us now consider each of the deadly sins in turn, examining its destructiveness to self and others as well as its biblical precedents and some examples from the best of Western literature.

I. Gluttony

Gluttony is included in virtually all lists of the deadly sins. It refers to the desire for excess of sensorial fulfillment, which can include an excess of food, drink, and other euphoric stimulants.

Why is gluttony destructive? It holds its victims in the spell of sensorial pleasure, preventing them from reaching higher levels of meaning and purpose in life, giving rise to the phenomenon of living to eat instead of eating to live. When gluttony casts its spell, it seeks out as much as it can get to the point where luxuriating in sensorial pleasures is almost insatiable. One seeks out the very best cuisine, wine, after-dinner drinks in the best restaurants with the best views, and so forth. These luxuriating events are not necessarily gluttony if they are special occasions or occasional treats. Gluttony is the negative interior disposition of a person that captures his imagination and will, foreclosing other pursuits that may have greater meaning and fulfillment. Enjoying gourmet cuisine turns into gluttony when one puts it at the center of life—reminiscing about it, anticipating its next occurrence, and orienting one's time and energy around it.

Satiation of sensorial desires—food, alcohol, and euphoric stimulants—can become addictive, and when they do, they can lead to extreme declines in health, family life, work performance, and social efficacy. Thus, gluttony can be destructive of self and others. The stronger the addiction and habit, the more difficult it is to break, and the more destructive it will be for oneself and others. When one becomes fixated and concerned only with the next luxurious sensorial event, it will consume one's imagination, creativity, and social respectability. Though gluttony does not have the extreme antisocial potential of anger, envy, and pride, its addictions can lead to neglect of family members, squandering of resources, arrested maturity, superficiality, and continual distraction.

Gluttony is viewed as a dangerous vice in both the Old and New Testaments. The Book of Proverbs advises strongly:

> When you sit down to dine with a ruler, observe carefully what is before you; and put a knife to your throat if you are a man given to appetite [gluttony]. Do not desire his delicacies, for they are deceptive food. Do not toil to acquire wealth. (23:1–4)

The author recognizes how luxurious food can become a preoccupation, leading to superficiality and a subordination of ourselves (and life's purpose) to mere food and the individuals who can provide it for us. Saint Paul sees gluttony as undermining the self-mastery for which Christ has destined us as children of God:

> "All things are lawful for me," but I will not be enslaved by anything. "Food is meant for the stomach and the stomach for food—and God will destroy both." (1 Cor 6:12–13)

In the Letter to the Philippians, Paul goes further in counterpoising gluttony to his relationship with Christ:

For many, of whom I have often told you and now tell you even with tears, walk as enemies of the cross of Christ. Their end is destruction, their god is the belly, and they glory in their shame, with minds set on earthly things. But our commonwealth is in heaven. (3:18–20)

Paul sees gluttony as one of the ways (along with lust) in which excess sensorial fulfillment can orient us toward the domain of the flesh, causing us to take our eyes off of our true dignity, nature, fulfillment, and destiny—the glorious body given to us through Jesus Christ.

Jami Attenberg's 2012 novel, *The Middlesteins*, illustrates the above fixation on sensorial pleasure.[4] The central figure, Edie Middlestein, is a former successful attorney and a loving mother and friend. Yet her obsession with eating causes a radical decline in her life—the loss of her job, then the loss of her husband, and now the loss of her health—to the point of killing her. Her children and in-laws who care about her rally to her support, but she cannot seem to help herself; she cannot resist finding another delicious morsel to feed her habit and bring her "peace of mind".

Though Attenberg reveals the destructiveness of Edie's gluttony to her job, marriage, family, and health, she does not make this the central focus of the novel; rather, she probes into the reasons for Edie's self-destructive obsession, and the ways it affects her family members. As with many cases of gluttony, the obsessed victim is not a hedonist (like a Roman epicurean at the vomitorium who focuses solely on euphoric self-indulgence), but rather a complex individual who uses food, as one would use alcohol and drugs, to manage the stresses and challenges of inner turmoil produced by a difficult life. To be sure, there are many hedonistic individuals focused on the euphoria of sensorial self-indulgence, but Edie is not one of them. Though the destructive effects of her gluttony are the same as the hedonist, she has almost unconsciously slipped into it while hedonists *choose* to forsake any higher-level meaning in life (e.g., achievement, contribution, family, and faith) for the sake of the next party and its continuous euphoria.

---

[4] Throughout this presentation of the book, I use parts of the following book review of *The Middlesteins*: Julie Orringer, "Suburban Sprawl: The Middlesteins", *New York Times*, December 27, 2012, https://www.nytimes.com/2012/12/30/books/review/the-middlesteins-by-jami-attenberg.html.

Edie grew up with parents who virtually set her up for obsessive euphoric self-medication. Her mother could not resist feeding her out of mistaken sense of love—"Here, dear, have another matzo ball." Her father also contributed to the mix because of his background—a Jewish immigrant from the Ukraine who nearly starved on his journey to Chicago, inducing an ongoing anxiety about getting enough to eat. The stage was set: Edie would use food as a way of overcoming anxiety and lifting her spirits. As the challenges of her life increased, she gained so much weight that her law firm discharged her with an excellent pension (to prevent her from filing suit), and her husband, who could no longer watch her destroy herself, abandons her. The one bright note is that Edie's family cared enough about her to help her in her time of need, even to the point of procuring remediative surgery and staying in the kitchen throughout the night before the surgery to prevent her from eating yet another snack that would adversely affect the surgery.

Clearly, gluttony—obsessive overeating for the purpose of euphoria—is *tragic*, whether it be caused by the free choice of a hedonist who has abandoned higher meaning in life for the sake of pleasure, or a person like Edie who has unconsciously appropriated the habit of excessive euphoric overeating to medicate herself and lift her spirits. Gluttony's effects are destructive to self and others, and can lead to an acute underliving of life. Though the reasons for their gluttony are quite different, both Edie and the hedonist are faced with a similar moral challenge: they must desire—nay, will—to make a change in their lives in order to prevent further waste of life, self-destructiveness, and destructiveness of others who care. This act of the will—that stands at the foundation of curbing an insatiable desire for sensorial overindulgence, and to replace it with higher-level desires for achievement, contribution, love, and faith—will be very difficult indeed. Yet without this act of the will, there can be no relief from gluttony's course of self-destruction. Though difficult, this act of the will is not impossible, and it can be strengthened and efficacious with the help of reinforcement, collective wisdom, and prayer.

Twelve-step programs, such as overeater's anonymous, cannot make the decision to change (the act of the will) for the addict, but they can help the addict to do the following:

- Recognize (instead of denying) his problem
- Refute his rationalizations
- Gain insight into the causes of his problem
- Encourage his acts of self-control through wise fellowship
- Avail himself of supernatural grace through prayer

There are literally millions of success stories that have been aided by these programs, but at the heart of all of them is the decision of the addict himself to control one's sensorial appetite and to commit one-self to a better future—not only a decision to refrain from denial and rationalization (i.e., to seek authenticity and truth) but also the de-cision to pursue the virtues of temperance and fortitude. When this decision toward truth and virtue is made, the Lord can help tremen-dously through prayer and grace.

Recall from above that the effectiveness of grace is in good part dependent on our desiring and choosing it. Furthermore, grace builds on nature. Thus, as we grow stronger in the virtues of temperance and fortitude by practicing them and making them a habit, we make them part of our nature—our "second nature". Philosophers since the time of Aristotle have associated virtue with habit, and habit with "second nature". The genius of twelve-step programs is the recognition of the power of "truth to self", free choice, and virtue such as self-control and fortitude—and to build faith and prayer onto this strong natural foundation. As the millions of success stories testify, this formula is incredibly successful, so long as individuals can hold out for enough time to break the spell of the addiction. It is sometimes best to stay in a treatment center that curbs the possibility of obtaining the addictive substance during the initial period of withdrawal, and then to remain vigilant in meetings (accountability sessions) and support groups to help bolster the act of the will and the development of temperance and fortitude. As time passes, the spell of addiction will wane—and then wane considerably, though it will never go away. An addict must continue to be vigilant even when the compulsion to satisfy the addic-tion has almost disappeared.

Though the culture does not make gluttony alluring, the avail-ability of delicious fast foods, sugars, and carbohydrates can initiate a habit like Edie's where food is used to self-medicate and lift the spir-its. When peer pressure to stay thin lessens, a developing routine of seeking pleasure to alleviate stress can turn into a full-time habit. What does this mean? Young people who will be best prepared to move beyond the spell of Level One euphoria and the destructiveness of euphoric addiction are those who are educated and trained in the virtues of prudence, temperance (self-control), and fortitude. When these virtues are combined with faith, they will have a remarkably effective shield to avoid the pitfalls of the first deadly sin, and move to higher levels of meaning and purpose in life.

II. Greed (Avarice)

Like gluttony, greed is grounded in an excessive worldly desire. Where gluttony is the excessive desire for sensorial euphoria, greed is the excessive desire for material possessions and wealth. Though greed does not cause physical addiction, it does cause psychological obsession to the point of being insatiable—so insatiable that one is willing to cheat, steal, defraud, and exploit the vulnerable in order to obtain more material goods than one actually needs. Though greed is focused on material goods (Level One), it is connected with the egocentric desire to have more (in order to be more) than others (Level Two).

Greed begins when an individual covets more than he needs because he thinks that excessive possessions will grant him comparative advantage, esteem, and status, and that he might have to take ethical shortcuts in order to satiate his desire. Nevertheless, he seems to ignore or suppress these innate murmurings of conscience in order to experience the elation and ego satisfaction coming from material goods. The elation seems to come from a sense of being enhanced—of becoming more—through possessions and wealth. He does not seem to recognize that material goods do not add to his creative, loving, contributive, moral, and transcendent self, but only to things possessed outside the self.

The elation coming from additional material goods with which to enhance the outer self leads to a forgetfulness of the inner self—the qualities that ultimately define the goodness, generativity, and love of a human being, enabling him to be contributive and imitate the heart of God. The more one pursues the adornments of the outer self, the more one forgets the inner self, which opens the door to heartlessness (particularly toward the marginalized and poor), exploitation of others, "legal cheating", and "legal stealing". These practices that violate the Ten Commandments and scriptural writ enhance egocentricity and delimit compassion—inhibiting the path to salvation. For this reason, Saint Thomas Aquinas noted that "greed is a sin against God ... inasmuch as man forsakes things eternal for the sake of temporal things."[5] Aquinas considers a sin against God to be most serious, because it inhibits the path to salvation in its quest for the things of the world.

How does this occur with greed? If one gives in to the lure of greed, it takes over more and more of the human psyche, and it can become the dominant perspective from which one views self, the world, and others. As it continues to seduce the individual, it blocks out empathy, respect, and compassion—and as it grows, even conscience and the desire for relationship with God. The insatiability of greed makes it expansive. The more one gets, the more one wants. As long as the individual gives in to its allurement, it grows in intensity—one can never be satisfied with the previous level of satisfaction. One "needs" a bigger house, a fancier car, more property, better clothes, more jewelry, and so forth.

Is there any way out of the seduction of greed? There is—a crisis of meaning: emotional crisis, existential crisis, economic crisis, relationship crisis, family crisis, and community crisis. As many saints have noted, crisis can be the best thing that ever happened to a person because it causes a rethinking of life's meaning, fulfillment, and destiny, which in turn can lead to the discovery—or in many cases the rediscovery—of the goodness of love, family, integrity, and God. Without such crises, greed's spell can be so powerful that it prevents the discovery of all higher purpose, dignity, fulfillment, and destiny. This point is illustrated well in both the Scriptures and literature, particularly Charles Dickens' *A Christmas Carol*.

We will begin with Scripture, which addresses greed at great length—far more than gluttony because it is more detrimental to the soul. We will begin with the Old Testament passages that probe the heart and futility of greed in depth, particularly those in the Psalms, Proverbs, and other Wisdom literature.

---

[5] *Summa Theologica* II-II, q. 118, a. 1, ad 2.

In Psalm 49, the psalmist asserts the futility of greed, indicating that the greedy man's heart takes so much satisfaction in his wealth that he trusts in it instead of the Lord. Yet his wealth cannot ransom him from Sheol (the domain of death), but only the Lord. In allowing his wealth to occupy his complete attention, and ignoring the Lord who can ransom him from death, he risks an eternity in the domain of the dead, which is, as the Psalmist notes, incredibly foolish:

> Why should I fear in times of trouble, when the iniquity of my persecutors surrounds me, men who trust in their wealth and boast of the abundance of their riches? Truly no man can ransom himself, or give to God the price of his life, for the ransom of his life is costly, and can never suffice, that he should continue to live on for ever, and never see the Pit.... Their graves are their homes for ever, their dwelling places to all generations, though they named lands their own. Man cannot abide in his pomp, he is like the beasts that perish. This is the fate of those who have foolish confidence, the end of those who are pleased with their portion. Like sheep they are appointed for Sheol [the underworld realm of the dead]; Death shall be their shepherd; straight to the grave they descend, and their form shall waste away; Sheol shall be their home. (Ps 49:5-9, 11-14)

The Book of Proverbs and other Wisdom literature (e.g., Ecclesiastes, Sirach, and Wisdom) do not accentuate the eternal significance of allowing one's heart to be completely consumed by greed; rather, they focus on how obsession with wealth is a waste of life and human creativity, lowering one's meaning in life to mere accumulation of property, which is foolishness (the opposite of wisdom):

> He who trusts in his riches will wither, but the righteous will flourish like a green leaf. (Prov 11:28)

> A good name is to be chosen rather than great riches, and favor is better than silver or gold. (Prov 22:1)

> He who loves money will not be satisfied with money; nor he who loves wealth, with gain: this also is vanity. (Eccles 5:10)

The New Testament reflects Jesus' extreme concern for those who give themselves over to greed. Not only is greed the antithesis of love; it has a consumptive property that beckons its victim to itself to the point of indentured servitude. Those who give themselves over to the accumulation of wealth will very likely serve it, and in so doing will block out love and faith as higher meanings and fulfillment in life. By doing this, a man trades his soul for mere accumulation of material goods, which is pitiable. Jesus makes this clear in two passages:

> No one can serve two masters; for either he will hate the one and love the other, or he will be devoted to the one and despise the other. You cannot serve God and mammon. (Mt 6:24)

> "Take heed, and beware of all covetousness; for a man's life does not consist in the abundance of his possessions." And he told them a parable, saying, "The land of a rich man brought forth plentifully; and he thought to himself, 'What shall I do, for I have nowhere to store my crops?' And he said, 'I will do this: I will pull down my barns, and build larger ones; and there I will store all my grain and my goods. And I will say to my soul, Soul, you have ample goods laid up for many years; take your ease, eat, drink, be merry.' But God said to him, 'Fool! This night your soul is required of you; and the things you have prepared, whose will they be?' So is he who lays up treasure for himself, and is not rich toward God." (Lk 12:15–21)

In Robert Bolt's *Man for All Seasons*, one is reminded of Saint Thomas More's use of Scripture when he confronts Richard Rich, who has falsely accused him (consigning him to death) in order to obtain lordship over Wales. More asks him, "It profits a man nothing to give his soul for the whole world ... but for Wales, Richard?"

Jesus' teaching is clear: one risks freely rejecting God and Heaven by allowing oneself to be consumed with the goods of this world. One must break the spell of greed to find life's higher purpose and to open oneself to the Lord, who can save us.

The Bible's clear pronouncement on the dangers of covetousness and greed is supported and complemented by classical and contemporary literature. It focuses on the negativity and destructiveness of greed to self, others, and the culture. Shakespeare's *Macbeth* is a prime example of the destructiveness of unmitigated greed and lust for power that destroys Macbeth and his wife—and nearly destroys his friends and country (examined in detail in the next chapter, Section III). In *Les Miserables*, Victor Hugo counterpoises the generosity of Jean Valjean to a greedy couple (the Thénardiers) who know no limit to exploitation of the poor to satisfy their greed. They take the daughter of a poor woman and reduce her to indentured servitude, ultimately ransoming her to Valjean for a ridiculous price. As the novel ends, they reach their "true fulfillment" by becoming slave traders in the New World. Their greed makes their lives into a force of darkness, pain, and destructiveness with no end in sight as they proceed into eternity.

A contemporary film depicting the seductive and addictive dimensions of greed—as well as its power to destroy the self and others—is Oliver Stone's and Stanley Weiser's 1987 film *Wall Street*.[6] The film's two central characters are Bud Fox (an up-and-coming stock broker whose greed moves him to near catastrophe) and Gordon Gekko (a diabolical supertrader who is the master of greed, a destroyer of companies and lives, and the "mentor" of Bud). Gekko is so imbued in greed that he has forsaken his conscience and has given himself over to it, declaring in a famous speech, "Greed, for lack of a better word, is good!"

Bud so desperately wants to become a protégé of Gekko (to procure the luxurious Manhattan lifestyle he seems to offer) that he begins gradually compromising his ethical standards to please and be rewarded by him. First, he divulges insider information to Gekko on a company—Bluestar Airlines, where his father works as head of the union. He involves himself in corporate spying to give Gekko additional information to enhance his wealth. He then learns the art of straw trading, to further enrich Gekko and himself. Finally, he involves himself in an insider-trading and straw-trade scheme with Bluestar Airlines, to reach a new height of wealth. At this point, he learns that Gekko is about to betray him, his father, and all the workers on the airline by selling off the assets of the company, firing its employees, and taking advantage of the company's overfunded pension fund.

Unlike Gekko, Bud has a qualm of conscience. He cannot betray and destroy his family and friends to satisfy his greed and relationship with Gekko. The gravity of harm that was to occur because of him

---

[6]See the plot summary for *Wall Street* on IMDb.com at https://www.imdb.com/title/tt0094291/plotsummary.

breaks the spell of greed; he decides to suffer the consequences of going against Gekko by undercutting Gekko's shares in Bluestar and secretly advising his British rival, Sir Larry Wildman, to buy them. When Gekko discovers Bud's betrayal of him, he turns him over to the Securities and Exchange Commission (SEC) for prosecution by providing information on Bud's illegal dealings. In the process of being prosecuted by the SEC, Bud decides to turn state's evidence against Gekko, and at the end of the film, both appear to be headed for long prison terms.

The moral of *Wall Street* goes far beyond the adage that there is no honor among thieves. It exposes the fallacy of Gekko's initial conviction that "greed, for lack of a better word, is good", showing that greed's cravings compels its victims to ignore their consciences, to undermine their ethical principles, to abuse family and friends, and to give away their souls for mere material wealth and self-aggrandizement. If allowed to follow its depraved logic to its natural end, greed will lead to heartlessness (like that of Gordon Gekko) opening upon complete betrayal of family, friends, colleagues, and economic welfare. Even if greed's victim can resist this final seduction and destruction, it still leaves in its wake tremendous harm and destruction, which may, in due time, come back to haunt its protagonist. Indeed, financial journals are filled with the names of those who have paid the price for undermining trust, betraying fiduciary responsibility, and breaking the law, such as Ivan Boesky, Michael Milken, Kenneth Lay, Bernie Madoff—and so many more.

Charles Dickens provides one of the very best literary studies of the heart and mind of greed in virtually all of his novels concerned with England during the Industrial Revolution. Perhaps the two most notable characters consumed by greed in the annals of Western literature are Uriah Heep (in *David Copperfield*) and Scrooge (in *A Christmas Carol*). Uriah Heep is the soul of greed motivated by envy. His every move is designed to acquire more power and possessions by any possible means—lying, stealing, and creating a completely false self-caricature (calling attention to his humility and generosity, which are virtually nonexistent). His devious machinations enable him to take over the business and household of Mr. Wickfield (who was an aging alcoholic). Thanks to Heep's secretary, Mr. Micawber, David discovers the fraud, which in turn interrupts Heep's plans to marry

Wickfield's daughter Agnes. Ultimately, Heep's greed and envy are his undoing, and he winds up in prison for attempting to defraud the Bank of England.

The epitome of greed is best illustrated by Ebenezer Scrooge in Dickens' *A Christmas Carol*. He describes him as follows:

> The cold within him froze his old features, nipped his pointed nose, made his eyes red, his thin lips blue, and he spoke out shrewdly in his grating voice.[7]

As the novella begins, Scrooge, who hates Christmas celebrations, turns down two petitioners asking for funds to help the poor on Christmas Eve, and he refuses an invitation to Christmas dinner from his nephew Fred, using the derogatory expression "Bah humbug." His clerk, Bob Cratchit, asks him for the day off, which annoys Scrooge, but because of social custom, he finally agrees to it. Though Scrooge appears to be almost irredeemable, he is given a remarkable chance to turn his life around by transforming his greed into generosity and genuine concern for humanity. As he sleeps, he is visited by the ghost of his former business partner, Jacob Marley, who is wearing chains and dragging money boxes. Marley tells Scrooge that his fate will be worse if he does not reform his selfish attitudes that paved the way for Marley's bleak destiny.

Scrooge is then visited by the Ghost of Christmas Past, who brings him back to scenes of his past life where he relives the scene of when his fiancée, Belle, ended their relationship because of Scrooge's inattentiveness out of hyperconcern for money. Scrooge is then shown a scene of her in a happy Christmas gathering with her new husband and family. Though perturbed by the visit, Scrooge remains resolute in his greed and hardness of heart.

He is then visited by the Ghost of Christmas Present, where Scrooge sees several scenes of Christmas joy as well as the difficulty of Bob Crachit (whose son, Tiny Tim, will die imminently if he is not able to obtain care). He then visits two exceedingly sad children—Ignorance and Want. Scrooge is even more perturbed by this visit, which fills him with some regret about the departure of Belle and

---

[7] Charles Dickens, *A Christmas Carol* (New York: Simon & Brown, 2010), p. 7.

a slight sense of longing for joy and companionship on Christmas. Nevertheless, his heart remains unchanged.

Finally, he is visited by the last ghost—the Ghost of Christmas Yet to Come, where he witnesses the aftermath of a man's death. No one will show up to his funeral unless lunch is provided. He asks if anyone would feel any loss at the man's death, and the ghost tells him only people who are rejoicing that they will have more time to repay their debt. The ghost then shows him his own grave, at which point Scrooge awakens, having a remarkable change of heart. He sees the emptiness, loneliness, and meaninglessness of a life that forsakes goodness, compassion, and contribution for the sake of an insatiable desire for more money. This moves him to action. He accepts Fred's invitation and spends Christmas with him and his family, buys a turkey for Bob Cratchit's Christmas dinner, and gives him a raise in the hopes of helping his son, Tiny Tim.

Though one might view Scrooge's change of heart as a bit artificial, because he is able to benefit from a privilege that most greedy people will not have—the visits by the four ghosts—Dickens' conversion story (perhaps a Christian allegory) has an undercurrent of realism. Those consumed by greed to the point of heartlessness and exploitation are frequently visited by crises sometimes brought on by a curious turn of events, rejection by families, economic downturns, depression and psychological problems, and even trouble with the law. These crises act very much like the four ghosts appearing to Scrooge in that they cause disruption of life, turbulence of soul, and a reexamination of what makes life worth living. As with the ghosts, crises do not force anyone to take action; they only challenge the greedy individual to action. They, like Scrooge's ghosts, can lead either to despair or to genuine change of heart—to contribute rather than to exploit, to bring joy rather than despair, to foster human relationships rather than destroying them. It then remains for the individual to make a decision and act on it.

Some might think that Scrooge's ghosts did not challenge him to genuine change of heart, because they appealed to his vanity to have someone care about the value of his life and to mourn his passing. Yet this is not unrealistic. Most people consumed by greed who confront a crisis, and its call to a change of heart, are initially moved by these more selfish feelings in their attempt to extricate themselves from loss, anxiety, and depression. As they work through their challenges and feelings, they discover the superficiality and negativity of their lives. This in turn calls them, as it did Scrooge, to change their view of happiness, purpose, dignity, fulfillment, and ultimate destiny. If they do change, they will not be disappointed. After this metanoia, only one thing remains—to develop goals, virtues, and prayer to solidify that change so that regression will be difficult, if not quasi-impossible. We will consider this last point of development of goals, virtue, and prayer in the next volume.

C. S. Lewis provides yet another example of greed's capacity to intoxicate its victims in his tale *The Great Divorce*.[8] The book describes a bus ride from Hell to the outskirts of Heaven, where individuals are given the opportunity to choose Heaven, but most decide to go back to Hell because of one or more of the deadly sins. The sin of greed is illustrated by a man who gets out of the bus and notices golden apples everywhere, seemingly free for the taking. Yet because he is a ghost at the outskirts of Heaven, and reality in Heaven is far more substantial, the golden apples are heavy and the area over which he must travel is hard on his insubstantial feet and hands. This requires an enormous effort for him to procure but one small golden apple to bring back to Hell, where it would be "worth something" because of its rarity. His greed so transfixes his attention on the advantage he could get in Hell that he does not notice the far better opportunity of sharing not only as many golden apples as he could want, but also limitless beauty, love, and joy with God and others in Heaven.

Braving and enduring every imaginable hardship, he manages to carry the tiny golden apple toward the bus, but he is confronted by an angel who tries to break the spell of greed and present him with the enormous beauty and goodness of the reality that he is about to abandon. Lewis puts it this way:

> I [the narrator] could hardly help admiring this unhappy creature when I saw him rise staggering to his feet actually holding the smallest of the apples in his hands. He was lame from his hurts, and the weight bent him double. Yet even so, inch by inch, still availing himself of every scrap of cover, he set out on his via dolorosa to the

---

[8] C. S. Lewis, *The Great Divorce* (New York: MacMillan, 1946).

bus, carrying his torture. "Fool. Put it down," said a great voice suddenly. It was quite unlike any other voice I had heard so far. It was a
thunderous yet liquid voice. With an appalling certainty ... and I saw
now ... a bright angel who stood, like one crucified, against the rocks
and poured himself perpetually down towards the forest with loud
joy. "Fool," he said, "put it down. You cannot take it back. There is
not room for it in Hell. Stay here and learn to eat such apples. The
very leaves and the blades of grass in the wood will delight to teach
you." Whether the Ghost heard or not, I don't know. At any rate,
after pausing for a few minutes, it braced itself anew for its agonies
and continued with even greater caution till I lost sight of it.[9]

Lewis recognized that the spell of the deadly sins is so intoxicat-
ing that it could lead us to actually choose Hell rather than Heaven.
As we shall see below and in the next chapter, greed is not the only
deadly sin leading to such an eternally fatal choice—all of them present the same haunting possibility.

III. Lust

Lust (*luxuria*) generally refers to an intense desire and therefore can
refer to "lust for power" as much as "intense desire for sexual gratification". However, its use within the deadly sins is focused specifically
for the habit of giving in to one's intense longings for sexual gratification. It is seen as the root cause of infidelity, promiscuity, licentious-
ness, and in the contemporary world, sexual addiction (whether that
be manifest in unrestrained use of pornography or unrestrained pursuit of sexual gratification). As such, lust frequently is the cause of broken relationships, broken marriages, unsuccessful family life, and their
deep and oftentimes devastating negative emotional consequences.

Lust is perhaps the most prevalent deadly sin in contemporary
Western culture. The almost unrestricted availability of Internet pornography, the cultural belief in the harmlessness of casual sex, the
continuous references and suggestions of sexuality in every form of
media and the culture's frequent promotion of sexual gratification as
a healthy and fulfilling end in itself, leads to a barrage of suggestions

[9] Ibid., p. 18.

and stimulation that is hard for anyone to resist, let alone those who are young and inexperienced in building friendships and generative relationships (explained in detail in Volume III, Chapter 3). It has gotten to the point where many young people find themselves helpless to resist even when they want to! It is hard to know what a pervasive cultural solution might be. However, there is a solution in every *individual* who truly wants to follow the teaching of Christ, develop genuinely generative marital relationships, avoid the devastation of broken commitments, and build a healthy family and enduring friendships—the commitment to chasteness through the grace and imitation of Jesus. We will address this virtue only briefly below in this section, and then in more detail in Volume II, Chapter 4, and Volume III, Chapter 2.

Before looking more deeply at the destructiveness to self and others caused by lust, we will want to examine the ideal of romantic love—*eros*. Sometimes this ancient term refers only to romantic or sexual *passion*, but that is not its full meaning in any major classical work of philosophy. The full meaning extends to the friendship and commitment underlying romantic love, which takes on a very special significance in Christianity—the exclusive highest priority, indissoluble commitment, and fidelity needed for strong faith-filled families.

Eros, in its concern for romance and romantic feelings, is a complex phenomenon much broader than sexual feelings and satisfaction. It involves many dimensions of the psyche, including intimacy, generativity, the reception of generativity, anticipation of deep friendship and commitment, the perception of beauty, complementarity of function, anticipation of family, and a sense of adventure. Hence, *eros* has a very wide range of feelings and psychological engagement coming from both personal maturity and decisions about life's meaning.

In my discussion of the four levels of happiness (see Volume I of the Quartet, and Volume II, Appendix I, of this Trilogy), I explained that a Level One and Two view of happiness/purpose tends to emphasize *personal* gratification and satisfaction of *self*, while Levels Three and Four tend to emphasize empathy, contribution, and transcendental purpose. Thus, a person who has a Level One or Level Two meaning in life, who is likely to be less personally mature, will have a very different, more superficial, view of *eros* than a person in

Levels Three and Four, who is more mature and is open to an intimate, generative, and committed relationship.

In my discussion of "freedom from" and "freedom for" (see Volume I, Chapter 4, of the Quartet), I showed that individuals on
Levels One and Two are likely to have a view of "freedom from",
which focuses on immediately attaining strong urges and desires,
escaping commitment, "keeping their options open", and resenting
unreciprocated sacrifices. Conversely, individuals on Levels Three
and Four are likely to view freedom as "freedom for", which focuses
on the most pervasive, enduring, and deep purpose in life—one that
goes *beyond* self and makes a genuine contribution to family, friends,
community, organizations, church, the Kingdom of God, and even
the culture. In this view, constraint and commitment for the sake
of achieving life's higher purpose is seen as worthwhile. Likewise,
foreclosing options to pursue some truly good directions is deemed
essential, and unreciprocated sacrifices are accepted and expected.
Once again, these different views of freedom radically affect individuals' views of a romantic relationship, as well as their feelings and
expectations from it.

We may now give a general profile of the focus and expectations
for a romantic relationship regarding the Level One-Two and Level
Three-Four perspectives. As might be expected, the Level One-Two
perspective of *eros* emphasizes what is more apparent, immediately
gratifying, intense, and ego-fulfilling. Hence, its focus is predomi-
nantly on sexuality, beauty, gender complementarity, and romantic
excitement and adventure. Furthermore, its expectations are fairly
short-term and focused on immediate gratification, keeping options
open, increased levels of romantic excitement, and avoiding commitments and unreciprocated sacrifices. As a consequence, it resists
movement to Level Three-Four, and the intimacy and generativity
intrinsic to them (discussed below).

In contrast to this, a Level Three-Four perspective of *eros* focuses
on making a difference beyond the self—and in mature individuals, on making the most pervasive, enduring, and deep contribution
possible. It is also open to empathy and care for others (in its quest
to make an optimal positive contribution to the world). Though it
does not abandon the dimensions of *eros* emphasized in Levels One
and Two (sexuality, beauty, gender complementarity, and romantic

excitement), it contextualizes these desires within concomitant desires for intimacy, generativity, complementarity, collaboration, common cause, deep friendship, loyalty, commitment, and family. A Level Three-Four perspective is not enough to bring about these desires; there must also be psychological stability and personal development and maturation. When these factors are co-present, the expectations of romantic relationships broaden and deepen. As a consequence there is a willingness to foreclose options, to invest more fully in the romantic relationship (and ultimately to make this relationship exclusive). There is willingness to make the other a "first priority" in the expenditure of physical and emotional resources, which anticipates a lifelong commitment as well as unreciprocated sacrifices. The following chart summarizes the outlooks of both perspectives.

LEVEL	FOCUS	EXPECTATIONS
Eros *(Romantic Love)* Three and Four	Openness to the importance and inclusion of intimacy, generativity, complementarity, collaboration, common cause, deep mutual friendship, long-term commitment, and family (Note: sexuality, beauty, and romantic excitement are still important, but contextualized by the above.)	Pervasive, enduring, and deep meaning, foreclosing of options to secure "best option", mutually supportive communion, constraints for the sake of intimacy, depth, and commitment, unreciprocated sacrifice
Eros *(Romantic Love)* One and Two	The emphasis is on sexual feelings and gratification, beauty of the other, romantic adventure, excitement of the relationship, and control within the relationship.	Immediate and heightened gratification, fulfillment of the desire to be admired and loved, keeping options open, greater levels of excitement, and no unreciprocated sacrifices

When romantic relationships occur in Level Three-Four individuals who are stable and mature, the intimate friendship becomes deeper and deeper. When friendship (*philia*) is reciprocated, it tends to deepen and become more committed. When we commit more of our time, future, and physical and psychic energy to a friend, and that friend reciprocates with a deeper commitment to us, the friendship

becomes closer, more supportive, more fulfilling, and more emotionally satisfying. When it is appropriate, this deep friendship can
incite intimacy, generativity, and romantic feelings, which, in turn,
can deepen the friendship even more—but now it is not just a deep
friendship; it is an *intimate romantic* deep friendship. This distinctive
kind of friendship can continue to deepen until both parties are not
only ready for, but desirous of, making the other their *number-one
priority*. From a logical point of view there can only be one "first
priority"—everything else is a contradiction. Hence the desire to
make a deep intimate friend a "first priority" is tantamount to wanting an *exclusive* commitment—which cannot be given to anyone else.

Furthermore, this deep friendship anticipates a *lifelong* commitment in which the couple enters into common cause—that is, to do
some good through their mutual efforts for the world *beyond* themselves. The most significant dimension of common cause for a couple who are intimately related (anticipating sexuality) is the creation
of a *family*. Love moves *beyond* itself—we seek to do the good for
the other, the community, the world, and the Kingdom of God. Just
as loving individuals move beyond themselves, so also loving cou-
ples move beyond themselves. Though it is very important that the
couple have their "alone time" to develop their closeness, affection,
generativity, and mutual support, it is likewise important that they
do not *stay* within the relationship *alone*. A couple staring into each
other's eyes can be as mutually self-obsessed as Narcissus looking at
his image in the pool—they can drown in the waters below their
beautiful self-images. This illustrates the need for intimate friendships to move from "*within* the relationship" to "*beyond* the relationship". The deeply committed romantic relationship cultivates
a complementary and collaborative strength—a synergy to move
beyond itself to make a positive difference through common cause.
Family is the most fundamental aim of such a relationship. But there
can be many other objectives as well—for community, church, culture, Kingdom of God, and so forth. Though the most fundamental
objective (family) must come first, it too must move beyond itself, to
make a positive difference in ways that will not undermine its depth
and cohesiveness.

In sum, the ideal of a Level Three-Four romantic relationship is
to bring intimate friendship to its highest level, to make the intimate

friend a "first priority" through an exclusive and lifelong commitment to enter into mutually supportive and collaborative common cause toward family and other positive objectives that will serve not only friends, but community, culture, church, and the Kingdom of God.

We can now see an inherent conflict between Level One-Two *eros* and Level Three-Four *eros*. The emphasis on beauty, adventure, and sexual feelings in Level One-Two *eros*, without the dimensions of generativity, friendship, and commitment, can incite individuals to be both sexually permissive and promiscuous. Sexual stimulation (from sexual activity to pornography) is frequently addictive.[10] Sexuality can become an end in itself, and when it does, romantic desires can be accentuated only by more sexual activity, more partners, or more excitement (e.g., amplified by aggressiveness, risk, and alcohol/drugs).[11] These activities can enhance sexual addiction[12] and desensitize the individual to higher dimensions of relationship and psychic satisfaction (e.g., intimacy, generativity, collaboration, common cause, friendship, commitment, exclusivity, and family). As a result, the long-term practice of Level One-Two *eros* can become addictive, callous, and aggressive,[13] leading to objectification ("thingification") of the other, "using" the other as an object of gratification, and dominating the other for ego satisfaction. This can lead to a state of mind

---

[10] Activation of the reward pathways (dopamine system) in the lower brain by sexual activity, pornography, aggression, and drugs all form memories and habits of pleasure that can become gradually addictive.

See Donald Hilton, "Pornography Addiction—A Supranormal Stimulus Considered in the Context of Neuroplasticity", *Socioaffective Neuroscience and Psychology* 3 (July 19, 2013): 1–18, https://www.ncbi.nlm.nih.gov/pmc/articles/PMC3960020/.

Frances Prayer, "What Drives a Sex Addict? Is Sex Addiction about Love or an Insatiable Craving?", *Psychology Today*, October 7, 2009, pp. 1–4, http://www.psychologytoday.com/blog/love-doc/200910/what-drives-sex-addict.

[11] Both sexual activity and aggression activate reward pathways in the hypothalamus. There is also evidence of interrelationship between sexual desires and aggression (even violence) through the hypothalamus.

If sexuality is connected to generative (higher cerebral) functions, it will likely mitigate the aggressive components originating in the hypothalamus. See D. Lin et al., "Functional Identification of an Aggression Locus in the Mouse Hypothalamus", *Nature* 470 (February 10, 2011): 221–26. Ewen Callaway, "Sex and Violence Linked in the Brain", *Nature*, February 9, 2011, http://www.nature.com/news/2011/110209/full/news.2011.82.html.

[12] See Hilton, "Pornography Addiction", pp. 1–18, and Prayer, "What Drives a Sex Addict?", pp. 1–4.

[13] See ibid.

in which intimacy, generativity, and mature friendships are hard to recapture. The addictive quality of lower brain activities can make it difficult to move from Level One-Two to Level Three-Four happiness and meaning. The longer individuals reinforce Level One-Two *eros*, the more difficult it will be for them to grow in levels of maturity and development, and to seek genuinely intimate, generative, and exclusive romantic relationships. Hence, it is difficult to maintain and deepen marital and family relationships with a narrow Level One-Two perspective and focus.

We may now return to the topic of lust, which might be viewed as unrestrained Level One-Level Two *eros*. In this sense, lust is not only an underestimation and undermining of *eros'* true potential and power; it is also an agent of the destruction of true *eros* (Level Three-Level Four). As noted above, this narrow lower kind of *eros* stunts personal maturity, creates sexual addictions, and moves toward narcissism, promiscuity, and infidelity, giving rise to broken relationships, commitments, marriages, and families. Lust (an exclusively Level One-Two view of *eros*) has three additional fatal flaws. First, it objectifies ("thingifies") the other who loses his sense of dignity, belovedness, intrinsic respectability, mystery, and transcendental depth. Though every mature person wants to be viewed in terms of these positive characteristics, lust reduces the "lover's" gaze to seeing mere *objects* of gratification, physical beauty, and status. Thus, lust prevents us from respecting as we ought, loving as we ought, and working for family and common cause. A relationship adversely affected by lust is likely to be short-lived and insufferably self-involved.

It might be objected that some beloveds want to be viewed as mere objects of beauty and gratification. Yet, if this truly were the case, one can only feel pity for someone who wants to ignore and reject their depth, mystery, transcendental powers, and unique belovedness—to reduce themselves to the status of mere objects, playthings, and players. True friends of such individuals will never play to or take advantage of this shallow self-image, but rather will help them to elevate their self-image toward their uniquely lovable and transcendent dignity, purpose, fulfillment, and destiny.

The second fatal flaw of lust is its momentum toward narcissism, because it frequently puts the emphasis not on love, but on being loved; not on giving oneself, but on receiving from the other; not on satisfying the other, but on being satisfied by the other. Evidently, this narcissistic worldview cannot sustain a mature friendship—let alone a marriage—over the long term. Rather, it is likely to *undermine* "freedom for", "commitment", "mature friendships", and marriages.

The third fatal flaw of lust is its tendency to move *away* from exclusive commitments and deep friendships to *multiple*, uncommitted, passionate relationships. Therefore, it prevents people from entering into marital commitments with the awareness and freedom to keep them. When people do enter into marriage with a dominant Level One-Two perspective of *eros*, lust continuously challenges it and frequently undermines it. It is hard enough to maintain a marital commitment in both mind and heart in today's permissive culture, with its encouragement of continuous sexual gratification and ego-comparative fulfillment, without imbuing our imaginations with unrestrained romantic passion. Therefore, we will have to fight against these temptations and cultural stimuli by replacing them with good images, ideals, and habits (virtues). We will have to be realistic about the blindness to consequences that lust frequently causes (see discussion about Leo Tolstoy's novel *Anna Karenina* below); we also need to be vigilant about confronting temptation at its very beginning in order to begin the long process of deepening chastity and charity in our lives. (This will be taken up in detail in Volume II, Chapters 4–6.)

Given the darkness and negativity caused by lust, it should come as no surprise that the Bible specifically prohibits it, particularly in the preaching of Jesus. Adultery (unlawful intercourse with a partner who is committed to another by marriage) is prohibited in the Ten Commandments (Ex 20:14; Deut 5:18) and also in the Code of Holiness[14] (Lev 20:10). Adultery was considered so serious that it was punishable by death, generally stoning (Ezek 16:40). There are multiple condemnations of adultery in Wisdom literature (Prov 2:16; 7:1–27; 23:27–28; 30:20). Jesus repeats and reinforces the prohibition of adultery (Mt 5:27; Mk 10:19; Lk 18:20), but adds considerably to it, indicating that the *desire* for adultery and illicit fornication (lust) is evil as well:

---

[14] The Code of Holiness is in Leviticus, Chapters 17—26.

You have heard that it was said, "You shall not commit adultery." But I say to you that every one who looks at a woman lustfully has already committed adultery with her in his heart. If your right eye causes you to sin, pluck it out and throw it away; it is better that you lose one of your members than that your whole body be thrown into hell. And if your right hand causes you to sin, cut it off and throw it away; it is better that you lose one of your members than that your whole body go into hell. (Mt 5:27–30)

Jesus very clearly extends the prohibition of adultery to the *desire* for illicit sexual union because he is aware that if these passions are unrestrained, it will lead to all the above consequences—to actual adultery and the undermining of self, others, and the relationships between them. As we shall see in the case of Leo Tolstoy's novel *Anna Karenina* (and so many other well-known literary figures like *The Great Gatsby*[15]), the entertainment of adulterous desires captivates the imagination and causes a controlling self-blinding to adultery's devastating consequences. In the midst of this, lust powerfully fuels the passions to the point where acting upon them seems irresistible. At that point, the darkness takes over.

Anna Karenina weaves together several deep and complex themes— including love, forgiveness, Christian faith, sinfulness, and guilt. Yet, its focus seems to center on the deadly sin of lust and infidelity manifest in the lives of Princess Anna Karenina and her illicit lover, Count Alexei Vronsky.[16] Tolstoy presents Anna as an almost perfect woman from the vantage point of external beauty, charm, vivaciousness, and personality. Men and women alike fall in love with Anna's external appearance almost irresistibly. Yet on the inside, Anna has a character flaw to which she allows virtually free reign—unrestrained romantic

---

[15] In F. Scott Fitzgerald's classic work, J. Gatsby's obsession with Daisy leads to an affair, resulting in a landslide of terrible consequences—broken marriages, ruptured relationships among friends, and ultimately, to Gatsby's murder by the husband of a woman who was the mistress of Daisy's husband, Tom. The message is similar to *Anna Karenina*'s, except seen through the eyes of a male narrator, Nick Carraway. See F. Scott Fitzgerald, *The Great Gatsby* (New York: Charles Scribner's Sons, 1925).

[16] In addition to the text of *Anna Karenina* by Leo Tolstoy, I drew from *The Anna Karenina Companion: Includes Study Guide, Historical Context, Biography, and Character Index* (CreateSpace Independent Publishing Platform, 2012; currently, out of print). A free Project Gutenberg e-book (2020) of Leo Tolstoy's novel is available on their website at http://www .gutenberg.org/files/1399/1399-h/1399-h.htm.

passion. Though Anna believes that she is committed to "love", her view of it is quite narrow and immature. She believes that the strength of her feelings justifies ignoring and even rejecting other dimensions of love—her commitment to her husband (Count Alexei Karenin), her son (Sergei "Seryozha" Karenin), and her illegitimate daughter (with Vronsky), Annie. Her feelings and passions become so central that the deep hurt she will cause to her husband and children, the loss of their reputation within Russian society, the principles of her Orthodox Christian faith (which do not appear to have ever been strong), and the sensitivities of her family and friends, pale in comparison. Giving way to these strong passions, she catapults headlong into an affair with Count Vronsky.

As the story develops, Anna's romantic passions first become an object of scandal. Her husband, Karenin, is a good man and generous provider who has done nothing to deserve Anna's growing disdain. He explains to her that their reputation is being seriously jeopardized, and that she should call the affair off. However, Anna's soul is so filled with "love" of Vronsky that she cannot imagine a life without him. She ignores Karenin's requests, trying to justify her infidelity and betrayal by blaming *him* for being boring, and for forsaking *his* passion for mere reputation and convention. Anna is so blinded by her passion she does not recognize either her inauthenticity or the devastation she is causing to family members and friends around her—so blinded that she doesn't even acknowledge the terrible social consequences that are about to befall her. As with so many other tragic characters, her moral flaw begins to control the events around her, ultimately becoming fatal.

After Anna confesses her infidelity to Karenin, he asks her to stop the affair, but Anna cannot help herself. She pursues Vronsky with even greater passion, provoking Karenin to seek a divorce, which would have ruined Anna's reputation. When Anna almost dies giving birth to her daughter, Annie (with Vronsky), Karenin comes to visit her and is genuinely moved with compassion. He forgives Anna for her infidelity, assures her that he will drop the divorce, and then forgives Vronsky for his part in the affair. This act of compassion, forgiveness, and magnanimity stands in such contrast to the infidelity and inauthenticity of Anna and Vronsky that Vronsky is moved to commit suicide—though he is unsuccessful in his attempt to do so. Anna, however, is not moved in the same way. Instead, she resolves that she cannot live with her husband (despite his compassion and generosity) and must follow her passion to live with Vronsky, convincing him to elope with her in Europe, thus leaving behind Karenin, Seryozha, and the rest of her family.

At first, Anna's and Vronsky's romantic adventure seems like veritable bliss. Yet, it has no solid foundation beyond the strong feelings that they have for one another. They have abandoned the idea of love as commitment for good beyond themselves. Furthermore, Anna does not see Karenin's forgiveness and generosity as a manifestation of love for her—true love that can span the chasm of hurt and betrayal that she has initiated. So when the intensity of passion begins to die down—as it almost always does—Vronsky begins to find himself bored by the object of his former passion. In an ironic turn, Anna now faces the same boredom and disinterest from Vronsky that she had formerly seen in her husband and used as an excuse to leave him and elope with Vronsky. This causes Anna to seek Vronsky's time and affections desperately, to the point where she is suffocating him, causing him to pull away from her even more. Additionally, they have no way of finding social relationships and amusement with their Russian peers in Europe because their elopement without divorce has caused scandal. Though Vronsky tries to amuse himself by taking up painting, it is clearly not the kind of pursuit around which his soldierly life can be centered, and so he lapses into even greater dissatisfaction in his relationship with Anna.

Unable to bear the social snubbing of their peers in Europe, Anna and Vronsky return to St. Petersburg. They stay in a luxurious hotel, but in separate rooms. At this juncture, the veil of passion over Anna's rational faculties begins to lift. She begins to see that the social consequences of her unrestrained passion are quite real indeed. Though she tries to maintain her belief that these consequences are nothing compared to her passion for Vronsky, she begins to feel progressively more isolated. Vronsky, who enjoys considerably more freedom for social interaction, exacerbates Anna's feelings of isolation. In the blindness of passion, Anna had abandoned her relationships with family, friends, and society, but now feels quite alone. She does not appear to feel regret for her past actions and certainly has no intention of asking for forgiveness from her husband, son, and friends; so, her social isolation continues to grow. Instead of reversing course, she turns to even greater passion—desperately pleading with Vronsky to refrain from even the smallest trips for business, for she has only Vronsky to alleviate her loneliness, and she strongly suspects he has other lovers to whom he is giving his romantic affections. Anna's passion has now degenerated into jealousy, anger, and despair—three other deadly sins.

In an attempt to reclaim some of her former social status (to alleviate her loneliness), Anna decides to attend a gala event at a theatre in St. Petersburg, where many of her former social peers will be present. Though Vronsky pleads with her not to go, Anna's blindness to the social consequences of her reckless actions causes her to believe that everything will turn out okay. The evening is a complete disaster: Anna is roundly snubbed by her former friends, and one of them storms out in protest. Devastated, Anna and Vronsky decide to leave St. Petersburg and move into Vronsky's country estate.

While at the estate, Anna's jealousy and bitterness grows, and she and Vronsky begin to argue repeatedly. Anna starts taking morphine to help her sleep, but this only enhances her confusion and discouragement. The two leave Vronsky's estate and go to Moscow, where the loneliness, jealousy, anger, desperation, confusion, and despair intensify. After several weeks, Anna and Vronsky have a terrible argument, leading her to believe that their relationship is finished. As her feelings of desperation and discouragement increase, she begins to contemplate suicide. After sending a telegram to Vronsky asking him to return, and visiting her friends Dolly and Kitty, Anna is overcome by her jealousy, bitterness, and confusion—and so she decides on a course of suicide. As she looks around her she can only see the bad news, the bad news of her life, her friends, and even people simply walking down the street. In a final act of desperation, she throws herself in front of a train, ending her life in the same way as a railway worker who accidentally fell in front of a train on the occasion when she first met Vronsky.

Of course, lust does not always lead to complete destruction or suicide—or to murder and physical injury (as portrayed in countless volumes of popular magazines and cable television programs). Nevertheless, as explained above, it stunts the growth of romantic love, preventing it from developing into genuine generativity, exclusive commitment, and self-sacrifice for family. Indeed, it almost always undermines and destroys these things. As such, it leaves in its wake profoundly immature individuals, broken relationships and families, dashed expectations, and emotional destructiveness of every kind. If allowed to grow, lust leads to the same kind of blindness experienced by Anna—blindness about hurt to others, separation from children and friends, and separation from church and society.

What can we learn from Anna's story? Firstly, we will want to see through the myth of lust's so-called beauty. As we have seen, lust causes blindness to its negative and evil consequences, but when the blindness comes to an end, the real future, with its emotional and spiritual darkness and devastation, catches up with us. Secondly, it is always best to challenge the urges of lust at their beginning, when they may be strong, but still manageable. Allowing those urges to grow will almost always become unmanageable—following upon blindness, inauthenticity to self, and the hypocrisy of blaming others for our misdeeds.

Thirdly, the mythical beautiful world painted by unrestrained romantic passion will almost certainly come to a hurtful end because of the narcissism of one or both parties, the jealousies and anger generated by inauthenticity and infidelity, and the confusion and destructiveness caused by the rupturing of commitments and families. As will be seen in Volume II, there is but one way of contending with the passion of lust after its early detection—prayer, the virtue of chastity, and the sacraments.

IV. Sloth (Acedia)

Sloth (acedia) has the general meaning of disinclination toward exertion, but in the Judeo-Christian tradition, it refers to spiritual apathy—a complete lack of concern for oneself, others, the community, the society, and the Kingdom of God. It is seen as one of the most serious deadly sins, because it reflects a general disinclination toward care, love, contribution, and faith that open upon our true dignity, purpose, and eternal destiny. It stands at the root not only of underliving life, but of wasting it—along with our talents and the potential to develop them to make an optimal positive difference to the families, friends, colleagues, acquaintances, institutions, communities, and churches with which we associate. Unlike the other deadly sins that require tempering of our passions, sloth reflects that absence of passion—healthy passion coming from beliefs, convictions, ideals, principles, empathy, and conscience. Oftentimes, sloth can become so deep that one not only does not care, but does not care that he does not care. When this occurs, the individual relegates himself to wasting his life and assents to the status of a "ne'er-do-well", jeopardizing his salvation. He will be like the individual in Jesus' Parable of the Talents who did nothing with the talent he was given and buried it in the ground for fear of his master. Jesus responds:

> You wicked and slothful servant! You knew that I reap where I have not sowed, and gather where I have not winnowed? Then you ought to have invested my money with the bankers, and at my coming I should have received what was my own with interest. So take the talent from him, and give it to him who has the ten talents. For to every one who has will more be given, and he will have abundance; but from him who has not, even what he has will be taken away. And cast the worthless servant into the outer darkness, where there will be weeping and gnashing of teeth. (Mt 25:26–30; cf. Lk 19:11–27)

The verdict rendered to the slothful servant stands in direct contrast to the two servants who made the best use out of the talents they had been given. They are given great abundance (with the implication of salvation) for using their gifts to make an optimal positive difference to others, to community, the culture, and the kingdom. But the slothful servant loses *everything* he had since he did not care about making a positive difference to anyone or anything beyond himself. What's worse is that he knows he is responsible to a master (God) who wants him to use his talents to make a positive difference; yet he ignores this implicit mandate and completely wastes the potential of the talent he has been given. The servant's callous disregard of the master's expectations earns the disdain of the master, who simply cannot believe that the servant would let his time and his gifts come to nothing. Jesus' message about the seriousness of the sin of sloth is clear: if we don't care about completely wasting our lives and talents, then we should care about what the Lord who gave us our lives and talents expects of us; and if we do not even do that, then we rightfully earn the disregard of the Lord Himself. Stated differently, if we do not care that we do not care—and we do not care about what the Lord thinks about our apathy and laziness—then we may be given a future similar to the life we have created in our past: a wasteland, filled with emptiness and darkness. Though at first glance sloth appears to be a lesser sin than the more aggressive sins—lust, greed, anger, envy, and pride—the Lord teaches otherwise; for the sin of sloth can lead to the undermining of all virtue, particularly the virtue of love—charity, contribution, compassion, and self-sacrifice.

English literature is replete with examples of ne'er-do-wells who waste their lives, take advantage of others, and bring down unsuspecting good people who give them an unwise benefit of the doubt. It is difficult for an author to place such characters at the center of a narrative, because protagonists and antagonists are supposed to *do* something, to which slothful characters cannot bring themselves. Thus, they are frequently relegated to significant side characters who play into the narrative through the negativity they create in taking advantage of others.

In E. M. Forster's work *Room with a View*, one of the main side characters, Cecil Vyse, when asked by the vicar, Mr. Beebe, about his profession responds as follows:

> I have no profession. It is another example of my decadence. My attitude—quite an indefensible one—is that, so long as I am no trouble to any one I have a right to do as I like. I know I ought to be getting money out of people, or devoting myself to things I don't care a straw about, but somehow, I've not been able to begin.[17]

Cecil has both title and resources from his family, and he has appropriated enough education to appear witty and sarcastic. Instead of orienting his life toward contribution or good for anyone or any cause, he has contented himself with the "profession of leisure". Much like the servant who buried his talent in the ground, Cecil tries to excuse his admitted decadence by claiming that anything beyond leisure would be a vulgar pursuit of money or a worthless cause. This rationalization for wasting his life, title, and family

---

[17] E. M. Forster, *A Room with a View* (London: Edward Arnold, 1908), pp. 109–10.

resources, though wholly inadequate, is sufficient to give peace to the slothful Cecil.

Cecil believes that his title, wit, and resources will be sufficient to solidify an engagement with Lucy Honeychurch, a beautiful upper-class lady who is touring Florence with her chaperone cousin, Charlotte Bartlett. Unbeknownst to Cecil, a rather awkward, but loveable commoner, George Emerson, also encounters Lucy (along with his father) in Florence. Though George has none of the exterior appeal of Cecil (title, monetary resources, status, and high-level education), he is sincere, loving, and passionate—and is genuinely concerned for Lucy and her happiness. As the fates would have it, Lucy and George encounter one another coincidentally—twice in Florence and once in England, where George expresses his sincere love for Lucy. When Lucy returns to England from Florence, she finds herself engaged to Cecil, who has perfected the vice of sloth as well as "putting on airs". Lucy again encounters George by coincidence in Windy Corner in the English countryside. Once again they kiss, and Lucy is moved by George's sincere love for her. She reveals to him her engagement to Cecil, to which George responds that Cecil only views her as "an object for the shelf", and that he is incapable of loving her enough to respect her and allow her independence. Though Lucy initially tells George that he must leave—a request with which he complies— she has one more chance encounter with George's father after see-ing Cecil for who he really is. She breaks off her engagement with Cecil and returns to George, ultimately marrying him. Though Cecil possesses all the good fortune an English lady could ever want, his decadence, slothfulness, insincerity, vanity, and arrogance make him rather dark and ugly on the inside. Despite the exterior glitter and gold, his soul's emptiness, coldness, and lovelessness burst through, alarming not only Lucy, but anyone else who could possibly care for him. Though he will probably never find love, he will always be able to content himself with his cynical arrogance—"I have no profession. It is another example of my decadence."

Forster critiques the sin of sloth by revealing the decadence, heart-lessness, and loneliness it cultivates. Though its victims are convinced of their remarkably good fortune to be born into a perpetually easy life, they suffer from insipient meaninglessness, loneliness, and alien-ation, because they do very little for the world and the people around them and even less for the culture and the Kingdom of God. They know in their inmost being that their lives mean next to nothing both objectively and in the hearts of people around them. They are like unnoticeable transparent beings who consume more than they contribute and lower others to their level instead of raising them to a higher dignity and destiny. As a result, despite their feigned happiness, they are quite empty, lonely, and alienated—the unfortunate fruits of the nothingness to which they have devoted themselves.

V. Vanity

Though vanity (*vanagloria*) has been included in the sin of pride (*superbia*), since the time of Pope Gregory I (d. 604) many lists of the deadly sins—including those of the originator Evagrius Ponticus and John Cassian (who transmitted the list to the West)—kept it separate because of its difference from another, more sinister, dimension of pride: lust for power and dominion. I belong to this camp for the same reason: the substantial differences between the two sins. Though the cause of *vanagloria* and *superbia* is the same (egocentricity), their effects and manifestations are different.

In general, "vanity" refers to an excessive self-love and/or an excessive desire to be loved, admired, or recognized by others. This excessive love of self, as well as the desire for adulation and recognition, frequently aims at becoming a central focus of attention within the lives of an increasingly large sphere of people. If it is allowed to grow uninhibitedly, one will seek to become *the central* focus of attention in people's lives—and if allowed to reach its "fulfillment", it will lead to self-idolatry, where the perpetrator seeks to replace God and family at the center of his and other's lives. As vanity begins to grow within the soul, its victim can hear the refrain of the evil queen in the Disney fairy tale *Snow White and the Seven Dwarfs*—"Mirror, mirror on the wall, who's the fairest of them all?" As it reaches out to its fulfillment, it longs to be like John Lennon exclaiming, "We're [the Beatles] more popular than Jesus."[18]

---

[18] Maureen Cleave, "How Does a Beatle Live? John Lennon Lives Like This", an interview with John Lennon, *London Evening Standard*, March 4, 1966.

Through it all, there is an undercurrent of darkness, emptiness, self-delusion, and impending demise—much like the Greek mythical figure Narcissus, who fell so deeply in love with the image of his face reflected in a pool that he lost interest in all other dimensions of life, until he died from starvation.

In the Bible the English word "vanity" frequently means "futility" ("transitoriness", "passing away", or "fading away"). This is not what is intended by Evagrius Ponticus and John Cassian in their original lists of the deadly sins. They meant "vainglory", a belief that one deserves to be admired because of one's perceived superior beauty, status, or talent. This is translated in New Testament Greek as *kenodoxia*—literally, "empty glory". If "glory" is the object of admiration and awe, then vainglory is the belief that one be admired for a false reason—that is, admiring an empty object of glory. Wisdom literature and the New Testament teach that worldly beauty, worldly success, worldly talent, and worldly status are all passing away—and therefore are false objects of admiration or esteem. As theologians have stated for centuries, "Sic transit gloria mundi"—"Thus passes the glory of the world"—therefore, it is unworthy of our profound admiration, and completely unworthy of our worship.[19] Though Jesus does not speak specifically of *kenodoxia*, He speaks about the same idea when using the phrase "exalts himself"—"whoever exalts himself will be humbled, and whoever humbles himself will be exalted" (Mt 23:12). Jesus warns against self-exaltation and extols the opposing virtue—humble-heartedness (being "poor in spirit")—as the first Beatitude (Mt 5:3). Humble-heartedness is foundational for all the Beatitudes and therefore for charity (*agapē*), and self-exaltation (the opposite of humble-heartedness) leads in the opposite direction—away from *agapē*.

Jesus taught resistance to self-exaltation by using wisdom instruction, showing through parable and example that it is foolish and will lead to shame before others. In Luke 14:8–11, Jesus says:

---

[19] Thomas à Kempis (d. 1471) seems to have been the first to state this truth with the precise Latin phrase, but the truth behind the phrase was recognized by Evagrius Ponticus and his successors who reflected on the deadly sins. Later, the phrase was integrated into the papal induction ceremony three times, a custom that was not carried forward after 1963. See Thomas à Kempis, *The Imitation of Christ* (Project Gutenberg, 1999), bk. 1, Chapter 3, http://www.gutenberg.org/cache/epub/1653/pg1653-images.html.

When you are invited by any one to a marriage feast, do not sit down in a place of honor, lest a more eminent man than you be invited by him; and he who invited you both will come and say to you, "Give place to this man," and then you will begin with shame to take the lowest place. But when you are invited, go and sit in the lowest place, so that when your host comes he may say to you, "Friend, go up higher"; then you will be honored in the presence of all who sit at table with you. For every one who exalts himself will be humbled, and he who humbles himself will be exalted.

Jesus' teaching is clear—vanity (self-exaltation) is foolish and will likely result in shame. Furthermore, it undermines humble-heartedness, and so undermines charity, the will of God, and a disposition of a soul needed for the Kingdom of God.

Before examining how vanity leads to the downfall of its victims, it may do well to illustrate how vanity works through two vignettes from C. S. Lewis' *The Great Divorce*. The first addresses vanity arising out of external appearance. Recall from above that *The Great Divorce* is about a bus ride from Hell to Heaven where the ghosts coming from Hell are met by heavenly friends who try to talk them into coming to Heaven. In this vignette, Lewis describes a woman ghost who had ventured a little way into the outskirts of Heaven and discovered that her appearance, which was extraordinarily good by the standards of the world and Hell, was vastly inferior to the appearance of the solid luminescent humans in Heaven. This comparative inferiority and the shame that it brought incited her to flee back to the bus (going back to Hell) before she would be noticed. Her friend from earth, now transformed in heavenly splendor, comes to meet her, but she is so ashamed that she cannot bear to be seen by him. Addressing her earnestly, out of a purely good and loving motive, he tries to talk her into proceeding toward Heaven (rather than going back to the bus); but her vanity blinds her to his loving motives and all she can think about is her comparative inferiority and shame. The dialogue between them proceeds as follows:

"Go away!" squealed the Ghost. "Go away! Can't you see I want to be alone?" "But you need help," said the Solid One. "If you have the least trace of decent feeling left," said the Ghost, "you'll keep away. I don't want help. I want to be left alone. Do go away. You know I can't walk fast enough on these horrible spikes to get away from you. It's abominable of you to take advantage." "Oh, that!" said the Spirit. "That'll soon come right. But you're going in the wrong direction. It's back there—to the mountains—you need to go. You can lean on me all the way. I can't absolutely carry you, but you need have almost no weight on your own feet: and it will hurt less at every step." "I'm not afraid of being hurt. You know that." "Then what is the matter?" "Can't you understand anything? Do you really suppose I'm going out there among all those people, like this?" "But why not?" "I'd never have come at all if I'd known you were all going to be dressed like that ..." "How can I go out like this among a lot of people with real solid bodies? It's far worse than going out with nothing on would have been on earth. Have everyone staring through me." "Oh, I see. But we were all a bit ghostly when we first arrived, you know. That'll wear off. Just come out and try." "But they'll see me." "What does it matter if they do?" "I'd rather die." "But you've died already. There's no good trying to go back to that." The Ghost made a sound something between a sob and a snarl. "I wish I'd never been born," it said. "What are we born for?" "For infinite happiness," said the Spirit. "You can step out into it at any moment...." "But, I tell you, they'll see me." "An hour hence and you will not care. A day hence and you will laugh at it. Don't you remember on earth—there were things too hot to touch with your finger but you could drink them all right? Shame is like that. If you will accept it—if you will drink the cup to the bottom—you will find it very nourishing: but try to do anything else with it and it scalds ..." but suddenly it cried out: "No, I can't. I tell you I can't. For a moment, while you were talking, I almost thought ... but when it comes to the point.... You've no right to ask me to do a thing like that. It's disgusting. I should never forgive myself if I did. Never, never. And it's not fair. They ought to have warned us. I'd never have come. And now—please, please go away!" "Friend," said the Spirit. "Could you, only for a moment, fix your mind on something not yourself?" "I've already given you my answer," said the Ghost, coldly but still tearful.[20]

Apparently this woman's vanity prevented her from choosing infinite happiness to prevent a few hours of shame that mattered to

[20]Lewis, *Great Divorce*, pp. 21–22.

no one except herself. Vanity about her appearance blinded her to her true self, dignity, and destiny—and above all, to her true beauty. She could not imagine what she would become for fear of being thought comparatively inferior even for a few hours.

The second vignette concerns creative and intellectual vanity. The narrator observes a ghost (coming from Hell) who was a famous artist on earth. He is greeted by a spirit (from Heaven) who was a friend and another famous artist on earth. The ghost is amazed by the beauty of Heaven and can think only of painting it, but his heavenly friend tries to dissuade him from it because painting can never exceed the beauty, reality, and goodness of anything that is part of the heavenly domain—and so a painting would be meaningless. This cuts to the heart of the ghost who has defined himself almost exclusively by his artistic talent, and the great fame it has brought to him. His spirit friend tells him that in Heaven fame too is meaningless, because everyone is equally famous—equally glorified—and their goodness comes not from some comparative advantage and talent, but from the inner beauty of their being, a unique manifestation of the goodness, lovability, and beauty of God. This agitates the ghost, at which point the following dialogue ensues:

"Of course," said the Ghost, as if speaking to itself, [I assume that] "there'll always be interesting people to meet...." [in Heaven]

"Everyone will be interesting" [said the spirit].

"Oh-ah-yes, to be sure. I was thinking of people in our own line. Shall I meet Claude? Or Cezanne? Or—."

"Sooner or later—if they're here."

"But don't you know?"

"Well, of course not. I've only been here a few years. All the chances are against my having run across them.... There are a good many of us, you know."

"But surely in the case of distinguished people, you'd hear?"

"But they aren't distinguished—no more than anyone else. Don't you understand? The Glory flows into everyone, and back from everyone: like light and mirrors. But the light's the thing." "Do you mean there are no famous men?" "They are all famous. They are all known, remembered, recognised by the only Mind that can give a perfect judgment." "Of, of course, in that sense ..." said the Ghost. "Don't stop," said the Spirit, making to lead him still forward. "One must be content with one's reputation among posterity, then," said the Ghost. "My friend," said the Spirit. "Don't you know?" "Know what?" "That you and I are already completely forgotten on the Earth?" "Eh? What's that?" exclaimed the Ghost, disengaging its arm. "Do you mean those damned Neo Regionalists have won after all?" "Lord love you, yes!" said the Spirit, once more shaking and shining with laughter. "You couldn't get five pounds for any picture of mine or even of yours in Europe or America to-day. We're dead out of fashion." "I must be off at once," said the Ghost. "Let me go! Damn it all, one has one's duty to the future of Art. I must go back to my friends. I must write an article. There must be a manifesto. We must start a periodical. We must have publicity. Let me go. This is beyond a joke!" And without listening to the Spirit's reply, the spectre vanished.[21]

Once again, Lewis illustrates how ego gratification, comparative advantage, and fame can blind us to the reality of our true selves, dignity, destiny, goodness, and beauty. The ghost is so enamored of his talent, recognition, and status that he cannot fathom being equivalent to everyone else in his true nature and glory. After receiving the "bad news" about being only one among many in an unparalleled state of splendor, he breaks loose from his heavenly friend to return to eternal gloom where he can live as a mere shadow of what would have been his heavenly splendor—with his reputation intact.

As with other deadly sins, particularly greed, lust, and pride, vanity has an addictive quality that impels its victims to seek greater and more rapid fulfillment until it strains the limits of even the most beautiful and popular individuals. It is an unquenchable fire that probes every possible avenue to gain the admiration and love it seeks; yet as it does so, it undermines its willing adherents in three major ways.

First, it replaces the true identity of its victim with a façade—a false identity that is admirable or beautiful to the external observer, but lacking in interior significance and substance. In order to become more externally appealing, one has to appropriate a chameleon nature capable of changing not only one's appearance, but also one's core identity—that is, one's intrinsic lovability, spiritual powers, principles, ideals, religious beliefs, dignity, meaning in life, and fulfillment—in

---

[21] Ibid., pp. 29–30.

order to become an ever more significant center in the lives of an ever
increasing number of people. Eventually, the exterior image completely replaces the core identity of its beautiful and popular victim.
As this occurs, victims ironically feel an increasing sense of emptiness,
loss, and loneliness amid an increasing sense of popularity and adulation. As the façade grows, the substance diminishes nearly to the point
of nothingness—and the victims feel it.

Unfortunately, by this time, they are almost powerless to extricate
themselves from the emptiness and loss of meaning and substance.
Only one thing can save them, and it is not themselves (the first savior they are inclined to turn to)—but only the Lord of unconditional
love who would reach into the depths of complete emptiness to help
refashion an identity completely given over to mere appearances.
Without a radical act of faith, those who give themselves over to vanity are likely to be perpetually lost in the emptiness and meaninglessness of their own making. They must be able to muster the humility
of Peter, who after walking toward Jesus on the water finds himself
drowning, then reaches up and cries, "Lord, save me" (Mt 15:30).

A second major way in which vanity undermines its willing adherents is to make them believe that the appearance (the façade) is the
"identity" in which people are interested—the only one that can be
shown to others in the external world. Not only do the victims of
vanity disvalue and abandon their true substantive identity in their
own minds (their intrinsic lovability, spiritual powers, principles, ideals, religious beliefs, dignity, meaning in life, and hope for transcendent fulfillment); they convince themselves that no one else cares
about these qualities either. As the power of vanity overshadows the
psyche, it reinforces the fiction that all people, particularly family
and friends, are just like them. They are interested much more in
their popularity than in their goodness and unique lovability; much
more in their talents than in their spiritual nature and religious beliefs;
much more in their outward beauty than in their principles, ideals,
and desire to serve and love others—much more interested in the
victim as a "thing" rather than a person. Once the conviction sets
in, and the victim believes that family, friends, and everyone else is
interested much more in associating with their elevated fame, talent,
and beauty than in their friendship, goodness, and transcendent soul,
they abandon the latter to the former in their own hearts and will

show the former only to others and the world. Indeed, they hide their inner selves from others so that others may admire the external façade in its place.

Obviously, this has major negative consequences. First, one cannot afford to ever decrease in external beauty, talent, and popularity— for this would constitute a complete loss of the adulation one so desperately needs for meaning and identity, and therefore, a complete loss of identity and the self. Aging becomes a gradual suicide. As one ages, one's true family and friends are the only ones left to support and sustain the goodness, lovability, and transcendent identity of the beloved. Regrettably, the victim of vanity frequently rejects this real love, because it makes the lover an equal—or fleetingly superior—to him as beloved, which is too hard to take. Reversing this belief would take a radical act of humility, which is exceedingly difficult for the victim to initiate from within himself alone. Such humility frequently requires the help of an unconditionally loving God, which, in turn, requires faith.

Another consequence of hiding one's substance and core identity from others and the world is the shame that comes when one is confronted by misfortune, sickness, or aging. Of course, we can do everything possible to hide these "problems"—from plastic surgery to the best coiffeurs and clothing—but ultimately, little manifestations of weakness, unattractiveness, and frailty begin to emerge, which gives rise to shame, a painful shame. Individuals who have a strong core identity—sense of intrinsic lovability, spiritual awareness, principles, and so forth—do not feel this shame nearly as acutely; however, vanity's victims do; and the more radically they have abandoned their core identity, the more acutely they feel the pain of shame—to the point of self-torment and hiding from others.

The third major way in which vanity undermines its willing adherents is to immerse them in the negative emotions of what I call "the comparison game" (see Volume I, Chapter 3, of the Quartet). In Volume II, Appendix I, of this Trilogy, I give a brief description of these emotions—jealousy, fear of failure, fear of loss of esteem, inferiority, depression, ego sensitivities, self-pity, resentment toward others for withholding adulation, ego-rage, ego-blame, and pervasive emptiness due to a lack of contributive and transcendent meaning and fulfillment. Rather than repeat the explanation, suffice to say that these negative emotional conditions—whether they be felt by losers, winners, or something in between—is psychologically painful not only to vanity's victims, but to all the people they touch. The bouts of anger, depression, self-pity, blame, contempt, resentment, and jealousy cast darkness over the whole interpersonal network of vanity's victims, creating an ethos of misery, fighting, and despair—an ethos into which an evil spirit can embed itself and bring still further misery. The solution to this miserable condition is to move one's identity fulcrum away from dominant ego-comparative identity (which opens the door to vanity's power) to a dominant contributive identity and/or transcendent identity. If one is already powerfully under the sway of vanity, it will probably be essential to make a radical act of faith in God through prayer and grace to make the transition.

Given the power of vanity to undermine our identity, relationships with others, emotional state, and even our ability to accept salvation when it is offered to us on a veritable silver platter, we will want to make every effort to move away from it with every human and providential power. If possible, we will want to nip it in the bud near its inception—or even at the inception of a dominant ego-comparative identity. Certainly, it is nothing to be trifled with, for the longer we entertain it, the more we allow it to take hold of our souls, even to the point of destroying our core identities, our families and friends, and even our relationship with God.

Before leaving this topic we will want to consider one final dimension of vanity's power—the power of delusion. We have already addressed the capacity of lust to blind Jay Gatsby and Anna Karenina and the power of greed to blind Ebenezer Scrooge, Bud Fox (*Wall Street*), and Uriah Heep. The blinding power of vanity can certainly match these deadly sins—and surpass them.

One of the most pure examples of this power is found in the 1950 film noir classic *Sunset Boulevard* (which is periodically revitalized in London and Broadway theaters—and has been rereleased in 2017 with Glenn Close).[22] At the center of the film is a former famous silent-film star, Norma Desmond, who is so completely seduced by her past beauty, popularity, and fame, that she could never get

---

[22] See Tim Durks, "Filmsite Movie Review: Sunset Boulevard (1950)", AMC Filmsite, 2020, https://www.filmsite.org/suns.html.

beyond it. She believes that she still retains that same beauty and popularity and sits in her mansion awaiting an invitation to return to the
silver screen. Her former husband, Max von Mayerling, who after
being divorced by her became her butler, writes fan letters to her to
help her keep the myth alive, lest she fall into another depression and
succeed in a suicide attempt.

As fate would have it, a second-rate screen writer, Joe Gillis, who
is trying to evade creditors who are attempting to repossess his car,
turns into what he thinks is the driveway of a deserted mansion and
disguises his car. Norma calls him because she's mistaken him for
someone else. When they meet inside, Joe tells her that he is a script
writer, at which point she discloses that she has written a screenplay
for her comeback called *Salome*. Joe reviews the poorly written script
and indicates that he could improve it significantly as a "script doctor". Norma hires him and insists that he stay at the mansion to work
and live with her.

As the weeks pass, Norma convinces herself that Joe sees her as
having the same beauty, charm, and energy she possessed thirty
years before. She begins to fall gradually in love with him, and at a
New Year's Eve party, at which he is the only guest, she professes
her love. Joe tries to extricate himself kindly from this misappre-
hension but infuriates Norma, who slaps him and storms to her
room. At this juncture Joe decides to leave the mansion, but when
he phones Max to tell him to pack his clothes, Max informs him
that Norma has tried to commit suicide with Joe's razor blades.
Feeling compassion toward her, he returns.

Norma, believing that the screenplay for *Salome* has been perfected,
and that her comeback is to be imminently revealed, sends the script
to her former director, Cecil B. DeMille. Again, as the fates would
have it, another employee of Paramount Studios, Gordon Cole, starts
calling Norma, and she mistakenly thinks he is calling her on behalf
of Mr. DeMille to stage her comeback as Salome. However, he is
interested only in using her very unusual car for an upcoming film
at Paramount. Since she won't speak directly with Gordon Cole,
because she believes she should deal only with Mr. DeMille personally, she does not realize the mistake and has Max drive her to
the Paramount Studio to see him. When she arrives, Mr. DeMille
receives her with great respect but avoids mentioning his disinterest

in the script and her as a future star. She leaves the studio believing that her comeback is imminent and undergoes several beauty treatments to prepare for it.

Norma discovers another manuscript of Joe's having a female coauthor, Betty Schaefer, who she surmises may have more than a working interest with Joe. She calls Betty to tell her that Joe has been living with her and impugns his reputation. When Betty comes to the mansion to see for herself, Joe does not dissuade her by exposing Norma's delusions. After Betty leaves, Joe decides to go back to his old life at a newspaper and packs to leave. Norma again threatens to commit suicide but Joe disregards it. She then threatens him with a gun, but he ignores that as well and then tries to tell her the truth about the vainglorious lie she has been living, including the mistake at Paramount and the fake fan letters written by Max. Norma is so convinced by her delusion that she cannot accept what Joe has said, and instead of returning to reality, she decides to end passionately the threat to her fantasy. She shoots him three times, and he falls into her swimming pool.

In the final scene, the police and reporters arrive at the mansion to investigate Joe's death, but Norma feels no fear because the reality of her fantasy has reached new heights. With encouragement from Max, she is convinced that the newspapers and film crews are there to report on her new comeback at Paramount as Salome. Max stages her arrival into the living room by shouting, "Action!" after which Norma descends down her grand stairway and announces her comeback, concluding, "All right, Mr. DeMille, I'm ready for my close-up."

Though Norma is an extreme caricature of the blindness of vanity, she illustrates how powerful vainglorious self-delusion can be—not only with respect to self-impairment and self-destruction, but also the impairment, injury, and destruction of others. It is a hard lie to overcome and a hard spell to break, leaving in its wake the broken lives of people who truly care for the real person—not merely a popular façade.

The destructive power of vanity can come to new heights in our current culture, particularly through social media. Millennials and Gen Xers are becoming progressively more superficial—isolated from their core identities—through continuous attempted improvements of their self-image on Snapchat and Facebook. Visitors to these sites obtain little insight into the true person, but must content themselves with a myriad of photographs and posts designed to convey an image of beauty and success that betray very little virtuous, transcendental, self-sacrificial, and religious substance.

What is more pitiable, and more serious, is the apparent belief in this myth by the hosts who designed them. They are not only falling in love with their created self-image—a classic manifestation of narcissism—but also enjoying their superficial images more than the reality of their self-reflective transcendental nature and any objectively good or loving definition they could bring to it. This narcissistic self-lobotomy is likely to cause a severe underliving of life, underestimation of dignity, and, if such can be imagined, a disinterest in eternal salvation.

To compound the problem, these social media technologies have produced "group think", which has the two-sided problem of robbing these individuals of their freely chosen self-identity while reinforcing their venture into superficiality and valuelessness. Furthermore, the culture of social media, which is morphing into the culture of young people itself, is becoming more superficial over time, and when it is compared with the principles, beliefs, and ideals of the Greatest Generation (who on the whole had less education), it seems to have lost its capacity for self-sacrificial love and commitment.

As if matters could not get worse, a journal of the American Medical Association, *JAMA Facial Plastic Surgery*,[23] has reported a steadily increasing trend in what is becoming known as "Snapchat dysmorphia". Most everyone is aware of the widespread practice of taking "selfies" at every imaginable status-bearing occasion—even quite risky ones. It now seems that the filters used by Snapchat to "clean up" these selfies are causing a large number of young people (even as young as fourteen) to desire and seek facial plastic surgery to alter their appearance to look like their Snapchat version. This not only exacerbates the narcissism and superficiality of selfies and social media, but also is leading to another destructive phenomenon.

---

[23] See Susruthi Rajanala, Mayra Maymone, and Neelam Vashi, "Selfies—Living in the Era of Filtered Photographs", *JAMA Facial Plastic Surgery*, August 2, 2018, https://jamanetwork .com/journals/jamafacialplasticsurgery/article-abstract/2688763.

Doctors and psychologists are quite concerned about the increasing incidence of serious self-esteem problems (similar to anorexia) and increasing addiction to facial plastic surgery to alleviate perceived imperfections. Contrary to what might be supposed, having these plastic surgeries does not enhance self-esteem, but rather makes the individual progressively more critical of their appearance, moving them to seek additional surgeries to become their ideal self. The cycle is so compelling that body dysmorphic disorder (a mental illness classified on the obsessive-compulsive spectrum) is affecting tens of thousands of our young people at an accelerating rate. There is currently no end or even diminishment in sight.

It seems that the deadly sin of vanity has undermined everything of substance in our culture, threatening its future as well as the individuals within it. We might even say that vanity is the "preferred deadly sin" within our culture, and that Satan has done remarkably well in playing to this Achilles heel—so much so that many in the culture might literally prefer, like C. S. Lewis' characters, to choose Hell before enduring a slight diminishment of its empty satisfactions. If we are to restore core identity, true dignity, and interest in eternal salvation not only to those we love, but also to the culture itself, we will have to find progressively more creative ways to bring intellectual, religious/spiritual, and moral conversion into individual and cultural consciousness. This is the subject of Volume II and the conclusion to this Trilogy (in Volume III).

VI. Conclusion

The five deadly sins addressed in this chapter arise out of a dominant interest in Level One (pleasure-material) happiness and Level Two (ego-comparative) happiness, and as we have seen, they are self-destructive and injurious to others, society, and the Kingdom of God. Evidently, they are prime gateways used by the Evil One to seduce us into his darkness, destruction, and alienation from God.

The longer we engage in these deadly sins, the more we want them, and to satisfy our increased desire, we have to get more of them. Thus, we find ourselves progressively more transfixed by these sins, becoming almost obsessed in our pursuit of them. The Evil

One takes advantage of this negative transformation by intensifying temptations, deceits, and suggestions for even greater satisfaction. As this progresses, we become less and less concerned for the people around us. We become not only insensitive to them, but also willing to use and abuse them for the satisfaction of our enflamed passion.

As this downward spiral proceeds, we find ourselves becoming ever more distant from God and the spiritual life. Though we may feel some increase in spiritual emptiness, alienation, loneliness, and guilt, we try to shrug it off as if God were irrelevant and his commandments foolish. At this point, we are in real spiritual danger. Therefore, we need to do everything possible to awaken from our seduction, recognize the deception and danger in it, and fight it not only with the virtues of prudence, temperance, and fortitude (addressed in Chapter 4), but also with the supernatural grace of the sacraments, prayer, and the truth of Christ interpreted by the Church (to be addressed in Volume II of this Trilogy).

Chapter Six

The Deadly Sins—Part II

Anger, Envy, and Pride

Introduction

Though the previous five deadly sins can certainly lead to self-destruction and destruction of others, they are less aggressive and voracious than the final three deadly sins we will discuss in this chapter: anger, envy, and pride. As we shall see, these sins can become incendiary and even explosive, leading to permanent injury and even the deaths of multiple individuals, and sometimes large groups. Though each of these sins is different in its commission and objective, all three have a common root: vengeance. Anger seeks vengeance for a seemingly justifiable harm; envy seeks vengeance for an unintended slight or comparative advantage by another; and pride seeks power and dominion for its own sake, and wreaks vengeance on anyone who is unwilling to submit to subjugation.

As we shall see in Volume II of this Trilogy, the commandment most often urged by Jesus in the New Testament is forgiveness. At first glance, we might think this to be an unusual prioritization, but after studying the next three deadly sins, Jesus' wisdom will become abundantly clear; for forgiveness borne out of faith and love is the key to reversing the blinding, driving, and destructive power of anger, envy, and pride. Forgiveness may seem quite simple, but when injustice is felt, it can be quite difficult to achieve, and sometimes seemingly impossible. At this juncture, faith in Jesus and the help of the Church will be indispensable.

I. Anger

Prior to the time of Jesus, anger was not interpreted as necessarily negative. Some stoic philosophers (e.g., Galen and Seneca) viewed anger as a weakness and even a kind of madness, and Plato viewed it as one of the unruly passions undermining our rational soul.[1] Other philosophers view anger more positively. Aristotle, for example, views anger as a natural emotion arising out of a perpetrated injustice that seeks retribution in order to restore the equity of justice. He further notes, when anger achieves its just retribution, it is better than the sweetest honey.[2] The Old Testament views anger in a similar light, addressing it in the context of Yahweh's anger far more often than human anger. In that context, Yahweh's anger is aroused by the disobedience of Israel and also by foreigners who interfere with His plans. Since His anger arises out of His justifiable indignation (His moral will), it is always just, and so also the retribution and punishments He inflicts on Israel out of this anger.[3] Since Yahweh's anger arises out of righteous indignation, similarly motivated human anger is also justifiable.[4] Many of the psalms express anger toward adversaries and enemies, and call upon God to exact vengeance and retribution against those enemies—in the belief that God will avenge our injustices just as He takes vengeance on Israel for disobedience (see Ps 37; 55—59; 94; 109; 137). Nevertheless, Wisdom literature cautions against inciting anger in others (Prov 6:34; 15:1; 16:14) and yielding to unrighteous anger (Ps 37:7-9; Prov 15:18; 16:32; 19:19; 24:19; 27:4).

Jesus supersedes the permissibility of righteous anger in the Old Testament, implying that God does not take vengeance on His enemies and, therefore, on our enemies. He loves His enemies (Mt 5:44),

[1] In *Phaedrus*, Plato relates an allegory of a charioteer (representing reason, the highest part of the soul) driven by two horses: a white one (representing the inclination toward virtue and piety) and a black one (representing the unruly passions, including anger). The black horse is constantly pulling and veering, acting in a disordered way, causing the charioteer to use the white horse to keep it in line in the pursuit of the good. Plato, *Phaedrus* 246a–254e, trans. R. Hackforth, in *The Collected Dialogues of Plato*, ed. Edith Hamilton and Huntington Cairns (Princeton, N.J.: Princeton University Press, 1961).

[2] Aristotle, *Rhetoric* 2, 2.

[3] John L. McKenzie, *Dictionary of the Bible* (New York: Macmillan Publishing, 1965), pp. 32–34.

[4] Ibid.

and He causes good things to happen to them (Mt 5:45). As explained in Volume IV (Chapter 2) of the Quartet, Jesus does not portray God as angry or punishing. Indeed, He presents God as "Abba" (meaning "daddy", which conveys the trust and delight of a child for his affectionate, patient, understanding father); as the Father of the Prodigal Son (Lk 15:11–32); and as the Shepherd who rejoices in finding the lost sheep (Lk 15:4–6). Since God is not angry, does not seek retribution, and shows mercy unconditionally (Mt 5:44–45; Lk 15:11–32), then we too must strive to be like our Heavenly Father in refraining from anger (Mt 5:22), refraining from vengeance (Mt 5:38–42), and showing mercy unconditionally (Mt 18:21–22). Jesus goes even further than this, advocating that we should love our enemies as our Heavenly Father loves His enemies (Mt 5:43–48).

Bearing this general context in mind, you may now look more closely at Jesus' prohibition of anger in the Sermon on the Mount:

> You have heard that it was said to the men of old, "You shall not kill; and whoever kills shall be liable to judgment." But I say to you that every one who is angry with his brother shall be liable to judgment; whoever insults his brother shall be liable to the council, and whoever says, "You fool!" shall be liable to the hell of fire. (Mt 5:21–22)

In this passage, Jesus intentionally links anger to the fifth commandment, the prohibition against killing, suggesting that anger is the interior attitude that gives rise to the most serious sin against individuals. Thus, for Jesus if one wants to avoid the disposition giving rise to the most heinous sin of killing, one will want to avoid anger, its interior source. If we put the prohibition against anger in the wider context of the fifth antithesis (the prohibition against vengeance, i.e., "An eye for an eye and a tooth for a tooth" [Mt 5:38–39]) and the sixth antithesis (the prohibition against hating enemies and the admonition to love them [Mt 5:45–48]), we can see an implicit interior causal chain leading from anger to destruction of others and the self: Anger (even justifiable anger arising out of unjust harms) leads to hatred and the desire for vengeance, which in turn leads to the destruction of others, even to killing them intentionally. This highly negative interior disposition also leads to self-destruction, rendering us incapable of love through being consumed by hatred and vengeance. Given these consequences, Jesus gives the strongest possible admonition and warning against anger, indicating that its consequences can be so dark and evil as to lead to "judgment" (implying judgment according to the same nonmerciful criterion we have used against the injustices of others).

Jesus also links anger to insult (particularly the worst kind of insult in Semitic society, "You fool", suggesting pure contempt for the other). How is insult related to anger? Evidently, insult stirs up anger, and the desire for retribution, in others. Thus, for Jesus, it is just as serious, if not more serious, to stir up anger and vengeance intentionally in others by insult and contempt as it is for us to allow anger, hatred, and the desire for vengeance to grow within ourselves.

Jesus does not leave much room for righteous indignation even though it is justifiable in the Old Testament, because righteous indignation is based on the primacy of justice (equity, i.e., "An eye for an eye and a tooth for a tooth"), while His teaching is based on the primacy of mercy, forgiveness, and compassionate love. The moment Jesus supersedes justice with mercy and forgiveness, He supersedes the legitimacy of "just retribution", and the moment He does this, He also supersedes the legitimacy of the emotion that empowers the desire for "just retribution and vengeance": anger. In this regard, He is completely logically consistent, from cause to effect. If we accept Jesus' teaching on the primacy of mercy, forgiveness, and compassionate love (the criterion by which *we* would want to be judged), then we must also extend the primacy of mercy and forgiveness (over just retribution) to others (see Mt 7:2, 12; 18:21–35, the Parable of the Unmerciful Servant). This teaching is nothing more than minimal justice and the Golden Rule: treat others the way you want to be treated (Mt 7:12). Now if we extend the primacy of mercy and forgiveness to others, then we will want to obey the commandment of Jesus to refrain from anger and its negative interior consequences— hatred and the desire for vengeance. If we do this, we will avoid a world of hurt and destruction to others—and destruction to self.

Perhaps the best literary illustration of the destructiveness of justified anger is Shakespeare's well-known tragedy *Hamlet*.[5] Shakespeare

---

[5] I drew from an e-book of *Hamlet* by William Shakespeare (Project Gutenberg, 2019). The e-book is available for free on Project Gutenberg's website at http://www.gutenberg .org/files/1524/1524-h/1524-h.htm. For additional information regarding plot summary, see "Hamlet: Synopsis and Plot Overview of Shakespeare's Hamlet", Shakespeare Birthplace Trust (website), accessed July 2, 2020, https://www.shakespeare.org.uk/explore-shakespeare /shakespedia/shakespeares-plays/hamlet/.

sets up the tragic story by showing the audience that if *anyone* had a
right to be angry and seek retribution, it is Prince Hamlet whose father
(King Hamlet of Denmark) has been murdered by his uncle Claudius
(who poured poison into his ear) so that Claudius could marry his
mother and take the crown. The ghost of Hamlet's father first appears
to three sentries (Hamlet's friends) on the ramparts of Elsinore castle.
They tell Hamlet about it, and he resolves to see the ghost for himself,
for he is despondent about his father's death. The ghost reveals the
cruel manner in which Hamlet's uncle Claudius has killed him, and
how quickly he moved to marry his mother and take the crown. As if
Hamlet were not already completely outraged, the ghost makes Hamlet promise that he will avenge him by killing Claudius.

Since Hamlet is not certain about the ghost's identity, he concocts
a plot to determine Claudius' guilt. Using a group of traveling actors
(brought to Elsinore by Hamlet's friends Rosencrantz and Guildenstern), he writes a short play depicting events very similar to those in
which his uncle Claudius was supposedly involved. When Claudius
sees the play, he rushes out of the room, convincing Hamlet of his guilt.

Queen Gertrude, Hamlet's mother, requests that Hamlet come
to her room to give an explanation of his behavior, which results in
a terrible fight. Polonius (chief counselor to the king) decides to
hide behind a tapestry during the exchange, but accidentally makes
a noise. Hamlet, suspecting that it is his uncle Claudius, is filled with
rage and stabs wildly at the tapestry, killing the figure behind it. This
gives rise to the first unnecessary tragedy born of Hamlet's "justifiable" anger. Hamlet discovers the mistake, but instead of feeling
remorse that might have led to a reconsideration of his recklessly
destructive path, he shows greater rage toward his mother, demand-
ing that she stop sleeping with Claudius. He drags Polonius' body out
of the room, ending act 3.

Claudius sends Hamlet to England with Rosencrantz and Guildenstern, giving a note to the king of England to execute Hamlet, but
Hamlet escapes when his ship is attacked by pirates with whom he
successfully negotiates a release, enabling him to return to Denmark.
In the meantime, Ophelia, the daughter of Polonius, is driven mad
by the tragic death of her father. Hamlet loves Ophelia and is engaged
to her. While he is on his journey to England and back to Denmark,
Ophelia's madness worsens, and she wanders the halls of Elsinore

listless and alone. She is found drowned, seemingly by suicide—the second unnecessary tragedy incited by Hamlet's rage. Though Hamlet professes to love Ophelia, the tragedy does not dampen his rage and desire to exact vengeance on Claudius.

When Hamlet returns from his interrupted journey to England, he is fully aware of the note that Claudius has left with Rosencrantz and Guildenstern and is renewed in his vigor to exact retribution. When Claudius hears that Hamlet has returned to Denmark safe and sound, he has to devise another plan to have Hamlet killed so that he can remain king of Denmark and married to Gertrude. He has Laertes (the son of Polonius, who, like Hamlet, is outraged at the unjust death of *his* father at the hands of Hamlet) challenge Hamlet to a fencing match. He gives Laertes a poison-tipped foil, but just in case Laertes cannot make contact with Hamlet, he sets out a cup of poisoned wine with which to congratulate Hamlet if he wins the match. In the first part of the match, Hamlet avoids contact with Laertes' foil, at which point his mother picks up the cup of poisoned wine to congratulate Hamlet on his success. Claudius, realizing that she is about to poison herself, tries to stop her but is too late. She drinks the wine and declares that she has been poisoned—the third unnecessary tragedy incited by Hamlet's "justifiable" anger. In the confusion, Laertes seizes the opportunity to slash Hamlet with the poisoned foil, assuring Hamlet's impending death—the fourth unnecessary tragedy. Hamlet and Laertes struggle, causing the two to exchange foils, after which Hamlet stabs Laertes with his own poisoned weapon—the fifth unnecessary tragedy.

At this point Shakespeare introduces a glimmer of hope and light by having Laertes reconcile with Hamlet. This act of forgiveness causes Laertes to reveal Claudius' plot against Hamlet. Hamlet rushes toward Claudius and runs him through with the poison sword, finally completing the act of vengeance that he has been seeking throughout the play. As he lay dying, an announcement is made that Prince Fortinbras of Norway is marching toward Denmark on his way to Poland. Hamlet names him as successor to the throne in view of the fact that the entire Danish royal family will soon be dead, as well as its chief counselor and his children. Hamlet dies with his friend Horatio, whom he begs to refrain from suicide so he can tell the whole story of Prince Hamlet.

As Shakespeare implies, anger is a powerful negative passion, whether justified or unjustified. Its stepchildren, hatred and vengeance, lead to madness and destructive consequences—both intended and unintended. There is only one way out of its grasp, the one suggested by Jesus: a radical incisive act of forgiveness similar to the one displayed belatedly by Laertes. Hamlet's *justified* anger has led to the deaths of two innocent people (Polonius and Ophelia, his betrothed); the death of two excusably complicit people, his mother (who wanted to remain married to Claudius) and Laertes (who is complicit with Claudius only because of his own sense of justified anger); and one victim of injustice swept up into the chaos of justified rage, Hamlet himself. All this death and destruction, including the end of the Danish royal family and court, was to procure vengeance against the one completely guilty party: King Claudius. Shakespeare's tragedy validates the teaching of Jesus that anger, even when justified, frequently leads to needless pain, destruction, and death. In order to avoid it, we must take on the virtue that counters it—the good habit and discipline of forgiveness in imitation of Christ.

One more point should be considered. Contemporary psychological studies show that the suppression or repression of anger can lead to depression or explosive behavior.[6] Suppression generally refers to a *conscious* attempt to prevent anger from surfacing into the conscious psyche while repression is an *unconscious* (frequently neurotic) attempt to do this. In the end, the effects of both actions are psychic exhaustion and depression. In the long term, both actions are likely to be unsuccessful, possibly giving rise to a surge of anger more volatile than would have occurred without suppression or repression.

If these studies are correct, would this not contradict Jesus' admonition to refrain from anger in all its forms? No. Jesus is not asking us to suppress or repress anger, but to dispel anger through radical forgiveness, supported by the Holy Spirit. Forgiveness is not a blocking action; it is a "letting go" of an inexcusable injustice intentionally perpetrated on us by another. This abandonment of our just claim against another is quite different from retaining the just claim while trying to block its aggressive negative effects from reaching our

---

[6] See Francis Hsu, *Suppression versus Repression: A Limited Psychological Interpretation of Four Cultures* (Chicago: Northwestern University Press, 1949).

consciousness. Forgiveness tries to nip the *cause* of anger in the bud, but suppression/repression allows the cause to produce its unsettling effects, while trying to prevent them from causing disturbance within the conscious psyche. The first strategy, if successful, stops the surge and momentum of destructive psychic energy, but the second allows the surge to continue, causing the psyche to battle it to the point of either exhaustion or depression.

Forgiveness has another advantage over suppression/repression: it allows for the action of divine grace. In Christianity, forgiveness is practiced within a context of prayer and faith that anticipates the action of the Holy Spirit to help us let go of what is objectively inexcusable and unjust. Spontaneous prayers (short, easily remembered incisive prayers) can be used to galvanize our faith, which allows the Holy Spirit to move through our freedom to empower difficult acts of forgiveness. I have a favorite, particularly effective spontaneous prayer that helps me invite the Lord into my psyche when I need His help to let go of injustice: "Lord, You are the just judge; You take care of it." When I am filled with indignation (and even rage) at an injustice perpetrated by another, I repeat this prayer again and again until I am able to give the whole situation as well as the perpetrator over to the Lord's justice and mercy. I then pray for the perpetrator. As I do this, I can feel my psyche letting go of the injustice and my desire for retribution. Slowly but surely this "letting go into the justice and mercy of God" settles the mounting feelings of anger without my suppressing/repressing them. Though I may take the emotions to bed with me at night, they begin to subside gradually when I place the injustice (and my just claim) into the hands and heart of God for His, rather than my, action. I've done this dozens of times and can assure you that it is one of the most powerful experiences of God's action and the Holy Spirit you will experience. Try it for yourselves, and you will find not only a freedom from anger and suppression/repression, but also the reality and efficacy of God's grace.

II. Envy

Envy (*invidia*) is resentment toward another person who appears to have an advantage or some benefit that one does not have. This resentment frequently leads to hatred for the other individual and a desire not only to take the advantage or benefit for oneself, but also to deprive the other of it—and make them pay an additional penalty for "unjustly" possessing it. Frequently, envious individuals believe that they have been treated unfairly (by life, God, or others) simply because another person possesses an advantage, benefit, or opportunity that they did not receive. They have an expectation that a good life requires equal advantages and opportunities, and that others' comparative advantage is therefore unjust. This sense of being treated unfairly causes resentment within the disadvantaged individual, and frequently enough, he blames the advantaged individual (unjustly) for the perceived injustice toward him. He believes that this "unjust treatment" gives him license to hate the other individual, to deprive the individual of his advantage, and if possible, to take the advantage for himself. The ensuing harm from both the misguided hatred and desire to hurt the advantaged individual can be quite severe, and sometimes, it can be directed toward whole groups of people who are perceived to be advantaged.

Envy is distinct from jealousy. The former arises out of a perceived lack of benefit (felt to be an injustice) that engenders hatred and retributive action. The latter generally arises out of a sense of losing someone who an individual believes should be loyal to him (e.g., losing the loyalty or fidelity of a spouse or good friend to another person or cause). Hence, jealousy involves three people: the jealous person, the object of jealousy, and the interloper who is causing the jealousy, by wooing the beloved from the jealous person. Envy, on the other hand, is restricted to two people: the agent of envy and the object of envy. No doubt, some agents of envy can feel envy toward hundreds, if not thousands, of people, but their resentment is not caused by a third person wooing away a former beloved.

Envy is also distinct from covetousness, though not completely. Covetousness is associated more with greed, the desire to possess something or somebody because it is beautiful and will enhance one's image and reputation. Envy, as noted above, arises out of a perceived advantage of another person with an accompanying sense of injustice, leading to resentment, hatred, and the desire to hurt the other and take his advantage for oneself. Though these are distinct passions with distinct misguided objectives, there is one main similarity: to obtain something that does not properly belong to the covetous or envious person. Envy, as many philosophers and Church Fathers have taught, is worse than covetousness and greed because it generally seeks to do harm to the advantaged other, while covetousness/greed is satisfied simply with the possession of the object desired.

Many ancient philosophers and poets recognize the destructiveness of envy to both the agent and its intended victim.[7] The Roman poet Ovid (writing between 10 B.C. and A.D. 17) presents the most lurid description of its destructive power:

> Soon as she [Envy] saw the goddess gay and bright,
> She fetch'd a groan at such a cheerful sight.
> Livid and meagre were her looks, her eye
> In foul distorted glances turn'd awry;
> A hoard of gall her inward parts possess'd,
> And spread a greenness o'er her canker'd breast;
> Her teeth were brown with rust and from her tongue,
> In dangling drops, the stringy poison hung.
> She never smiles but when the wretched weep,
> Nor lulls her malice with a moment's sleep,
> Restless in spite: while watchful to destroy,
> She pines and sickens at another's joy;
> Foe to her self, distressing and distrest,
> She bears her own tormentor in her breast....
> On mortals next, and peopled towns she falls,
> And breathes a burning plague among their walls....
> For envy magnifies what-e'er she shows....
> Giv'n up to envy (for in ev'ry thought
> The thorns, the venom, and the vision wrought)
> Oft did she call on death, as oft decreed,
> Rather than see her sister's wish succeed.[8]

Ovid understood well how envy breeds resentment, hatred, malice, harm, and death. He also recognized how envy consumes herself

---

[7] See David Konstan and N. K. Rutter, *Envy, Spite, and Jealousy: The Rivalrous Emotions in Ancient Greece* (Edinburgh: Edinburgh University Press, 2003).

[8] Ovid, *Metamorphoses* 2, trans. Sir Samuel Garth et al. (A.D. 1; MIT Classics, 1994), http://classics.mit.edu/Ovid/metam.2.second.html.

while she is attempting to annihilate her victims, whose joy and positive demeanor infuriate her. She will never be satisfied; as she annihilates one victim, she looks for others who may experience greater joy, advantage, and opportunity than herself. Eventually, her loathing for others will be turned on herself, for her complete dedication to hatred cannot escape the occasional look into a mirror—and there she will find complete disgust even with herself.

Envy figures quite prominently in the Bible and lies at the center of two important initial narratives in Genesis: the story of Adam and Eve, and the story of Cain and Abel. As most readers know, the words of the serpent to Eve are not simply designed to provoke covetousness—that is, a desire for the forbidden fruit of the tree— but resentment toward God for not sharing all of His wisdom and powers with her and her husband. Notice how the crafty serpent (the devil) uses the statement: "You will not die. For God knows that when you eat of it your eyes will be opened, and you will be like God, knowing good and evil" (Gen 3:5). It is meant to suggest that God self-interestedly deprived them of being like Him, and that they have a right to be like Him. This provokes the question, "Why would God want to prevent us from becoming like Him? Is He worried about us being His equal?" We can feel the envy beginning to percolate in the soul of Eve—"He has an unfair advantage and opportunity that He has purposely kept away from us. It's unfair." Now study the narrative for yourself:

> Now the serpent was more subtle than any other wild creature that the LORD God had made. He said to the woman, "Did God say, 'You shall not eat of any tree of the garden'?" And the woman said to the serpent, "We may eat of the fruit of the trees of the garden; but God said, 'You shall not eat of the fruit of the tree which is in the midst of the garden, neither shall you touch it, lest you die.'" But the serpent said to the woman, "You will not die. For God knows that when you eat of it your eyes will be opened, and you will be like God, knowing good and evil." So when the woman saw that the tree was good for food, and that it was a delight to the eyes, and that the tree was to be desired to make one wise, she took of its fruit and ate; and she also gave some to her husband, and he ate. Then the eyes of both were opened, and they knew that they were naked. (Gen 3:1–7)

Evidently, the serpent is trying to actualize a trifecta of envy, greed, and pride; but envy lies at the center of the temptation because the serpent wants Eve to believe that God has withheld something very important from them so that He can always remain superior to them. Thus, he appeals to greed (to obtain something desirable that does not belong to them), then to pride (to become like God); finally, to complete his evil, he appeals to envy—to take from the Creator the advantage of which He deprived them.

In the well-known story of Cain and Abel, Cain gives free reign to his envy and decides to kill his brother as repayment for Abel's being favored by God. The author skillfully describes how envy starts, grows, and progresses toward its ultimate destructive climax:

> Now Abel was a keeper of sheep, and Cain a tiller of the ground. In the course of time Cain brought to the LORD an offering of the fruit of the ground [an offering of average produce], and Abel brought of the firstlings of his flock and of their fat portions [the best of the best of what he had to offer]. And the LORD had regard for Abel and his offering, but for Cain and his offering he had no regard. So Cain was very angry, and his countenance fell. The LORD said to Cain, "Why are you angry, and why has your countenance fallen? If you do well, will you not be accepted? And if you do not do well, sin is lurking at the door; its desire is for you, but you must master it." Cain said to Abel his brother, "Let us go out to the field." And when they were in the field, Cain rose up against his brother Abel, and killed him. Then the LORD said to Cain, "Where is Abel your brother?" He said, "I do not know; am I my brother's keeper?" And the LORD said, "What have you done? The voice of your brother's blood is crying to me from the ground. And now you are cursed from the ground, which has opened its mouth to receive your brother's blood from your hand." (Gen 4:2–11)

The author understood the dynamics of envy quite well. Cain was unwilling to share the finest portion of his produce with the Lord while Abel was willing to do so. When God rewarded Abel for acting well and did not reward Cain because he tried to hold back the best for himself, Cain became angry—that is, resentful toward his brother for obtaining God's favor. God tries to mitigate Cain's anger by explaining that it is *his* (Cain's) fault, not Abel's, that he showed favor to Abel and not to him. He even tells Cain that if he does well, he too will find His favor, and then warns him that if he does not do well, "sin is lurking at the door", and it wants *him*. Cain's resentment is so great that he ignores God's offer to show him favor if he acts rightly in the future, and decides to kill his brother (disregarding God's warning about the danger of so doing), because simply getting what Abel has is not enough. He will only be satisfied when he punishes Abel for having already won God's favor.

We might be thinking, "Who would ignore God's warning and turn down His offer of grace, simply to punish his brother for winning God's favor before him?" An envious person would do precisely that, for as the biblical author suggests, envy is not logical, practical, prudent, or satisfied with mere equality or justice; envy's resentment and hatred can only be satisfied by vengeance, malice, and destruction; and so Cain acts against his best interests, perpetrating the ultimate injustice upon his brother and risking punishment by God, simply to make his brother pay for getting a richly deserved reward for acting rightly before God. If we conclude that this is the action of a mad man, we will have learned the point being made by the biblical author: envy renders us mad, and, as Ovid recognized, she is madness herself.

Wisdom literature continues the biblical reflection on the madness, addictiveness, and curse of envy. God corrects Job by telling him that "anger kills the foolish man, but envy slays the simple minded" (Job 5:2, my translation). In the Book of Proverbs we hear: "A sound heart is the life of the flesh: but envy the rottenness of the bones" (Prov 14:30, KJV), and "Wrath is cruel, and anger is outrageous; but who is able to stand before envy?" (Prov 27:4, KJV).

Jesus does not specifically mention envy in the Gospels, but as we have seen above, He prohibits anger in all its forms (Mt 5:22) and extols its opposing virtues—forgiveness from the heart, not judging others, self-sacrificial love, and love of enemies—on countless occasions. In the Sermon on the Mount, Jesus instructs His disciples to turn the other cheek when struck unjustly by another (Mt 5:38–40). He also advocates loving our enemies and doing good for those who hate us (Mt 5:43–48). We also see Jesus' admonition to forgive "seventy times seven" (Mt 18:22) and the prohibition against judging others (Mt 7:1–5). Jesus also assures His followers that every perceived injustice will be equalized in the Kingdom of Heaven:

Blessed are you poor, for yours is the kingdom of God. Blessed are you that hunger now, for you shall be satisfied. Blessed are you that weep now, for you shall laugh. Blessed are you when men hate you, and when they exclude you and revile you, and cast out your name as evil, on account of the Son of man! Rejoice in that day, and leap for joy, for behold, your reward is great in heaven. (Lk 6:20–23)

In saying this, Jesus undermines the motivation for envy—for no comparative advantage will be permanent, and all will enjoy the fullness of happiness with God and the beatific vision forever. Therefore if we have faith in the promises of Jesus, we can find a way out of envy, and indeed a good reason for never engaging in it, for it has no lasting power and engaging it threatens the very eternal salvation that will equalize every perceived disadvantage and injustice.

Jesus presents another teaching that undermines the motivation for envy from the opposite angle. He tells His followers to be wary of riches, status, and power in this world, because they may present a significant disadvantage to entering into the Kingdom of God. Using a typical rabbinical teaching technique of hyperbolic allusion, Jesus warns "the rich" (which refers not only to material wealth, but also to talent and worldly status and power) that their perceived advantage may make it more difficult for them to enter into the Kingdom of God, like a camel trying to pass through the eye of a needle (Mt 19:24).

In sum, Jesus does not speak directly about the darkness and destructiveness of envy (as does the Old Testament); rather, He gives an assurance of consummate joy and equality in the Kingdom of God that undercuts the motivation for envy, followed by a teaching that warns both rich and poor alike and warns that riches may present a significant inhibition to the highest, most enduring human dignity, destiny, and fulfillment: eternity with the unconditionally loving God.

Though Jesus does not teach about the evil and dangers of envy directly, Mark indicates that Jesus knew the underlying sin of the chief priests who betrayed Him, "for he perceived that it was out of envy that the chief priests had delivered him up" (Mk 15:10). So it seems that Jesus was well aware of envy and its dangers, but decided to take the high road above and around it to help his followers avoid its darkness and downfall. The rest of the New Testament returns to a direct critique of envy and to its inclusion in lists of prohibited acts that jeopardize salvation (see Acts 7:9, 13:45, 17:5; Rom 1:29; Phil 1:15; 1 Tim 6:4; Tit 3:3).[9]

Edmund Spenser gives a wonderful allegorical interpretation of the deadly sins and their counterpoised virtues in his classic *The Faerie Queen*; and like Ovid, he is particularly graphic in his description of envy:

> And next to him [Avarice] malicious Envy rode
> Upon a ravenous Wolf, and Still did chaw
> Between his cankred Teeth a venemous Tode,
> That all the Poison ran about his Jaw;
> But inwardly he chawed his own Maw
> At Neighbour's Wealth, that made him ever sad;
> For Death it was, when any good he saw,
> And wept, that cause of Weeping none he had:
> But when he heard of Harm, he wexed wondrous glad.
>
> All in a Kirtle of discolour'd Say
> He clothed was, ypainted full of Eyes
> And in his Bosom secretly there lay
> An hateful Snake, the which his Tail upties
> In many Folds, and mortal Sting implies.
> Still as he rode, he gnash'd his Teeth, to see
> Those heaps of Gold with griple Covetise,
> And grudged at the great Felicity
> Of proud Lucifera, and his own Company.
>
> He hated all good Works and vertuous Deeds,
> And him no less, that any like did use:
> And who with gracious Bread the Hungry feeds,
> His Alms, for want of Faith, he doth accuse;
> So every Good to Bad he doth abuse:
> And eke the Verse of famous Poet's Wit

---

[9] In Acts 7:9, 13:45, and 17:5 the Greek word used is *zēloō*, which is translated as "jealous" or "envious". We are using it in the second sense. See Johannes P. Louw and Eugene A. Nida, *Greek-English Lexicon of the New Testament: Based on Semantic Domains*, 2nd ed., vol. 1 (New York: United Bible Societies, 1996), p. 759.

He does backbite, and spightful Poison spues
From leprous Mouth, on all that ever writ:
Such one vile Envy was, that first in row did sit.[10]

This allegorical description is so dark and ugly, we need not comment any further, for it speaks not only about envy's destruction of others, the good, the wise, and the innocent, but also envy itself, the hateful companion of Lucifera—named after the devil himself.

Shakespeare takes envy quite seriously. Shylock is moved by envy in *The Merchant of Venice*; so also Richard III in the tragic history bearing his name. Cassius, who convinces Brutus to assassinate Caesar by forged letters and false claims, is motivated almost solely by envy of Caesar's popularity, success, and power in Shakespeare's *Julius Caesar*. Yet there is no better characterization of envy in the whole of English literature than Iago in Shakespeare's tragedy *Othello*.[11] In view of this, we will want to look more deeply into his character and his relationships with Othello and other "friends" whom he destroys. Othello is a Moorish general in the Venetian army who promotes Cassio to be his lieutenant over Iago, an ensign who considers himself to be a better soldier than Cassio. This slight fills Iago with envy toward Cassio and hatred for Othello, whom he believes has treated him unjustly. Iago's envy and hatred know no bounds, and he is willing to hurt and destroy anyone who might be an opportune pawn in his plot to take revenge on both Cassio and Othello. After stewing and brewing about how to take his revenge, he forges a plot that he is fully aware comes from the depths of Hell. Spewing disdain toward Othello who has slighted him, he resolves to go ahead with it, almost bragging to himself how evil and monstrous his plot truly is:

[10]Edmund Spenser, *The Faerie Queene*, ed. John Hughes (Cambridge, Mass.: Cambridge University Press, 1715), bk. 1, canto 4, http://spenserians.cath.vt.edu/TextRecord.php?textsid=68.

[11]I drew from an e-book of *Othello* by William Shakespeare (Project Gutenberg, 2019). The e-book is available for free on Project Gutenberg's website at http://www.gutenberg.org/files/1531/1531-h/1531-h.htm. For additional information regarding plot summary, see "Othello: The Moor of Venice; Synopsis and Plot Overview of Shakespeare's Othello: The Moor of Venice", Shakespeare Birthplace Trust (website), accessed July 2, 2020, https://www.shakespeare.org.uk/explore-shakespeare/shakespedia/shakespeares-plays/othello-moor-venice/.

The Moor is of a free and open nature,
That thinks men honest that but seem to be so,
And will as tenderly be led by the nose
As asses are.
I have't. It is engender'd. Hell and night
Must bring this monstrous birth to the world's light.[12]

Iago now becomes the central player in the tragedy as prime antagonist. Discovering that Othello has secretly eloped with Desdemona, the daughter of a prominent senator, Iago uses his first pawn (Roderigo) to inform Desdemona's father of the elopement, hoping to provoke his rage and indignation toward Othello. When Roderigo informs Desdemona's father, he is indeed enraged and goes to Othello's house to seek his head. Upon arriving, he is confronted by Venetian soldiers from the duke's palace who prevent him from violently confronting Othello.

At that moment, news arrives that the Turks are about to invade Cyprus, and so Othello is asked to go to the duke's residence to advise the senators. Desdemona's father follows Othello to the residence, where he accuses Othello of seducing Desdemona by witchcraft; however, Othello successfully defends himself by convincing the senators that Desdemona fell in love with him, which is confirmed by her. It seems that Othello has averted Iago's first attempt at treachery, but he is prepared to do far more.

Iago sees his next opportunity, an even better one, because it can ensnare Cassio along with Othello when Othello and his retinue—Desdemona, Cassio, Iago, Emilia (Iago's wife), Roderigo, and others—are sent to Cyprus to fight the Turks. As fate would have it, a storm wipes out the entire Turkish fleet, and so the defenders are left without a fight. Othello leaves to consummate his marriage with Desdemona, and Iago initiates his new plot, beginning with Cassio, whom he envies for receiving the promotion to lieutenant. He gets Cassio drunk and persuades Roderigo to pick a fight with him. Montano tries to stop the fight and is wounded in the attempt. When Othello returns and discovers what happened, he demotes Cassio, which brings no end of delight to Iago. Yet he cannot stop

---

[12] Act I, scene 3.

himself there. He hopes to implicate Cassio in an adulterous affair with Othello's new wife, in anticipation of bringing Cassio to ultimate ruin. He does not seem to care that Desdemona will be an innocent victim of his envy toward Cassio and his hatred for her husband. He sees his opportunity when Desdemona drops a handkerchief that was Othello's first gift to Desdemona. Emilia (Iago's wife) gives the handkerchief to Iago without knowing his true purpose. In the meantime, Iago convinces Othello to be suspicious of Cassio and Desdemona. As Iago suspected, Othello, believing in the goodness of humanity, trusts him—not only becoming suspicious of his wife's infidelity, but enraged at Cassio for his supposed betrayal. All Iago needs to do now is use the dropped handkerchief to confirm the false accusation of adultery in Othello's mind.

Iago plants the dropped handkerchief in Cassio's quarters, after which he encourages Cassio to speak plainly about his amorous relationship with Bianca while Othello is listening. Iago skillfully prevents Othello from hearing Bianca's name and convinces Othello that Cassio was speaking about his new wife, Desdemona. This is later confirmed in Othello's mind when Bianca discovers the handkerchief in Cassio's quarters and claims in front of Othello that it belongs to another lover. When Othello recognizes the handkerchief, he vows to kill Desdemona and asks Iago to kill Cassio.

Iago, of course, does not want to kill Cassio or be blamed for it, so he persuades his favorite pawn, Roderigo, to do the job for him. When Roderigo attacks Cassio at night, Cassio wounds him, and so Iago feels compelled to slash Cassio, hitting him in the legs. Since Iago is able to keep his identity hidden, he joins Cassio's companions when he cries for help, pretending that he has come to Cassio's aid. To prevent Roderigo from disclosing his treachery, Iago stabs him and kills him—an innocent victim needed to carry out his plot and protect himself. To prevent any blame from being cast on him, Iago blames Bianca for the plot to kill Cassio—his second innocent victim.

In the meantime, persuaded of Desdemona's guilt, Othello strangles her in bed—the third innocent victim in Iago's scheme. When Emilia arrives, Othello tells her of the handkerchief that Bianca discovered, confirming her adultery and betrayal. Emilia recognizes what her husband has done and reveals the whole matter to

Othello, after which Iago kills her for "betraying him"—the fourth
innocent victim. Once Othello recognizes that he has killed his innocent wife because of Iago's treachery, he stabs him but does not
kill him, preferring him to suffer throughout his life. In desolation
for killing his wife and preferring not to endure the indignity of
a trial and imprisonment, Othello commits suicide—the fifth and
intended innocent victim of Iago. The play ends with Lodovico
(Desdemona's high-ranking cousin) instructing Cassio to punish
Iago appropriately.

One might think that Shakespeare has taken extreme literary
license in creating Iago's incredibly evil character. After all, who
would realistically take such personal risks, engender the murder of
five innocent victims, and blame an innocent lover for a capital
offense to avenge a perceived unjust slight? Yet, Shakespeare creates
this narrative for good reason: to convey the irrational hatred and
destructiveness of two deadly sins—envy and anger, which have
completely infected a supposed colleague and friend of the victims.
Shakespeare knew that this spilling of innocent blood for the sake
of vengeance (moved by anger and envy) is not unusual, for he was
a student of Roman and English history, particularly its monarchs.
The "moral of his story" is the same as the descriptions of envy in
the Bible, Ovid, and Spenser: envy is an almost uncontrollable irrational passion, opening upon intense hatred and vengeance that is
bent on the destruction of its intended victims as well as the innocent pawns that can be used along its vicious way. In the end, it
will destroy and consume itself within its willing subject, leaving
behind completely unnecessary devastation and despair. This should
be ample enough warning to confront envy at its inception and, if
possible, to bring the gift of Jesus to bear against it—faith and hope
in the ultimate justice and love that will occur in His promised resurrection to eternal life.

III. Pride (*Superbia*)

Pride (*superbia*) in the most general sense refers to egocentricity that
leads not only to self-absorption but to the exclusion, neglect, and
even derision of others. It can include or exclude vanity (which, as

we saw in the previous chapter, is concerned with self-image, recognition by others, and perceived status). Since we have already treated vanity independently of pride, we will here restrict ourselves to the other major dimensions of pride: the will to be superior, the will to power, and the will to dominion.

A. Explanation of Pride and Its Five Stages of Destructiveness

In Volume I of the Quartet (throughout Chapters 1–4), we discussed dominant ego-comparative (Level Two) identity. As noted there, winners in the comparison game can content themselves with mere vanity (being given recognition, adulation, and superior or, even, celebrity status). Frequently, this is not enough. One not only wants to be the center of attention and recognition but also inherently superior and even the center of power and dominion. This urge or lust aims at making one's perceived superiority felt by the external world. It can be subtle and Machiavellian[13] or exceedingly strong and self-delusional—even to the point of acting like a messiah (an anointed savior) or a demigod. Yet, *superbia* need not rise to the level of a despotic dictator like Hitler or Stalin; it can be manifested in dominating and Machiavellian leaders of every sort—political, business, military, educational, and even religious. Furthermore, it need not be restricted to high-level leaders; it can also be found in middle managers who "lord it over others and make their authority over them felt" (see Mt 20:25). This can come not only from a sense of superiority and contempt for others, but also from a sense of inferiority disguised as superiority for the sake of saving face or ego-comparative advantage. In either case, the motivation and result are the same: the motivation is ego-comparative advantage for its own sake, and the result is the domination of another for the sake of that advantage. Thus, the practitioners of pride need not be

---

[13] Machiavellian refers to the attitude recommended by Niccolò Machiavelli to political leaders in his sixteenth-century classic work *The Prince*. He contends there that the prince (the person in power) may do anything—including unethical, underhanded, devious, threatening, and even violent courses of action—in order to remain in power. The term has come to mean "devious, underhanded, and cunning schemes and actions to maintain one's power and advantage".

"winners" in the comparison game; they can also be "drawers" and even "losers" who have carved out a path to some form of power advantage, whether by good fortune, Machiavellian tactics, or brutal politics. Once they have the advantage, they make their power and authority felt.

If the belief in one's inherent superiority—whether it come from objective ego-comparative advantage in the external world or a projection of superiority onto feelings of inferiority—is strong enough, then it will naturally seek fulfillment by exercising that superiority over others (i.e., seeking legitimate authority) or dominating others (imposing authority over others who are perceived to be weak by allowing domination to occur). If this belief in inherent superiority is not counterbalanced by empathy and genuine care for others, it will tend toward narcissism that excludes not only care for others, but also respect for them. As this grows, the narcissistically proud person becomes progressively more insensitive to others' needs and then to their right to individual, political, and economic justice, and finally to their right to life.

From the above we may adduce five stages of growth in pride that are concomitantly five stages in the decline of empathy, conscience, care, and love:

1. Dominant ego-comparative (Level Two) identity
2. An increasingly strong belief in one's inherent superiority (whether this be based on a ego-comparative advantage or on projections to cover over inferiority feelings)
3. The desire to make one's belief in inherent superiority felt within the external world
4. A desire to press one's advantages in the external world to their fullest limit (regardless of whether this violates one's conscience and feelings of empathy and care—or violates others' rights to life, liberty, property, and minimum justice); at this point, the urge to dominate overshadows and suppresses one's conscience and feelings of empathy and care
5. The choice to be despotic—that is, to exercise one's power over others in an absolute, oppressive, and even cruel way not for any external advantage, but simply to exercise "godlike" authority over others

When one reaches this final stage, it is generally accompanied by the belief that one is a messiah or has been "chosen" by a nonmoral providence (e.g., by a Hegelian "world spirit") to rule as a god or demigod. To maintain this delusion, the subject must believe that he has transcended good and evil—or rejected the idea of good and evil.[14]

In Chapter 4, we presented three internal powers that oppose the progression from the early to later stages of pride (and other temptations): conscience, empathy, and religion. I believe that these three powers have their origin in a supernatural or transcendent cause for reasons explained in Volume II of the Quartet (Chapters 1–4, and 6). For the moment, suffice to say that one has to marginalize these three powers in order to make "progress" in the stages of pride, particularly in the move from the belief in one's inherent superiority (stage two) to the exercise of narcissistic, uncaring, unjust, and despotic authority over others (stages three, four, and five). Hitler, for example, used the nonmoral view of God and religion of Hegel (the "world spirit" developed in *The Philosophy of Right*[15]) to bolster his belief in being messianically chosen by a nonmoral providence. He also used Freidrich Nietzsche's view of the superman's transcendence of good and evil through *The Will to Power*[16] to justify his negation of good and evil and empathy/care for the weak.[17]

[14]Adolf Hitler, for example, believed that he was messianically chosen by a nonmoral world spirit (which he probably borrowed from Hegel's *Philosophy of Right* and *Phenomenology of Spirit*). He also was highly influenced by Friedrich Nietzsche's *Will to Power* and *Beyond Good and Evil* (for source information, see note 16 below). See the 1943 report *Analysis of the Personality of Adolph Hitler: With Predictions of His Future Behavior and Suggestions for Dealing with Him Now and After Germany's Surrender*, prepared by Dr. Henry A. Murray, from the Harvard Psychological Clinic, for the U.S. Office of Strategic Services, https://archive .org/details/AnalysisThePersonalityofAdolphHitler/page/n1/mode/2up. Also, see William L. Shirer and Ron Rosenbaum, *The Rise and Fall of the Third Reich: A History of Nazi Germany* (New York: Simon & Schuster, 2011), pp. xxii–xxiv.

[15]See G. W. F. Hegel, *Philosophy of Right*, trans. S. W. Dyde (Kitchener, Ont.: Batoche Books, 2001), pp. 8, 47–52, 266–69.

[16]Friedrich Nietzsche, *The Will to Power*, trans. Walter Kaufmann (New York: Vintage Books, 1968). See also Friedrich Nietzsche, *Beyond Good and Evil*, trans. and ed. William Kaufman (New York: Dover Publications, 1997).

[17]See Yvonne Sherratt, *Hitler's Philosophers* (New Haven: Yale University Press, 2013), pp. 16–32, 41–43, 52 (for Hegel), and pp. 16–30, 42–52, 70–71 (for Nietzsche).

Similarly, Vladimir Lenin,[18] Friedrich Engels,[19] Joseph Stalin,[20] and the Bolshevik party effectively used Marx's atheism[21] to justify their rejection of religion as well as Marx's dialectical materialism to justify their historical ascendency to despotic authority.[22] They were also able to use Marx's moral relativism and reduction of good and evil to the "evil of capital" to justify their marginalization of conscience and moral good and evil.[23] Virtually every despotic ruler and despotic social movement finds a theoretical and practical way to rationalize the marginalization of God, religion, empathy, and conscience, allowing for the ascendency to the absolute, arbitrary, and cruel use of power.

Even religious despots, like Jim Jones and David Koresh, have to marginalize conscience, principles of good and evil, empathy, and a personal relationship with a just and loving God. Though this may seem counterintuitive, many cult leaders search out religious texts from their traditions that are quite ancient in origin (e.g., texts from the oldest strands of the Old Testament that have been superceded by later prophets and by Jesus, such as the requirement for vengeance against defeated enemies in 1 Samuel 13—15). They used these texts to justify the religious suspension of ethical norms. This leads to religious intolerance, harsh punishments for cultic violations, and a cruel/angry view of God.[24] If religious leaders violate wholesale their

[18] See Vladimir Ilyich Lenin, "The Attitude of the Workers' Party to Religion", *Proletary*, no. 45, May 13 (26), 1909, http://www.marxists.org/archive/lenin/works/1909/may/13.htm.

[19] See Friedrich Engels, *Anti-Duhring* (India: Leopard Books, 1878).

[20] See James Thrower, *Marxist-Leninist "Scientific Atheism" and the Study of Religion and Atheism in the USSR* (New York: Walter de Gruyter, 1983).

[21] See, for example, Marx's declaration that "religion is the sigh of the oppressed creature, the heart of a heartless world, and the soul of soulless conditions. It is the *opium* of the people" (italics in original). See Karl Marx, *A Contribution to the Critique of Hegel's Philosophy of Right* (Paris, 1844), https://www.marxists.org/archive/marx/works/1843/critique-hpr/intro.htm#05.

[22] See ibid., and Karl Marx and Friedrich Engels, *Manifesto of the Communist Party* (Radford, Va.: Wilder Publications, 2007).

[23] See David S. Levin, "The Moral Relativism of Marxism", *Philosophical Forum* 15, no. 3 (1984): 249ff.; see also Nicholas Churchich, *Marxism and Morality: A Critical Examination of Marxist Ethics* (Cambridge, Mass.: James Clarke, 1994).

[24] Jesus was well aware of the devil's capacity to quote Scripture, as He personally witnessed during His temptations in the desert (Mt 4:1–11; Lk 4:1–13). Shakespeare notes this through the wisdom of Antonio in *The Merchant of Venice*, "The devil can cite Scripture for his purpose. An evil soul producing holy witness is like a villain with a smiling cheek, a goodly apple rotten at the heart. O, what a goodly outside falsehood hath!" (act 1, scene 3, in Project Gutenberg, 1998, http://www.gutenberg.org/cache/epub/1515/pg1515-images.html).

own ethical code (or reduce ethics to their own decrees) and lack a sincere relationship with God, they are, as Jesus noted, nothing more than wolves in sheep's clothing (Mt 7:15) and "bad fruit" (Mt 7:16–20). Jesus judges their insincere, false, and utilitarian misuse of religion straightforwardly: "Every tree that does not bear good fruit is cut down and thrown into the fire" (Mt 7:19).

Many literary, philosophical, and political writers have contended that pride is the worst of all the deadly sins, not only because it has egocentricity and narcissism at its "heart", but also because it naturally tends toward self-idolatry, the divinization of self, which seeks to replace the true God with one's delusional divinized self-image. This dimension of pride makes it destructive of self and others, and brings it into the center of Satan's plan to continue and amplify the sin that separated him from God and the blessed.

Evidently, we are not the true God—and if we even begin to exaggerate our self-importance to that level, we verge on the grossest kind of delusional narcissism for the pure pursuit of power. Succeeding in this masquerade requires depriving other people of the true grace of God, falsely pretending to have the key to ultimate fulfillment, dignity, and destiny, and using the victims as pawns in an undeniably satanic scheme. Though this dreadful state of affairs may seem to have the power to endure, it soon implodes as resistance grows against the audacious pretense and its inability to be truly divine. Even if sufficient resistance cannot be harnessed to overthrow the despot (as happened to Macbeth, Hitler, and David Koresh), the despot will not be able to avoid growing old and then dying. As this process takes place, many despots suffer from continuous nightmares and bouts of depression. Elizabeth I could not escape the torment within herself after executing the earl of Essex and Mary, Queen of Scots. According to Anna Whitelock:

> Elizabeth suffered bouts of depression that drove her to seek sanctuary, away from the public glare of the court, among her women in the privy chamber. When Sir John Harington, her godson, arrived at court he was shocked by what he saw. His letter to a friend paints a vivid picture of the unmasked queen. "So disordered is all order," that she had not changed her clothes for many days, she was "quite disfavoured, and unattired, and these troubles waste her much." She now kept a sword close by her and, as Harington described, "constantly

paced the privy chamber, stamping her feet at bad news and thrusting her rusty sword at times into the arras [tapestry] in great rage."[25]

Adolf Hitler suffered from the same depression, anger, nightmares, and suicidal tendencies, according to the psychological profile developed of him by Henry Murray, based on O.S.S. intelligence reports that came from inside the Third Reich. He notes there:

> Every new act of unusual cruelty, such as the purge of 1934, has been followed by a period of anxiety and depletion, agitated delection and nightmares, which can be interpreted only as the unconscious operation of a bad conscience. Hitler wants nothing so much as to arrive at the state where he can commit crimes without guilt feelings; but despite his boasts of having transcended Good and Evil this has not been possible. The suicidal trend in his personality is eloquent testimony of a repressed self-condemning tendency.[26]

We now need to return to the less extreme manifestations of pride, and consider its seemingly more benign starting point: the first and second stages mentioned above. It should be noted that this seemingly benign starting point is deceptive, because pride tends to grow first in the mind, then in ambition and will, and then in dominating and destructive power. Aristotle describes this more moderate form of pride accurately in *Rhetoric* after defining anger and envy ("spite"):

> Insolence ["pride"] is also a form of slighting, since it consists in doing and saying things that cause shame to the victim, not in order that anything may happen to yourself ["to get something for yourself" as in greed], or because anything has happened to yourself ["to get vengeance" as in anger], but simply for the pleasure involved [the pleasure of shaming someone in order to feel superior]. (Retaliation is not "insolence", but vengeance.) The cause of the pleasure thus enjoyed by the insolent man is that he thinks himself greatly superior to others when ill-treating them. That is why youths and rich men are insolent; they think themselves superior when they show insolence.[27]

---

[25] Anna Whitelock, "Elizabeth I: The Monarch behind the Mask", *BBC History Magazine*, June 1, 2013, www.historyextra.com/article/elizabeth-i/elizabeth-i-monarch-behind-mask.

[26] Murray, *Analysis of the Personality of Adolph Hitler*.

[27] Aristotle, *Rhetoric* 1378b, in *Basic Works of Aristotle*, ed. and trans. Richard Mckeon (New York: Random House, 1941), p. 1381.

One can sense Aristotle's disdain for the proud person who causes shame or injury to someone simply for the pleasure of feeling superior. He seems to hint that this offense is worse than greed, because the greedy person does not want to injure a person for mere pleasure (as in sadism or narcissism), but is motivated only by his insatiable desire for wealth. He suggests further that pride is worse than anger, for the angry man shames or injures a person because he himself has been shamed or injured, and so he is "justly" seeking revenge. The proud man undermines and injures others for the sheer pleasure of injuring them, which makes him feel superior.

B. The Destructiveness of Pride in the Bible

The Bible is filled with warnings about pride—not only because it arises out of a completely false and inauthentic inflated self-image, but also because of its destructiveness to others, and to the divine order and plan, leading to self-idolatry. The references are so extensive that we will only be able to give a few examples of this "worst of all sins".

We have already seen the primary appeal to pride in the serpent's temptation of Eve to disobey God's command in Genesis 3:1–7: "For God knows that when you eat of it [the fruit of the forbidden tree] your eyes will be opened, and you will be like God, knowing good and evil" (Gen 3:5). Though the serpent is trying to incite envy to obtain the outcome of abject disobedience to God, he uses pride as his essential stepping stone to getting there: "if you eat of this fruit, you will become like God."

Much of the First Book of Samuel is devoted to the transformation of Saul from a humble man (9:21) to an overweeningly proud king who flagrantly disobeyed the Lord, set up a monument to himself, and lied to Samuel about his misdeeds (15:10–23). Since Saul disobeyed God, God chose another man for Samuel to anoint—David, the youngest son of Jesse. And when Samuel anointed him, the Spirit left Saul and rushed upon David—though Saul did not yet know that David had been anointed by Samuel. Nevertheless, he felt the loss of God's Spirit, and so by God's providential action, Saul's servants brought David to him as a skilled harpist who would bring him consolation (16:1–23).

David's prowess in battle began with the killing of Goliath and continued to grow throughout his campaigns as military leader against the Philistines (17:1–58). After a particularly important battle, Saul heard the women of Israel chanting, "Saul has slain his thousands, and David his ten thousands" (18:7). Saul's pride was badly injured, and he envied the accolades that the crowds gave to David. So as Scripture reports, "an evil spirit from God rushed upon Saul" (18:10); while David was present, he tried to kill him by thrusting him with his spear twice, but David avoided him (18:11). Saul interpreted these events as the Spirit of God protecting David, so he began to fear him (18:12); but since his pride and envy knew no bounds, he ignored his fear of both God and David.

Saul then tried to kill David by placing him at the forefront of his armies, but the Lord continued to protect him, and he grew in honor among the Israelites because of his courage and military feats (18:13–16). David married Saul's daughter Michal (18:17–30) and was best friends with Saul's son Jonathan. Despite all this, Saul's pride and envy stirred him again to persecute and kill David. Jonathan challenged his father's motives by telling him that David had done no wrong to him and indeed had done him and Israel only good. Saul paid no heed to this challenge and ignored the implicit accusation that he was acting out of pride and envy in direct contrast to the justice of the Lord, and so he continued in his relentless attempts to kill David. Finally, his own daughter (David's wife) had to help David out the window and deceive her father to protect him. Jonathan again challenged his father about the injustice of his actions, but Saul was bent on killing him, driven to the point of madness by his hurt pride (19:1–17).

Saul then stooped to new lows, persecuting anyone who helped David in his flight, and massacring eighty-five priests because they provided David with a sword and the help of the prophet Gad (22:6–23). During Saul's relentless pursuit of David, the Lord enabled David to situate himself in the same cave that Saul used. David spared Saul's life, taking only a piece of his cloak to prove his encounter with him instead of killing him. When Saul exited the cave, David indicated that he had had him within his power, but had mercy on him, showing him the piece of his cloak (24:1–11). Though Saul showed gratitude and remorse for a moment, his pride and envy eventually set him back on a course to kill David.

Once again, the Lord enabled David to approach Saul and his men while they were sleeping. David took Saul's spear and water jug to show that the Lord had once again put Saul under his power, and that David had shown him mercy. Though Saul acknowledged this in gratitude, David recognized that he could not be trusted, and decided to live in the land of the Philistines to gain protection from Saul. When he did this, Saul finally stopped his insane pursuit (26:1–25).

Since Saul felt that the priests, prophets, and mediums of the land could not be trusted, he had all the prophets and mediums driven out from the land of Israel (28:3). Clearly, his pride was out of control, and he was now using the authority God had given him to undermine God's purpose and presence in Israel. It is difficult to imagine what Saul could have been thinking when he was killing priests and banishing prophets. Had he completely lost touch with God? If not, did he not care about undermining God's purpose and presence in Israel? Could he have been unaware of the consequences of his actions? It seems that pride and envy had left him with a completely distorted sense of God, reality, and himself. His resentment and hatred stemming from his inability to outshine and control David had taken away his soul. As Scripture describes it, "an evil spirit from God rushed upon Saul" (18:10).

At this juncture, events began to turn against Saul. His pride had alienated him not only from David, but also from God and the religious leaders he had banished. The Philistines once again rose up against Saul with a large army, but David would not be there to help him—indeed, he was marching with the Philistines who were attacking Saul's forces (though the Philistine officers forced him to return to his homestead). Saul consulted the only medium left in the land of Israel (after he had banished the rest), but had to do so in disguise, because she would be frightened of him if she knew who he was. She conjured the prophet Samuel, who told Saul that he and his sons would soon be killed (28:5–19). As the Philistines marched on Israel, the prophecy was proven true. Saul was surrounded by them, then his sons were killed; so rather than be taken captive by the Philistines, he fell on his own sword after being unable to convince his armor-bearer to thrust him through (31:1–4).

His pride and envy alienated him from God, the priests, and the prophets, as well as from David (his best leader) and thousands of his

people. He died alone on the hilltop by his own hand, recognizing
that his heirs were all dead, and that the house and kingdom of Saul
would come to ruin. The fruit of pride and envy proved once again
to be destruction, the destruction of friends, family, country, religion,
and ultimately, self.

Saul's story illustrates what Wisdom literature teaches over and
over again: "Pride goes before destruction, and a haughty spirit
before a fall" (Prov 16:18). Since this Wisdom teaching is so central
to the Christian understanding of the destructiveness of pride, it is
worth closer examination. Much of the Book of Proverbs is devoted
to warnings about pride and admonitions toward humility:

> When pride comes, then comes disgrace;
>   but with humility is wisdom. (11:2)
>
> Every one who is arrogant is an abomination to the LORD;
>   be assured, he will not go unpunished. (16:5)
>
> Before destruction a man's heart is haughty,
>   but humility goes before honor. (18:12)
>
> Haughty eyes and a proud heart,
>   the lamp of the wicked, are sin. (21:4)
>
> Do you see a man who is wise in his own eyes?
>   There is more hope for a fool than for him. (26:12)
>
> A man's pride will bring him low,
>   but he who is lowly in spirit will obtain honor. (29:23)

Much of the tenth and eleventh chapters of Sirach are devoted to
a denunciation of pride—which is mostly self-explanatory:

> Do not be angry with your neighbor for any injury,
>   and do not attempt anything by acts of insolence [i.e., pride].
> Arrogance is hateful before the Lord and before men,
>   and injustice is outrageous to both.
> Sovereignty passes from nation to nation
>   on account of injustice and insolence and wealth.
> How can he who is dust and ashes be proud?
>   for even in life his bowels decay....
> The beginning of man's pride is to depart from the Lord;
>   his heart has forsaken his Maker.

For the beginning of pride is sin,
  and the man who clings to it pours out abominations.
Therefore the Lord brought upon them extraordinary afflictions,
  and destroyed them utterly.
The Lord has cast down the thrones of rulers,
  and has seated the lowly in their place....
Pride was not created for men,
  nor fierce anger for those born of women....
The wisdom of a humble man will lift up his head,
  and will seat him among the great. (10:6–9, 12–14, 18; 11:1)

We see the same themes mentioned often in the Psalms: "In the pride of his countenance the wicked does not seek him; all his thoughts are, 'There is no God'" (10:4). "For though the LORD is high, he regards the lowly; but the haughty he knows from afar" (138:6).

The prophets also denounced and warned against pride. Isaiah reiterates the Lord's rejection of the proud: "The LORD of hosts has a day against all that is proud and lofty, against all that is lifted up and high.... And the haughtiness of man shall be humbled" (2:12, 17). "The LORD of hosts has purposed it, to defile the pride of all glory, to dishonor all the honored of the earth" (23:9).

Jeremiah condemns the pride of Israel that has led to their wavering faith and weakening hearts: "Thus says the LORD: Even so will I spoil the pride of Judah and the great pride of Jerusalem. This evil people, who refuse to hear my words, who stubbornly follow their own heart and have gone after other gods to serve them and worship them, shall be like this waistcloth, which is good for nothing" (13:9–10).

Daniel likewise condemns pride: "When [Nebuchadnezzar's] heart was lifted up and his spirit was hardened so that he dealt proudly, he was deposed from his kingly throne, and his glory was taken from him" (5:20).

We may now turn to the New Testament. As with envy, Jesus does not give a specific condemnation of pride in the Gospels, because He assumes that His audience is aware of the wholesale denunciation of it by every part of the Old Testament. Instead, He extols the opposite virtues of humility, compassion, charity, meekness (gentleheartedness), and the love of enemies—equating these with the heart of His Heavenly Father. We might infer from this that the opposite of these virtues—pride—is contrary to the heart of His Heavenly Father, and therefore describes the nature of their common opponent: Satan. As noted above, Jesus teaches that self-exaltation is foolish indeed, and such people will be humbled both now and in the future.

Jesus also gives an implicit condemnation of pride in His repeated condemnation of the Pharisees' self-righteousness, which arises out of their overweening spiritual pride. He illustrates the destructiveness of this pride in His Parable of the Tax Collector and the Pharisee. The prayer of the Pharisee (prayed to himself) reveals the "perfect" status he has accorded to himself while he is hypocritically condemning the tax collector:

> Two men went up into the temple to pray, one a Pharisee and the other a tax collector. The Pharisee stood and prayed thus to himself, "God, I thank you that I am not like other men, extortioners, unjust, adulterers, or even like this tax collector. I fast twice a week, I give tithes of all that I get." But the tax collector, standing far off, would not even lift up his eyes to heaven, but beat his breast, saying, "God, be merciful to me a sinner!" I tell you, this man went down to his house justified rather than the other; for every one who exalts himself will be humbled, but he who humbles himself will be exalted. (Lk 18:10–14)

Jesus also formalizes His teaching about the illicitness of pride in the use of power—both worldly and ecclesial power—that attacks *superbia* at its "heart":

> You know that the rulers of the Gentiles lord it over them, and the great ones make their authority over them felt. But it *shall not* be so among you. Rather, whoever wishes to be great among you *shall* be your servant; whoever wishes to be first among you *shall* be your slave. Just so, the Son of Man did not come to be served but to serve and to give His life as a ransom for many. (Mt 20:25–28, NAB; italics added)

The word "shall" is used three times (italicized above) to translate *estai*, which conveys a mandatory or imperative sense—"you shall not ..." This command is so important that Jesus uses Himself as the model for the disciples' future conduct and leadership. He is not only saying, "Do as I say," but "Do as I do." By using his eschatological title, "the Son of Man", Jesus here is not speaking to them simply as teacher and friend, but as Lord and definitive judge.

There is another implicit condemnation of pride in all four Gospels, though it does not come from Jesus Himself, but rather from the outrageous and destructive conduct of one of Jesus' apostolic twelve companions—Judas Iscariot. We have already seen how pride led to the destructiveness and ultimate demise of Saul, Adolf Hitler, Jim Jones, and David Koresh, among many others in world history. In the midst of all these, Judas Iscariot is perhaps one of the most poignant instances of the destructiveness of pride—to self, others, the world, and God's side of the cosmic struggle between good and evil. Judas was close to the loving antithesis of pride (Jesus), yet fell headlong into pride's seduction, inauthenticity, and destructive power. If pride could usher in Judas' seduction by Satan (Lk 22:3; Jn 13:27) while he witnessed Jesus' miraculous power and the effects of His loving ministry, we cannot underestimate what it might do to us if we allow ourselves to become separated from Jesus and His teaching.

So how did Judas, the companion of Jesus, become His betrayer, handing Him over to His enemies with a kiss (Mt 26:47–49; Mk 14:43–45; Lk 22:47–48)? In my view, the cause is not simply Satan; it was Judas' disposition of heart that made him vulnerable to Satan—a disposition that would cause him to elevate his will over the will of Jesus, and even to resent the will of Jesus. This disposition of heart, I would submit, has all the indications of pride as we have described it above. One might wonder how I came to this conclusion since we know so little about Judas from the Scriptures. I suppose it might be best described as a process of eliminating other plausible explanations. In order to describe this briefly, we must begin with what we *do* know about Judas. Five points are germane:

1. He was one of the twelve apostles selected by Jesus and presumably witnessed dozens of Jesus' exorcisms and miracles, including raising the dead.
2. He would have also witnessed Jesus' ministry of forgiveness and consolation to sinners as well as his ministry to the poor, the sick, the grieving, and even his friends. Judas was the holder of the purse; therefore, he collected donations from those

supporting Jesus and distributed them to the poor and others as Jesus instructed.

3. Judas was greedy and dishonest, and so helped himself to the common purse (Jn 12:6), apparently unaware that Jesus and the other disciples knew what he was doing.

4. There was probably tension between Judas and Jesus, perhaps even resentment of Jesus by Judas—evidenced not only by his betrayal of Jesus to the chief priests, but also by John's attribution of the protesting of the woman's anointing of Jesus' feet to Judas.[28]

5. Another sign of tension between Judas and Jesus is his offer to hand Jesus over to the chief priest *before* they offer him money (Mk 14:10–11; Lk 22:4–5; cf. Mt 26:15–16),[29] and that he hands Jesus over to them with a kiss—a snake behind the handshake, indicating disdainful duplicity, if not resentment and hatred.

This small set of facts about Judas suggests that he not only was greedy and dishonest, but also was alienated from Jesus—looking for a way, indeed anxious, to betray him. His duplicitous kiss is not simply a way of cloaking his active betrayal; it is also a way of showing Jesus the falsity of his affection, perhaps a sign of disdain or contempt. Judas not only seems alienated from Jesus, but also disgruntled or angry, seeking some way of putting Jesus in His place or exacting retribution. It is impossible to know why Judas might have felt this way. Perhaps he felt overshadowed by Jesus, or controlled by Jesus, or not respected properly by Jesus. Whatever the case, Judas decided to set himself up over and against Jesus, to set his will above Jesus', and to hurt him rather than help him.

He may not have known that the chief priests would follow through on their desire to kill Jesus. Perhaps he thought that they

---

[28] In their Gospels, Mark attributes the protest to some people who were present (14:4). Matthew attributes the protest to the disciples in general (26:8), but John attributes the protest to Judas (12:4–6), attributing dishonest motives to Judas as well. This may be John's way of indicating not only Judas' greed, but also tension between him and Jesus.

[29] It should be noted that Mark and Luke indicate that Judas decided to betray Jesus before the chief priests agreed to pay him; only Matthew suggests that Judas betrayed Jesus in order to get thirty pieces of silver, because of greed (26:15–16). John never even mentions the thirty pieces of silver; he only intimates that Judas is alienated from Jesus and this occasions the devil's entrance into him (13:27).

would just admonish or punish him, or that Jesus would be able to extricate himself from them. Yet he must have known that his betrayal would hurt Jesus, His ministry, and even the other apostles who were His companions. It is hard to imagine that he could have wished Jesus and the apostles harm for mere money, especially after seeing Jesus' miraculous power, authoritative preaching, and loving ministry to sinners and the sick. In my view, he wished Jesus and the apostles harm because he was angry or resentful, and the only likely reason for this, in view of Jesus' love for him (and His divine prophetic powers), is that he had felt hurt himself, perhaps belittled or humbled before Jesus' authority and power.

If this conclusion is correct, then the cause of Judas' anger and resentment is not merely feeling hurt by Jesus' authority and power; it is *Judas' attitude* toward that authority and power. Judas did not look upon Jesus' miraculous power and authoritative teaching as a sign of His divinity, provoking obedience; he viewed it as competition with his own ego and autonomy, provoking a battle of the wills leading to disobedience. It seems that Judas was put off, even jealous, of Jesus' miraculous power and authoritative teaching instead of being impressed, edified, and led to belief.

Sometime after he began his discipleship with Jesus, he began to feel unimportant or insignificant in Jesus' light, and so his jealousy, resistance, anger, and resentment grew to a point of no return. He would not be happy until he received the respect that he deserved from Jesus, until he had subjected Him to harm by betraying Him with a kiss. If these conclusions are correct, then Judas seems to have followed the profile of Saul, following the stages of *pride* to their tragic conclusion—from hurt pride to jealousy to anger to resentment to unjust vengeance and to self-destruction.

A student at Georgetown once asked me how one might gauge the extent to which one is egotistical or proud. I indicated that there are many ways of knowing this; but the most obvious is the degree to which one's pride is hurt and his anger provoked when he encounters someone who is thought to be superior to him by others that he respects. If the reaction is like Saul's reaction to the song of the women about him and David—"Saul has slain his thousands, and David his ten thousands" (1 Sam 18:7)—then this probably indicates a degree of ego and pride that could well get one into trouble. If one reacts explosively to someone else's acknowledged superiority or to subtle slights, he may have enough ego-centrality, and even ego-idolatry, to cause destruction to others, the culture, the community, the Kingdom of God, and ultimately to himself. This seems to have been the profile of not only Saul and Judas Iscariot but also the political and religious demigods, such as Hitler, Lenin, Stalin, Jim Jones, David Koresh, and other cult leaders, whose lives could have done much good, but instead caused vast destruction, ultimately leading to their own demise.

C. The Destructiveness of Pride in Literature

So much of contemporary literature is concerned with the destructiveness of ego-centrality, ego-idolatry, the will to power, the will to be the highest, and the will to dominate, that simply listing these works would be overwhelming. Therefore I will eschew the desire to be comprehensive and briefly consider three classic works devoted to this subject:

- Edmund Spenser's *Faerie Queen*, Book 1 (1590)
- John Milton's *Paradise Lost*, Book 1 (1667)
- William Shakespeare's *Macbeth* (1608)

Let us begin with Edmund Spenser's *Faerie Queen*.

Spenser provides an allegorical interpretation of pride that he equates with Queen Lucifera, named after the fallen angel Lucifer (Satan), who was banished from Heaven (see Rev 12:7–12). In the following passage, the Redcross Knight (representing Christian virtue and divine law) after having defeated the pagan dark knight Sansjoy in the presence of Queen Lucifera, is brought to her palace (the Palace of Pride) amid the applause of the crowds to recover from the wounds of battle. The palace is beautiful to look at from the outside—ablaze with gold and gems, and on the inside filled with seemingly successful and powerful people. While the Redcross Knight is recovering, a witch named Duessa (representing falsity, deceit, and shame, a relative of the Queen of Darkness) pretends to weep over him, to win his confidence, though she has no sympathy or love within her.

As the Redcross Knight is recovering, his dwarf discovers a dungeon in the basement of the Palace of Pride, where very famous and powerful people who had once occupied the palace are now being imprisoned, tormented, and dying. The knight and his dwarf hastily leave the palace before his wounds are healed, surprising Duessa when she returns to the palace from her visit to Hell. Spenser describes the scene, giving us a warning about pride's deceit and ultimate aim of destruction as follows:

> The false Duessa leaving noyous Night,
> Return'd to stately Palace of Dame Pride;
> Where when she came, she sound the Fairy Knight
> Departed thence, albe his Woundes wide,
> Not throughly heal'd, unready were to ride.
> Good cause he had to hasten thence away;
> For on a Day his wary Dwarf had spy'd,
> Where in a Dungeon deep huge Numbers lay,
> Of caytive wretched Thralls, that wailed Night and Day.
> A rueful Sight, as could be seen with Eye;
> Of whom he learned had in secret wise
> The hidden Cause of their Captivity,
> How mortgaging their Lives to Covetise,
> Through wasteful Pride, and wanton Riotise,
> They were by Law of that proud Tyranness
> Provok'd with Wrath, and Envy's false Surmise,
> Condemned to that Dungeon merciless,
> Where they should live in Woe, and die in Wretchedness.[30]

Earlier in the *Faerie Queene*, Spenser tells us that the ultimate objective of pride is dominion over others, to be lord of oneself and others, requiring the rejection of the true Lord who rules not by domination and subjugation, but by love. It is this desire to be lord of self and others that causes the high angel Lucifer to be expelled from Heaven, and what motivates Lucifera to host her many willing victims in the Palace of Pride. They wish to be dominators, but what they don't

---

[30] Spenser, *Faerie Queen*, bk. 1, canto 5, http://spenserians.cath.vt.edu/TextRecord.php?textsid=69.

realize is that they have put themselves under the power of the queen of dominators in order to reach their objective. Though the queen allows them to enjoy their revelry, wrath, envy, and vanity for a while, she ultimately comes around to exacting the price of her hospitality: the dungeon underneath the palace, where she can dominate them forever. Spenser names many of the famous individuals who populate the dungeon later in the canto: the great king of Babylon (King Nebuchadnezzar, who conquered Judah, was sent it into exile, and destroyed the Temple), Semiramis (the queen of Syria, who was reputed to be exceedingly powerful and lustful, adored as a goddess), and Cleopatra (the famous queen of Egypt, who eloped with Antony of Rome, who took her own life by allowing a cobra to bite her). In doing so, Spenser shows how pride fuels the other deadly sins, in particular, envy, wrath, lust, vanity, and greed.

Let us now consider John Milton's seventeenth–century epic poem *Paradise Lost*, which considers the inner workings of the sin of pride through the self-justification of its chief advocate, Satan, before the other fallen angels (Mammon, Beelzebub, Belial, and Moloch). Though Milton considers pride from many other angles, particularly in the original sin of Eve and Adam, the speeches made by Satan to his fellow fallen angels best exemplify the pure state of pride that could move an angelic being to resent and reject the Creator who fashioned him in love. A few passages from book 1 of this epic poem will hopefully entice the reader to probe more deeply into this worst of the deadly sins.

Our first passage presents Satan's attitude toward the Creator and Jesus, His Son, after he has lost the battle in Heaven and finds himself in Hell with his allies. Instead of feeling regret, if for nothing else than the miserable situation into which he has been consigned by his rebellious actions, he feels nothing but rage and resentment toward "the victor"; in unyielding refusal to acknowledge his sovereignty over creation, he rallies his fallen allies to an eternal war with the supremely good Being he hates without measure:

> What though the field be lost?
> All is not lost; the unconquerable Will,
> And study of revenge, immortal hate,
> And courage never to submit or yield:

And what is else not to be overcome?
That Glory never shall his wrath or might
Extort from me. To bow and sue for grace
With suppliant knee, and deifie his power
Who from the terrour of this Arm so late
Doubted his Empire, that were low indeed,
That were an ignominy and shame beneath
This downfall; since by Fate the strength of Gods
And this Empyreal substance cannot fail,
Since through experience of this great event
In Arms not worse, in foresight much advanc't,
We may with more successful hope resolve
To wage by force or guile eternal Warr
Irreconcileable, to our grand Foe,
Who now triumphs, and in th' excess of joy
Sole reigning holds the Tyranny of Heav'n.[31]

Satan appeals to a complete and icy inversion of the heart's logic by seeing "hope" in his defeat; now he has gained enough hate to muster the courage and force of an *eternal* war, and experience to predict how his enemy might counter him in the future. He tells his troops to find within themselves their unconquerable will, the desire for revenge, and unmitigated hatred so that they may wrest an eternal advantage from their miserable condition: the "advantage" of proclaiming that they will *never* "bow and sue for grace with suppliant knee, and deifie his power". The implication of this speech makes one shudder, for the eternity of Satan's miserable condition does not come from God, but from *his* desire to dishonor the Triune God eternally, to resent and hate him eternally, and to rebel against Him eternally. Satan, not God, is responsible for the eternity of his misery, because he prefers to draw his banal satisfaction of eternal resentment and hatred from his unmitigated force of free will, his unmitigated will to rebellious power.

Our second passage reveals the source of Satan's eternal resentment and hatred of the Creator who fashioned him in love. He declares

<hr />

[31] John Milton, *Paradise Lost* (Project Gutenberg, 2011), bk. 1, http://www.gutenberg.org /cache/epub/20/pg20-images.html.

that he deserves better than honoring God as his Creator and the Son of God as his Lord, because as he falsely and inauthentically asserts to his allies, he is *self*-begot and *self*-raised. As such, he deserves to be treated as an equal, not as a creature who would show gratitude and love for being brought lovingly into being:

> When this creation was? rememberst thou
> Thy making, while the Maker gave thee being?
> We know no time when we were not as now;
> Know none before us, self-begot, self-rais'd
> By our own quick'ning power, when fatal course
> Had circl'd his full Orbe, the birth mature
> Of this our native Heav'n, Ethereal Sons.
> Our puissance is our own, our own right hand
> Shall teach us highest deeds, by proof to try
> Who is our equal: then thou shalt behold
> Whether by supplication we intend
> Address, and to begirt th' Almighty Throne
> Beseeching or besieging. This report,
> These tidings carrie to th' anointed King;
> And fly, ere evil intercept thy flight.[32]

Satan here appears to be deceiving even himself, appearing to be convinced by the dazzling logic in his ontological argument for his own divinity. He tells his allies that since they are eternal beings, then it cannot be proved that there was a point at which they were nothing, and therefore that they were created by a higher being than themselves. He uses the remarkable timeless attribute through which they were created to show the difficulty of proving the existence of a *higher* or *highest* creator. The self-deception is remarkable because this argument works only from the perspective of the lower being, an angel, but not from the perspective of the higher being, the Supreme Being, who knows that its essence is in all ways unrestricted, and therefore unique.

The supreme irony is that *any* rational being can prove the unrestrictedness and uniqueness of an uncaused reality because it can be proven from the requirement for an uncaused cause, which is

---

[32] Ibid.

necessarily (by nature) unrestricted and unique.[33] In view of this, Satan must be at least partially aware of the falsity of his claims, but *chooses* to remain in a culpably false projection of self through a Nietzschean will to divine power. The problem is, only God can make this self-proclamation truthfully; so every other self-proclamation is nothing more than bad faith expressed resolutely and hypocritically to oneself. We can here feel the insipient despair of the ultimate and hypocritical lie to self, incited by pride.

Our final passage concerns the key point in Satan's argument. Though he grudgingly admits that he and his allies are in an unhappy place, they have a satisfaction that more than compensates for it: the freedom to be absolute ruler in a domain unoccupied by God. Satan thus rallies his troops to make their eternal choice and to proclaim that it is "better to reign in Hell, then to serve in Heav'n."

> Here [in Hell] at least
> We shall be free; th' Almighty hath not built
> Here for his envy, will not drive us hence:
> Here we may reign secure, and in my choyce
> To reign is worth ambition though in Hell:
> Better to reign in Hell, then serve in Heav'n.
> But wherefore let we then our faithful friends,
> Th' associates and copartners of our loss
> Lye thus astonisht on th' oblivious Pool,
> And call them not to share with us their part
> In this unhappy Mansion, or once more
> With rallied Arms to try what may be yet
> Regaind in Heav'n, or what more lost in Hell?[34]

As usual, Satan falsely attributes his own motive, envy, to the Creator and His only-begotten Son. He tells his band of "disciples" to

---

[33] I have given several such proofs, including a contemporary metaphysical proof of God, in *New Proofs for the Existence of God: Contributions of Contemporary Physics and Philosophy* (Grand Rapids, Mich.: Eerdmans, 2010), Chapter 3. See also Robert Spitzer, *The Soul's Upward Yearning: Clues to Our Transcendent Nature from Experience and Reason* (San Francisco: Ignatius Press, 2015), Appendix II; and Robert Spitzer, *Credible Catholic Big Book*, vol. 1, *Evidence of the Nature and Existence of God* (Magis Center, 2017), CredibleCatholic.com, https://www.crediblecatholic.com/pdf/7E-P2/7E-BB1.pdf.

[34] Milton, *Paradise Lost*, bk. 1.

bear up bravely on the "oblivious Pool", not only because they can reign "supreme" away from their sovereign, but also because of their "hope" of regaining their lost position in Heaven. After saying this, he seems to catch a highly unusual glimmer of truth to self—"or what more lost in Hell?"

In my view, Milton has explored profoundly the complete self-deception of *pride* and its capacity to engender a choice for eternal misery through anger, resentment, and hatred toward the truth of creaturehood before the unconditionally loving God.

We may now turn to our final literary appraisal of pride: Shakespeare's tragedy *Macbeth*.[35] After a dramatic opening scene in which three witches set their sights on Macbeth and we hear the report of Macbeth's valiant defeat of the traitor Macdonwald, the play proceeds to a scene in which Macbeth and his friend Banquo are discussing their victory. As they are walking along, three witches hail them and deliver a remarkable prophesy to Macbeth. Though these witches may have been inspired by the three fates, Shakespeare has transformed them in their ugliness and intention into demonic powers whose pleasure and purpose is the demise of mankind.[36] They tell Macbeth that he is about to receive two promotions: first, he is to become Thane of Cawdor in place of Macdonwald (the traitor he defeated), and second, he will then become king of Scotland.

[35] I drew from an e-book of William Shakespeare's *Macbeth* (1606; Project Gutenberg, 1997). The e-book is available for free on Project Gutenberg's website at http://www.guten berg.org/cache/epub/1129/pg1129-images.html. For additional information regarding plot summary, see "Macbeth: Synopsis and Plot Overview of Shakespeare's Macbeth", Shakespeare Birthplace Trust (website), accessed July 2, 2020, https://www.shakespeare.org.uk /explore-shakespeare/shakespedia/shakespeares-plays/macbeth/.

[36] Several scholars believe that Shakespeare made this demonic adaptation of the witches to cultivate the favor of his patron King James I, who himself had written a book on witchcraft, and to gain the interest of his audience who had an interest in the occult. See Amanda Mabillard, "The Relationship between Macbeth and the Witches", Shakespeare Online, accessed April 20, 2020, http://www.shakespeareonline.com/faq/macbethfaq/macbethdarkness.html. I do not believe that Shakespeare made this association for these practical reasons alone. He had a view of the supernatural and of a cosmic struggle between good and evil that comes out in preternatural forces, like ghosts, in *Hamlet* and *Macbeth*. Shakespeare's public faith was Protestant, but then again, he had no choice to be otherwise since Elizabeth I made Catholicism unlawful. Nevertheless, his parents were very likely covert Catholics who influenced him in his religious upbringing. See Amanda Mabillard, "What Was Shakespeare's Religion?", Shakespeare Online, accessed April 20, 2020, http://www.shakespeare-online.com /faq/shakespearereligion.html.

Though Banquo and Macbeth are uncertain about the veracity of these predictions, Macbeth begins to feel inflated by the prospect—his mind filled with desire and temptation. Banquo then asks the witches about his future, to which the witches respond:

FIRST WITCH. Lesser than Macbeth, and greater.
SECOND WITCH. Not so happy, yet much happier.
THIRD WITCH. Thou shalt get kings, though thou be none.[37]

Banquo asks a curious question that seems to refer to the witches who had just vanished, but also refers to the prophesies that they have delivered: "Were such things here as we do speak about?/ Or have we eaten on the insane root/That takes the reason prisoner?"[38] Macbeth has clearly eaten of the root of pride that delivers the prospect of kingship with the authority of the witches' prophesy. All that is required to transform it into the insanity "that takes the reason prisoner" is a verification from another thane who comes on the scene to deliver the message that Macbeth has been made Thane of Cawdor by King Duncan. After hearing it, Macbeth is enchanted—or better, bedeviled—by the power and glory of his impending kingship.

King Duncan comes to greet and congratulate Macbeth on his victory and tells him that he will stay with Macbeth at his castle that night. He states that he has named his son Malcom as his rightful heir.

Macbeth sends a letter about this to his wife, Lady Macbeth, who is far more susceptible to pride and unbridled ambition; she begins plotting the downfall of both King Duncan and his son so that her husband might become king. As she hatches her plot she prays to "the spirits" to be deprived of conscience, womanly feelings, compassion, mercy, and decency so that she can follow through on her insidious and brutal plan:

> The raven himself is hoarse
> That croaks the fatal entrance of Duncan
> Under my battlements. Come, you spirits
> That tend on mortal thoughts, unsex me here

---

[37] Act 1, scene 3.
[38] Ibid.

And fill me from the crown to the toe top-full
Of direst cruelty! Make thick my blood,
Stop up the access and passage to remorse,
That no compunctious visitings of nature
Shake my fell purpose nor keep peace between
The effect and it! Come to my woman's breasts,
And take my milk for gall, your murthering ministers,
Wherever in your sightless substances
You wait on nature's mischief! Come, thick night,
And pall thee in the dunnest smoke of hell
That my keen knife see not the wound it makes
Nor heaven peep through the blanket of the dark
To cry, "Hold, hold!"[39]

She then conceives a plot in which Macbeth is to get Duncan's chamberlains drunk, and then enter the room of Duncan to stab him while he sleeps. In the morning when the chamberlains awake, they can be unjustly blamed for the outrage. When Macbeth hears of the brutality of the plot, he begins to have second thoughts. Lady Macbeth minimizes his objections, then pushes him and insults him until he finally relents and accedes to his role in the intended brutality.

As Macbeth proceeds to Duncan's room to kill him, he has a vision of a bloody dagger that piques his conscience and unnerves him. Nevertheless feeling compelled to finish the task given him by Lady Macbeth, he kills Duncan in his bed. Emerging from the room with bloody hands and still shaken by the vision of the dagger, he cannot go back to the scene to place the daggers near the chamberlains, and so Lady Macbeth finishes her bloody work. She then tells Macbeth to cool down, to resist the promptings of conscience, and to wash his hands:

Why, worthy Thane,
You do unbend your noble strength, to think
So brainsickly of things. Go, get some water
And wash this filthy witness from your hand.
Why did you bring these daggers from the place?

[39] Act I, scene 5.

They must lie there. Go carry them, and smear
The sleepy grooms with blood.
MACBETH. I'll go no more.
I am afraid to think what I have done;
Look on't again I dare not.
LADY MACBETH. Infirm of purpose!
Give me the daggers. The sleeping and the dead
Are but as pictures; 'tis the eye of childhood
That fears a painted devil. If he do bleed,
I'll gild the faces of the grooms withal,
For it must seem their guilt.[40]

Lady Macbeth is so drunk with ambition and the prospect of royal power that she shuts down her conscience, along with every urging of justice and love. Beyond this, she goads her husband into doing the same by insulting his "noble strength", calling him "infirm of purpose", and accusing him of being childish—" 'tis the eye of childhood / That fears a painted devil."

Though Macbeth is not nearly as power hungry and cruel, he is still guilty of allowing his wife to goad him out of following his conscience, particularly when he has had a haunting supernatural apparition of the bloody dagger. In this sense Lady Macbeth is correct: Macbeth is weak, even to the point of allowing his wife to goad him out of his conscience and religious sensibility. Even as he does so, his conscience and religious sensibility grow progressively weaker so that he feels little compunction about killing the innocent chamberlains who he fears might divulge his terrible actions. After that, he descends to the level of his wife and orders the killings of four other people, including his friend Banquo. Ultimately, we become what we do. If we choose murder, even by being goaded into it, we become murderers, and the grizzly habit becomes our second nature.

The plot continues. After Macbeth kills the chamberlains and word gets to Duncan's sons, they flee from Scotland, fearing that they too may be killed. In their absence, Macbeth is made king because he is a close relative of the now deceased King Duncan. Macbeth has

---

[40] Act 2, scene 2.

now become the moral equivalent of his wife and will do just about anything to maintain his power. He begins to feel anxious about his kingship because of the witches' prediction that Banquo's progeny would also be kings. Since Banquo, and more importantly, his son Fleance, will be leaving the vicinity, he hires two assassins, and then a third, to kill them. Though the assassins kill Banquo, his son escapes, thereby allowing the witches' prediction to stay in effect.

Later when Macbeth hosts a banquet for the nobility, he is "treated" to yet another supernatural portent: the ghost of Banquo sitting in Macbeth's chair. Macbeth not only feels fear and guilt at the ghost's presence, but also anxiousness about the future of his kingly power. He trembles at the sight of the ghost and angrily tells him to go away. Since Macbeth is the only one who can see him, his guests think that he has gone mad; eventually, the ghost leaves and Macbeth returns to normal. When the ghost reappears, Macbeth again becomes fearful and angry, and Lady Macbeth has to dismiss the guests.

Is the ghost merely a projection of Macbeth's guilty conscience or a real preternatural portent? For Shakespeare, it is irrelevant, for in both cases Macbeth is confronted by the depravity of his unscrupulous actions. This is Shakespeare's point: no one can escape being judged by one's own actions, not just in the life to come, but in many cases, here and now. The more unjust and depraved the action, the more likely the confrontation will take place in the present, through mind, spirit, or both. Macbeth's pride, lust for power, and abandonment of conscience has literally come back to haunt him, and his spirit descends into the darkness and madness that he has created by his deeds.

When Macbeth comes to his senses, he goes back to the witches to obtain clarification about their previous predictions. They give him a cautionary prediction to beware of Macduff, and then two reassuring predictions: that no man born of a woman shall harm him, and that Macbeth will be safe until Great Birnam Wood comes to Dunsinane Hill. Macbeth is relieved, but asks one further question about Banquo's progeny inheriting the throne. The witches show him a vision that indicates they will. Macbeth concludes from this that the only way to secure his throne is to get rid of the threat: Macduff. At this juncture, Macbeth's conscience is completely eroded and his lust for power has led to paranoia, so he orders the wholesale murder of

Macduff and his household. Macduff escapes to England, but Macbeth's assassins kill the rest of Macduff's household.

In act 5, the two principal characters reverse roles. Lady Macbeth, who was formerly more power hungry, unconscionable, and cruel than Macbeth, suddenly feels the weight of judgment upon her. This reversal of character seems to correspond to the principle that the more unconscionable and heinous one's actions, the more likely one is to be confronted and harshly judged by them in this lifetime. So, Lady Macbeth begins to feel darkness, emptiness, and guilt accompanied by nightmares, like Elizabeth I, Hitler, and so many of history's other great tyrants. She begins to walk in her sleep and see imaginary blood on her hands that she tries vigorously to remove. She carries a candle with her to dispel the darkness around her and rubs her hands for long periods of time, trying to rid herself of the blood, exclaiming:

> Out, damned spot! Out, I say! One- two- why then 'tis time to do't. Hell is murky. Fie [ecch!], my lord, fie! A soldier, and afeard? What need we fear who knows it, when none can call our power to account? Yet who would have thought the old man [King Duncan whose murder she instigated] to have had so much blood in him.... Here's the smell of the blood still. All the perfumes of Arabia will not sweeten this little hand. Oh, oh, oh![41]

Though Lady Macbeth believes that no human being knows what she has done, and apparently does not believe in a divine being who would be able to do so, she finds herself convicted by her own conscience, rising up like an alter ego to judge her for her depravity. Eventually, she will succumb to it and apparently commit suicide offstage.

While Lady Macbeth convicts herself through the agency of conscience and justice, Macbeth, who has "successfully" overridden *his conscience*, will be convicted by divine providence whose intention is to rescue Scotland from the tyrant and restore beneficence and order to its people. This is done through the hands of two survivors: Macduff, who has heard about the death of his family and rides to confront Macbeth, and Malcolm (Duncan's son), who escaped to England and has now raised an English army for the same purpose.

---

[41] Act 5, scene 1.

They are supported by the Scottish nobility who are also appalled by Macbeth's tyranny, and so he is convicted on every side. As the opposing army approaches Dunsinane Castle, they cut down boughs from the trees of Birnam Wood to disguise themselves, fulfilling yet another one of the witches' prophesies. Before the opposing army arrives, Macbeth hears of his wife's apparent suicide and is struck with emptiness and depression, leading to his famous lament about the meaninglessness and stupidity of life:

> She should have died hereafter;
> There would have been a time for such a word.
> Tomorrow, and tomorrow, and tomorrow
> Creeps in this petty pace from day to day
> To the last syllable of recorded time;
> And all our yesterdays have lighted fools
> The way to dusty death. Out, out, brief candle!
> Life's but a walking shadow, a poor player
> That struts and frets his hour upon the stage
> And then is heard no more. It is a tale
> Told by an idiot, full of sound and fury,
> Signifying nothing.[42]

Interestingly, Macbeth feels no qualm of conscience. His emptiness and despair seem to arise out of the turn of fortune in his life: his wife's suicide and the opposing army approaching him. Nevertheless, he bolsters his confidence in his continued kingship by recalling the witches' predictions about the movement of Birnam Wood and not being harmed by a man born of a woman. Suddenly a messenger comes, informing Macbeth that the opposing army has disguised themselves with boughs from the trees of Birnam Wood, fulfilling one of the witches' predictions and striking fear into his heart. Yet he is still convinced of his invincibility because of the witches' prediction that he would not be harmed by a man born of a woman.

The English forces begin to defeat Macbeth's army, but he continues to fight, confident that he cannot be harmed. When he is confronted by Macduff, Macduff informs Macbeth that he was not born

---

[42] Act 5, scene 5.

naturally, but "was from his mother's womb / Untimely ripp'd"[43] (by caesarean section). Macbeth sees his impending doom immediately before Macduff kills, beheads him, and displays his head for all to see. The final judgment of divine providence, "that calls upon us, by the grace of Grace",[44] is then proclaimed by the just heir to the throne: King Duncan's son, Malcolm:

> What's more to do,
> Which would be planted newly with the time,
> As calling home our exiled friends abroad
> That fled the snares of watchful tyranny,
> Producing forth the cruel ministers
> Of this dead butcher and his fiend-like queen,
> Who, as 'tis thought, by self and violent hands
> Took off her life; this, and what needful else
> *That calls upon us, by the grace of Grace*
> We will perform in measure, time, and place.
> So thanks to all at once and to each one,
> Whom we invite to see us crown'd at Scone.[45]

Macbeth's frame of mind closely resembles that of other tyrants, such as Adolf Hitler, who might be said to be similarly judged by divine providence. As he received news that the Russian forces were approaching from the East and the Anglo-American forces from the West, he remained confident in his messianic destiny (supported by cocktails of methamphetamines). When the Russians were hours away from his bunker, he committed suicide with his new bride, Eva Braun, and had his body burned (though the Russians claimed they had discovered his skull, like Macbeth's head, in the ashes).

What is to be gleaned from the tragedy of Macbeth? Firstly, as with all other tragedies, it speaks of the blinding, driving, and destructive power of the deadly sin of pride. All the deadly sins have this blinding, driving, and destructive power, evidenced in the spell of lust (that bewitched Anna Karenina), the spell of greed (that charmed Bud in

---

[43] Act 5, scene 8.
[44] Act 5, scene 9.
[45] Ibid.; italics added.

Wall Street), the spell of anger (that transfixed *Hamlet*), the spell of vanity (that enchanted Norma Desmond in *Sunset Boulevard*), the spell of envy (that gripped Iago in *Othello*), and hard as it may be to imagine, the spell of sloth (that absorbed Cecil Vyse in *Room with a View*). Yet pride seems to have an even greater power to blind, drive, and destroy that leads to the outrageous crimes of not only literary characters like Macbeth and his wife, but real historical figures, such as Saul, Judas Iscariot, Hitler, and Stalin. This is why pride is selected from among the other deadly sins to characterize the sin of the devil himself in both the Bible (Gen 3:1–14; Rev 12:7–12) and in literature (Queen Lucifera in the *Faerie Queen*, and Satan in *Paradise Lost*).

Secondly, the tragedy of Macbeth shows how pride can overcome and erode conscience if free agents allow it to do so. If they *do* allow it to do so, they can expect it to reap a whirlwind of destruction, including their own self-destruction, whether this be caused by the judgment of conscience or Providence or by the human community. In the end, giving leeway to the awful seduction of pride will do nothing but cause darkness, emptiness, destruction, and evil. As the witches of Macbeth intimate (and Milton's Satan decrees), pride is the open door to the demonic, and the entryway for Satan into our minds, hearts, and spirits.

Thirdly, we will need the help of the concerned providential God, whom Shakespeare calls "the grace of Grace" and Milton identifies as "the Son of God", to help us extricate ourselves from pride's grip. Pride is nothing to be trifled with, for it looks so innocuous at first, and as it grows, it progressively blinds us to its ever-increasing power over us. When we allow pride, with its seductions of status, ambition, power, dominion, and insipient self-idolatry, to have even a little entryway, it begins its hypnotic spell, and we soon forget the goodness and love of our Creator and Redeemer, allowing our relationship with Him to go to sleep like Lady Macbeth's conscience.

When we are so spellbound, how can we be dislodged in our freedom from our course of self-destruction? As Jesus said, "With men this is impossible, but with God all things are possible" (Mt 19:26). Providential help can present itself through a perfectly natural occurrence of suffering (caused by ourselves, others, or nature), or occasionally by a supernaturally induced one (like Paul getting knocked to the ground and blinded by light when Jesus spoke to him [Acts 9:3–4, 8; 26:13–14]). When this occurs we can be sure that God will surround that suffering with His providence, by calling us through the voice of a friend or stranger, through the words of Scripture or literature, through a "chance" encounter—to return to faith and love, particularly to humble-heartedness, gentle-heartedness, and peace. Though God frequently uses suffering (whether caused by ourselves, others, or nature) to reveal the way out of pride's blinding and destructive power, He need not do so and often uses other means such as new opportunities, friendships, "chance" encounters with the Church, or other means to make us aware of his sublime, saving, and loving Spirit, sent out to inspire, guide, and protect us.

We will know when we encounter God's Spirit because the spell of pride will be temporarily and surprisingly broken, perhaps shattered; and when this occurs, whether it be caused by deprivation, suffering, opportunity, new friends, or a direct encounter with the Church, we need to act upon it by allowing ourselves to sense the goodness, wisdom, and love of what is being presented to us and follow it. Frequently, when pride's spell is broken, it will be accompanied by an awareness of the emptiness and darkness of the life we pursued while under pride's spell; and when this happens, we will feel what we think is fear, but it will not be like any other fear (which causes panic, adrenaline, and the heart to race). Rather, it will be like what Rudolf Otto calls "horror" (which causes coldness and a shudder as the heart slows down and the blood drains from one's face), the horror that comes from listening to a ghost story.

The evil of pride's spell goes beyond any ghost story; and when we feel the horror of that evil, we must reach out spontaneously as Peter did when he was drowning, pleading, "Lord, save me" (Mt 14:30). He will surely reach out and save us just as He saved Peter; but when He does, we must try to stay on the road of His teaching, especially the road of the Beatitudes and in particular through membership in the Church community. If we stay on the road through the Church community—through her teaching, sacraments, community, and spiritual encouragement—we will begin, as Augustine did, to love the Word of the Lord ever more deeply, and as this occurs, to be astonished and revolted by the life of pride we left behind. At this point, we will not want to forget to give thanks to the Lord, who rescued us from a fate literally worse than death, an eternity of self-idolatry separated from love and surrounded by darkness. Augustine expressed this gratitude and love beautifully in the *Confessions*:

> Late have I loved you,
> Beauty so ancient and so new,
> Late have I loved you!
> Lo, you were within,
> but I outside, seeking there for you,
> and upon the shapely things you have made
> I rushed headlong—I, misshapen.
> You were with me, but I was not with you.
> They held me back far from you,
> those things which would have no being,
> were they not in you.
> You called, shouted, broke through my deafness;
> you flared, blazed, banished my blindness;
> you lavished your fragrance, I gasped; and now I pant
>   for you;
> I tasted you, and now I hunger and thirst;
> you touched me, and I burned for your peace.[46]

IV. Conclusion

As we conclude this volume, it should be stressed that the deadly sins are not the final word—neither are the temptations, deceits, and desolations of the Evil One. As noted in Chapter 2, Jesus is victorious over Satan and has left us with everything we need to resist and defeat him successfully in our lives, thereby assuring our path to salvation. Jesus' vehicles of grace include the Church (with her teaching Magisterium, sacraments, community, and rites of blessing and exorcism), the Holy Spirit dwelling within our hearts, and the Word of Jesus given in the Gospels. Therefore, we have nothing to fear, for as Jesus assured us, "Be of good cheer, I have overcome the world" (Jn 16:33).

---

[46] Saint Augustine, *Confessions* 10, 27, trans. Henry Chadwick (New York: Oxford University Press, 2009), p. 184.

Jesus' victory and His vehicles of grace must be accompanied by our free acts of the will to use these graces. Hence, we must join and participate in the Church, particularly in the sacraments of the Holy Eucharist and Reconciliation, reading the Word of God, seeking out the Church's teaching, and engaging in spiritual and moral conversion. The Church's Magisterium and the saints have given us great wisdom over the centuries on how to benefit from these graces and to expedite our spiritual and moral conversion. Though this will be the topic of the next volume (*The Way Out of Darkness: The Church, Spiritual Conversion, and Moral Conversion*), it may do well to illustrate here, through a brief personal reflection, the profundity and beauty of Jesus' path out of darkness through the Church.

My life experience, study of philosophy and psychology, and reading of classic literature have converged into a single felt and thought conviction: the deadly sins are frightening attitudes indeed, and if they become habitual, they are terrifying. What is most frightening is the thought that continually rolls through my mind as I reflect upon my life: "There but for the grace of God go I."[47] What has really scared me about the eight deadly sins in both reflection and experience is how Judas, after witnessing the Lord's divine power and love again and again, allowed his pride to supersede obedience and love ("there but for the grace of God go I"); how easily Bud was seduced into a life of greed by Gordon Gecko that almost resulted in complete disaster for his family and friends ("there but for the grace of God go I"); how easily Anna Karenina was swept into the persistent belief that her illicit relationship with Count Vronsky was beautiful and good as it shattered her husband, son, and friends ("there but for the grace of God go I"); and how persistently Prince Hamlet believed that his anger and vengeance were justified when it led to the destruction of so many innocent people ("there but for the grace of God go I").

What do *I* mean by the "grace of God"? The best way of describing it is an interwoven complex of graces and challenges working through the marvelous hand of providence and life within the Catholic Church. If I had to delineate those graces, I would specify the following in the order in which they typically occur:

---

[47] Attributed to the sixteenth-century English Reformer John Bradford, but recognized by Saint Paul in 1 Corinthians 15:8–10.

- The gift (grace) of faith occurring through the Church
- The blessing of suffering and weakness calling me to transformation
- The inspiration of the Holy Spirit, helping me to understand both the privileges and challenges of life
- The call of the Lord to moral conversion, to a firm resolve to resist temptation and become the "new man"
- My free choices to enter more and more deeply into spiritual and moral conversion that galvanize the graces mentioned above

I will briefly explain each of these five components of "the grace of God".

The Catholic Church has been the conduit of faith for me from the day of my Baptism to the present. My mother, who was a daily communicant, conveyed the faith beautifully and maturely, and my catechism classes at Sacred Heart Church galvanized the Holy Spirit within me from the first grade onward (described in Volume II, Chapter 5, of the Trilogy). Throughout my childhood, and even in my times of doubt during adolescence, the influence of the Church through good priests and teachers inspired me continuously, keeping me steady when many times I could have veered seriously off course. Suffice it to say that the sacraments of the Holy Eucharist and Reconciliation, special liturgies such as Good Friday, the teaching of the Catholic Church, and the inner gifts of the Holy Spirit directed, protected, consoled, and enchanted me to know, love, and follow the Lord ever more deeply. When I was young, I mistakenly thought that faith was only an act of the will, but in college, after reflecting back, I knew I would have had no faith were it not for the teaching and sacraments of the Church, the inner movement of the Holy Spirit, and my parents, teachers, and priests who introduced me to the Person of Jesus Christ. Faith certainly has a dimension of free choice and will, but it is also a tremendous gift and complex grace. This grace was the beginning of my spiritual/religious conversion, and it moved me ever more deeply into the love and life of the Lord.

God's grace also worked in and through suffering and weakness in my life. I have addressed this in some detail in Volume IV of the Quartet, but I might summarize by saying that in the light of faith, suffering and weakness are absolutely indispensable for both spiritual and moral conversion. It was suffering that continuously broke the spell of egocentricity, superficiality, and the deadly sins, suffering that interrupted destructive momentums, caused me to question and reflect, opened me to the inspiration of the Holy Spirit, and led me back to the Lord through the Word and sacraments of the Church. In the light of faith, suffering is an unimaginably beautiful blessing, for the wisdom of the Cross defeats the darkness of pride, the temptations of Satan, and the foolishness of mere sensuality and ego-comparative purpose. As Saint Paul tells us, the wisdom of the Cross allows Christ to grow stronger in us (2 Cor 12:7–12), propelling us not only to our salvation, but to the desire and capacity to help others to their salvation.

As we shall see in Volume II (Chapter 3), the inspiration of the Holy Spirit sweeps into our lives during times of suffering, waking us at 3:00 A.M. to call us ever so firmly, yet gently, out of the darkness through deeper spiritual and moral conversion. When these graced inspirations come to us, it is incumbent upon us to listen and plan some steps to follow them. Inasmuch as these inspirations entail a change of life, they will not be easy to implement; yet *persistence* in starting anew, availing ourselves of the sacraments of the Holy Eucharist and Reconciliation, and fidelity to our contemplative prayer, *will* ultimately bear fruit. Yes, most progress will be in "baby steps", but a lot of baby steps add up to a transformation from what Saint Paul called the "old man" to the "new man" (Eph 4:22, 24; Col 3:9–10).

Our free choices work through all the above dimensions of "the grace of God", and this ultimately rescues us from the grip of Satan and the deadly sins. On saying this, it must also be emphasized that important as our free choices and actions are, they will be virtually powerless to rescue us from the deadly sins and the temptations of Satan without the gifts and graces of the Church (described above). For this reason, the next volume of the Trilogy is essential, because it tells us how to avail ourselves of the graces given to us by Jesus through His commissioning and gifts of the Holy Spirit to Saint Peter and his successors.

Volume II begins with examining the evidence for the Catholic Church as the definitive interpreter of the words of Jesus and the ongoing inspiration of the Holy Spirit (Chapter 1), then addresses the sacramental and liturgical life, which is the conduit of supernatural grace, strength, and inspiration (Chapter 2), and then explores the interior (contemplative) life given through the Mystical Body of Christ and the Holy Spirit (Chapter 3). We then move from this foundation of spiritual/religious conversion to moral conversion, first exploring the theological virtues (Chapter 4), then techniques for resisting temptation, such as the Examen Prayer, and other dimensions of moral conversion (Chapters 5 and 6), completing our journey with a deep look at the merciful love of God and the Sacrament of Reconciliation (Chapter 7).

I encourage readers not only to read Volume II of this Trilogy, but to enter into the Church more actively and to pursue at least some of the pathways to spiritual and moral conversion. Though this will no doubt take a commitment of time and energy, it will be the best investment in self-realization you could ever make, for it will significantly increase your purpose in life, sense of dignity, contribution to the world, and contribution to the Kingdom of God—not to mention setting you on a firm path to salvation. If readers are hesitant about pursuing spiritual and moral conversion because of doubts about God, the soul, and Jesus, I would ask that you delve into Volumes II and III of the Quartet, and supplement it with other resources mentioned in those works. There is more than enough evidence to support the Christian faith, as well as spiritual and moral conversion through the Church. If ever there was a true and lasting meaning in life, conversion within the Catholic Church certainly captures and inspires it.

APPENDIX

Scientifically Validated Miracles Associated with the Blessed Virgin Mary, Saints, and the Holy Eucharist

Introduction

Some scientists might deny the possibility of a miracle because they mistakenly believe that miracles require the suspension of inviolable physical laws. Though there is no reason why God—as a supernatural creative being—would not be able to suspend the laws of nature, it is not necessary to explain miracles this way. C. S. Lewis put it quite succinctly—"The divine art of miracle is not an art of suspending the pattern into which events conform but of feeding new events into that pattern."[1] God does not need to suspend the laws of nature to make His extraordinary presence manifest—He need only add a transnatural power to those occurring in nature.

Perhaps the greatest miracle is not the manifestation of transnatural power, but the fact that nature itself not only has regularity, but that this regularity is describable by mathematics in a most surprising, indeed completely unexpected, way. The Nobel Prize-winning physicist and mathematician Eugene Wigner recognized this remarkable coincidence of natural laws and mathematics, referring to it as a "miracle" or the scientist's "article of faith". "It is, as Schrödinger has remarked, a miracle that in spite of the baffling complexity of the world, certain regularities in the events could be discovered."[2]

---

[1] C. S. Lewis, *Miracles: A Preliminary Study* (New York: HarperOne, 1947), p. 95.

[2] Eugene Wigner, "The Unreasonable Effectiveness of Mathematics in the Natural Sciences", *Communications in Pure and Applied Mathematics* 13, no. 1 (February 1960), http://www.dartmouth.edu/~matc/MathDrama/reading/Wigner.html.

Wigner later goes on to describe a fourfold miracle in the connection between classical physics, quantum physics, higher-level mathematics, and the human mind's ability to recognize it:

> Finally, it now begins to appear that not only complex numbers but so-called analytic functions are destined to play a decisive role in the formulation of quantum theory. I am referring to the rapidly developing theory of dispersion relations.
>
> It is difficult to avoid the impression that a miracle confronts us here, quite comparable in its striking nature to the miracle that the human mind can string a thousand arguments together without getting itself into contradictions, or to the two miracles of the existence of laws of nature and of the human mind's capacity to divine them.[3]

Though Wigner was using the term "miracle" loosely here, this fourfold, nonnecessary coincidence of physics, mathematics, aesthetics, and the human mind is completely inexplicable in terms of logic, mathematics, and physics themselves. Wigner and Schrödinger leave us to draw our own conclusions, but people of faith will see rigorous rationality and creative serendipity in this fourfold coincidence, which has all the earmarks of creative intellection coursing through nature—and intellection pointing toward a supernatural mind.

More recently, Michio Kaku (one of the founders of string theory) has articulated a new approach to the same "miracle" within the natural universe manifesting supernatural intellection. He assumes that the pre-Big Bang universe is in the hyperdimensionality of M-theory (eleven-dimensional string theory) and further postulates the need for primitive semiradius tachyons to create free spaces for interaction within the universe. If his view of the pre-Big Bang universe is correct (and we do not have confirmation of this), then this universe with its primitive semiradius tachyons would be such an elegant manifestation of extreme complexity (like a matrix) that Kaku can

---

[3] Ibid.

see only one ultimate solution-resolution—a divine mind capable of mathematical superintellection.[4]

Impressive as the miracle of mathematical-physical laws may be, the divine intellect has also seen fit to manifest his supernatural intellect and power in the world by, as C. S. Lewis notes, "feeding new events into the patterns of nature". The Lord does this to manifest His presence in the world, which is particularly noteworthy in the actions of Old Testament prophets, such as Moses, Elijah, and Elisha, and above all, through Jesus and the disciples who continue to work them in His name to this very day.

This kind of miracle is rare; otherwise, it would not be differentiateable from natural patterns and therefore not a "miracle". Yet these miracles occur every day throughout the world by the power of the Holy Spirit in the name of Jesus. We need only make a simple Internet search to see literally hundreds of testimonies to contemporary miracles attributed to the Holy Spirit and the name of Jesus.[5]

The most remarkable and scientifically validated contemporary miracles have occurred through the appearance of the Blessed Virgin Mary and the intercession of Catholic saints. These miracles are also done through the power of the Holy Spirit in the name of Jesus, but they have, as it were, a third agent: the Virgin Mary or a saint. This "sharing" of power and glory by the Lord shows that even though the Lord is center stage, He does not want to be the whole show, but

---

[4] See Barbara Hollingsworth, "String Theory Co-Founder: Sub-Atomic Particles Are Evidence the Universe Was Created", CNSNews.com, June 17, 2016, http://www.cnsnews .com/news/article/barbara-hollingsworth/string-theory-co-founder-sub-atomic-particles -are-evidence-0. Hollingsworth's article contains quotes made by Michio Kaku according to an article published by the Geophilosophical Association of Anthropological and Cultural Studies.

[5] There are multiple sites that publish nonvalidated accounts of miracles by the Holy Spirit in the name of Jesus, such as Christian-Faith.com (http://www.christian-faith.com/true -stories-testimonies-of-jesus-christ/); ApologeticsPress.org (http://www.apologeticspress.org /sitesearch.aspx?q=miracles); and GodIsReal.Today (http://www.godisreal.today/modern -day-miracles/). There are also many good books about contemporary miracles done through the Holy Spirit and the name of Jesus, such as Craig Keener, *Miracles: The Credibility of the New Testament Accounts*, 2 vols. (Grand Rapids, Mich.: Baker Academic, 2011). See also Jeff Doles, *Miracles and Manifestations of the Holy Spirit in the History of the Church* (Seffner, Fla.: Walking Barefoot Ministries, 2008).

rather, in conformity with His unconditionally loving will, shares His healing power and glory with His beloveds.

We will first examine some well-known Marian apparitions (and the medically validated miracles associated with them) and then examine some scientifically validated miracles associated with contemporary saints: Saint Padre Pio, Blessed Fulton J. Sheen, and Pope Saint John Paul II.

I. Three Marian Apparitions

The Church is quite careful about approving Marian apparitions as valid because a validation that is subsequently falsified would undermine her credibility. Perhaps this is why the apparition at Medjugorje has not been approved despite its initiation in 1981. The Church's long-standing criteria (administered by the Congregation for the Doctrine of the Faith in the 1978 document *Normae Congregationis*) are as follows:

- There must be moral certainty, or at least great probability, that something miraculous has occurred, something that cannot be explained by natural causes, or by deliberate fakery.
- The person or persons who claim to have had the private revelation must be mentally sound, honest, sincere, of upright conduct, and obedient to ecclesiastical authority.
- The content of the revelation or message must be theologically acceptable, morally sound, and free of error.
- The apparition must yield positive and continuing spiritual assets—for example, prayer, conversion, and increase of charity.

Over the last five centuries, there have been nine Marian apparitions approved by the Church. We will discuss three of them that have undergone particular historical and scientific scrutiny:

1. The apparition of Our Lady of Guadalupe
2. The apparition of Our Lady of Lourdes
3. The apparition of Our Lady of Fatima

A. The Apparition of Our Lady of Guadalupe

According to several well-attested accounts (see below), the Blessed Virgin Mary appeared to a native Aztec, Juan Diego, on December 9, 1531. She asked him to ask his bishop, Juan de Zumarraga, to build a church atop Tepeyac Hill (now within the confines of Mexico City). Juan Diego did as he was instructed; but after relating his story to Zumarraga, the bishop did not believe him. The Blessed Virgin Mary appeared again to Juan Diego that same day (December 9) and asked him to return to the bishop. On December 10, Juan Diego returned to Zumarraga, but he still had doubts and asked Juan Diego to return to the hill and ask the Virgin for a miraculous sign. He did as he was instructed, and the Lady promised a sign the next day (December 11). However, before Juan Diego could return to the hill on December 11, his uncle Juan Bernardino became quite ill and Juan Diego stayed with him to find medical assistance and a priest. On December 12, when Juan Diego left his uncle to find a priest, the Virgin met him on the road and assured him that his uncle would be cured and told him to proceed to the hill, where he would find the sign required by Bishop Zumarraga. He went to Tepeyac Hill and found Castilian roses growing there (not native to Mexico); he gathered them and put them in his tilma. When he returned with the roses to Bishop Zumarraga and opened his cloak to allow the roses to fall, the picture of the Lady of Guadalupe appeared on the tilma. Apparently, the roses and the image were sufficient to convince Bishop Zumarraga to build the first church (and sanctuary for the image) atop of Tepeyac Hill.

Some scholars have challenged the veracity of this story because it was not found either in the writings of Bishop Zumarraga or in an ecclesiastical report about the image. However, in 1995, Jesuit historian Xavier Escalada published a four-volume encyclopedia on the image and history of Our Lady of Guadalupe, in which he reports and analyzes a hitherto unknown sheet of parchment dated 1548 called "*Codex Escalada*".[6] The parchment contains an illustrated story of the

---

[6]See Arturo Rocha Cortes, ed., "Documentos Mestizo", Codice 1548 o 'Escalada'" (the *Codex Escalada* 1548), Códice (1548), *Boletín Guadalupano*, Año II, Núm. 35 (Noviembre 2003): 5, 6 y 7.

vision of Juan Diego and is signed by Antonio Valeriano and Bernardino de Sahagun. These signatures were authenticated by Banco de Mexico and Charles E. Dibble. The authentication of the signatures, along with the parchment, illustrations, language, and style, validate both the parchment and the existence and vision of Juan Diego.[7]

The image itself has many extraordinary attributes that border on the miraculous, and probably indicate it. Four attributes have been scientifically tested in the twentieth and twenty-first centuries:

1. The material of the tilma has maintained its chemical and structural integrity for almost five hundred years. This is quite remarkable, considering that most replicas of tilmas with the same chemical and structural composition last only *fifteen years* before analyzable decomposition occurs. Furthermore, the tilma was displayed without protective glass for its first 115 years and was subjected to soot, candlewax, incense, and touching throughout its history. There is currently no scientific explanation for its physical and chemical longevity.[8]

2. Though there are several parts of the cloth that have been painted subsequent to the original image (e.g., the moon underneath the Virgin's feet, the angel holding the cloth, and the rays coming from the image), the original image of the Virgin herself does not appear to have been painted by an artist at the time. There is no sketch underneath it, no brush strokes, and no corrections, and it appears to have been produced in a single step. These features were identified by Dr. Philip Serna Callahan (biophysicist and NASA consultant), who photographed the image under infrared light.[9]

[7] See Alberto Peralta, "El Codice 1548: Critica a una supesta Fuente Guadalupana del Siglo SVI", *Artículos* (Proyecto Guadalupe, 2003); Stafford Poole, "History versus Juan Diego", *The Americas* 62, no. 1 (July 2005): 1–16, http://muse.jhu.edu/issue/9974; and Stafford Poole, *The Guadalupan Controversies in Mexico* (Stanford, Calif.: Stanford University Press, 2006).

[8] See Giulio Dante Guerra, "La Madonna di Guadalupe: 'Inculturazione' Miracolosa", *Christianita*, 1992, pp. 205–6.

[9] See P. Callahan, *The Tilma under Infrared Radiation: CARA Studies in Popular Devotion*, vol. 2, *Guadalupe Studies, nᵛ 3* (Washington, D.C.: Center for Applied Research in the Apostolate, 1981), pp. 6–13. See also Thomas Mary Sennott, "The Tilma of Guadalupe: A Scientific Analysis", MiracleHunter.com, 2015, http://www.miraclehunter.com/marian_apparitions/approved_apparitions/guadalupe/article_11.html.

3. According to Nobel Prize-winning biochemist Richard Kuhn, who analyzed a sample of the fabric, the pigments used were from no known natural source, whether animal, mineral, or vegetable. Given that there were no synthetic pigments in 1531, this enigma remains inexplicable.[10] Dr. Callahan also noted that the original image on the tilma had not cracked, flaked, or decayed over the course of five hundred years, while the paint and gold leaf had flaked or deteriorated considerably. This phenomenon has not yet been scientifically explained— and may not be able to be so explained.

4. The eyes of the Virgin have three remarkable qualities that cannot be explained through known technology in 1531— and would be difficult to replicate with today's technology enhanced by computers, ophthalmologic knowledge, and digital photography.

- Engineer Jose' Aste Tonsmann has amplified an image of the pupils of the Blessed Virgin Mary by twenty-five hundred times and can identify not only what appears to be the image of Bishop Zumarraga, but also several other witnesses of the miracle reflected there.
- The images in the pupils also manifest the triple reflection called the Samson-Purkinje effect, which was completely unknown at the time of the image's formation.[11]
- The image in the eyes of the Virgin follow the curvature of the cornea precisely in the way it occurs in a normal human eye.[12]

The first ophthalmologist to identify both the Samson-Purkinje effect and the precise corneal curvature in the images in both of the Virgin's eyes was Dr. Javier Torroella Bueno in 1956. Dr. Rafael

---

[10] See the comments of engineer Jose' Aste Tonsmann of the Mexican Center of Guadalupan Studies during a conference at Pontifical Regina Apostolorum Athenaeum in 2001. Reported in "Science Sees What Mary Saw from Juan Diego's Tilma", Zenit, 2001, available at CatholicEducation.org, https://web.archive.org/web/20100620110845/http://www.catholiceducation.org/articles/religion/re0447.html.

[11] "The Mystery in Our Lady's Eyes", Sancta.org, accessed April 20, 2020, http://www.sancta.org/eyes.html.

[12] Ibid.

Torrija Lavoignet made a detailed examination of the Virgin's eyes with an ophthalmoscope and confirmed Dr. Bueno's findings, noting other remarkable similarities to human eyes.[13] Since that time, the eyes have been examined by more than twenty ophthalmologists confirming the conclusions of the original examination. As noted above, Dr. Jose' Aste Tonsmann (formerly of Cornell University working at IBM) amplified the Virgin's eyes by a factor of twenty-five hundred times and used a series of filters to eliminate "noise" in the amplified images. He not only confirmed the precise corneal curvature and the Samson-Purkinje effect, but also several other figures behind Bishop Zumarraga (the front figure pictured with a beard), all of whom were looking at the tilma in amazement.[14]

The above five enigmas in the tilma of Juan Diego are scientifically inexplicable today and certainly cannot be explained by the artistic and preservation capabilities between 1531 and 1900. In view of this, it is reasonable and responsible to believe that this tilma had more than an extraordinary origin—indeed, a supernatural one.

In addition to the seemingly miraculous origin of the image, there have been many miracles associated with the tilma over the last several centuries, some concerned with healing, and one concerned with the tilma's remarkable survival when a bomb was placed underneath it by a Mexican secularist in 1921. Despite the fact that a brass crucifix was completely bent over, and the altar was damaged, the tilma was left unharmed.[15] This is among the many healings that have taken place over the centuries through the tilma, or replicas that have touched the original.

In conclusion, devotion to Our Lady of Guadalupe portrayed on the remarkable tilma in the cathedral atop Tepeyac Hill has been a most remarkable source of conversion to Catholicism throughout Mexico. It has also been a source of strength and grace for the Catholic religion, particularly in times of persecution and secularism. The

[13] Ibid.

[14] Jose' Aste Tonsmann, *El secreto de sus ojos* (Mexico City: Editorial Diana, 1981). Readers interested in some of Dr. Tonsmann's photographs will want to consult "The Mystery in Our Lady's Eyes", http://www.sancta.org/eyes.html.

[15] See D. A. Brading, *Mexican Phoenix: Our Lady of Guadalupe; Image and Tradition across Five Centuries* (Cambridge, Mass.: Cambridge University Press, 2001), p. 314; Poole, *Guadalupan Controversies*, p. 110.

message of our Lady to Juan Diego, filled with love and affection for the native people of the Western hemisphere, has inspired tens of thousands of people beyond the boundaries of Mexico; she is now considered to be the patroness of all the Americas.[16] Her image can be found all over the United States as well as other non-Mexican countries in Latin America. The influence of this single devotion has been so great that Pope Benedict XIV in 1754 wept and uttered the words of Psalm 147 when he looked upon it for the first time: "God has not dealt in like manner with any other nation" (see 147:20).

B. The Apparition of Our Lady of Lourdes

The appearance of the Blessed Virgin Mary to Bernadette Soubirous at the Grotto of Lourdes in 1858 is probably the most well-known Marian apparition in history—more because of the thousands of miraculous cures that have taken place through the water of the Grotto than the apparition itself.

On February 11, 1858, just outside of Lourdes, France, Bernadette Soubirous (a fourteen-year-old girl without much formal education), her sister Toinette, and a friend Jeanne Abadie were searching for kindling and bones in a cave. Just as she had taken off her shoes and stockings, a Lady, small in stature, dressed in white with a blue sash around her waist and holding a gold rosary, appeared to her. Bernadette tried to make the sign of the cross but was so scared that she could not, at which point the Lady asked her to pray the Rosary with her, restoring her calm. Bernadette was the only one to see and hear the apparition.

When Toinette returned home, she told their mother, provoking both parents to punish them for telling such a "story". Nevertheless, Bernadette was drawn back to the cave, and the Lady appeared to her again. Bernadette brought holy water with her and sprinkled it on the apparition to see if she would shrink from it, but the Lady only smiled, at which point Bernadette told her that if she was not of God, she would have to go away. The Lady smiled and bowed

---

[16] See Carl Anderson, *Our Lady of Guadalupe: Mother of the Civilization of Love* (New York: Doubleday Religion, 2009).

and Bernadette went into a kind of ecstasy—sensing her holiness and love. Her companions witnessed this ecstasy, which seemed to last long after the apparition.

Bernadette returned a third time to the Grotto, and the Lady gave her instructions to return several times throughout the upcoming two weeks. On February 20, the Lady taught her a prayer and asked for penance for the conversion of sinners.

Bernadette returned to the Grotto on several other occasions accompanied by hundreds of people. The official Lourdes website lists the major points of the apparitions as follows:

[*Sunday, February 21.*] The Lady appeared to Bernadette very early in the morning. About one hundred people were present. Afterwards the Police Commissioner, Jacomet, questioned her. He wanted Bernadette to tell what she saw. Bernadette would only speak of "AQUÉRO" ("that thing" in local dialect).

[*Tuesday, February 23.*] Surrounded by 150 persons, Bernadette arrived at the Grotto. The Apparition reveals to her a secret "only for her alone".

[*Wednesday, February 24.*] The message of the Lady: "Penance! Penance! Penance! Pray to God for sinners. Kiss the ground as an act of penance for sinners!"

[*Thursday, February 25.*] Three hundred people were present. Bernadette relates; "She told me to go, drink of the spring (. . . .) I only found a little muddy water. At the fourth attempt I was able to drink. She also made me eat the bitter herbs that were found near the spring, and then the vision left and went away." In front of the crowd that was asking "Do you think that she is mad doing things like that?" she replied; "It is for sinners."

[*Saturday, February 27.*] Eight hundred people were present. The Apparition was silent. Bernadette drank the water from the spring and carried out her usual acts of penance.

[*Sunday, February 28.*] Over one thousand people were present at the ecstasy. Bernadette prayed, kissed the ground and moved on her knees as a sign of penance. She was then taken to the house of Judge Ribes who threatened to put her in prison.

[*Monday, March 1.*] Over one thousand five hundred people assembled and among them, for the first time, a priest. In the night, Catherine Latapie, a woman from Loubajac, 7 kilometres away, went to the Grotto, she plunged her dislocated arm into the water of the spring: her arm and her hand regained their movement.[17]

Several additional cures occurred at the Grotto (seven of which were considered medically inexplicable—and therefore miraculous), which drew even more people to the cave. This caused a great deal of controversy within both the Church and the town. A decision was made in March to barricade the Grotto, which had the effect of bringing it to the attention of the national press and national government. Bernadette was not to be deterred, and so visited the barricaded Grotto at night on several other occasions. On one such occasion (March 25, 1858) the Lady declared that she was "the Immaculate Conception". Her last apparition occurred on July 16, 1858.

The controversy concerning the closure of the Grotto became a national issue, compelling Emperor Napoleon III formally to reopen the Grotto on October 4, 1858. The Catholic Church was concerned about the immense popularity of the Grotto and the potential for people to be misled, and so the bishop assembled an ecclesiastical committee in November 1858 to assess the veracity of Bernadette's apparitions.[18] On January 18, 1860, the bishop, following the advice of the committee, declared the apparition to be authentic. Bernadette was canonized as a saint in 1933. Today, almost four million pilgrims per year visit the shrine, and hundreds receive extraordinary and miraculous cures.

1. The Miraculous Cures

From the time of Blessed Mary's first apparition to Bernadette Soubirous, the water from the Lourdes Grotto has been a source of miraculous healings, both for those who have visited the Grotto and even for those who used the water in remote places. Since the

[17] "The Apparitions", Lourdes Sanctuaire (website), accessed April 20, 2020, https://www.lourdes-france.org/en/apparitions/.

[18] For a list of criteria needed to approve Marian apparitions, see Section I above.

time of Bernadette, over seven thousand miraculous cures have been reported to the Lourdes Medical Bureau by pilgrims who have visited Lourdes (which does not include miracles that have taken place outside of Lourdes). There were so many purported cures associated with the water and Grotto of Lourdes that the Catholic Church decided to set up the Lourdes Medical Bureau to be constituted by and under the leadership of physicians and scientists alone. The forerunner of the bureau was started by doctors affiliated with the Grotto in 1883. Pope Pius X formally constituted the Medical Bureau we know today in 1905. The objective of the bureau is to render a judgment that a particular cure was near instantaneous, efficacious throughout the remainder of life, and in all other ways, scientifically inexplicable. The bureau is constituted by twenty physicians and scientists. Its records are open to any physician or scientist who wants to make their own investigation or challenge to any particular case recognized by the above criteria as "miraculous".

Since 1883, only seventy cases have been recognized as "miraculous" according to the strict standards of the bureau. But this does not mean that the seven thousand other cures were not miraculous by other standards. These cases simply cannot be shown to be *completely* scientifically inexplicable, though their occurrence could be truly extraordinary and possibly, or even probably, miraculous. The seventy cases approved by the Lourdes Medical Bureau have been inspected by large numbers of physicians and scientists, and the vast majority of them have been shown to be permanent and inexplicable cures.[19]

Though many of the seven thousand cases are truly remarkable, we will examine only three that had an impact far beyond the individual's receiving a miraculous cure:

1. The case of Marie Bailly, attested to by the Nobel Prize-winning physician Alexis Carrel (1902)

---

[19] For a list of the seventy miraculous healings recognized by the Church at this time, see "Miraculous Healings", Lourdes Sanctuaire (website), accessed April 21, 2020, https://www .lourdes-france.org/en/miraculous-healings/. Books and websites have been written about particular cases, but readers desiring more information on the seventy cases will have to visit the Lourdes Medical Bureau.

2. The case of Gabriel Gargam (1901)
3. The case of John Traynor (1923)

2. Marie Bailly and Alexis Carrel—1902

The first case concerns Marie Bailly, attested to by the Nobel Prize-winning physician Alexis Carrel. This case was examined by Father Stanley Jaki, O.S.B., who received doctorates in physics and theology, was a notable contributor to the history and philosophy of science, and was a Templeton Prize winner.[20] This case is as much about Dr. Carrel as the recipient of the miraculous healing: Marie Bailly. Dr. Carrel won the Nobel Prize for techniques he perfected in vascular surgery, and *Scientific American* credited him with "having initiated all major advances in modern surgery, including organ transplants".[21]

In 1902 a physician friend of Dr. Carrel invited him to help take care of sick patients being transported on a train from Lyons to Lourdes. Carrel, at that time, was an agnostic who did not believe in miracles, but consented to help out, not only because of friendship, but also an interest in what natural causes might be allowing such fast healings as those taking place at Lourdes. On the train, he encountered Marie Bailly, who was suffering from acute tuberculous peritonitis with considerable abdominal distension with large hard masses.[22] Though Marie Bailly was half-conscious, Carrel believed

[20] Stanley Jaki made a thorough examination of Dossier 54 on this case at the Lourdes Medical Bureau. He gives the physician depositions (from Carrel and two other physicians) in the dossier, as well as an analysis of it, in his introduction to a new edition of Alexis Carrel's *The Voyage to Lourdes*. This was published by his own publishing company (New Hope, Ky.: Real View Books, 1994); it is available for purchase online at http://www.realviewbooks.com/. Father Jaki summarized the main parts of this case in a lecture given for the Catholic Medical Association on September 13, 1998, which was published by the Catholic Medical Association in February 1999. See Stanley Jaki, "Two Lourdes Miracles and a Nobel Laureate: What Really Happened?", CatholicCulture.org, accessed April 21, 2020, https://www.catholicculture.org/culture/library/view.cfm?recnum=2866.

[21] See Jaki, "Two Lourdes Miracles".

[22] Dr. Carrel wrote about this cure himself in *Voyage to Lourdes*, using as the main protagonist Dr. Lerrac ("Carrel spelled backwards") and changing the name "Marie Bailly" to "Marie Ferrand" in the story. It is a complete description of what Dr. Carrel saw on his train ride to Lourdes. See Alexis Carrel, *The Voyage to Lourdes*, trans. Virgilia Peterson (New York: Harper Brothers, 1950). An online version of this edition is available free of charge at http://www.basicincome.com/bp/files/The_Voyage_to_Lourdes.pdf.

that she would pass away quite quickly after arriving at Lourdes—if not before. Other physicians on the train agreed with this diagnosis.

When the train arrived at Lourdes, Marie was taken to the Grotto, where three pitchers of water were poured over her distended abdomen. After the first pour, she felt a searing pain, but after the second pour, it was lessened; after the third pour, she experienced a pleasant sensation. Her stomach began to flatten and her pulse returned to normal.[23] Carrel was standing behind Marie (along with other physicians) and was taking notes as the water was poured over her abdomen; he wrote: "The enormously distended and very hard abdomen began to flatten and within 30 minutes it had completely disappeared. No discharge whatsoever was observed from the body."[24] Marie then sat up in bed, had dinner (without vomiting), and got out of bed on her own and dressed herself the next day.[25] She then boarded the train, riding on the hard benches, and arrived in Lyons refreshed. Carrel was still interested in her psychological and physical condition, and so asked that she be monitored by a psychiatrist and a physician for four months.[26] After that, Marie joined the Sisters of Charity—to work with the sick and the poor in a very strenuous life—and died in 1937 at the age of fifty-eight.[27]

When Carrel witnessed this exceedingly rapid and medically inexplicable event, he believed he had seen something like a miracle; but it was difficult for him to part with his former skeptical agnosticism, so he did not yet return to the Catholic faith of his childhood. Furthermore, he wanted to avoid being a medical witness to a miraculous event because he knew that if it became public, it would ruin his career as a medical faculty member at Lyons.

Nevertheless, Marie Bailly's cure seemed so evidently miraculous (being so rapid, complete, and inexplicable) that it became public in the news media in France and throughout the world. Reporters indicated that Carrel did not think the cure was a miracle, which forced Carrel to write a public reply stating that one side (some believers) was jumping to a miraculous conclusion too rapidly and the other

---

[23] See Jaki, "Two Lourdes Miracles".
[24] Ibid.
[25] Ibid.
[26] Ibid.
[27] Ibid.

side (the medical community) had unjustifiably refused to look at facts that appeared to be miraculous.[28] Carrel implied that Bailly's cure may have been miraculous.

As Carrel feared, his advocacy of the possibility of Bailly's miraculous cure led to an end of his career at the medical faculty of Lyons, which ironically had a very good effect on his future, because it led him to the University of Chicago and then to the Rockefeller University. In 1912, he received the Nobel Prize for his work in vascular anastomosis. Carrel returned to Lourdes many times, and on one occasion, he witnessed a second miracle, the instantaneous cure of an eighteen-month-old blind boy. Despite these two miracles, Carrel could not bring himself to affirm the reality of miracles conclusively, real divine supernatural intervention manifest in the world. In 1938, one year after the death of Sister Marie Bailly, Carrel became friends with the rector of the Major Seminary in Rennes, who told him to consult with a Trappist monk who was a well-known spiritual director and friend of Charles de Gaulle: Father Alexis Presse, with whom he began a dialogue. In 1942, Carrel announced that he believed in God, the immortality of the soul, and the teachings of the Catholic Church. Two years later, in 1944, as Carrel was dying in Paris, he sent for Father Presse, who administered the Last Rites of the Church to him. He had not been able to let go of the miracles of Lourdes, and they had led him to continue his inquiry into his spiritual nature and Christian revelation. Ultimately, he would find himself joined to the Lord through the Church of his childhood.

3. Gabriel Gargam—1901

Our second case, that of Gabriel Gargam, occurred in 1901.[29] He was born in 1870 to practicing Catholic parents, but lost his faith at the age of fifteen and no longer practiced it. Later in life he became a postal sorter; during the course of his work in 1899, the train on which he had been sorting collided head on with another train, traveling at fifty

---

[28] Ibid.

[29] See Elaine Jordan, "The Lourdes' Miracle of Gabriel Gargam", TraditioninAction.org, April 13, 2013, http://www.traditioninaction.org/religious/h106_Lourdes.htm. Adapted from Paul Glynn, *Healing Fire of Christ: Reflections on Modern Miracles—Knock, Lourdes, Fatima* (San Francisco: Ignatius Press, 2003).

miles per hour. He was thrown fifty-two feet from the train and was badly injured. After eight months, he was at the point of death—a mere seventy-eight pounds with gangrenous feet and unable to take solid food. He could be fed only once every twenty-four hours by a tube, and he required two nurses to take care of him. His condition was well-attested not only by his physicians, but by those involved in the lawsuit he filed against the railroad; the court records and physicians' testimonies still exist today.[30]

Gargam spent two years in bed, unable to be moved from his room. Though his aunt (a religious sister) and his mother begged him to go to Lourdes, he refused to do so, preferring to suffer his fate in his room. Finally, he relented and consented to the trip, but being moved on a stretcher and riding on the train almost killed him. When he arrived at Lourdes, he was in dire condition; he went to confession and received a piece of Holy Communion, and then he was brought to the waters in the Grotto. The strain was so great that he fell into a swoon and his attendants believed him to be dead, so they put him on a carriage, put a cloth on his face, and began to wheel him back to the hotel. On the way there, a Eucharistic procession was passing by. The priest leading the procession saw the sorrowful crowd around Gargam, and he blessed them with the Holy Eucharist, at which point Gargam's legs began to move under the sheets. He then sat upright by his own power (which he had not been able to do for two years), and then proceeded to get off the carriage and walk around by his own power. The astonished crowd accompanied him back to his hotel where he sat down to eat a hearty meal (though he had not taken solid food for two years).[31]

On August 20, 1901, Gargam was examined by sixty physicians, all of whom pronounced him completely cured. They could not explain his cure through any known form of physical causation, a judgment that still holds true today. Gargam also underwent a spiritual metamorphosis, consecrating himself to the Blessed Virgin Mary and the service of the sick at Lourdes. He lived a normal healthy life until his death at eighty-three years of age.[32]

[30] Jordan, "The Lourdes' Miracle".
[31] Ibid.
[32] Ibid.

4. John Traynor—1923

The third case, John Traynor, occurred in 1923.[33] Traynor was raised a Catholic and was a bonafide World War I hero who was severely injured during the war. In 1915, in a third battle where he received severe wounds, he was sprayed with machine gun fire. A bullet lodged under his collarbone, he was wounded in the chest, and another bullet hit his head (which caused a permanent hole, revealing his pulsating brain that was later blocked by a silver plate). As a result of these injuries, Traynor's right arm was paralyzed (and his muscles atrophied), his legs were partially paralyzed, and he was epileptic (from the wound in his head). He was not able to do anything and had to be moved from his bed to his wheelchair, sometimes suffering four epileptic fits per day.

In 1923, Traynor's diocese of Liverpool organized a pilgrimage to Lourdes. Traynor, who had a sincere devotion to the Blessed Virgin Mary, wanted to go, though his physicians, wife, the government ministry of pensions, and even the priest organizing the pilgrimage begged him to stay home. They thought the trip would be suicide, and they were almost correct. Traynor was wheeled to the train in Liverpool and suffered tremendously on the trip to Lourdes. When he arrived, he was almost dead; one woman wrote to his wife, indicating that he would be buried at Lourdes. During his stay, he was taken to the baths nine times, and on the occasion of his tenth time (July 25, 1923), his legs felt agitated in the bath. After the bath, he was placed in the wheelchair to receive a Eucharistic blessing from the bishop of Rheims, who was passing by in a Eucharistic procession. After being blessed by the Host, his arm (which had been paralyzed for eight years) grew so strong that he was able to burst through his bandages. He then regained the use of his legs (which had been partially paralyzed for eight years, preventing him from standing and walking). He got out of his chair and walked several steps, but his

---

[33] See Patrick O'Connor, "I Met a Miracle: The Story of Jack Traynor" (Catholic Truth Society, 1943); reproduced by FaithandFamily.org.UK by permission of the Catholic Truth Society, accessed April 21, 2020, http://www.faithandfamily.org.uk/publications/jack_traynor.htm. See also Glynn, *Healing Fire of Christ*, p. 260; Ruth Cranston, *The Mystery of Lourdes* (London: Evans Brothers, 1956), p. 118; "Miracles of Lourdes", website of Our Lady of the Rosary Library, accessed April 21, 2020, https://olrl.org/stories/lourdes.shtml.

attendants put him to bed for the evening because they were afraid he might hurt himself. During the night, he leapt out of his bed, knelt down to finish a Rosary, and ran out his door to go to the Grotto, to the utter amazement of everyone watching. He knelt down in the Grotto to finish his prayers, but seemed to suffer a temporary lapse of memory about his condition prior to going into the bath for the tenth time. The healing not only cured his paralysis and epilepsy; it seemed to mask the memory of his former misery. Two days later, while riding on the train back to Liverpool, Archbishop Keating of Liverpool came into his compartment and reminded him of his former condition—only then was his memory revived; both he and the archbishop broke down in tears.[34]

His cure was so complete that he went into the coal and hauling business (lifting two-hundred-pound sacks of coal), and he pledged himself to service at the Grotto of Lourdes every summer. He died on the eve of the Feast of the Immaculate Conception in 1943 (twenty years after his cure). A large number of conversions occurred in Liverpool as a result of the obvious miracle.[35]

In 1926, the Lourdes Medical Bureau certified that Traynor was instantly and permanently cured in a completely scientifically inexplicable way. Not only was the paralysis in his arm and legs completely cured, but he regained the muscle and tendons in his skeletal arm. Moreover, the permanent hole in his temple healed completely, leaving no mark but a slight indentation. He received a certificate from Dr. McConnell of Liverpool, attesting that he had not had an epileptic fit since 1923. All these cures occurred simultaneously and instantly.[36] A movie is currently being made by his great-great-grandson about the miracle and will be available sometime in the near future.[37]

5. Conclusion

As previously noted, there are many other miraculous cases of healings associated with Lourdes beyond the above three—seventy of

---

[34] See ibid.

[35] See ibid.

[36] See ibid.

[37] See Eleanor Barlow, "Liverpool 'Miracle' Soldier's Story to Be Told in Documentary Directed by Great-Great-Grandson", *Echo News* (Liverpool), June 11, 2016, http://www.liverpoolecho.co.uk/news/liverpool-news/liverpool-miracle-soldiers-story-told-11455815.

them officially judged a miracle by the Lourdes Medical Bureau, and literally thousands of others that are truly extraordinary, but not susceptible of being judged *completely* scientifically inexplicable. In view of this, it is highly likely that an extraordinary power—indeed, a supernatural power—appears to be continuously present and operative at the Grotto of Lourdes. The evidence is so extensive that even slight openness to the existence of God and God's action in the world would lead one to draw this conclusion, at least prospectively.

If one concludes to the presence of divine power and healing at Lourdes, what would this mean beyond the obvious conclusion of God's existence and action in the world? One conclusion might be that God is love, for this is not only evident in the actual cures that take place multiple times every year at the Grotto, but also in the loving service of so many people who have dedicated their time, and even their lives, to helping sick pilgrims to bathe in these waters of hope. But what about those who do not receive a cure? What happens to them? The vast majority, though perhaps initially disappointed, find themselves spiritually renewed by the prayer, spiritual witness, and loving service at the Grotto. The experience causes them to refocus, not on receiving a cure in this world, but on their eternal salvation with the loving God who is so extraordinarily present at the sanctuary and the Grotto. Very few pilgrims leave the Grotto embittered. Quite the opposite—they are edified, spiritually rejuvenated, and focused on life with God, which they now know includes an element of the Cross to help them along the way. Acceptance of the Cross as an integral means to the purification of love, and its ultimate purification in Heaven, is perhaps the hardest dimension of human existence. Yet Lourdes, even when cures do not occur, has the remarkable effect of inciting us quite rapidly toward this acceptance. Lourdes is clearly about the love of God manifest in healing, service, and most blessedly in the acceptance of the Cross of Jesus Christ.

How else does this remarkable story and Grotto affect us? There is the most obvious point of all—not only is God the Father and the risen Jesus present, but also the Blessed Virgin Mary. The modern age seems to have so much difficulty accepting the involvement of the Blessed Virgin Mary in the work of divine providence and salvation. Yet as we have seen at Guadalupe and now at Lourdes, Blessed Mary has a way of appearing to people much like herself when she was a young woman in Nazareth. As noted earlier, the Persons of the Blessed Trinity are not interested in monopolizing the providential stage; they desire to share it with the Blessed Mother, and with saints such as Bernadette Soubirous, and even men of medicine like Alexis Carrel.

The Blessed Virgin Mary's vital presence at Lourdes shows her centrality in the order of salvation by God's will. We might ask why He would want her to have such an important role in providence and salvation. One answer might be, as illustrated by Guadalupe and Lourdes, that He seeks a feminine and motherly voice in the manifestation of His care and salvific intention. Mary's motherly affection toward Juan Diego and Bernadette shows this essential dimension as well as the dimension of family in God's providential plan and love. This motherly dimension is truly important for those who are suffering and need the kind of encouragement and solace that only a mother can give. This motherly care and solace richly complements the unconditional love of the prodigal son's Father (Abba) and the unconditional brotherly love of Jesus Himself.

Some people might object that this constitutes "Mariolatry", a divinization and worship of Mary. Far from it! Catholics are not interested in divinizing or worshipping Mary, but only acknowledging her vital role in the order of salvation—not only in first-century Nazareth, but throughout history. When the Father made all of us adopted children through His Son, Jesus, He also made us adopted children of Jesus' Mother, Mary. She accepts us within the divine-human family she initiated through her consent to be the Mother of His Son. We are her children, not just in the first century, but for all time—and the miracles of Guadalupe and Lourdes confirm this logic of familial love.

One last observation: when the Blessed Virgin Mary appeared to Bernadette Soubirous, she announced herself as "the Immaculate Conception". This is another doctrine that non-Catholics believe to be extrabiblical and somewhat difficult to believe. Though the Bible does not explicitly mention Mary being free of original sin at the time of her conception, the Church believed that this followed from her sinlessness, almost universally attested by the Church Fathers. On this basis, the doctrine was declared by Pope Pius IX in 1854 in the papal bull *Ineffabilis Deus*. Given the veracity of the many miracles that have occurred at Lourdes, it is reasonable to assign the same veracity to Bernadette's account of the apparitions, which implicitly confirms the veracity of the Immaculate Conception by Mary's own words. This doctrine confirms God's long-standing providential plan to choose Mary as the Mother of His Son, and to keep her from being affected by concupiscence—one of the effects of the fall. This would protect Mary's capacity to raise Jesus with a perfected love. This doctrine makes complete sense. If the Son of God is to become incarnate as a baby (because He is fully human), then it seems fitting that His Mother be able to raise Him in accordance with the fullest potential for human love. Though Bernadette may not have recognized the significance of Mary's announcement (at the age of fourteen without formal education), she became a conduit to confirm an important doctrine about God's foreknowledge, unconditional love, providence, and intention to save.

C. The Apparition of Our Lady of Fatima

In the spring of 1916, three Portuguese shepherd children—Lucia Santos and her cousins Jacinta and Francisco Marto—were visited three times by an apparition of an angel who identified himself as "the Angel of Peace".[38] They said that the angel taught them prayers and encouraged them to spend time in adoration. On May 13, 1917, the children were visited for the first time by the Blessed Virgin Mary at the Cova da Iria in Fatima, who appeared to them as exceedingly radiant. She wore a white mantle edged with gold and carried a rosary, telling the children to devote themselves to the Holy Trinity and to daily recitation of the Rosary for an end to the First World War.

Though Lucia had asked her two cousins to keep the apparition secret, Jacinta told her mother, who in turn told it to several neighbors, which made the children's apparition quite public. On June 13, 1917, the children experienced the second apparition, at which time the Blessed Virgin Mary revealed that Jacinta and Francisco would die soon, but that Lucia would live longer to spread the message of peace from Fatima. This prediction proved to be true. Francisco

---

[38] See "Apparitions of the Angel of Portugal", EWTN.com, 2017, https://www.ewtn.com/fatima/angel-of-portugal.asp. For information regarding the three apparitions, click on the button for each apparition.

died in 1919 and Jacinta died in 1920 during the world flu pandemic; Lucia lived to be ninety-seven, dying on February 13, 2005, after spending most of her life in a discalced Carmelite monastery.

On August 13, 1917, officials of the Portuguese government intercepted the children, who were returning to the Cova da Iria, and interrogated them because hundreds of people were flocking to the Cova, and officials considered the three secrets that the Blessed Virgin Mary had revealed to the children to be politically disruptive. On August 19, the children received the fourth apparition, in a pasture near the Cova where the Blessed Virgin Mary promised that an extraordinary miracle would occur on October 13. The Virgin visited the children one more time prior to October 13 with a similar message about praying the Rosary for world peace.

On October 13, 1917, a huge crowd of around fifty thousand people gathered at the Cova da Iria to witness the great miracle that the Blessed Virgin Mary promised would occur on that date. It had been raining and then it began to clear. Lucia shouted, "Look at the sun." The sun appeared to be rotating on its own axis, throwing out a variety of colors, and then it appeared to approach the earth, causing many to believe that the world was ending. It then returned to its normal state. Though the ground had been quite wet from the rain prior to the miracle, the sun's activity during the miracle dried the ground significantly, baffling many of the engineers and scientists present. The miracle was variously described by reporters, doctors, and scientists. Dr. Domingos Pinto Coelho, reporting for the Catholic newspaper, described the event as follows:

> The sun, at one moment surrounded with scarlet flame, at another aureoled in yellow and deep purple, seemed to be in an exceedingly swift and whirling movement, at times appearing to be loosened from the sky and to be approaching the earth, strongly radiating heat.[39]

A reporter from the Lisbon paper, O Dia, saw it this way:

> The silver sun, enveloped in the same gauzy grey light, was seen to whirl and turn in the circle of broken clouds.... The light turned a

[39] Cited in John de Marchi, The Immaculate Heart: The True Story of Our Lady of Fatima (New York: Farrar, Straus and Young, 1952), p. 147.

beautiful blue, as if it had come through the stained-glass windows of a cathedral, and spread itself over the people who knelt with out-stretched hands.... People wept and prayed with uncovered heads, in the presence of a miracle they had awaited. The seconds seemed like hours, so vivid were they.[40]

Dr. Almeida Garrett, professor of natural sciences at Coimbra University, described it as follows:

The sun's disc did not remain immobile. This was not the sparkling of a heavenly body, for it spun round on itself in a mad whirl, when suddenly a clamor was heard from all the people. The sun, whirling, seemed to loosen itself from the firmament and advance threateningly upon the earth as if to crush us with its huge fiery weight. The sensation during those moments was terrible.[41]

The Italian priest John de Marchi, I.M.C., spent seven years researching the Fatima accounts of both the apparitions and the miracle of the sun, obtaining hundreds of testimonies to the phenomenon, and presented them in three important works:

- *The Immaculate Heart: The True Story of Our Lady of Fatima*[42]
- *The True Story of Fatima*[43]
- *Fatima: From the Beginning*[44]

In addition to the large group of witnesses at the Cova de Iria, several witnesses reported seeing the solar phenomenon in the surrounding area, some as far as eighteen to forty kilometers from the Cova. De Marchi found no witnesses outside the forty-kilometer perimeter of the Cova. The vast majority of those present attested to the sun's highly unusual and beautiful activity, giving various reports of how it seemed to look. De Marchi found no one present who denied it.[45]

[40] Cited in ibid., p. 143.
[41] Cited in ibid., p. 146.
[42] Ibid.
[43] John de Marchi, *The True Story of Fatima* (St. Paul, Minn.: Catechetical Guild, 1956).
[44] John de Marchi, *Fatima: From the Beginning* (Fatima, Portugal: Missoes Consolata, 1981).
[45] De Marchi, *Immaculate Heart*, p. 143.

How can this event be explained? It could not have been an astronomical phenomenon because it was not witnessed by anyone beyond forty kilometers from the Cova da Iria. Therefore, it had to be either a highly unusual local *atmospheric* phenomenon or a supernatural phenomenon acting like a gigantic spinning lens or prism suspended in the atmosphere. If it was caused by atmospheric conditions, such conditions would be exceedingly unusual in human recorded history. Though some scientists, such as Steuart Campbell, have suggested that the phenomenon might be explained by a large cloud of stratospheric dust (similar to one that created a reddening effect on the sun in China in 1983),[46] it does not explain how the phenomenon made the sun spin on its own axis, approach the earth, and then recede to its original position. Even if it could, the fact that the children predicted the precise time and place for such a highly unusual atmospheric event goes beyond natural explanation.[47]

The atmospheric explanation requires a convergence of a large number of highly unusual factors whose spontaneous occurrence would be very difficult to explain by natural causation. Even if one attributes the phenomenon to purely natural causes, the convergence of so many highly unusual atmospheric conditions, to produce a rotating disc approaching and then receding from the earth on the precise day predicted by the children, strongly suggests that the phenomenon had a supernatural dimension. Recall C.S. Lewis' definition of a miracle: "The divine art of miracle is not an art of suspending the pattern into which events conform but of feeding new events into that pattern."[48]

Alternatively, the phenomenon could be explained on a purely supernatural basis, as a sort of transphysical round lens or prism suspended in the atmosphere spinning on its own axis, approaching the earth and then receding back to its original position. In either case, if the fifty thousand witnesses were not deluded by mass hallucination, it seems that something supernatural took place at the Cova da Iria on October 13, 1917.

---

[46] See Steuart Campbell, "The 'Miracle of the Sun' at Fatima", *Journal of Meteorology* 14, no. 142 (October 1989).

[47] Stanley Jaki, the well-known Benedictine professor of physics and philosopher of science, notes that the children's prediction alone shows the supernatural origin of the phenomenon. See Stanley Jaki, *God and the Sun at Fatima* (Frasier, Mich.: Real View Books, 1999).

[48] C.S. Lewis, *Miracles: A Preliminary Study* (New York: HarperOne, 1947), p. 95.

The explanation of mass hallucination has been proffered by some critics, especially because the event was religious and the witnesses were expecting a miracle to occur. Yet such an explanation is highly dubious because of the large number of witnesses who ranged from believers to skeptical nonbelievers and included physicians, scientists, reporters, churchmen, attorneys, and other people of high education and repute. Furthermore, those who witnessed the event eighteen to forty kilometers away could not have been under the same "spell" as those in the Cova da Iria. Finally, the fact that the phenomenon dried wet ground (from a lengthy preceding rain) in a very short time shows that the event was not only in the minds of the participants. According to de Marchi, "Engineers that have studied the case indicated that an incredible amount of energy would have been necessary to dry up in a few minutes, the pools of water that had formed on the field."[49] De Marchi concludes to the high improbability of mass hallucination as follows:

> The prediction of an unspecified "miracle", the abrupt beginning and end of the alleged miracle of the sun, the varied religious backgrounds of the observers, the sheer numbers of people present, and the lack of any known scientific causative factor make a mass hallucination unlikely.[50]

In view of the combination of circumstances—the children's accurate prediction, the drying effect of the phenomenon, the highly unusual nature of the phenomenon (particularly the spinning, approaching, and receding of the sun), the large number of witnesses from various backgrounds and education, and the witnesses from as far away as eighteen to forty kilometers—it is reasonable and responsible to conclude to the presence of supernatural power at the Cova da Iria on October 13, 1917, whether the event was produced by a convergence of highly unusual atmospheric factors or had a purely supernatural cause (such as a transphysical spinning lens or prism).

There have been many healing miracles connected with the Cova da Iria and the intercession of Our Lady of Fatima. Unfortunately, these miracles have not been as assiduously documented and

---

[49] Ibid., p. 150.
[50] Ibid., pp. 278–82.

medically confirmed as those at Lourdes; therefore, I do not mention them here. The miracle of the sun is sufficient to speak of the authenticity of the apparitions.

II. Validated Miracles through the Intercession of Contemporary Saints

There are many well-documented, medically confirmed miracles by objective scientific panels that occurred in the twentieth and twenty-first centuries in connection with the canonization of some well-known saints: Saint Padre Pio, Pope Saint John Paul II, Pope Saint John XXIII, Blessed Fulton J. Sheen, and so forth. As the reader may know, one such miracle is required for beatification and a second miracle is required for canonization (declared sainthood). The diocese in which the miracles occurred is responsible for convening an objective scientific panel to judge whether a miracle is beyond any natural explanation. Examples of such miracles include instantaneously cured long-term malignancies, the instantaneous regeneration of dead tissue, and instantaneous cure of blindness or long-term paralysis. I will present only three such miracles here, one concerned with Padre Pio, another with Fulton J. Sheen, and another with John Paul II. If readers are interested in dozens of other scientifically confirmed miracles of this kind, they need only do a Google search for the canonization miracles of their favorite saints (e.g., "canonization miracles of St. John Paul II"). Normally, a description of the miracle and the procedures used to validate its nonnatural (supernatural) origin are given in abundant detail.

A. A Miracle Attributed to Saint Padre Pio

During his lifetime, Padre Pio performed a large number of miracle cures, about which several books have been written.[51] Nevertheless, I

---

[51] See, for example, Franciscan Friars of the Immaculate, *Padre Pio: The Wonder Worker* (New Bedford, Mass.: Our Lady's Chapel, 1999), and Renzo Allegri, *Padre Pio: Man of Hope* (Ann Arbor, Mich.: Charis Books, 2000).

will limit myself to a miracle connected with Padre Pio's beatification, because this kind of miracle must be approved by a diocesan scientific board, a diocesan theological tribunal, a Vatican scientific board, and a Vatican tribunal. I have also taken the miracles for Blessed Fulton J. Sheen and Pope Saint John Paul II from the proceedings concerned with their beatification, to assure the same quality of investigation and medical-scientific scrutiny.

The miracle used for Saint Padre Pio's beatification process was the case of Consiglia De Martino, a married woman with three children from Salerno, Italy.[52] On October 31, 1995, Consiglia began to feel acute pain, followed by a very fast-moving growth in her neck. It quickly reached the size of a grapefruit, causing her and a friend to call their husbands to go to the Riuniti Hospital in Salerno. After ordering two CAT scans, the examining physician determined that she had suffered from diffuse lymphatic spilling of approximately two liters (two quarts), resulting from a rupture of the lymphatic canals. Consiglia was told that she would have to have a very difficult and complicated surgical intervention as soon as possible, and so the doctor scheduled the surgery for November 3.

Consiglia began to pray immediately to Padre Pio, and phoned his monastery at San Giovanni Rotondo, where she spoke with Fra Modestino Fucci (a brother who was Padre Pio's friend and who had been promised by him before he died that he would be helping him with intercessory prayers). He prayed at the tomb of Padre Pio on November 1 and 2. During that time, prior to the surgical intervention, physicians gave no medical treatment to Consiglia.

On November 2, Consiglia noticed a marked decrease in pain followed by a rapid diminution of the swelling in her neck. The following day, Consiglia was examined by physicians prior to the scheduled surgery. They noticed immediately the disappearance of the swelling in her neck and ordered X-rays of that area as well as her abdomen. The X-ray showed not only the complete cure of the rupture of the

[52] See Father Paolino Rossi, "After Much Study, a Miracle", CatholicCulture.org, from the magazine *Inside the Vatican*, April 1999, pp. 5–7, https://www.catholicculture.org/culture/library/view.cfm?id=1018&CFID=71847156&CFTOKEN=25822477. See also the website Cacciopploi.com, accessed April 21, 2020, at http://caccioppoli.com/The%20path%20of%20Padre%20Pio%20to%20sainthood,%20the%20miracle%20of%20Consiglia%20De%20Martino,%20the%20miracle%20of%20Matteo%20Pio%20Colella.html.

thoracic duct (the largest lymphatic vessel of the lymphatic system) that caused the lymphatic spilling, but also the complete disappearance of the large two-quart liquid deposit in her neck as well as other liquid deposits in her abdomen. The surgery was canceled, and a CAT scan was ordered for November 6, which confirmed the results of the X-ray taken on November 3. Evidently, Consiglia had been immediately and inexplicably cured of a complex and dangerous condition without any medical intervention whatsoever. She attributed the cure to Padre Pio, to whom she, her family, and Fra Modestino had been praying. Successive examinations of Consiglia showed no long-term effects of the condition.

The diocesan investigation of the miracle took place from July 1996 to June 1997 in the Salerno curia. Two ex officio experts and a medical consultant studied the published documentation and unanimously declared the "extraordinary and scientifically inexplicable" nature of the cure. On April 30, 1998, the five-member Medical Committee of the Congregation for the Causes of Saints (CCS) at the Vatican declared unanimously that "the healing of the traumatically ruptured thoracic duct of Consiglia De Martino on November 3, 1995 is scientifically inexplicable."[53] After the positive conclusion of the Medical Committee, "on October 20, 1998 the assembly of Cardinals and Bishops members of the Congregation for the Causes of Saints approves the Consiglia De Martino case as a miracle."[54]

B. A Miracle Attributed to Blessed Fulton J. Sheen

A miracle used in the process of the beatification of Archbishop Fulton J. Sheen took place on September 16, 2010, in Peoria, Illinois, when James Fulton Engstrom, a newborn baby of Bonnie and Travis Engstrom, was found to be stillborn.[55] During the delivery, James'

[53] See the website Caccioploi.com.
[54] Ibid.
[55] See Peter Jesserer Smith "Archbishop Fulton Sheen Alleged Miracle Passes Major Vatican Test", *National Catholic Register*, March 7, 2014, http://www.ncregister.com/daily-news/archbishop-fulton-sheen-alleged-miracle-passes-major-vatican-test. See also Madeleine Teahan, "Fulton Sheen and the Miracle of Baby James", *Catholic Herald*, July 1, 2014.

umbilical cord became knotted, cutting off blood, oxygen, and nutriment from the baby during the delivery process. When he emerged, James was apparently stillborn. Unlike healthy babies, he was pulseless, his arms and legs flopped to the sides, and he was blue in color. Since Bonnie Engstrom had decided on a home delivery, the midwife and others had to perform CPR on the baby in anticipation of an ambulance to take him to the hospital. After twenty minutes, the ambulance arrived and took the lifeless child to the hospital. Upon arriving, doctors again tried to revive him through resuscitation and epinephrine injections; after sixty-one minutes, they were about to declare him deceased. Throughout the ordeal, his parents and some family friends prayed through the intercession of Archbishop Fulton J. Sheen for the life of the child.

At the moment the doctors were about to call the death of James, his heart started to beat for the first time, at a normal heartbeat of 148 beats per minute. This in itself was extraordinary because James moved from lifelessness to ordinary cardiac activity instantaneously. However, this is only part of the story. After sixty-one minutes of cardiac arrest and significant oxygen deprivation (except for the times during which CPR was administered), doctors expected James to suffer from massive organ failure. When this did not occur, they predicted that he would be severely disabled, noting that he would probably have cerebral palsy, requiring him to be strapped to a wheelchair with feeding tubes for the rest of his life, and consigning him to blindness and virtually no mental activity. Contrary to all expectations, James did not manifest any of these deficiencies or symptoms, but very clearly continued to develop like a normal child.

A seven-member panel of medical specialists assembled in Peoria (the place of the miracle) to examine all medical records associated with the case as well as James himself. They concluded in March 2014 that James' recovery and development could not be explained through any scientifically known natural causation. Given the circumstances, he should have been either dead or severely disabled. A panel of theologians was subsequently convened that rendered a decision attributing James' restoration to health as a miracle occurring through the intercession of Archbishop Fulton J. Sheen.

C. A Miracle Attributed to Pope Saint John Paul II

The second miracle leading to the canonization of Pope John Paul II concerned a fifty-year-old woman from Santiago, Costa Rica: Floribeth Mora Diaz.[56] She suffered a brain aneurysm in April 2011. After a series of tests in a hospital, including a brain scan, and after a three-hour operation, the doctors told her that her condition was inoperable and terminal and that she would have only one month to live.

After receiving the bad news, Floribeth went home and was consigned to bed to keep her comfortable for the remainder of her short life. She had a strong devotion to Pope John Paul II and so began praying for his intercession so that she could live to be with and help her husband and four children. The beatification of Pope John Paul II was scheduled to take place on May 1, 2011, and Floribeth decided to watch the events on T.V. After watching the beatification she went to sleep, at which time she had a vision of John Paul II speaking to her, saying, "Get up! Don't be afraid!" Much to the surprise of her husband, she got out of bed and told him that she felt well—and that this had occurred after a vision of Pope John Paul II. Floribeth subsequently underwent several medical tests—including new brain scans—which left her neurologist and other doctors completely stupefied by her recovery. They declared that her virtually instantaneous cure on May 1 at 2:00 A.M. was scientifically inexplicable by any known natural agency. Later, a commission of medical physicians was assembled by the Vatican who brought Floribeth to Rome in secret and admitted her to a hospital for a new examination, comparing her current state of health to neurological records and scans from before her cure on May 1, 2011. They also concluded

---

[56] For an interview with the head physician, see Harriet Alexander, "John Paul II Sainthood: Was the Recovery of Brain-Injured Woman Really a Miracle?", *Telegraph*, July 5, 2013, https://www.telegraph.co.uk/news/worldnews/europe/vaticancityandholysee/10162835 /John-Paul-II-sainthood-was-the-recovery-of-brain-injured-woman-really-a-miracle.html. For an interview with Floribeth Mora Diaz, see Pepe Alonso, "Mora's Miracle: The Costa Rican Woman Who Was Healed through John Paul II's Intercession", *National Catholic Register*, September 26, 2013, http://www.ncregister.com/daily-news/moras-miracle-the-costa -rican-woman-who-was-healed-through-john-paul-iis-in. For a general description, see also Marta Jimenez, "Woman Healed by John Paul II's Intercession Recounts Miracle", *Catholic News Agency*, April 25, 2014, https://www.catholicnewsagency.com/news/woman-healed-by -john-paul-iis-intercession-recounts-miracle.

that her cure was scientifically inexplicable. This paved the way for the theological commission and Pope Francis to declare Pope John Paul II to be a saint.

III. A Contemporary Eucharistic Miracle

A true Eucharistic miracle occurs at every Holy Mass when the priest utters the words of Consecration and the substance of the bread is transformed into the substance of Jesus' Body and the substance of the wine is transformed into the substance of His Blood. However, this term is sometimes used to refer to extraordinary empirical signs of Jesus' presence in the Eucharist, most notably, bleeding Hosts, or the transmutation of a consecrated Host into a piece of cardiac muscle tissue. The first reported Eucharistic miracle of the second (rarer) sort, the miracle of Lanciano, took place in the eighth century.

Eucharistic miracles are quite difficult to certify scientifically, because of problems certifying that the blood came from the Host or that the transmuted flesh was originally a consecrated Host. However, one notable exception to this difficulty occurred under the auspices of Pope Francis (at that time Bishop Jorge Bergoglio, the auxiliary bishop of Buenos Aires) on August 18, 1996, in the Church of Santa Maria y Caballito Almagro in Buenos Aires, Argentina.[57]

On that day in the evening, Father Alejandro Pezet, the priest who celebrated Mass that day, was told by a woman parishioner that a consecrated Host had been discarded on a candleholder in the back of the church. Unable to consume the Host, Father Pezet put it into a glass of water and into the tabernacle so that it would dissolve (the ordinary practice for respectfully handling such a Host). When he opened the tabernacle on August 26, he saw that the Host had been transformed into a piece of bloody tissue that was larger than the original Host. He informed Bishop Bergoglio of the occurrence,

---

[57]For documentation of forensic examination, genetic testing, and pathology report, as well as photographs, see Ron Tesoriero, *Reason to Believe* (Australia: Ron Tesoriero Publishing, 2007).

See also Mieczyslaw Piotrowski, "Eucharistic Miracle in Buenos Aires", *Love One Another!* 2010. For a summary of this article, see "Eucharistic Miracle Beheld by Pope Francis?", Aleteia.org, April 22, 2016, https://aleteia.org/2016/04/22/eucharistic-miracle-beheld-by-pope-francis/.

who asked him to have the Host professionally photographed. This occurred on September 6, 1996. It was decided to keep the Host in the tabernacle without publicizing it or its origin.

After three years, the bloody tissue had not decomposed (which is truly extraordinary and virtually impossible to explain through natural causation, particularly because no special attempt was made to preserve it). Since the original photographs revealed the complete lack of decomposition, Bishop Bergoglio asked that the bloody tissue be scientifically examined. According to an article written by Mieczyslaw Piotrowski, "On October 5, 1999, in the presence of the [Bishop's] representatives, scientist Dr. Ricardo Castanon Gomez took a sample of the bloody fragment and sent it to New York for analysis."[58] The article further states that since Dr. Gomez did not want to prejudice the scientific committee who would be examining the tissue in New York, he did not reveal its source. A team of five scientists was assembled, including the famous cardiologist and forensic pathologist Dr. Frederick Zugibe (author of many books on forensic pathology, deceased 2013[59]). Zugibe testified that

> the analyzed material is a fragment of the heart muscle found in the wall of the left ventricle close to the valves. This muscle is responsible for the contraction of the heart. It should be borne in mind that the left cardiac ventricle pumps blood to all parts of the body. The heart muscle is in an inflammatory condition and contains a large number of white blood cells. This indicates that the heart was alive at the time the sample was taken. It is my contention that the heart was alive, since white blood cells die outside a living organism. They require a living organism to sustain them. Thus, their presence indicates that the heart was alive when the sample was taken. What is more, these white blood cells had penetrated the tissue, which further indicates that the heart had been under severe stress, as if the owner had been beaten severely about the chest.[60]

---

[58] Piotrowski, "Eucharistic Miracle in Buenos Aires", cited in "Eucharistic Miracle Beheld by Pope Francis?"

[59] For a biography of Frederick Zugibe, see "Crucifixion and Shroud Studies: Medical Aspects of the Crucifixion", Crucifixion-Shroud.com, accessed July 2, 2020, www.crucifixion-shroud.com/bio.htm.

[60] Piotrowski, "Eucharistic Miracle in Buenos Aires", cited in "Eucharistic Miracle Beheld by Pope Francis?"

What is so remarkable about this testimony is not so much the fact that the tissues come from the wall of the left ventricle, but that white blood cells are present in large numbers in it, requiring that the tissue be removed when the heart was still alive and pumping. This feature precludes a great number of possible scenarios of fraud that a critic might propose—for it cannot be thought that officials in the Church had authorized the torture and death of a male with AB positive blood type (the same as on the Shroud of Turin and the Sudarium, face cloth of Oviedo), opened his chest while he was still alive (after torturing him), and removed the tissue from his beating heart. If this scenario is out of the question, then one must ask the origin of this tissue that came from the tabernacle where the desecrated Host was stored (as witnessed by the physician who extracted it, Dr. Ricardo Castanon Gomez). How did a piece of nondecomposing cardiac muscle tissue from the wall of the left ventricle with significant numbers of white blood cells (which had penetrated the tissue) make its way into the glass inside the tabernacle where the discarded Host had been stored in secret by Father Alejandro Pezet? How did this specific piece of tissue (which could only have come from a live, tortured subject) make its way into the tabernacle?

The major factors needed to avert the criticism of "pious fraud" are in place, because solid medical evaluation shows that the sample had not decomposed and cannot be obtained from a deceased subject (i.e., a cadaver). Short of the fantastic scenario mentioned above, this nondecomposing piece of tissue appears to be the result of a transmutation of a consecrated, discarded Host witnessed not only by Father Alejandro Pezet, but also by his bishop, Jorge Bergoglio (Pope Francis).

IV. Conclusion

The above three Marian apparitions (and the miracles associated with them), the three intercessory miracles of the saints, and the Eucharistic miracle witnessed by Pope Francis, are but a very small sample of miracles manifest in the twentieth century. They are recounted here because they have been subject to considerable scientific scrutiny by experts who are believers and nonbelievers. As noted above, the

Lourdes Medical Bureau has certified seventy miracles, the complete documentation for which is available through the bureau. Yet these seventy miracles do not exhaust the miracles of Lourdes; there are literally thousands of them that have not been subject to the above scientific scrutiny or could not be unanimously declared by believing and unbelieving scientists to be *completely* beyond scientific and natural explanation. The same holds true for healing miracles associated with the tilma of Our Lady of Guadalupe and the water and apparition of Our Lady of Fatima. Padre Pio performed dozens of miracles during his lifetime, and every canonized saint in the twentieth century had to be connected with at least two miracles judged to be completely scientifically and naturally inexplicable. Though Eucharistic miracles are much rarer, the above miracle associated with Pope Francis in Buenos Aires does not exhaust the domain of Eucharistic miracles.[61] Moreover, as noted above, there are literally thousands of miracles associated with charismatic healing services (in the name of Jesus) that have been catalogued and reported.[62]

The above miracles not only help to give credence to Christian faith, the risen Jesus, and His Real Presence in the Eucharist, but also ground the rich theology of the Blessed Virgin Mary and the saints that constitute the Mystical Body and the living tradition of the Catholic Church. It seems strange to me that some Christian denominations think that God would not want to share His glory and His Son's glorification with all of us—and allow our little unique sparks of glorified goodness and love to constitute His Son's Mystical Body. After all, all Christians acknowledge that God is unconditional love, and as such, He cannot possibly want to hoard His glory for Himself. His nature is to give it away, to share it, to create community, and to allow His infinite richness to be expressed like countless little finite expressions that come together in His providential weave like a gigantic tapestry.

The Christian view of God shouts out that He would not only share His glory, but delight in its being freely appropriated and

---

[61] For example, one has been recently reported in Poland. See "Check Out This New Eucharistic Miracle in Poland", *Catholic News Agency*, April 18, 2016, https://www.catholicnewsagency.com/news/check-out-this-eucharistic-miracle-in-poland-96162.

[62] For a list of websites that publish nonvalidated accounts of miracles by the Holy Spirit in the name of Jesus and a list of books about contemporary miracles done through the Holy Spirit and the name of Jesus, see note 5 in the introduction of this appendix.

magnified again with everyone in the Mystical Body. Hence, devotion and prayers to the Blessed Virgin Mary and the saints is perfectly consistent with His infinitely good and loving nature, and it enriches our experience of His goodness, glory, and love. Since we are finite in intellection and intuition, we cannot appropriate God's infinite glory, goodness, and love in a single intuitive moment. All we can do is appreciate finite manifestations of that glory in His incarnate Son, in the goodness and wisdom of Scripture, in the manifestations of the Blessed Virgin Mary, who has become our Mother, and in the lives of the saints, who, though imperfect, reflect in so many extraordinary ways God's glory, love, and goodness in their lives.

This fills our contemplative experience with great richness, for it breaks the Divine Light into a multifaceted spectrum, enabling us to appreciate ever more deeply not only the infinite goodness and love of God, but also His glory and beauty. Gerard Manley Hopkins expressed His glory and beauty in nature in his poems "God's Grandeur" and "The Wind Hover", but he also saw God's beauty manifest in the goodness and love of the saints in his poem "Kingfishers". Beginning with God's glory, beauty, and richness manifest in nature, he concludes with his recognition of a higher beauty manifest in justice and love:

> As kingfishers catch fire, dragonflies draw flame;
> As tumbled over rim in roundy wells
> Stones ring; like each tucked string tells, each hung bell's
> Bow swung finds tongue to fling out broad its name;
> Each mortal thing does one thing and the same:
> deals out that being indoors each one dwells;
> Selves—goes itself; *myself* it speaks and spells,
> Crying *Whát I dó is me: for that I came.*
> I say móre: the just man justices;
> Keeps grace: thát keeps all his goings graces;
> Acts in God's eye what in God's eye he is—
> Chríst—for Christ plays in ten thousand places,
> Lovely in limbs, and lovely in eyes not his
> To the Father through the features of men's faces.[63]

---

[63] Gerard Manley Hopkins, "As Kingfishers Catch Fire", in *Gerard Manley Hopkins: Poems and Prose* (London: Penguin Classics, 1953), p. 51.

What Hopkins understood is that Christ's glory is expressed not only in His goodness, love, and truth, but also in the beauty of His Person. Beauty awakens us, takes hold of us, and moves us deeply within our being, filling us with a sense of appreciation, awe, resonance, harmony, and fulfillment. It moves us at once to great excitement and great calm as if it is filling our deepest interior needs with a completion or fulfillment beyond our capacity to produce. Beauty takes hold of us—we do not take hold of it—and when the highest beauties of the divine Person, love, goodness, and truth take hold of us, they can move us not only to feelings of ecstasy, but also to an awareness of holiness, mystery, and communion with God. In the first volume of his trilogy *Glory*, Hans Urs von Balthasar expresses it this way:

> Before the beautiful—no, not really *before* but *within* the beautiful—the whole person quivers. He not only "finds" the beautiful moving; rather, he experiences himself as being moved and possessed by it.[64]

Von Balthasar's observation pertains to all beauty—from natural beauty to divine beauty; but when it applies to divine beauty, the feelings and consciousness awakened by it reach a supernatural height. This insight helps to reveal why God would share His glory with the Blessed Virgin Mary and the saints. It is not only because such sharing is consistent with His unrestricted goodness and love, but because it is part of His plan to awaken our sense of appreciation, awe, wonder, sacredness, and joy revealed in the beauty of the goodness and love of His Son's Mother and the saints. As we contemplate the life of the Virgin Mary and include her in our prayers— and further contemplate the lives of the saints, in their goodness, holiness, and love—we put a prism in front of the light of God's unrestricted glory, making it a myriad of interwoven colors and shapes, a veritable symphony of holiness and love. The above miracles not only serve to validate this view of the God of Jesus Christ, but also reveal the same beauty of goodness and love that they validate. Miracles—scientifically and naturally inexplicable events—are not only real; they validate the truth

---

[64] Cited in Edward T. Oakes and David Moss, eds. *The Cambridge Companion to Hans Urs von Balthasar* (Cambridge, Mass.: Cambridge University Press, 2004), p 270.

of God's presence, goodness, and love, and above all, they reveal His beauty, glory, mystery, holiness, and majesty—they fill us with wonder, awe, fascination, and delight, the very thing lacking in a purely mundane materialistic view of reality. If we are to enjoy their richness to the full, we will also want to practice devotion to the Blessed Virgin Mary (through the Rosary) and allow ourselves to be moved by lives of the saints who reflect the glory and grandeur of God.

BIBLIOGRAPHY

Alexander, Eben. "My Experience in Coma". *Journal of Neurosurgery* 21, no. 2 (2012). http://www.ebenalexander.com/my-experience -in-coma/.

Alexander, Harriet. "John Paul II Sainthood: Was the Recovery of Brain-Injured Woman Really a Miracle?" *Telegraph*, July 5, 2013. https://www.telegraph.co.uk/news/worldnews/europe/vatican cityandholysee/10162835/John-Paul-II-sainthood-was-the -recovery-of-brain-injured-woman-really-a-miracle.html.

Allegri, Renzo. *Padre Pio: Man of Hope.* Ann Arbor, Mich.: Charis Books, 2000.

Allen, Thomas B. *Possessed: The True Story of an Exorcism.* Lincoln, Neb.: iUniverse.com, 2000.

Alonso, Pepe. "Mora's Miracle: The Costa Rican Woman Who Was Healed through John Paul II's Intercession". *National Catholic Register*, September 26, 2013. http://www.ncregister.com/daily -news/moras-miracle-the-costa-rican-woman-who-was-healed -through-john-paul-iis-in.

Anderson, Carl. *Our Lady of Guadalupe: Mother of the Civilization of Love.* New York: Doubleday Religion, 2009.

Aquinas, Thomas, Saint. *Summa Theologica.* Edited and translated by Fathers of the English Dominican Province. Vols. 1–3. New York: Benziger Brothers, 1947.

Aristotle. *Rhetoric.* In *Basic Works of Aristotle.* Edited and translated by Richard Mckeon. New York: Random House, 1941.

Armstrong, Patti. "Parish Priest Aids Family in Fight against Demons". *National Catholic Register*, February 11, 2014. http:// www.ncregister.com/daily-news/parish-priest-aids-family-in-fight -against-demons.

Aromiekim. "Tibetan Buddhism: Ghosts, Demons, and Exorcisms". *Exorcise Me* (blog), January 28, 2015. https://exorciseme.word press.com/2015/01/28/tibetan-buddhism-ghosts-demons-and -exorcism/.

Augustine, Saint. *Confessions*. Translated by Henry Chadwick. New York: Oxford University Press, 2009.

―――. *De Moribus Ecclesiae Catholica (Of the Morals of the Catholic Church)*. Edited by Philip Schaff. Translated by Richard Stothert. Self-published, CreateSpace, 2015.

Baglio, Matt. *The Rite: The Making of a Modern Exorcist*. 1st ed. New York: Doubleday, 2009.

―――. *The Rite: The Making of a Modern Exorcist*. New York: Doubleday, 2010.

Barlow, Eleanor. "Liverpool 'Miracle' Soldier's Story to Be Told in Documentary Directed by Great-Great-Grandson". *Echo News* (Liverpool), June 11, 2016. http://www.liverpoolecho.co.uk/news /liverpool-news/liverpool-miracle-soldiers-story-told-11455815.

Barnes, Albert. "Albert Barnes' Notes on the Whole Bible", 1870 commentary on Matthew 16:18. StudyLight.org. Accessed April 8, 2020. https://www.studylight.org/commentaries/bnb/matthew-16 .html.

Beauregard, Mario. *Brain Wars: The Scientific Battle over the Existence of the Mind and the Proof That Will Change the Way We Live*. New York: HarperOne, 2012.

Benedict XVI. *Light of the World: The Pope, the Church, and the Signs of the Times; A Conversation with Peter Seewald*. Translated by Michael J. Miller and Adrian J. Walker. San Francisco: Ignatius Press, 2010.

Betty, Stafford. "The Growing Evidence for 'Demonic Possession': What Should Psychiatry's Response Be?" *Journal of Religion and Health* 44, no. 1 (Spring 2005): 13–30. http://www.ucs.mun.ca /~jporter/spiritualism/Stafford%20demonic%20possession.pdf.

Brading, D. A. *Mexican Phoenix: Our Lady of Guadalupe; Image and Tradition across Five Centuries*. Cambridge, Mass.: Cambridge University Press, 2001.

Brown, Michael. "An Interview with the Priest Involved in the Case behind *The Exorcist*". *Spirit Daily*. Accessed April 11, 2020. https:// www.spiritdaily.org/Halloran.htm.

Brown, Raymond. *An Introduction to New Testament Christology*. New York: Paulist Press, 1994.

Callahan, P. *The Tilma under Infrared Radiation: CARA Studies in Popular Devotion*. Vol. 2, *Guadalupe Studies, n° 3*. Washington, D.C.: Center for Applied Research in the Apostolate, 1981.

Callaway, Ewen. "Sex and Violence Linked in the Brain". *Nature*, February 9, 2011. http://www.nature.com/news/2011/110209/full /news.2011.82.html.

Carrel, Alexis. *The Voyage to Lourdes*. Translated by Virgilia Peterson. New York: Harper Brothers, 1950. http://www.basicincome.com /bp/files/The_Voyage_to_Lourdes.pdf.

————. *The Voyage to Lourdes*. New Hope, Ky.: Real View Books, 1994.

Catechism of the Catholic Church. 2nd ed. Washington, D.C.: Libreria Editrice Vaticana—United States Conference of Catholic Bishops, 2000. http://ccc.usccb.org/flipbooks/catechism/index.html.

Chesterton, G.K. *Orthodoxy*. Reprint of the 1908 edition, Project Gutenberg, 2005. https://archive.org/stream/orthodoxy16769gut /16769.txt.

Churchich, Nicholas. *Marxism and Morality: A Critical Examination of Marxist Ethics*. Cambridge, U.K.: James Clarke, 1994.

Churchill, Winston. "We Shall Fight on the Beaches". International Churchill Society, June 4, 1940. https://www.winstonchurchill .org/resources/speeches/1940-the-finest-hour/we-shall-fight-on -the-beaches.

Cleave, Maureen. "How Does a Beatle Live? John Lennon Lives Like This", an interview with John Lennon. *London Evening Standard*, March 4, 1966.

Clift, Jean Dalby, and Wallace Clift. *Symbols of Transformation in Dreams*. New York: Crossroad Publishing, 1984.

Collins, Adela Yarbro. "The Apocalypse". In *The New Jerome Biblical Commentary*, pp. 996–1016. Englewood Cliffs, N.J.: Prentice-Hall, 1990.

Cooper, Terry, and Cindy Epperson. *Evil: Satan, Sin, and Psychology*. Mahwah, N.J.: Paulist Press, 2008.

Cranston, Ruth. *The Miracle of Lourdes*. Doubleday Image, 1988.

————. *The Mystery of Lourdes*. London: Evans Brothers, 1956.

Cristiani, Leon. *Evidence of Satan in the Modern World*. Rockford, Ill.: Tan Books and Publishers, 1961.

————. *Evidence of Satan in the Modern World*. Charlotte, N.C.: Tan Books and Publishers, 1977.

De Marchi, John. *Fatima: From the Beginning*. Fatima, Portugal: Missoes Consolata, 1981.

————. *The Immaculate Heart: The True Story of Our Lady of Fatima.* New York: Farrar, Straus and Young, 1952.

————. *The True Story of Fatima.* St. Paul, Minn.: Catechetical Guild, 1956.

Dervic, Kanita, Maria A. Oquendo, Michael F. Grunebaum, Steve Ellis, Ainsley Burke, J. John Mann. "Religious Affiliation and Suicide Attempt". *American Journal of Psychiatry* 161, no. 12 (December 2004): 2303–8. http://ajp.psychiatryonline.org/doi/abs/10.1176/appi.ajp.161.12.2303.

Dickens, Charles. *A Christmas Carol.* New York: Simon & Brown, 2010.

Doles, Jeff. *Miracles and Manifestations of the Holy Spirit in the History of the Church.* Seffner, Fla.: Walking Barefoot Ministries, 2008.

Engels, Friedrich. *Anti-Duhring.* India: Leopard Books, 1878.

Faraday, Ann. *The Dream Game.* New York: Harper & Row, 1990.

Fitzgerald, F. Scott. *The Great Gatsby.* New York: Charles Scribner's Sons, 1925.

Fitzmyer, Joseph. *Luke the Theologian: Aspects of His Teaching.* New York: Paulist Press, 1989.

Forster, E. M. *A Room with a View.* London: Edward Arnold, 1908.

Fortea, Jose Antonio. *Interview with an Exorcist.* Westchester, Pa.: Ascension Press, 2006.

Freze, Michael. *The Rite of Exorcism: The Roman Ritual Rules, Procedures, Prayers of the Catholic Church.* Self-published, CreateSpace, 2016.

Gallagher, Richard E. "A Case of Demonic Possession—among the Many Counterfeits". *New Oxford Review* 75, no. 3 (March 2008). https://www.newoxfordreview.org/documents/a-case-of-demonic-possession/#.

————. "True and False Possessions, Revisited—in a Strange and Confusing Realm". *New Oxford Review,* May 2015. https://www.newoxfordreview.org/documents/true-false-possessions-revisited/#.

Glynn, Paul. *Healing Fire of Christ: Reflections on Modern Miracles— Knock, Lourdes, Fatima.* San Francisco: Ignatius Press, 2003.

Greyson, Bruce. "Seeing Dead People Not Known to Have Died: 'Peak in Darien' Experiences". *American Anthropological Association,* November 21, 2010. http://onlinelibrary.wiley.com/doi/10.1111/j.1548-1409.2010.01064.x/abstract.

Greyson, Bruce, and C.P. Flynn, eds. *The Near-Death Experience: Problems, Prospects, Perspectives*. Springfield, Ill.: Charles C. Thomas, 1984.

Groeschel, Benedict, C.F.R. "Mother Teresa Remembered". *First Things*, September 11, 2007. https://www.firstthings.com/web -exclusives/2007/09/mother-teresa-remembered.

————. *Spiritual Passages: The Psychology of Spiritual Development*. Valley, N.Y.: Crossroads Publishing, 1984.

Guerra, Giulio Dante. "La Madonna di Guadalupe: 'Inculturazione' Miracolosa". *Christianita*, 1992, pp. 205–6.

Hafiz, Yasmine. "Exorcism Conference at Vatican Addresses the Need for More Demon-Fighting Priests". *Huffington Post*, May 13, 2014. http://www.huffingtonpost.com/2014/05/13/exorcism -conference-rome-priests_n_5316749.html.

Haug, Werner, Paul Compton, and Youssef Courbage, eds. *Population Studies No. 31*. Vol. 2, *The Demographic Characteristics of National Minorities in Certain European States*. Strasbourg: Council of Europe Publishing, 2000.

Hegel, G.W.F. *Philosophy of Right*. Translated by S.W. Dyde. Kitchener, Ont.: Batoche Books, 2001.

Heiler, Friedrich. "The History of Religions as a Preparation for the Cooperation of Religions". In *The History of Religions*, edited by Mircea Eliade and J. Kitagawa, pp. 132–61. Chicago, Ill.: Chicago University Press, 1959.

Hilton, Donald. "Pornography Addiction—A Supranormal Stimulus Considered in the Context of Neuroplasticity". *Socioaffective Neuroscience and Psychology* 3 (July 19, 2013): 1–18. https://www.ncbi .nlm.nih.gov/pmc/articles/PMC3960020/.

Holden, Janice. *Handbook of Near Death Experiences: Thirty Years of Investigation*. Westport, Conn.: Praeger Press, 2009.

Hollingsworth, Barbara. "String Theory Co-Founder: Sub-Atomic Particles Are Evidence the Universe Was Created". CNSNews .com, June 17, 2016. http://www.cnsnews.com/news/article /barbara-hollingsworth/string-theory-co-founder-sub-atomic -particles-are-evidence-0.

Hopkins, Gerard Manley. "As Kingfishers Catch Fire". In *Gerard Manley Hopkins: Poems and Prose*, p. 51. London: Penguin Classics, 1953.

Hsu, Francis. *Suppression versus Repression: A Limited Psychological Interpretation of Four Cultures*. Chicago: Northwestern University Press, 1949.

Ignatius of Loyola, Saint. *The Autobiography of St. Ignatius*. Edited by J. F. X. O'Conor, S.J. New York: Benziger Brothers, 1900. https://books.google.com/books?id=T6dlAAAAMAAJ&q=manresa#v=snippet&q=manresa&f=false.

———. *Spiritual Exercises*. Translated by Elder Mullan, S.J. New York: P. J. Kenedy & Sons, 1914.

———. *The Spiritual Exercises of Saint Ignatius*. Translated by Anthony Mottola. New York: Image-Doubleday, 1989.

Isaacs, Craig. *Revelations and Possession: Distinguishing Spiritual from Psychological Experiences*. Kearney, Neb.: Morris Publishing, 2009.

Jaki, Stanley. *God and the Sun at Fatima*. Fraser, Mich.: Real View Books, 1999.

———. "Two Lourdes Miracles and a Nobel Laureate: What Really Happened?" Lecture given for the Catholic Medical Association on September 13, 1998, which was published by the Catholic Medical Association in February 1999. CatholicCulture.org. Accessed April 21, 2020. https://www.catholicculture.org/culture/library/view.cfm?recnum=2866.

Jeremias, Joachim. *New Testament Theology*. Vol. 1. London: SCM Press, 1971.

Jimenez, Marta. "Woman Healed by John Paul II's Intercession Recounts Miracle". *Catholic News Agency*, April 25, 2014. https://www.catholicnewsagency.com/news/woman-healed-by-john-paul-iis-intercession-recounts-miracle.

John of the Cross, Saint. *The Ascent of Mount Carmel*. In *The Collected Works of St. John of the Cross*, translated by Kieran Kavanaugh, O.C.D., and Otilio Rodriguez, O.C.D., pp. 73–292. Washington, D.C.: ICS Publications, 1979.

———. *The Collected Works of St. John of the Cross*. Translated by Kieran Kavanaugh, O.C.D., and Otilio Rodriguez, O.C.D. Washington, D.C.: ICS Publications, 2000.

———. *The Dark Night of the Soul*. In *The Collected Works of St. John of the Cross*, translated by Kieran Kavanaugh, O.C.D., and Otilio Rodriguez, O.C.D., pp. 293–389. Washington, D.C.: ICS Publications, 1979.

———. "The Living Flame of Love". In *The Collected Works of St. John of the Cross*, edited and translated by Kieran Kavanaugh, O.C.D., and Otilio Rodriguez, O.C.D., pp. 569–649. Washington, D.C.: ICS Publications, 1979.

———. *The Spiritual Canticle*. In *The Collected Works of St. John of the Cross*, translated by Kieran Kavanaugh, O.C.D., and Otilio Rodriguez, O.C.D., pp. 405–65. Washington, D.C.: ICS Publications, 1979.

Jordan, Elaine. "The Lourdes' Miracle of Gabriel Gargam". Tradition inAction.org, April 13, 2013. http://www.traditioninaction.org /religious/h106_Lourdes.htm.

Jung, C. G. *The Archetypes and the Collective Unconscious*. In *Collected Works of C. G. Jung*. Vol. 9, pt. 1, translated by R. F. C. Hull. Princeton, N.J.: Princeton University Press, 1981.

———. *Children's Dreams: Notes from the Seminar Given in 1936–1940*. Edited by Lorenz Jung and Maria Meyer-Grass. Translated by Ernst Falzeder. Princeton, N.J.: Princeton University Press, 2010.

Keener, Craig. *Miracles: The Credibility of the New Testament Accounts*. 2 vols. Grand Rapids, Mich.: Baker Academic, 2011.

Kelly, Edward F., Emily Williams Kelly, Adam Crabtree, Alan Gauld, Michael Grosso, and Bruce Greyson. *Irreducible Mind: Toward a Psychology for the 21st Century*. New York: Rowman & Littlefield, 2007.

Kelly, Emily. "Near-Death Experiences with Reports of Meeting Deceased People". *Death Studies* 25 (2001): 229–49.

Kelly, E. W., B. Greyson, and I. Stevenson. "Can Experiences Near Death Furnish Evidence of Life After Death?" *Omega: Journal of Death and Dying* 40 (2000): 39–45.

Kempis, Thomas à. *The Imitation of Christ*. Project Gutenberg, 1999. http://www.gutenberg.org/cache/epub/1653/pg1653-images .html.

Konstan, David, and N. K. Rutter. *Envy, Spite, and Jealousy: The Rivalrous Emotions in Ancient Greece*. Edinburgh: Edinburgh University Press, 2003.

Kreeft, Peter. *Everything You Ever Wanted to Know about Heaven—But Never Dreamed of Asking*. San Francisco: Ignatius Press, 1990.

Kwiatkowski, Marisa. "The Exorcisms of Latoya Ammons". *Indianapolis Star*, January 25, 2014. Updated October 31, 2019. http://www

.indystar.com/story/news/2014/01/25/the-disposession-of
-latoya-ammons/4892553/.

Lenin, Vladimir Ilyich. "The Attitude of the Workers' Party to Religion". *Proletary*, no. 45, May 13 (26), 1909. http://www.marxists.org/archive/lenin/works/1909/may/13.htm.

Levin, David S. "The Moral Relativism of Marxism". *Philosophical Forum* 15, no. 3 (1984): 249ff.

Lewis, C. S. *The Abolition of Man*. New York: HarperCollins, 1974.

———. *The Great Divorce*. New York: MacMillan, 1946.

———. *Miracles: A Preliminary Study*. New York: HarperOne, 1947.

———. *The Screwtape Letters*. New York: MacMillan, 1943.

———. *The Screwtape Letters*. Reprint of the 1941 edition, Quebec: Samizdat University Press, 2016. PDF e-book. http://www.samizdat.qc.ca/arts/lit/PDFs/ScrewtapeLetters_CSL.pdf.

———. *Surprised by Joy: The Shape of My Early Life*. New York: Harcourt, 1955.

Lin, D., M. P. Boyle, P. Dollar, H. Lee, E. S. Lein, P. Perona, and D. J. Anderson. "Functional Identification of an Aggression Locus in the Mouse Hypothalamus". *Nature* 470 (February 10, 2011): 221–26.

Lipka, Michael. "Millennials Increasingly Are Driving Growth of 'Nones' ". Pew Research Center, May 12, 2015. http://www.pewresearch.org/fact-tank/2015/05/12/millennials-increasingly-are -driving-growth-of-nones/.

———. "Why America's 'Nones' Left Religion Behind". Pew Research Center, August 24, 2016. http://www.pewresearch.org/fact-tank/2016/08/24/why-americas-nones-left-religion -behind/.

Lonergan, Bernard. *Method in Theology*. Edited by Robert M. Doran and John D. Dadosky. Vol. 14 of *The Collected Works of Bernard Lonergan*, edited by Frederick Crowe and Robert Doran. Toronto: University of Toronto Press, 1990.

Low, Robbie. "The Truth about Men and Church". *Touchstone: A Journal of Mere Christianity*, June 2003. http://www.touchstonemag.com/archives/article.php?id=16-05-024-v#ixzz4RjWtmadF.

Mabillard, Amanda. "The Relationship between Macbeth and the Witches". Shakespeare Online. Accessed April 20, 2020. http://www.shakespeare-online.com/faq/macbethfaq/macbethdarkness .html.

————. "What Was Shakespeare's Religion?" Shakespeare Online. Accessed April 20, 2020. http://www.shakespeare-online.com/faq /shakespearereligion.html.

Marx, Karl. *A Contribution to the Critique of Hegel's Philosophy of Right.* Paris, 1844. https://www.marxists.org/archive/marx/works/1843 /critique-hpr/intro.htm#05.

Marx, Karl, and Friedrich Engel. *Manifesto of the Communist Party.* Radford, Va.: Wilder Publications, 2007.

McGinn, Bernard. *The Essential Writings of Christian Mysticism.* New York: Random House/Modern Library, 2006.

McKenzie, John L. *Dictionary of the Bible.* New York: Macmillan Publishing, 1965.

Meier, John P. *A Marginal Jew: Rethinking the Historical Jesus.* Vol. 2, *Mentor, Message, and Miracles.* New York: Doubleday, 1994.

Milton, John. *Paradise Lost.* Project Gutenberg, 2011. http://www .gutenberg.org/cache/epub/20/pg20-images.html.

Nietzsche, Friedrich. *Beyond Good and Evil.* Translated and edited by William Kaufman. New York: Dover Publications, 1997.

————. *The Will to Power.* Translated by Walter Kaufmann. New York: Vintage Books, 1968.

Oakes, Edward T., and David Moss, eds. *The Cambridge Companion to Hans Urs von Balthasar.* Cambridge, Mass.: Cambridge University Press, 2004.

O'Connor, Patrick. "I Met a Miracle: The Story of Jack Traynor". Catholic Truth Society, 1943. Reproduced by FaithandFamily .org.UK by permission of the Catholic Truth Society. Accessed April 21, 2020. http://www.faithandfamily.org.uk/publications /jack_traynor.htm.

O'Mahony, Christopher, ed. *St. Thérèse of Lisieux by Those Who Knew Her.* Dublin: Pranstown House, 1989.

Orringer, Julie. "Suburban Sprawl: The Middlesteins". *New York Times,* December 27, 2012. https://www.nytimes.com/2012/12/30/books /review/the-middlesteins-by-jami-attenberg.html.

Osis, Karlis, and Erlendur Haraldsson. *At the Hour of Death: A New Look at Evidence for Life After Death.* 3rd ed. Norwalk, Conn.: Hastings House, 1997.

Ovid. *Metamorphoses 2.* Translated by Sir Samuel Garth et al. A.D. 1; MIT Classics, 1994. http://classics.mit.edu/Ovid/metam.2.second.html.

Page, Sydney. *Powers of Evil: A Biblical Study of Satan and Demons.* Grand Rapids, Mich.: Baker Books, 1995.

Parnia, Samuel, et al. "AWARE—AWAreness during REsuscitation—A Prospective Study". *Journal of Resuscitation*, October 6, 2014, pp. 1799–805. http://www.resuscitationjournal.com/article/S0300 -9572(14)00739-4/abstract.

Peck, Scott. *Glimpses of the Devil.* New York: Simon & Schuster, 2005.

Peralta, Alberta. "El Codice 1548: Critica a una supesta Fuente Guadalupana del Siglo SVI". *Artículos.* Proyecto Guadalupe, 2003.

Pieper, Josef. *Leisure: The Basis of Culture.* Translated by Gerald Malsbary. South Bend, Ind.: St. Augustine Press, 1998.

Piotrowski, Mieczyslaw. "Eucharistic Miracle in Buenos Aires". *Love One Another!* 2010. Summary of article: "Eucharistic Miracle Beheld by Pope Francis?", Aleteia.org, April 22, 2016. https://aleteia.org /2016/04/22/eucharistic-miracle-beheld-by-pope-francis/.

Plato. *Phaedrus.* Translated by R. Hackforth. In *The Collected Dialogues of Plato*, edited by Edith Hamilton and Huntington Cairns. Princeton, N.J.: Princeton University Press, 1961.

Pontifical Council for Justice and Peace. *Compendium of the Social Doctrine of the Church.* 2004; repr., Washington, D.C.: Libreria Editrice Vaticana—United States Conference of Catholic Bishops, 2005. http://www.vatican.va/roman_curia/pontifical_councils /justpeace/documents/rc_pc_justpeace_doc_20060526_com pendio-dott-soc_en.html.

Poole, Stafford. *The Guadalupan Controversies in Mexico.* Stanford, Calif.: Stanford University Press, 2006.

———. "History versus Juan Diego". *The Americas* 62, no. 1 (July 2005): 1–16. http://muse.jhu.edu/issue/9974.

Praveen, K. Parboteeah, Martin Hoegl, and John B. Cullen. "Ethics and Religion: An Empirical Test of a Multidimensional Model". *Journal of Business Ethics* 80, no. 2 (June 1, 2008): 387–98.

Prayer, Frances. "What Drives a Sex Addict? Is Sex Addiction about Love or an Insatiable Craving?" *Psychology Today*, October 7, 2009, pp. 1–4. http://www.psychologytoday.com/blog/love-doc /200910/what-drives-sex-addict.

Rajanala, Susruthi, Mayra Maymone, and Neelam Vashi. "Selfies—Living in the Era of Filtered Photographs". *JAMA Facial Plastic*

Surgery, August 2, 2018. https://jamanetwork.com/journals/jama facialplasticsurgery/article-abstract/2688763.

Ramsey, Paul. *Deeds and Rules in Christian Ethics*. Lanham, Md.: University of America Press, 1967.

Ring, Kenneth, Sharon Cooper, and Charles Tart. *Mindsight: Near-Death and Out-of-Body Experiences in the Blind*. Palo Alto, Calif.: William James Center for Consciousness Studies at the Institute of Transpersonal Psychology, 1999.

Ring, Kenneth, and Madelaine Lawrence. "Further Evidence for Veridical Perception during Near-Death Experiences". *Journal of Near-Death Studies* 11, no. 4 (Summer 1993): 223–29.

Rocha Cortes, Arturo, ed. " 'Documentos Mestizo' Codice 1548 o 'Escalada' " (the *Codex Escalada* 1548), Códice (1548). *Boletín Guadalupano*, Año II, Núm. 35 (Noviembre 2003): 5, 6 y 7.

Rossi, Paolino. "After Much Study, a Miracle". CatholicCulture .org. From the magazine *Inside the Vatican*, April 1999, pp. 5–7. https://www.catholicculture.org/culture/library/view.cfm?id =1018&CFID=71847156&CFTOKEN=25822477.

Russell, David S. *The Method and Message of Jewish Apocalyptic*. Old Testament Library. Philadelphia: Westminster, 1964.

Schneible, Ann. "Practical Help for the Demon-Possessed: Vatican Rolls Out New Exorcism Course". *Catholic News Agency*, April 10, 2015. http://www.catholicnewsagency.com/news/practical-help -for-the-demon-possessed-vatican-rolls-out-new-exorcism-course -36248/.

Second Vatican Council. Dogmatic Constitution on the Church. *Lumen Gentium*, November 21, 1964. http://www.vatican.va/archive /hist_councils/ii_vatican_council/documents/vat-ii_const_1964 1121_lumen-gentium_en.html.

Sennott, Thomas Mary. "The Tilma of Guadalupe: A Scientific Analysis". MiracleHunter.com, 2015. http://www.miraclehunter .com/marian_apparitions/approved_apparitions/guadalupe/article _11.html.

Shakespeare, William. *Hamlet*. Project Gutenberg, 2019. http://www .gutenberg.org/files/1524/1524-h/1524-h.htm.

———. *The Merchant of Venice*. Project Gutenberg, 1998. http://www .gutenberg.org/cache/epub/1515/pg1515-images.html.

————. *Othello: The Moor of Venice*. Project Gutenberg, 2019. http://www.gutenberg.org/files/1531/1531-h/1531-h.htm.

————. *The Tragedy of Macbeth*. 1606; Project Gutenberg, 1997. http://www.gutenberg.org/cache/epub/1129/pg1129-images.html.

Sherratt, Yvonne. *Hitler's Philosophers*. New Haven: Yale University Press, 2013.

Shirer, William L., and Ron Rosenbaum. *The Rise and Fall of the Third Reich: A History of Nazi Germany*. New York: Simon & Schuster, 2011.

Smith, Peter Jesserer. "Archbishop Fulton Sheen Alleged Miracle Passes Major Vatican Test". *National Catholic Register*, March 7, 2014. http://www.ncregister.com/daily-news/archbishop-fulton-sheen-alleged-miracle-passes-major-vatican-test.

Spenser, Edmund. *The Faerie Queene*. Edited by John Hughes. Cambridge, Mass.: Cambridge University Press, 1715.

Spitzer, Robert J. *Finding True Happiness: Satisfying Our Restless Hearts*. San Francisco: Ignatius Press, 2015.

————. "Free Will and Original Sin". In *Credible Catholic Big Book*. Vol. 2, *Evidence of Our Transphysical Soul*. Magis Center, 2017. CredibleCatholic.com. Chapter 7. https://www.crediblecatholic.com/pdf/7E-P1/7E-BB2.pdf.

————. *God So Loved the World: Clues to Our Transcendent Destiny from the Revelation of Jesus*. San Francisco: Ignatius Press, 2016.

————. *The Light Shines on in the Darkness: Transforming Suffering through Faith*. San Francisco: Ignatius Press, 2017.

————. *New Proofs for the Existence of God: Contributions of Contemporary Physics and Philosophy*. Grand Rapids, Mich.: Eerdmans, 2010.

————. "Purgatory". In *Credible Catholic Big Book*. Vol. 5, *Central Doctrines of the Catholic Church*. Magis Center, 2017. CredibleCatholic.com. Chapter 9. https://www.crediblecatholic.com/pdf/M5/BB5.pdf.

————. *The Soul's Upward Yearning: Clues to Our Transcendent Nature from Experience and Reason*. San Francisco: Ignatius Press, 2015.

Squires, Nick. "Surge in Satanism Sparks Rise in Demand for Exorcists, Says Catholic Church". *Telegraph*, March 30, 2011. http://www.telegraph.co.uk/news/religion/8416104/Surge-in-Satanism-sparks-rise-in-demand-for-exorcists-says-Catholic-Church.html.

Stevenson, Ian. "The Contribution of Apparitions to the Evidence for Survival". *Journal of the American Society for Psychical Research* 76 (October 1982): 341–58. Available on the website of the Division of Perceptual Studies at https://med.virginia.edu/perceptual-studies /wp-content/uploads/sites/360/2017/09/The-Contributions-of -Apparitions-to-the-Evidence-for-Survival_-Ian-Stevenson-1982 .pdf.

Tanquerey, Adolphe. *The Spiritual Life: A Treatise on Ascetical and Mystical Theology.* Translated by Herman Branderis. First published, 1930; repub., Rockford, Ill.: Tan Books, 2000.

Taylor, Charles. *Malaise of Modernity.* Concord, Ont.: House of Anansi Press, 1998.

―――. *A Secular Age.* Cambridge, Mass.: Harvard University Press, 2007.

―――. *Sources of the Self: The Making of the Modern Identity.* New York: Cambridge University Press, 1992.

Teahan, Madeleine. "Fulton Sheen and the Miracle of Baby James". *Catholic Herald,* July 1, 2014.

Teresa of Avila, Saint. "The Book of Her Life". In *The Collected Works of St. Teresa of Avila,* translated by Kieran Kavanaugh and Otilio Rodriguez, 1:31–308. Washington, D.C.: ICS Publications, 1976.

Tesoriero, Ron. *Reason to Believe.* Australia: Ron Tesoriero Publishing, 2007.

Thrower, James. *Marxist-Leninist "Scientific Atheism" and the Study of Religion and Atheism in the USSR.* New York: Walter de Gruyter, 1983.

Tolstoy, Leo. *Anna Karenina.* Project Gutenberg, 2020. http://www .gutenberg.org/files/1399/1399-h/1399-h.htm.

Tonsmann, Jose' Aste. *El secreto de sus ojos.* Mexico City: Editorial Diana, 1981.

Townsend, Tim. "Paranormal Activity: Do Catholics Believe in Ghosts?" *U.S. Catholic* 78, no. 10 (October 2013): 12–17. http:// www.uscatholic.org/articles/201309/paranormal-activity-do -catholics-believe-ghosts-27887.

Twelftree, Graham. *Christ Triumphant: Exorcism Then and Now.* Hodder & Stoughton, 1985.

Underhill, Evelyn. *Mysticism: A Study in the Nature and Development of Spiritual Consciousness.* Mineola, N.Y.: Dover Publications, 2002.

——————. *Mysticism: A Study in the Nature and Development of Spiritual Consciousness.* New York: Renaissance Classics, 2012.

Van Lommel, Pim. "Continuity of Consciousness". International Association for Near-Death Studies. Last updated April 25, 2015. http://iands.org/research/nde-research/important-research-articles/43-dr-pim-van-lommel-md-continuity-of-consciousness.html.

Van Lommel, Pim, Ruud van Wees, Vincent Meyers, and Ingrid Elfferich. "Near-Death Experience in Survivors of Cardiac Arrest: A Prospective Study in the Netherlands". *The Lancet* 358, no. 9298 (2001): 2039–45.

Vogl, Carl. *Begone Satan! A True Account of an Exorcism in Earling, Iowa, in 1928.* Charlotte, N.C.: Tan Books, 2010.

Whitelock, Anna. "Elizabeth I: The Monarch behind the Mask". *BBC History Magazine,* June 1, 2013. www.historyextra.com/article/elizabeth-i/elizabeth-i-monarch-behind-mask.

Wigner, Eugene. "The Unreasonable Effectiveness of Mathematics in the Natural Sciences". *Communications in Pure and Applied Mathematics* 13, no.1 (February 1960). http://www.dartmouth.edu/~matc/MathDrama/reading/Wigner.html.

Wolpe, Rabbi David. "Dybbuks, Demons and Exorcism in Judaism". *Jewish Journal,* June 27, 2012. http://www.jewishjournal.com/cover_story/article/dybbuks_demons_and_exorcism_in_judaism_20120627.

Wright, N. T. *Jesus and the Victory of God.* Minneapolis: Fortress Press, 1996.

NAMES INDEX

Abadie, Jeanne, 371
Abel (biblical figure), 318, 319–20
Abraham (biblical figure), 127
Adam (biblical figure), 91, 92–93, 97,
    105, 318–19, 344
Agnes of Jesus (Pauline Martin), 230
Alexander, Eben, 136
Alexander, Harriet, 392n56
Allegri, Renzo, 69n23, 229n31,
    388n51
Allen, Thomas, 152–55, 157n51, 163,
    164n71, 171
Alonso, Pepe, 392n56
Ambrose of Milan, Saint, 222–23
Ammons, Latoya, 147, 175–76
Anderson, Carl, 371n16
Antiochus Epiphanes, 91–92
Antony of Rome (Mark Antony), 344
Apostoli, Andrew, 231
Aquinas. See Thomas Aquinas, Saint
Aristotle, 198, 206, 268, 309, 332–33
Armstrong, Patti, 147n29
Aste Tonsmann, Jose', 369–70
Attenberg, Jami, 266–67
Augustine of Hippo, Saint, 22, 36, 53,
    207nn15–16, 222–23, 357–58

Baglio, Matt, 26n12, 140n19, 141n20,
    143, 144, 147–48, 156n50, 175, 176
Bailly, Marie, 374, 375–77
Balthasar, Hans Urs von, 398
Bandura, Albert, 31, 32
Barlow, Eleanor, 380n37
Barnes, Albert, 123
Beauregard, Mario, 136
Benedict XIV (pope), 371
Benedict XVI (pope; formerly Joseph
    Ratzinger), 17

Bergoglio, Jorge Mario (later Pope
    Francis), 26n12, 63, 393–95, 396
Bernadette, Saint (Bernadette
    Soubirous), 371–74, 382–83
Bernardino, Juan, 367
Betty, Stafford, 140n18, 145n26
Bischofberger, George, 167
Bishop, Raymond J., S.J., 153,
    154n45, 155, 161–63, 164n71,
    167, 170
Blatty, William Peter, 152, 178
Blessed Virgin Mary. See Mary
Bober, Frank, 153
Boesky, Ivan, 274
Bolt, Robert, 272
Bowdern, William, S.J., 153, 162–71
Bradford, John, 359n47
Brading, D.A., 370n15
Braun, Eva, 355
Brown, Michael, 164n70, 171n81
Brown, Raymond, 99n16
Bueno, Javier Torroella, 369–70
Burke, Edmund (Jesuit priest), 167

Cain (biblical figure), 318, 319–20
Callahan, Philip Serna, 368, 369
Campbell, Steuart, 386
Carrel, Alexis, 374, 375–77, 382
Castanon Gomez, Ricardo, 394, 395
Chalmer, David, 201
Chaucer, Geoffrey, 263
Chesterton, G.K., 139
Churchill, Winston, 191–92
Cleave, Maureen, 294n18
Cleopatra, 344
Close, Glenn, 302
Coelho, Domingos Pinto, 384
Compton, Paul, 240n36

Cooper, Sharon, 136n3
Cooper, Terry, 154, 171–73
Cortes, Arturo Rocha, 367n6
Courbage, Youssef, 240n36
Cranston, Ruth, 379n33
Cristiani, Leon, 148, 156n50, 176, 229n30
Cullen, John B., 217n21

Dante Alighieri, 263
David (biblical figure), 333–35, 341
de Gaulle, Charles, 377
de Marchi, John, I.M.C., 384n39, 385, 387
DeFilippis, Carmine, 148n30
DeMille, Cecil B., 303–4
Dervic, Kanita, 197n10, 217n20, 218n23
Dibble, Charles E., 368
Dickens, Charles, 29, 261, 263, 270, 274–76, 302
"Doe, Roland". See "Robbie Mannheim" possession case, in Subject Index
Doles, Jeff, 365n5
Dostoyevsky, Fyodor, 29, 261, 263
Durks, Tim, 302n22

Ecklund, Anna, 148, 175
Einstein, Albert, 199
Elijah (biblical figure), 365
Elisha (biblical figure), 365
Elizabeth I (queen of England), 331–32, 348n36, 353
Engels, Friedrich, 330
Engstrom, Bonnie and Travis, 390–91
Engstrom, James Fulton, 390–91
Epperson, Cindy, 154, 171–73
Escalada, Xavier, 367
Evagrius Ponticus, 262, 263, 294, 295
Eve (biblical figure), 91, 105, 318–19, 333, 344

Faraday, Ann, 180n96
Fitzgerald, F. Scott, 261, 263, 286, 302

Fitzmyer, Joseph, 92n6
Flynn, C.P., 136n6
Forster, E.M., 292–94
Fortea, Jose Antonio, 143
Francis (pope; formerly Jorge Mario Bergoglio), 26n12, 63, 393–95, 396
Freze, Michael, 140n19
Fucci, Modestino, 389–90
Fuller, Reginald, 121

Galen, 309
Gallagher, Richard E., 28, 148–52, 154
Gargam, Gabriel, 375, 377–78
Garrett, Almeida, 385
Glynn, Paul, 377n29, 379n33
Gregory I (pope), 262, 294
Greyson, Bruce, 136
Groeschel, Benedict, C.F.R., 71n29, 230–31
Guerra, Giulio Dante, 368n8

Halloran, Walter H., S.J., 153, 154, 163, 165, 167, 170–71, 173
Haraldsson, Erlendur, 137n13
Harington, Sir John, 331–32
Haug, Werner, 240n36
Hegel, Georg Wilhelm Friedrich, 329
Heiler, Friedrich, 216n18
Hilton, Donald, 283n10, 283n12
Hitler, Adolf, 176, 327, 329, 331, 332, 339, 342, 353, 355, 356
Hoegl, Martin, 217n21
Holden, Janice, 136
Hollingsworth, Barbara, 365n4
Hopkins, Gerard Manley, 397–98
Hsu, Francis, 314n6
Hughes, E. Albert, 153–54, 159–60, 168, 173, 178
Hugo, Victor, 272–73

Ignatius of Loyola, Saint
   on discernment of spirits, 29, 56–57, 69n25, 247, 258, 259
   on Holy Spirit, 69–70
   as moral master, 18

on mysticism and contemplative
life, 77n41
Spiritual Exercises, 56–57, 69n25,
77n41, 211, 218n22, 227, 247,
249–52
on tactics of Satan, 211, 218n22,
227, 228, 247, 249–55, 258,
259
Irenaeus of Lyon, Saint, 99n16
Isaacs, Craig, 64, 65n6, 66–68, 143,
146, 173, 180–81

Jacomet (Police Commissioner at
Lourdes), 372
Jaki, Stanley, O.S.B., 69n22, 375,
376n23, 386n47
James, Saint, 101, 122
James I and VI (king of England and
Scotland), 348n36
Jeremias, Joachim, 98
Jimenez, Marta, 392n56
John XXIII, Saint (pope), 388
John Cassian, Saint, 262, 294, 295
John of the Cross, Saint
Ascent of Mount Carmel, The, 70n28,
76, 81n43, 227n26
Dark Night of the Soul, The, 76n40,
227n26
on deceit and discouragement, 253
"Living Flame of Love, The",
70n28, 86
as moral master, 18, 70, 71n32,
73–79, 81, 82, 85–86, 226–27,
253
on mysticism and contemplative
life, 70, 71n32, 73–79, 81, 82,
85–86
Spiritual Canticle, The, 70n28,
73–74, 78–79, 85n45
on temptation, 226–27
John Paul II, Saint (pope), 63, 366,
388, 389, 392–93
John Vianney, Saint, 148n32, 229
Jonathan (biblical figure), 334
Jones, Jim, 330, 339, 342

Jordan, Elaine, 377n29, 378n30
Juan Diego, 367–71, 382
Judas Iscariot, 124, 126, 127–29, 194,
339–42, 356, 359
"Julia" (possession/exorcism case), 28,
104, 147, 148–52, 154, 175
Jung, Carl, 43, 134, 180n94, 180n97

Kaku, Michio, 364–65
Keating, Frederick, 380
Keener, Craig, 365n5
Kelly, Emily, 136
Konstan, David, 317n7
Koresh, David, 330, 331, 339, 342
Kreeft, Peter, 138
Kuhn, Richard, 369
Kwiatkowski, Marisa, 147n29

Las Casas, Bartolomé de, O.P., 36
Latapie, Catherine, 373
Lawrence, Madelaine, 136n3
Lay, Kenneth, 274
Lenin, Vladimir, 330, 342
Lennon, John, 294
Leo XIII (pope), 36
Levin, David S., 330n23
Lewis, C.S.
on deadly sins, 277–78, 296–99,
306
Great Divorce, The, 277–78, 296–99,
306
on Holy Spirit, 69
on miracles, 363, 365, 386
on reality of Satan, 139n17, 141–42
Screwtape Letters, The, 141–42, 199,
233–34
on tactics of Satan, 199, 233–34,
248, 249
Lin, D., 283n11
Lipka, Michael, 21nn3–4
Locke, John, 36
Lonergan, Bernard, 19–20, 22
Louw, Johannes P., 322n9
Low, Robbie, 239–40n36
Lucas, George, 43, 134

Mabillard, Amanda, 348n36
Machiavelli, Niccolò, 327n13
Madoff, Bernie, 274
Maginot, Michael, 147
Mannheim, Robbie. *See* "Robbie Mannheim" possession case, *in Subject Index*
Margaret Mary, Saint, 162
Mark Antony (Antony of Rome), 344
Martin, Pauline (Agnes of Jesus), 230
Martino, Consiglia De, 389–90
Marto, Francisco, 383–84
Marto, Jacinta, 383–84
Marx, Karl, 17, 241, 330
Mary (mother of Jesus), 24, 27, 31, 43, 46, 63, 77, 131, 167, 181, 242, 365–88, 396–99
Mary Magdalene, 100
Mary, Queen of Scots, 331
Maymone, Mayra, 305n23
McConnell, Dr. (of Liverpool), 380
McKenzie, John L., 309n3
Meier, John P., 100–101
Michael, Saint, 131, 170, 171
Michal (biblical figure), 334
Milken, Michael, 274
Milton, John, 29, 248, 342, 344–48, 356
Mora Diaz, Floribeth, 392–93
More, Thomas, Saint, 272
Moses (biblical figure), 365
Murray, Henry A., 329n14, 332

Napoleon III (emperor of France), 373
Narcissus (mythical figure), 282, 295
Nebuchadnezzar (king of Babylon), 337, 344
Nicola, John J., 153
Nida, Eugene A., 322n9
Nietzsche, Friedrich, 329, 347

O'Boyle, Patrick, 159
O'Connor, Patrick, 379n33

O'Flaherty, John, 167, 170
Orringer, Julie, 266n4
Osis, Karlis, 137n13
Ovid, 29, 317–18, 320, 322, 326

Padre Pio, Saint, 63, 69, 229, 366, 388–90, 396
Page, Sydney, 91n1, 91n3, 92n5, 93n8, 94n10, 99n15, 103n21, 107n23, 111n27, 121n33, 128
Parboteeah, K. Praveen, 217n21
Parnia, Samuel, 135
Paul, Saint
    conversion of, 48356–57
    on deadly sins, 265–66
    on grace, 359n47
    on Holy Spirit, 46, 55, 116
    on moral conversion, 25, 30, 32, 33, 36, 39, 40, 222, 224–25, 361
    on peace, 48
    on tactics of Satan, 28, 227–28
    on victory of Jesus over Satan, 38, 95, 121, 122, 125–26, 185
Paul of the Cross, Saint, 85
Peck, Scott, 147
Peralta, Alberto, 368n7
Peter, Saint, 24, 30, 31, 55, 101, 118, 119, 121–26, 129, 194, 242, 300, 357, 361
Pezet, Alejandro, 393, 395
Pieper, Josef, 81n44
Piotrowski, Mieczyslaw, 393n57, 394
Pius IX (pope), 382
Pius X (pope), 374
Plato, 309
Prayer, Frances, 283n10
Presse, Alexis, 377
Pseudo-Dionysius the Areopagite, 71n32

Rajanala, Susruthi, 305n23
Ramsey, Paul, 54
Ratzinger, Joseph (later Pope Benedict XVI), 17

Reppetti, William, S.J., 153
Ribes (judge at Lourdes), 372
Rich, Richard, 272
Riesinger, Theophilus, 148
Ring, Kenneth, 135–36
"Roland Doe". *See* "Robbie
    Mannheim" possession case, *in*
    Subject Index
Rossi, Paolino, 389n52
Rowling, J.K., 43, 134
Russell, David S., 92n5, 93n9
Rutter, N.K., 317n7

Sahagun, Bernardino de, 368
Samuel (biblical figure), 333, 335
Santos, Lucia, 383–84
Saul (biblical figure), 333–36, 339,
    341–42, 356
Schell, Albert, 167
Schneible, Ann, 26n12
Schrödinger, Erwin, 363, 364
Schulze, Luther, 158–59
Semiramis (queen of Syria), 344
Seneca, 309
Sennott, Thomas Mary, 368n9
Shakespeare, William
    on anger, 311–14
    on deadly sins, 261, 263, 272,
        311–14, 323–26, 330n24, 331,
        342, 348–56, 359
    on envy, 323–26
    on greed, 272
    Hamlet, 29, 236n35, 311–14, 348n36,
        356, 359
    Julius Caesar, 323
    King Lear, 215
    Macbeth, 29, 215, 272, 331, 342,
        348–56
    Merchant of Venice, The, 323, 330n24
    Othello, 29–30, 215, 323–26, 356
    on pride, 330n24, 331, 342, 348–56
    religious beliefs of, 348n36
    Richard III, 215, 323
    on tactics of Satan, 215, 220, 236n35

Sheen, Blessed Fulton J., 63, 366, 388,
    389, 390–91
Sherratt, Yvonne, 329n17
Smith, Peter Jesserer, 390n55
Socrates, 223
Soubirous, Bernadette, Saint, 371–74,
    382–83
Soubirous, Toinette, 371
Spenser, Edmund, 29, 263, 322–23,
    326, 342–44, 356
Squires, Nick, 27n12
Stalin, Joseph, 176, 327, 330, 342, 356
Stevenson, Ian, 136n5, 137
Stone, Oliver, 273
Suarez, Francisco, S.J., 36

Tanquerey, Adolphe, 65n5, 68
Tart, Charles, 136n3
Taylor, Charles, 243n39
Teahan, Madeleine, 390n55
Teresa of Avila, Saint, 18, 70, 71n32,
    72, 73, 82, 248, 253, 259
Teresa of Calcutta, Saint, 85, 229–31
Thérèse of Lisieux, Saint, 85, 229–30
Thomas, Gary, 148
Thomas à Kempis, 295n19
Thomas Aquinas, Saint, 36, 54–55,
    71n32, 207n15, 245, 262–63, 270
Thrower, James, 330n20
Tolkien, J.R.R., 43, 44, 134, 190–91
Tolstoy, Leo, 29, 261, 263, 285,
    286–90, 302, 355, 359
Torrija Lavoignet, Rafael, 369–70
Townsend, Tim, 138n14
Traynor, John, 375, 379–80
Twelftree, Graham, 120

Underhill, Evelyn, 39, 65n7, 66n9,
    68, 71n29, 86

Valeriano, Antonio, 368
van Lommel, Pim, 135, 136
Van Roo, William, 163, 165, 167, 168
Vashi, Neelam, 305n23

Vianney, Saint Jean, 148n32, 229
Virgil, 29, 261
Virgin Mary. *See* Mary
Vogl, Carl, 148

Weiser, Stanley, 273
Whitelock, Anna, 331–32

Wigner, Eugene, 363–64
Wright, N. T., 20, 24, 99, 106

Yarbro Collins, Adela, 130–31

Zugibe, Frederick, 394
Zumarraga, Juan de, 367, 369, 370

SUBJECT INDEX

"Abba", God as, 193, 310, 382
acedia. *See* sloth
addiction, 265–69, 283–84
adultery, 35, 285–90
Adversus Haereses (Irenaeus of Lyon), 99n16
affective consolation and desolation, 247–56
agapē/caritas, 49–50, 57, 59–61, 71n33, 295
Alcoholics Anonymous, 240
alternate personalities, emergence of, in possessions, 143, 144, 146, 149–50, 168, 171–72, 173
Amazing Parish, 195n9
American Medical Association, 305
American Psychiatric Association, 150n36, 197, 217, 218, 221, 233, 238
angels
    fallen angels story, 89, 92n5, 93n9, 110–11, 117, 344–48
    Fatima, "Angel of Peace" at, 383
    Satan/demon disguised as angel of light, 28n14, 95, 188–89, 227, 247, 256–59
    "sons of God" in Genesis, 89, 92n5
anger, 309–15
    destructiveness of, 314, 355–56
    forgiveness as means of dispelling, 314–15
    individual tendencies toward, 212

Names of individual persons are listed in the separate Names Index, with the exception of the Persons of the Trinity and Satan—these are in the Subject Index.

literary examples of, 311–14
philosophers' views of, 309
positive views of, 309
psychiatrists' views of, 314
scriptural approaches to, 309–11
vengeance at root of, 308
Anna Karenina (Tolstoy), 285, 286–90, 302, 355, 359
apparitions, ghosts, or spirits of the dead, 137–38
apparitions, miraculous. *See* Marian apparitions; miracles, visions, and revelations
archetypal theory, 180n94
"As Kingfishers Catch Fire" (Gerard Manley Hopkins), 397–98
The Ascent of Mount Carmel (John of the Cross), 70n28, 76, 81n43, 227n26
avarice. *See* greed

Beatitudes, 58–60, 71n33, 193, 295, 321
Beatles, 294
beauty, 397–99
Beelzebul. *See* Satan
Beelzebul accusation (in New Testament), 106–10, 111
Begone Satan! (Vogl), 148
Beyond Good and Evil (Nietzsche), 329n14
biological reductionism, 241, 247
bipolar disorder, 151, 173, 206
blaspheming Holy Spirit, as unforgiveable sin, 109–10
blind people, NDEs of, 135–36
body dysmorphic disorder, 306
Bolsheviks, 330

Bride/Bridegroom imagery, 73–74, 79, 85, 86

Called and Gifted, 195n9
Called Out of Darkness (Spitzer). See Trilogy
cardinal sins or vices. See deadly sins
cardinal virtues, 191n3, 207–11, 215
caritas/agapē, 49–50, 57, 59, 71n33, 295
catechetics, intellectual conversion in, 21–22
Catechism of the Catholic Church, 193n6, 194, 243n38
Catholic Church. See Church
Catholic Medical Association, 375n20
CCS (Congregation for the Causes of Saints), Medical Committee, 390
"Charlie Charlie" game, 141
chastity, as virtue, 279, 285, 290
Christian mysticism. See mysticism and contemplative life
Christian-Faith.com, 365n5
Christmas Carol, A (Dickens), 270, 274–77, 302
Church
  grace of God in, 359–61
  Happiness/Purpose Levels and commitment to, 216, 219–21
  initiation of, under Peter, 119, 121–26
  Marian apparitions validated by, 366, 373
  miraculous cures at Lourdes validated by, 374
  occultism and Satanism, concerns about rise of, 26n12, 141n20
  participation in, against powers of evil, 187, 188, 191, 193–95, 196–200
  power over demons given to, 90, 119–26
  religious commitment, Satan's efforts to undermine, 231–34

religious conviction and ethical behavior, connection between, 216–18, 239–40
  ridiculing and marginalizing of, 243–44
  saints, canonization process for, 388
  social ethics of, 36–37
  in Spitzer's Trilogy, 30–37
Code of Holiness, 285
Codex Escalada, 367
"comparison game", negative emotions of, 301–2
Confession. See Reconciliation, Sacrament of
Confessions (Augustine of Hippo), 22, 222–23, 358
Congregation for the Causes of Saints (CCS), Medical Committee, 390
Congregation for the Doctrine of the Faith, 366
consolation and desolation. See under deceit and discouragement
contemplative life. See mysticism and contemplative life
conversion
  intellectual, 20–22, 23–24
  Levels 1–4 of (See specific entries at Level)
  moral, 24–26, 30–33, 37, 190, 191, 216, 225, 360
  progress in, 18–19, 37–40
  spiritual, 22–24, 30–33, 190, 191, 216, 225
  three dimensions of, 19–24
cosmic emptiness, alienation, and loneliness
  experience of, 22–23
  sloth leading to, 294
  as tactic of Satan, 187, 217, 218, 221, 225–26, 238, 240, 241, 244
cosmic struggle between good and evil, 43–44, 45, 89, 93n19, 103, 134–35, 139–40
covetousness, distinguished from envy, 316–17

CredibleCatholic.com, 22nn5–6,
188n1, 203n13, 242, 243nn37–38,
244, 347n33
Crucifixion. *See* Passion and death
of Jesus
cultural or large-scale temptation,
237–46, 304–6

Dark Night of the Soul, The (John of
the Cross), 76n40, 227n26
dark nights of the soul, 75–76,
83–85, 226–27, 229–31, 251n44,
253–54
Darwinism, 241
David Copperfield (Dickens), 274–75,
302
deadly sins, 29–30, 261–62. *See also*
anger; envy; gluttony; greed; lust;
pride; sloth; vanity
availability of stimuli for, 213
destructiveness of, 306–8, 355–56,
358–59
grace of God and, 359–61
historical development of concept
of, 262–64
illuminative stage of contemplative
life and, 78–80
individual propensities to, 212
as interior attitudes, 234–35, 261–62,
341
Level One and Two persons and,
264
near occasions of, 205
purgative stage of contemplative
life and, 74, 77
victory of Jesus over, 358–59
deceit and discouragement, 246–59
affective and spiritual consolation/
desolation, 247–52
false consolations for Level Three
persons, 254–56
fervor, devil taking advantage of,
256–58
of Level One and Two persons,
246, 250

of Level Three persons, 227–28,
251–59
major decisions in times of
desolation, avoiding, 252–54,
258–59
occultism and, 156
in spiritual feelings, 247, 252–56
as tactic of Satan, 188
temptation of Jesus in the desert
and, 94–97
ulterior motives, increased
awareness of, 258–59
Declaration of Independence (U.S.),
36
demonic possession. *See* possession
and exorcism
denial of spiritual evil, 26–27
desire, 205–7
desolation and consolation. *See under*
deceit and discouragement
devil, the. *See* Satan
*Diagnostic and Statistical Manual of
Mental Disorders*, 150
dignity, human, 36, 37, 190
discernment of spirits
angel of light, Satan/demon
disguised as, 28n14, 95, 188–89,
227, 247, 256–59
guidance of Holy Spirit in, 56–57
Ignatius of Loyola on, 29, 56–57,
69n25, 247, 258, 259
discouragement. *See* deceit and
discouragement
dissociative identity (multiple
personality) disorder, 149, 151,
171–72
divine goodness, recognition of. *See*
reality of divine goodness and
spiritual evil
Dynamic Catholic, 195n9

eight deadly sins. *See* deadly sins
enemies, love of, 309–10
1 Enoch 6—9, 92n5, 93n9, 117
2 Enoch 29:3, 92n5, 93n9

entitlement culture, 245–46
envy, 315–26
  defined, 315–16
  destructiveness of, 316, 317, 326,
    356
  individual tendencies toward,
    212
  jealousy and covetousness
    distinguished, 316–17
  scriptural and literary examples,
    317–26
  vengeance at root of, 308
eros (romantic love), 279–84
ethical behavior and religious
  conviction, connection between,
  216–18, 239–40
ethical minimalism, 36
Eucharist, sacrament of, 30, 31,
  166–67, 168–71, 359, 360, 361
Eucharistic miracles, 393–95, 396
Evidence of Satan in the Modern World
  (Cristiani), 148, 176, 229n30
evil, recognition of. See reality of
  divine goodness and spiritual evil
Evil: Satan, Sin, and Psychology
  (Cooper and Epperson), 154
Examen Prayer, 31, 32, 362
existence of God, proofs of, 20–21,
  45, 346–47, 381
exorcism. See possession and exorcism
Exorcist, The (book and film), 28, 147,
  152, 164n70, 178

Facebook, 239, 240, 305
Faerie Queen, The (Spenser), 263,
  322–23, 342–44, 356
faith, as gift or grace, 360. See also
  science/reason and faith
fall, the, 89, 93, 97, 105–6, 203, 383
fallen angels story, 89, 92n5, 93n9,
  110–11, 117, 344–48
Fatima: From the Beginning (de Marchi),
  385
Fatima, Marian apparition at, 63, 69,
  383–88, 396

fervor, devil taking advantage of,
  256–58
flu pandemic (1918–1920), 383–84
foreign languages, possessed persons
  speaking, 145, 150, 159, 167, 171
forgiveness
  anger, as means of dispelling,
    314–15
  Jesus' prioritization of, 308
fortitude, 207–11, 214, 236–37, 268
four higher powers (rational desire,
  conscience, empathy, and faith),
  207–11, 214–15
free will, 200–204
  deadly sin, overcoming, 359
  faith and, 360
  grace of God and, 360, 361
  Holy Spirit working through, 196
  mortal sin requiring, 193–94
  possession and, 175–76, 177–78,
    181–82
  reality of divine goodness/spiritual
    evil and, 105, 106, 181–82
"freedom from" versus "freedom
  for", 280
Freudianism, 241

Gen Xers, 304–5
ghosts, apparitions, or spirits of the
  dead, 137–38
Glimpses of the Devil (Peck), 147
Glory (Balthasar), 398
gluttony, 264–69
  availability of stimuli and, 213
  defined, 264–65
  destructiveness of, 264–67
  individual tendencies toward, 212
  overcoming, 267–69
  scriptural and literary examples,
    265–67
God the Father
  as "Abba", 193, 310, 382
  Jesus' revelation of, 193, 310
  in Old versus New Testament,
    309–10

possession allowed by, 175–78
power allowed to Satan after fall
    by, 97
temptation of Jesus in the desert
    and, 93–94
Gödel's Theorem, 201
GodIsReal.Today, 365n5
Golden Rule, 36, 311
good judgment, Holy Spirit and
    peace necessary for, 50–51
Good Samaritan, Parable of, 193
good thief, at Crucifixion, 32, 33,
    193, 194
goodness, recognition of. See reality of
    divine goodness and spiritual evil
grace of God, 315, 356, 359–61
Great Divorce, The (Lewis), 277–78,
    296–99, 306
Great Gatsby, The (Fitzgerald), 286,
    302
Greatest Generation, 305
greed, 269–78
    availability of stimuli and, 213
    defined, 269
    destructiveness of, 269–70, 355–56
    individual tendencies toward, 212
    overcoming, 270, 276–77
    scriptural and literary examples,
        270–78
group/mass hysteria, 135, 173
"group think", 305
Guadalupe, Marian apparition at, 63,
    367–71, 382, 396
guidance and inspiration of Holy
    Spirit, 51–57, 187, 188, 190, 196,
    361

Hamlet (Shakespeare), 29, 236n35,
    311–14, 348n36, 356, 359
Happiness, Suffering, and Transcendence
    (Spitzer). See Quartet
Harry Potter series (Rowling), 43, 134
higher powers (rational desire,
    conscience, empathy, and faith),
    207–11, 214–15

Holy Spirit, 27, 46–63
    agenda and purpose of, 57
    blaspheming, as unforgiveable sin,
        109–10
    deceit and discouragement,
        attempting to overcome, 250–53
    forgiveness and, 315
    good judgment, peace necessary
        for, 50–51
    inspiration and guidance of, 51–57,
        187, 188, 190, 196, 361
    Jesus' gift of, 45, 46
    leading Jesus into desert, 93
    Level One individuals and, 219
    Level Two individuals and, 222,
        223
    peace brought by, 47–51, 57
    persecution, peace in times of,
        49–50
    prudence and, 236
    Sensus Fidei provided by, 53–55
    suffering, peace in times of, 48–49
    transformational power of, 57–61
    trusting in, 58
    words of help and edification given
        by, 51–53
    working with, 61–63
holy water, 101, 146, 150, 159, 162,
    164, 170, 173, 371
homicide. See killing
human dignity, 36, 37, 190
human freedom. See free will

illuminative stage of contemplative
    life, 71–72, 78–81, 82–83
imaginary playmates, children's
    experience of, 64–65, 180n94
Imitation of Christ, The (Kempis),
    295n19
Immaculate Conception, doctrine of,
    382–83
Immaculate Heart, The (de Marchi),
    384n39, 385
Ineffabilis Deus (1854), 382
Inferno (Dante), 263

inspiration and guidance of Holy
    Spirit, 51–57, 187, 188, 190, 196,
    361
Institutes (Cassian), 262
intellectual conversion, 20–22, 23–24,
    196–99
Intentional Discipleship, 195n9
Internet, 19, 26n12, 198, 213, 225,
    234, 238, 240, 242, 278, 365
intertestamental period, 91–92
Interview with an Exorcist (Fortea), 143

J (Johnnine tradition), 100n18
JAMA Facial Plastic Surgery (journal),
    305
jealousy, distinguished from envy, 316
Jeremiah 13:9–10, 337
Jerusalem, Council of, 31, 122
Jesus Christ. *See also* Passion and
    death of Jesus; teachings of Jesus
    about Satan; victory of Jesus over
    Satan
    on anger and forgiveness, 309–11,
        314–15
    as Bridegroom, 73–74, 79, 85, 86
    cosmic struggle between good and
        evil, awareness of, 89, 93n9
    incarnation of Son of God in, 45
    intellectual conversion to, 20–21,
        23–24
    merciful love of, 32–33
    miracles of, 365
    mission and purpose of, 89–91, 92
    as new Adam, 92–93
    prioritization of forgiveness by, 308
    temptation in the desert, 90, 92–98,
        111, 330n24
Jewish tradition
    Book of Revelation and, 130–32
    defeat of Satan, lack of, 98
    fallen angels in, 89, 92n5, 93n9,
        117
"Julia" possession/exorcism case, 28,
    104, 147, 148–52, 154
Julius Caesar (Shakespeare), 323

kenodoxia, 295. *See also* vanity
killing
    Cain and Abel, 318, 319–20
    prohibition of, 35
King Lear (Shakespeare), 215

L (special Luke), 100
Lanciano, miracle of, 393
Lazarus and the Rich Man, Parable
    of, 116
Level One happiness/purpose
    consolation and desolation at,
        249–50
    cultural or large-scale temptation
        at, 239
    deadly sins associated with, 264,
        269, 284, 285, 306
    deceit and discouragement of
        persons at, 246, 250–52
    entitlement culture and, 245
    eros or romantic love at, 279–84
    individual tendencies toward deadly
        sin at, 212, 213, 214–15
    temptation of persons at, 218–19
    transitioning from, 19, 22, 23, 234
Level Two happiness/purpose
    consolation and desolation at,
        250
    cultural or large-scale temptation
        at, 239
    deadly sins associated with, 264,
        284, 285, 306
    deceit and discouragement of
        persons at, 246, 252
    entitlement culture and, 245
    eros or romantic love at, 279–84
    individual tendencies toward deadly
        sin at, 212, 213, 214–15
    pride and, 327, 328
    temptation of persons at, 219–24
    transitioning from, 19, 22, 23, 234
Level Three happiness/purpose
    consolation and desolation at, 251,
        253, 254–56
    cultivating friends at, 246

cultural or large-scale temptation at, 239, 240, 241

deadly sins associated with, 284

deceit and discouragement of persons at, 227–28, 251–59

eros or romantic love at, 279–84

individual tendencies toward deadly sin at, 215

nonreligious individuals at, 216–18

temptation of persons at, 224–29

transitioning from, 22, 23

Level Four happiness/purpose

consolation and desolation at, 251, 253, 254

cultivating friends at, 246

cultural or large-scale temptation at, 239, 240, 241

deadly sins associated with, 284

eros or romantic love at, 279–84

failure to transition to, 216–17

individual tendencies toward deadly sin at, 215

living in, 39–40

temptation of persons at, 229–31

transitioning to, 22, 23

levitation or excessive weight, in possessions, 145, 150, 157

"Living Flame of Love, The" (John of the Cross), 70n28, 86

Lord of the Rings (Tolkien), 43, 44, 134, 190–91

Lorenz-Einstein transformation, 248–49

Lourdes, 63, 371–83

Immaculate Conception, doctrine of, 382–83

Marian apparition at, 371–73

meaning and purpose of, 381–83

miraculous cures associated with, 69, 373–81, 396

persons not cured at, 381

validation of, 373

Lourdes Medical Bureau, 69n21, 374, 375n20, 380, 381, 396

love

agapē/caritas, 49–50, 57, 59, 71n33, 295

eros (romantic love), 279–84

as gift of self, 96

Passion and death of Jesus, unconditional redemptive love of, 126–32

tactics of Satan, God's unconditional love as protection against, 187–89, 192, 193–94

Lucifer. See Satan

Lumen Gentium (1964), 53

lust, 278–90

adultery, 35, 285–90

availability of stimuli and, 213

defined, 278

destructiveness of, 284–85, 289–90, 355

eros (romantic love) versus, 279–85

individual tendencies toward, 212

overcoming, 279, 285, 290

prevalence in contemporary Western culture, 278–79

scriptural and literary examples, 285–90

M (special Matthew), 100

Macbeth (Shakespeare), 29, 215, 272, 331, 342, 348–56

Machiavellianism, 327

Magis Center, 21–22, 242–43

Man for All Seasons, A (Bolt), 272

Manichaeism, 222, 223

Margaret Mary, Saint, relic of, 162

Marian apparitions, 63, 69, 366–88, 396. See also Fatima; Guadalupe; Lourdes

Mariolatry, 382

Marxism, 17, 241, 330

mass/group hysteria, 135, 173

maturity, spiritual, 187–95

meditation versus contemplation, 81

Merchant of Venice, The (Shakespeare), 323, 330n24

Metamorphoses (Ovid), 317–18
Michelson-Morley experiment, 199
Middlesteins, The (Attenberg), 266–67
Millennials, 21n3, 304–5
miracles, visions, and revelations, 27,
    63–70, 363–99
  characteristics of authentic
    experiences, 65–70
  Eucharistic miracles, 393–95, 396
  evidence for, 24
  Marian apparitions, 63, 69, 366–88,
    396 (*See also* Fatima; Guadalupe;
    Lourdes)
  meaning and significance of, 395–99
  nature of, 363–66
  private, 63–64, 69
  psychological disorders
    distinguished, 64–67, 181
  public, 63, 69
  saints and, 63, 365, 388–93, 398,
    399
  "wholly Other", as experience of,
    65, 66, 68, 69, 82
Miserables, Les (Hugo), 272–73
moral conversion, 24–26, 30–33, 37,
    190, 191, 216, 225, 360
moral relativism, 17–19, 241, 246, 247
mortal sin, 193–94
motherly dimension of God, 382
multiple personality (dissociative
    identity) disorder, 149, 151,
    171–72
murder. *See* killing
Mustard Seed, Parable of, 58, 195
mysticism and contemplative life, 27,
    70–87
  active life versus, 72–73
  affective consolation and, 248–49
  contemplative orders and
    hermitages, 71nn30–31
  dark nights of the soul and, 75–79,
    83–85
  defined and described, 70–74
  illuminative stage, 71–72, 78–81,
    82–83

meditation versus contemplation,
    81
  passive dark night of the soul,
    75–76, 83–85
  passive thought, contemplation as,
    81–82
  presence and consolation of the
    Lord in, 81–83
  purgative stage, 71, 74–78
  unitive stage, 72, 85–87

narcissism
  lust and, 284–85, 290
  vanity and, 295
natural law and natural rights, 36, 139
Nazis and Nazism, 17, 192
near occasion of sin, 205
near-death experiences (NDEs), 45,
    135–37
New Testament. *See also Scripture
    Index*
  on anger, 309–11
  deadly sins in, 261–62
  on envy, 320–22
  on gluttony, 265–66
  on greed, 271–72
  on lust, 285–86
  physical illness versus possession in,
    104–5
  prioritization of forgiveness in, 308
  Satan and demons in, 89, 91–92
  on vanity, 295–96
New York Times, 220, 221
Nicomachean Ethics (Aristotle), 198
nonreligious ethical individuals,
    216–18, 223–24
Normae Congregationis (1978), 366

obedience, 95–97
occultism, witchcraft, and Satanism,
    26–27, 141, 144, 149, 152, 155–57,
    160–61, 174–78
Old Testament. *See also Scripture Index*
  anger of Yahweh in, 309
  deadly sins in, 261–62

on envy, 318–20, 321
on gluttony, 265
on greed, 270–71
on lust, 285
on pride, 333–37
Satan and demons in, 89, 91
original sin, 203
Othello (Shakespeare), 29–30, 215,
323–26, 356
ouija boards, 141, 155–57, 160–61,
174, 175
Our Father (Lord's Prayer), 112–13

parables, teachings of Jesus about
Satan in, 110n26, 113–19. *See also
specific parables*
Paradise Lost (Milton), 342, 344–48,
356
paranormal phenomena, 138, 143,
144–45, 147, 148n31, 149, 150,
151, 154–64, 171, 173
"Parson's Tale, The" (Chaucer), 263
Passion and death of Jesus
good thief, at Crucifixion, 32, 33,
193, 194
victory of Jesus over Satan in, 90,
105, 126–32
passive dark night of the soul, 75–76,
83–85, 226–27, 231, 251, 253
passive thought, contemplation as,
81–82
peace of Holy Spirit, 47–51, 56–57
Penance. *See* Reconciliation,
Sacrament of
persecution, peace of Holy Spirit in,
49–50
perseverance and spiritual maturity,
191–92, 361
personal ethics, 34–35
Phaedrus (Plato), 309n1
Phenomenology of Spirit (Hegel),
329n14
Philosophy of Right, The (Hegel), 329
physical illness versus possession, in
New Testament, 104–5

picture thoughts, 205
"pious fraud", 395
plastic surgery, 301, 305–6
poltergeist and psychokinetic activity,
145, 146, 150, 157, 158, 159, 161,
162, 171
Possessed: The True Story of an Exorcism
(Allen), 152–55, 163
possession and exorcism, 142–82.
See also "Robbie Mannheim"
possession case
alternate personalities, emergence
of, 104, 143, 144, 146, 149–50,
151
behavioral manifestations of, 143,
146
body but not soul affected by, 143,
176, 178–81
documented cases of, 147–73
effects on other people, 143, 144,
146–47
God's reasons for allowing, 175–78
good deriving from, 178
Jesus' ministry of, 90, 98–106
"Julia" case (2007), 28, 104, 147,
148–52, 154, 175
in non-Christian religions and
world cultures, 144–45n26
origins/causes of, 144, 149, 152,
155–57, 174–78
physical illness versus, 104–5
psychological disorders
distinguished, 143, 149, 150–51,
154, 158, 171–73, 180–81
reasons for studying, 28
rise of, in Jesus' time, 89
rise of, in modern world, 141
severe demonic oppression versus,
143–44
signs of demonic possession,
142–47
victims failing to remember, 149,
171, 176
prayer, and spiritual maturity, 188–90,
195

pride, 326–58
    defined, 326–27
    five stages of destructiveness of,
        327–33
    individual tendencies toward, 212
    Level Two personalities and, 212,
        327, 328
    literary examples, 342–56
    overcoming, 356–58
    scriptural examples, 333–42
    vanity, relationship to, 294, 326–27
    vengeance at root of, 308
Prince, The (Machiavelli), 327n13
Prodigal Son, Parable of, 32, 110n26,
    193, 194, 310, 382
prudence/prudential judgment,
    55–56, 207–11, 214, 235–36, 245
psychokinetic and poltergeist activity,
    145, 146, 150, 157, 158, 159, 161,
    162, 171
psychological disorders. See also specific
    disorders
    anger, suppression or repression
        of, 314
    authentic miracles, visions, and
        revelations distinguished, 63–67,
        181
    Diagnostic and Statistical Manual of
        Mental Disorders, 150
    possession distinguished, 143, 149,
        150–51, 154, 158, 171–73,
        180–81
    vanity leading to, 305–6
purgative stage of contemplative life,
    71, 74–78
Purgatorio (Dante), 263
Purgatory, 188

Q (Quelle), 92–93, 100–101, 107
quantum theory, 364
Quartet (Spitzer), 18–26, 43–45,
    241–42

racism, 241
rational desire, 206–11

reality of divine goodness and spiritual
    evil, 26–30, 43–88. See also deadly
    sins; Holy Spirit; miracles, visions,
    and revelations; mysticism and
    contemplative life; possession and
    exorcism; Satan; tactics of Satan;
    victory of Jesus over Satan
    cosmic struggle between good and
        evil, 43–44, 45, 89, 93n9, 103,
        134–35, 139–40
    free will and, 105, 106, 181–82
    presence of God within and to us,
        45–46
reason and faith. See science/reason
    and faith
Reconciliation, Sacrament of, 32–33,
    188, 193–95, 359, 360, 361
reductionism, biological, 241, 247
relativism, 17–19, 241, 246, 247
religious conversion. See spiritual
    conversion
religious conviction and ethical
    behavior, connection between,
    216–18, 239–40
religious objects, violent or blasphe-
    mous reactions to, in possessions,
    143, 145, 146, 150, 157, 159, 162,
    164, 166–67, 169, 173
Rerum Novarum (1891), 36
revelations. See miracles, visions, and
    revelations
Revelations and Possession (Isaacs),
    64n4, 65n6, 66n8, 66–67nn10–17,
    68n20, 143, 146n27, 173n93,
    180n95
Rhetoric (Aristotle), 309n2, 332–33
Richard III (Shakespeare), 215, 323
Rite, The (Baglio), 26–27n12, 140n19,
    141n20, 143, 144n25, 147–48,
    156n50, 175, 176
"Robbie Mannheim" possession case
    (1949), 104, 152–73
    conversion of Robbie to Catholicism
        and, 166, 178
    exit of demon in, 170–71

Exorcist, The (book and film) based on, 28, 147, 152
   family home in Maryland, exorcisms at, 168
   Hughes exorcism, 159–60
   older cases compared, 148n31
   origins/causes of possession, 155–57, 175, 177
   permissions for exorcisms in, 159–60, 162–63
   phenomena prior to beginning of exorcisms, 154, 155–63
   post-exorcism life of, 171, 176
   psychiatric assessment of, 171–73
   rectory of College Church, St. Louis University, exorcisms at, 165–67
   relatives' home in St. Louis, exorcisms at, 163–65
   series of thirty exorcisms by Bowdern, 155, 162–71
   sources and events, 152–55
   St. Alexius Hospital, St. Louis, exorcisms at, 168–71
Roman Empire, 89, 128–29
romantic love *(eros)*, 279–84
Room with a View, A (Forster), 292–94, 356
Rosary, 81, 162, 167, 371, 380, 383, 384, 399

saints. *See also specific saints, in Names Index*
   canonization process, 388
   doctrinal proclamations on, 31
   example of, 359
   intercession of, 27, 365, 387, 388–93
   miracles and healings associated with, 63, 365, 388–93, 398, 399
   private visions and revelations of, 63–64
Samson-Purkinje effect, 369–70
Satan, 28, 134–42. *See also* tactics of Satan; teachings of Jesus about Satan; victory of Jesus over Satan

angel of light, disguised as, 28n14, 95, 188–89, 227, 247, 256–59
cosmic struggle between good and evil, 43–44, 45, 89, 93n9, 103, 134–35, 139–40
evidence of reality of, 134–42 (*See also* possession and exorcism)
fallen angels story of, 89, 92n5, 93n9, 110–11, 117, 344–48
   in Milton's *Paradise Lost*, 344–48, 356
as murderer from the beginning, 127
names for, 91n2, 92n5, 113, 342
in Old and New Testaments, 89, 91–92
power allowed by God to, after fall, 97
pride as sin of, 356
as prince of this world, 128n37, 130
Scripture quoted by, 330n24
skepticism about existence of, 134, 135, 139, 140–41
Satanism. *See* occultism, witchcraft, and Satanism
schizophrenia, 63, 151, 172, 206
science/reason and faith
   antireligious cultural trends and, 243–44
   as defense against tactics of Satan, 196–99
   denial of spiritual evil and, 26–27
   miracles/visions/revelations and, 363–66
   skepticism about paranormal experience, immortal soul, and demons, 134, 135, 139, 140–41
   supposed contradiction between, 21, 232
Scientific American, 375
scratches, in possessions, 143, 146, 157, 158, 160–62, 164, 167, 168, 171
Screwtape Letters, The (Lewis), 141–42, 199, 233–34

Second Vatican Council, 53, 55
secularism, 243–44
selfies, 239, 305
self-transformation, 31–32, 34, 39
Sensus Fidei, 53–55
Sermon on the Mount, 112–13,
    261–62, 310, 320–21
seven deadly sins. *See* deadly sins
7 Essential Modules (The Magic
    Center), 22, 243n37, 244n40
severe demonic oppression versus
    possession, 143–44
sexual abuse, as explanation for
    possession symptoms, 173
sexuality, views of, 35, 278–79. *See
    also* lust
Sheep and Goats, Parable of, 116–19
Shroud of Turin, 20, 24, 198, 242,
    395
"Sic transit gloria mundi", 295
Silver Rule, 36
sin. *See also* deadly sins
    blaspheming Holy Spirit, as
        unforgiveable sin, 109–10
    mortal sin, 193–94
    near occasion of, 205
    original sin, 203
    possession due to being cursed not
        resulting in, 176
    against Ten Commandments,
        234–35, 261, 270, 285
situation ethics, 54
sloth, 290–94
    defined, 290
    destructiveness of, 290–92, 356
    fortitude versus, 236–37
    individual tendencies toward, 212
    scriptural and literary examples,
        291–94
Snapchat, 239, 305
Snow White and the Seven Dwarfs,
    294
social Darwinism, 241
social ethics, 33, 35–36

social media, 19, 35, 238–42, 244,
    304–5
socio-biology, 241
soul
    as apparition, ghost, or spirit,
        137–38
    as bride of Christ, 73, 79, 85, 86
    immortal soul, evidence of, 45,
        135–37
    possession not inhabiting, 143, 176,
        178–79
Sower, Parable of, 113–14, 118
spirits, apparitions, or ghosts of the
    dead, 137–38
Spiritual Canticle, The (John of the
    Cross), 70n28, 73–74, 78–79, 85
"spiritual churches", 232–33
spiritual consolation and desolation,
    249–56
spiritual conversion, 22–24, 30–33,
    190, 191, 216, 225
spiritual evil, recognition of. *See*
    reality of divine goodness and
    spiritual evil
Spiritual Exercises (Ignatius of Loyola),
    56–57, 69n25, 77n41, 211,
    218n22, 227, 247, 249–52
spiritual feelings, deceit and
    discouragement in, 252–56
spiritual maturity, 187–95
Star Wars (films), 43, 134
string theory, 364–65
substance abuse disorder, 173
Sudarium, 20, 395
suffering
    grace of God in, 360–61
    peace of Holy Spirit in, 48–49
    pride, overcoming, 357
    transformative power of, 57–61
Summa Theologica (Aquinas), 54–55,
    71n32, 207n15, 262–63, 270n5
sun, miracle of, at Fatima, 69,
    384–87
Sunset Boulevard (film), 302–4, 356

tactics of Satan, 28–29, 185–260. *See also* deceit and discouragement; temptation
  common defenses against, 187–90, 192–200
  free will and, 200–204
  reasons for studying, 185–86
  spiritual maturity and struggle with, 187–95
Talents, Parable of, 58, 195, 291–92
Tax Collector and Pharisee, Parable of, 110n26, 193, 194, 338
teachings of Jesus about Satan, 90, 106–19
  Beelzebul accusation, 106–10, 111
  "I saw Satan fall like lightning" statement, 110–12
  in parables, 110n26, 113–19
  Sermon on the Mount/Our Father, 112–13
telepathy, 145
temperance, 207–11, 214, 236, 268
temptation, 204–46
  cultural or large-scale temptation, 237–46, 304–6
  individual tailoring of, 211–18
  Jesus' temptation in the desert, 90, 92–98, 111, 330n24
  of Level One persons, 218–19
  of Level Two persons, 219–24
  of Level Three persons, 224–29
  of Level Four persons, 229–31
  moral commitment, undermining, 234–37
  origins and mechanism of, 205–7
  religious commitment, undermining, 231–34
  resisting, 208–11
  Satan's preparations for, 231–37
Ten Commandments, 234–35, 261, 270, 285
tilma of Juan Diego of Guadalupe, 367–70
Titus 3:3, 322

Tourette's syndrome, 173
trancelike states, in possessions, 143, 144, 146, 149, 150–51, 158, 161, 165–70, 172, 180
transcendence, evidence for, 20–21
transformational power of Holy Spirit, 57–61
Treatise on Government (Locke), 36
Trilogy (Spitzer), 18—37, 241–42, 359, 361–62
True Story of Fatima, The (de Marchi), 385
trusting in the Holy Spirit, 58
truth versus relativism, 17–19
twelve-step programs, 240, 267–68

unforgiveable sin, blaspheming Holy Spirit as, 109–10
unitive stage of contemplative life, 72, 85–87
Universal Declaration of Human Rights, 36
Unmerciful Servant, Parable of, 311

vainglory, 294–95. *See also* vanity
vanity, 294–306
  defined, 294–95
  destructiveness of, 295, 299–302, 304–6, 356
  individual tendencies toward, 212
  in modern culture, 304–6
  overcoming, 295–96, 300, 302
  pride, relationship to, 294, 326–27
  scriptural and literary examples, 295–99, 302–4
vengeance at root of anger, envy, and pride, 308
victory of Jesus over Satan, 27–28, 89–133. *See also* teachings of Jesus about Satan
  deadly sins defeated by, 358–59
  disciples and Church, power over demons given to, 90, 119–26
  Jewish literature, no parallel in, 98

victory of Jesus over Satan (*continued*)
  as mission and purpose of Jesus,
    89–91, 92
  Old and New Testaments, Satan
    and demons in, 89, 91–92
  by Passion and death of Jesus, 90,
    105, 126–32
  possession and exorcism, Jesus'
    ministry of, 90, 98–106
  Revelation on, 130–32
  spiritual battle between Jesus and
    Satan, 90
  temptation in the desert, defeat of
    Satan in, 90, 92–98, 111
visions. *See* miracles, visions, and
  revelations

Wall Street (film), 273–74, 302, 356,
  359
Weeds, Parable of, 114–16, 118, 195
"wholly Other", 65, 66, 68, 69, 82
Will to Power, The (Nietzsche), 329
Wisdom literature, 89, 270, 271, 285,
  295, 309, 320, 336
witchcraft. *See* occultism, witchcraft,
  and Satanism
words of help and edification given
  by Holy Spirit, 51–53
"world spirit", 329

Yeast and Flour, Parable of, 195

SCRIPTURE INDEX

Old Testament

Genesis
  1:27, 202
  3:1, 131
  3:1–7, 318, 333
  3:1–14, 356
  3:1–24, 89, 91, 127
  3:5, 221, 318, 333
  3:13–14, 131
  4:2–11, 319
  6:1–6, 89, 92n5, 93n9, 117
Exodus
  17:1–7, 95
  20:14, 285
Leviticus
  17—26, 285n14
  19:31, 156n49
  20:10, 285
Deuteronomy
  5:18, 285
  6:16, 95, 98
  8:1–3, 95
  8:3, 95
  18:10–12, 156, 175
1 Samuel
  9:21, 333
  13—15, 330
  15:10–23, 333
  16:1–23, 333
  17:1–58, 334
  18:7, 334, 341
  18:10, 334, 335
  18:11, 334
  18:12, 334
  18:13–16, 334
  18:17–30, 334
  19:1–17, 334

  22:6–23, 334
  24:1–11, 334
  26:1–25, 335
  28:3, 335
  28:5–19, 335
  31:1–4, 335
Job
  1:6–12, 89
  1:9–11, 131
  5:2, 320
Psalms, 89
  10:4, 337
  37, 309
  37:7–9, 309
  49, 271
  49:5–9, 271
  49:11–14, 271
  55—59, 309
  91, 95
  91:11–12, 95
  94, 309
  109, 309
  137, 309
  138:6, 337
  147:20, 371
Proverbs
  2:16, 285
  6:16–19, 262
  6:34, 309
  7:1–27, 285
  11:2, 336
  11:28, 271
  14:30, 320
  15:1, 309
  15:18, 309
  16:5, 336
  16:14, 309
  16:18, 336

Proverbs (*continued*)
 16:32, 309
 18:12, 336
 19:19, 309
 21:4, 336
 22:1, 271
 23:1–4, 265
 23:27–28, 285
 24:19, 309
 26:12, 336
 27:4, 309, 320
 29:23, 336
 30:20, 285
Ecclesiastes 5:10, 271
Sirach, 271
 10:6–9, 336–37
 10:12–14, 336–37
 10:18, 336–37
 11:1, 336–37
Isaiah, 89
 2:12, 337
 2:17, 337
 14:12, 92n5
 22:18–22, 122
 22:19, 122
 22:22, 122
 23:9, 337
Ezekiel 16:40, 285
Daniel
 5:20, 337
 7, 92n5

New Testament

Matthew (Gospel) 94, 100, 117
 3:13–17, 90
 4:1, 91n2
 4:1–11, 93, 330n24
 4:3, 91n2, 93
 4:4, 95
 4:5, 91n2
 4:6, 93, 95
 4:7, 91n2, 95, 97
 4:8, 97
 4:9, 97

 4:10, 91n2, 97, 98
 4:11, 91n2
 5:3, 295
 5:3–11, 71n33
 5:11, 50
 5:21–22, 310
 5:22, 310, 320
 5:27, 285
 5:27–30, 286
 5:37, 91n2, 112
 5:38–39, 310
 5:38–40, 320
 5:38–42, 310
 5:43–48, 310, 320
 5:44, 309
 5:44–45, 310
 5:45, 310
 5:45–48, 310
 6:13, 112
 6:14–15, 110n26
 6:24, 272
 7:1–5, 320
 7:2, 12, 311
 7:12, 36, 311
 7:15, 331
 7:16–20, 331
 7:19, 331
 9:6, 104
 9:32–33, 100
 9:34, 91n2
 10:19, 49
 10:25, 91n2
 12:22–24, 100
 12:22–32, 106–10
 12:24, 91n2
 12:26, 91n2
 12:27, 91n2
 12:28, 109
 12:29, 109
 12:32, 109
 13:1–23, 113–14
 13:18, 91n2
 13:24–30, 114–16, 195
 13:31–32, 58, 195
 13:33, 195

13:36–43, 114–16
13:38, 91n2, 114
13:39, 91n2
14:30, 357
15:21–28, 100
15:30, 300
16:17–19, 31, 121, 122
16:18, 118, 121, 122–23
16:19, 122
16:22, 124
16:23, 91n2, 124
18:21–22, 110n26, 310
18:21–35, 311
18:22, 320
19:24, 321
19:26, 356
20:25, 327
20:25–28, 338–39
23:12, 295
24, 119
25:14–30, 58, 195
25:26–30, 291
25:31–46, 116–19
25:40, 36
25:41, 91n2, 99, 118
26:8, 340n28
26:15–16, 340, 340n29
26:27–28, 96n12
26:34, 124
26:47–49, 339
26:56, 124
28:18, 97
28:18–20, 121
Mark (Gospel) 99, 100, 101, 107,
    340n29
1:9–11, 90
1:13, 91n2, 92–93
1:16–20, 101
1:23–28, 100, 101, 102
1:42, 104
2:27, 36
3:22, 91n2
3:22–29, 106–10
3:22–30, 99n16
3:23, 91n2

3:26, 91n2
4:1–20, 113–14
4:15, 91n2
4:30–32, 58, 195
5:1–20, 100
6:7–13, 119
7:24–30, 100
7:34, 104
8:33, 91n2
9:14–29, 100
10:19, 34, 285
13, 119
13:11, 49, 51
14:4, 340n28
14:10–11, 340
14:30, 124
14:43–45, 339
14:50, 124
15:10, 321
16:14–16, 121
Luke (Gospel) 95n11, 97n13, 100,
    122, 340n29
3:21–22, 90
4:1–13, 93, 330n24
4:2–3, 91n2
4:3, 93
4:4, 95
4:5, 91n2, 97
4:6, 97
4:7, 97
4:9, 93, 95
4:10–11, 95
4:12, 95, 97
4:13, 91n2
4:33–37, 102
6:20–23, 321
8:2, 100
8:4–15, 113–14, 191n2
8:12, 91n2
9:1–2, 119
10:17–20, 120
10:18, 91n2, 110–12
10:19, 91n2
11:5–13, 191n2
11:14–15, 100

Luke (Gospel) (*continued*)
  11:14–23, 106–10
  11:15, 91n2
  11:18, 91n2
  11:19, 91n2
  12:15–21, 272
  12:35–40, 191n2
  13:16, 91n2
  13:18–19, 58, 195
  13:20–21, 195
  14:8–11, 295–96
  15:4–6, 310
  15:11–32, 32, 110n26, 310
  15:21, 193
  16:19–31, 116
  18:1–8, 191n2
  18:9–14, 110n26
  18:10–14, 338
  18:13, 193
  18:20, 285
  19:11–27, 58, 195, 291
  21, 119
  21:12, 49
  22:3, 91n2, 124, 127, 339
  22:4–5, 340
  22:31, 91n2
  22:31–32, 124
  22:34, 124
  22:47–48, 339
  23:42, 193
  23:43, 32
  24:46–49, 121
John (Gospel)
  1:31–34, 90
  1:42, 122
  2:20, 53
  2:27, 53
  3:16–17, 32, 128
  6:70–71, 127
  8:28, 127
  8:39–43, 127
  8:44, 28n13, 91n2, 113, 127
  12:4–6, 340n28
  12:6, 340
  12:31, 91n2, 128

  12:32, 126
  13, 127
  13:2, 91n2, 124, 127, 128
  13:26–27, 127
  13:27, 91n2, 124, 128, 339, 340n29
  13:38, 124
  14:30, 91n2, 128
  15:13, 96n12, 128
  16:11, 91n2, 128
  16:32, 124
  16:33, 88, 358
  17:15, 91n2, 113, 129
  20:21–23, 121
  21:15–19, 31, 121
Acts
  1—10, 122
  1:8, 121
  3:19, 110n26
  7:9, 322
  8:28–30, 55
  9:3–4, 8, 357
  10:18–20, 55
  11:12, 55
  13:4, 55
  13:45, 322
  15:7–10, 122
  16:5–7, 55
  17:5, 322
  19:6–8, 55
  19:20–22, 55
  20:21–23, 55
  21:3–5, 55
  26:13–14, 357
Romans
  1:29, 322
  6:6, 25, 225
  7:15, 39, 227
  7:15–25, 32
  7:18–21, 39
  7:19, 33
  7:24–25, 33, 39, 227, 228
  13:13–14, 222, 223
1 Corinthians
  2:9–13, 46
  6:12–13, 265

13, 249, 255
15:5–6, 121
15:8–10, 359n47
2 Corinthians
  11:14, 28n14, 95
  12:7, 58
  12:7–12, 361
  12:8–10, 58
Galatians
  1, 121, 122
  2, 121
  2:9, 31
  5:19–21, 262
Ephesians
  1:7, 110n26
  2:15, 25, 225
  3:14–19, 40
  4:22, 25, 225, 361
  4:24, 25, 225, 361
  4:32, 110n26
  6:12–17, 38
  6:12–18, 125–26, 185–86
Philippians
  1:15, 322
  3:18–20, 256–66
Colossians
  1:13–14, 110n26
  3:9–10, 361
  3:9–11, 25, 225

1 Thessalonians 2:13, 53
1 Timothy 6:4, 322
Hebrews 13:15, 53
1 Peter
  1:7, 125
  2:9, 7
1 John 1:9, 110n26
Revelation
  12, 130–32
  12:1–6, 131
  12:4, 131
  12:5, 131
  12:7–12, 131, 342, 356
  12:9, 131
  12:10, 131, 228
  12:10–12, 132
  12:14, 131
  12:14–17, 131
  12:15, 132
  12:17, 131
  13—22, 132
  20:1–3, 118
  20:7–10, 118
  20:11–15, 132
  21:8, 262